AF600541

THE CATHOLIC UNIVERSITY OF AMERICA
CANON LAW STUDIES
No. 101

THE PROMOTER OF JUSTICE

HIS RIGHTS AND DUTIES

A DISSERTATION

Submitted to the Faculty of Canon Law of the Catholic University of America in Partial Fulfillment of the Requirements for the Degree of

DOCTOR OF CANON LAW

BY

REV. JOHN CARROLL GLYNN, J.C.L.
Priest of the Diocese of Hartford

THE CATHOLIC UNIVERSITY OF AMERICA
WASHINGTON, D. C.
1936

Nihil Obstat:

VALENTINUS T. SCHAAF, O.F.M., J.C.D.,

Censor Deputatus.

Washingtonii, D. C., die VII Maii, 1936.

Imprimatur:

✠MAURITIUS F. MCAULIFFE, D.D.,

Episcopus Hartfordiensis.

die IX Maii, 1936.

Printed by

THE PAULIST PRESS

New York, N. Y.

TO MY FATHER AND MOTHER

TABLE OF CONTENTS

PART II

COMMENTARY ON THE LEGISLATION OF THE CODE

CHAPTER VI

CHAPTER VII

CHAPTER VIII

FOREWORD

It is only with the publication of the New Code of Canon Law that the Promoter of Justice became a regularly established officer in the ecclesiastical judicature. Prior to that date he owed his existence entirely to local custom and legislation; where these did not exist he enjoyed no legal standing whatsoever. His duties varied according to the judgment of the individual Ordinary as to what the ambit of the office should include.

This lack of uniformity and definiteness has been remedied by the legislation of the Code which makes him the official plaintiff for the public good in all criminal cases and in the forensic defense of the public good in all contentious proceedings which may involve it either by reason of the nature of the case or by reason of circumstances. By abolishing the juridical institute of popular action, expressly as regards criminal and disciplinary proceedings and implicitly in relation to the remaining proceedings involving the public good, the prevailing common law has extended the rights and duties of the Promoter of Justice far beyond the narrow and indefinite competence he enjoyed under the pre-Code legislation. This reform in the procedural law effected by the Code has constituted him the public representative of the ecclesiastical fisc in the adjudication of all causes which may in any way jeopardize or compromise the common ecclesiastical welfare. It makes him the exclusive prosecutor in all criminal and disciplinary cases, the official protector and guardian of the ecclesiastical law as well as the legitimate agent of equity whose intervention in a given case may serve to forestall any injustice which a literal and strict interpretation of the otherwise just law would occasion to individuals subject to ecclesiastical jurisdiction.

The Code thus makes him an important officer of the ecclesiastical curia. The office and the extent of its right and duties, however, assumes an even greater degree of importance when these subjects are viewed in the light of recent contributions to the field of canonical literature. The Code has contented itself with a general statement of the rights and duties of the Promoter of Justice in contentious cases and as a consequence left a considerable degree of freedom in the interpretation of these rights and duties. The interpretations placed upon these general provisions of the law by the authors, the Roman Congregations and the present jurisprudence of the Roman Tribunals has accentuated the importance of this official in the procedural actions undertaken in any curia.

In view of this importance of the office and considering that, whereas the other officials of the curia have been the object of much and diversified writing, nothing expressly has appeared on the Promoter of Justice, the writer decided to select the office as the subject of this dissertation for his doctorate.

Since the subject embraces some thirty canons of the New Code of Canon Law, attention will be confined entirely to the Promoter of Justice to the absolute exclusion of all the related offices of Promoter provided in the common law. An effort will be made to delineate the historical background of the office to its present stage of development and to comment upon his rights and duties as they are set forth in the present law of the Code. This commentary will be made under the direction of the leading contemporary canonists and in the light of the most recent canonical jurisprudence evolved by the authors, the Roman Congregations and the Tribunals of the Holy See.

The writer wishes to take this occasion to express his gratitude to His Excellency, the Most Reverend Maurice F. McAuliffe, D.D., for the opportunity afforded for advanced study. He also acknowledges with sincere gratitude the helpful direction of the Faculty of the School of Canon Law and the assistance of all those who by their interest and encouragement have aided its completion.

MULTIPLICITY OF NAMES

It might be well before entering into a discussion of the historical background of the subject to note the various names by which the office of the Promoter of Justice has been designated at the various stages of its history. And while it is helpful to have uniformity of terminology throughout a paper, such will be impossible in this work for it will be necessary in quoting different documents to use the particular expression that obtained at the time the pronouncement was published. It will be sufficiently clear, however, that these titles refer to the office under consideration and form links in the chain of development through which the office evolved itself until it came forth in its much more fitting and illuminative title of the Promoter of Justice.

In the Councils of the Church,[1] in the decrees of the Roman Congregations,[2] in the allusions made to it by the Roman Pontiffs,[3] and in the commentaries of canonists writing before the Code,[4] we find the more common name of *promotor or procurator fiscalis.* After the promulgation of the Code, the authors use the terminology of the Code almost exclusively and designate the office as the Promoter of Justice. Occasionally one meets authors, as Wernz-Vidal, retaining the *promotor fiscalis* of the old law.[5] Again the English

[1] Concilium Magdeburgense, a. 1370, can. X—Mansi, 26, 574; *Concilium Romanum,* a. 1725, tit. XIV—*Coll. Lac.,* 1, 365; *Con. Quitense,* a. 1869, decr. II —*Coll. Lac.,* VI, 436; *Con. Plenarium Balto.* III, n. 301.

[2] S. C. EE. et RR., June 11, 1880—*A. S. S.,* XIII (1880), 328: Cum Magnopere S. C. Prop. Fide, 1883—*Collectanea S. C. Prop. Fide,* n. 1586, 170.

[3] Benedict XIV, *De Servorum Dei Beatificatione et Beatorum Canonizatione,* lib. I, cap. XVIII, n. 5, 113.

[4] Bouix, *De Judiciis Ecclesiasticis,* I, 475; S. B. Smith, *Elements of Ecclesiastical Law,* II, 131; Heiner, *De Processu Criminali Ecclesiastico,* 171; Lega, *De Judiciis Ecclesiasticis,* I, 176; Peregrinus, *De Fisco,* lib. IV, tit. IV, n. 41, 83.

[5] Wernz-Vidal, *Jus Canonicum,* VI, 96; De Becker, *De Matrimonio* (1931), 275; Creusen, "De jure denuntiandi invaliditatem matri.," *Nouvelle Revue Theologique,* 57 (1930), 521.

title of prosecutor is sometimes applied to designate the office.[6] Muniz retains the simple *fiscalis* in his commentary on the Fourth Book of the Code,[7] while Augustine translates it and employes the term "fiscal promoter."[8] Peregrinus[9] uses the terms *advocatus fisci* and *promotor fiscalis* interchangeably as does Lega.[10] It will be well to bear in mind that for these two writers the two titles have identical meanings. Their *advocati fisci* are the advocates described by Bouix[11] and not the *advocati fisci* of the Roman Law or the Decretals who indeed administered the temporalities of the fisc, but did not stand as proxy for it in litigious matters. Furthermore the public prosecutor mentioned by Benedict XIV is not absolutely identical with the present day Promoter.[12]

Of interest also are the names met with in the secular courts and which occasionally shed some light on the early beginnings of this ecclesiastical office, its counterpart. The more common names in the vernacular are: *ministère public, publico ministero,* director of public prosecutions, district attorney, Staatsanwaltscaft.[13]

THE OFFICE OF THE PROMOTER OF JUSTICE

Canon 1586 states: **"Constituatur in dioecesi promotor justitiae . . . pro causis tum contentiosis in quibus bonum publicum Ordinarii judicio in discrimen vocari potest, tum in criminalibus. . . ."** And again in Canon 1934 it is stated, **"Accusatio criminalis uni promotori justitiae, ceteris omnibus exclusis, reservatur."** Thus the New Code of Canon Law reaffirms and places its official approbation on this official whose appointment to every well regulated diocesan tribunal had already been prescribed by the

[6] Augustine, *A Commentary,* VII, 41; Woywod, *The Homiletic and Pastoral Review,* 33 (1933), 833.

[7] Muniz, *Procedimientos Ecclesiasticos,* III, 773.

[8] Augustine, *A Commentary,* VII, 381.

[9] Peregrinus, *De Fisco,* lib. IV, tit. IV, n. 41, 83.

[10] Lega, *Praelectiones de Judiciis Ecclesiasticis,* I, 172.

[11] Bouix, *De Judiciis Ecclesiasticis,* I, 476.

[12] Benedict XIV, *De Servorum Dei Beatificatione et Beatorum Canonizatione,* lib. I, cap. XVIII, n. 5, 113.

[13] Wernz-Vidal, *Jus Canonicum,* VI, 97.

Instruction of the Congregation of Bishops and Regulars of 1880.[14] In virtue of these two canons the ***promotor fiscalis*** or the ***procurator fiscalis,*** as he was known for three centuries under the old law, becomes a member of diocesan curia with the more fitting and descriptive title of Promoter of Justice. The Code, thereby, provides for his appointment to every well organized curia and reserves to him exclusively the official prosecution of all criminal causes before that curia.

Who, then, is this procurator of the public ecclesiastical society, whose appointment is ordained by the common law of the Church and what is the nature of his office? It is hardly necessary to observe that the word promoter is not used here in the same sense in which the English term is used today. Modern legal usage has practically reserved the word to designate a person engaged in establishing a joint stock corporation. Canon Law uses the term rather in the sense of a public official, who by virtue of his appointment is to foster the good order and the well being of a diocese by seeking out justice as often as this external good order has been jeopardized or publicly violated. In committing an offense or positing a scandalous action the delinquent has made himself amenable to the Church whose duty it is to correct and punish whenever it is necessary. But the Church is represented by the bishop, who therefore becomes the party seeking correction and satisfaction. He becomes the complainant against the accused, who is the defendant. Yet as the bishop is to sit in judgment against the accused the common law transfers his right of active prosecution to the Promoter of Justice and that for two reasons; first in the interests of justice; secondly, that he may not appear even to external appearance as judge in his own cause. The Promoter, then, is bound by his commission, general or particular, to assist the bishop in the defense and conservation of the good order of the diocese. He is in virtue of his office the public guardian and vindicator of the law as well as the diocesan censor of justice.[15] As

[14] Instr. S. C. EE. et RR., 11 Junii, 1880, art. XIII—*A. S. S.*, XIII (1880), 328.

[15] Noval, *De Processibus*, I, n. 140, 77; Wernz-Vidal, *Jus Canonicum*, VI, 101-102.

guardian of the law it will be his duty to see to it that all legislation, particular and general, is observed in the diocese; as vindicator of the law, it will fall upon him to denounce all imputable, public violations of that law to the proper authorities and to demand the proper punishment of the transgressors before the duly constituted tribunals of the diocese; as censor of the administration of justice, he must see to it that the courts of the diocese are not remiss or unfair in their administration of justice, proffering his own suggestions as to the actions taken by the judge, the defendant or the plaintiff in those causes which involve the public good.

His title in the old law, *procurator fiscalis,* affords a good insight into the nature and necessity of the office. A procurator both in the Roman Law and in the ecclesiastical sense of the word is within the limitations of the mandate of his appointment a true representative of the one making the appointment. Within these limits he is a person or agent who transacts business for or acts in the name of another.[16] In other words and to speak more fully, a procurator is one appointed by another called the principal to manage in whole or in part the affairs of that principal whether they be judicial or extra-judicial.[17] Hence a procurator differs from an advocate, because the latter merely assists a client who is present, while the former takes the place of the principal himself and may act for him in full capacity as plaintiff or defendant.

The Promoter of Justice is a procurator in the full sense of the term, subject always to the mandate of his principal, the bishop. He is, as the Instruction of 1880 calls him, the *procurator fiscalis* of the diocese for which he has been appointed.[18] This being the case the nature of the diocesan fisc must be examined in order to determine in what this custody or procuracy may consist. In its strict sense the fisc denotes an exchequer, the meaning commonly found in the classical authors. Ecclesiastical legislation, however, uses the term

[16] D. III, 3, *De Procuratoribus et Defensoribus;* D. I, 19, *De Officio Procuratoris Caesaris seu Rationalis;* c. 1-, X, *de Procuratoribus,* I, 38; c. 1-, *de Procuratoribus,* I, 19 in VI°.

[17] Schmalzgrueber, *Jus Universum Canonicum,* lib. II, tit. 38, n. 1.

[18] S. C. EE. et RR., 11 Junii, 1880, art. XIII—*A. S. S.,* XIII (1880), 328.

in its ordinary and technical sense. In this sense it is an artificial collection (*collectio ficta*) of all the property, the financial and personal rights pertaining to and conducive to the public weal of the diocese. This public fisc corresponds to the rights of patrimony in the private order of things. Whence it can be correctly described:

> patrimoniae rei publicae res omnia et jura ad peculiare ejus commodum pertinentia comprehendens, utilitatibus et necessitatibus publicis inserviens.[19]

In a word it is a non-collegiate person created by ecclesiastical law to act as a person and is endowed by law with all the rights of personality so that the fisc is said to contract, alienate, buy, sue, and be impleaded. This is effected through advocates and procurators.[20]

It is self-evident that such artificial persons created by law cannot act for themselves when their rights are called into question or when the exercise of these rights have been contravened by the actions of others. By its very nature it requires some person who can act *ex officio* as its representative to promote its best interests or to defend its challenged rights. The civil law supplies this need by providing that each fisc be administered by a procurator, a promoter or as he is sometimes called a *fiscalis*. So, likewise, the ecclesiastical law provides for the security of the ecclesiastical corporation, *i. e.*, the diocese, by appointing an official representative for it, whose duty it is to act in the name of the diocese in all judicial proceedings. The official thus instituted is called the diocesan promoter.

From what has been said thus far, it is evident that the Church in her regulations prescribing the appointment of this official is merely supplying a natural need and establishing an effective safe-

[19] Leurenius, *Forum Ecclesiasticum*, lib. III, tit. XXI, quaes. 460, n. 1.

[20] Bouix, *De Judiciis Eccl.*, I, 471; S. B. Smith, *Elements of Ecclesiastical Law*, II, 131; Leurenius, *Forum Ecclesiasticum*, lib. III, tit. XXI, quaes. 460, n. 1.

guard to secure her best interests. She recognizes the necessity of these ecclesiastical corporations and invests full authority over them in her Episcopate subject to the Roman Pontiff. To aid the already harassed and much preoccupied bishop, she provides for this second official who will aid, abet and promote the good order of his diocese by his straightforward and diligent supervision of the particular fisc to which he is appointed.

Wherefore the Promoter of the Diocesan Curia is an official lawfully appointed to guard and promote the rights of the diocese or diocesan fisc by acting as plaintiff or defendant in its stead. As will be seen from this definition, the duties of the diocesan promoter or attorney consist chiefly in, (1) prosecuting criminal offenses before the diocesan courts; for the good of the diocese demands that crimes be punished; [21] (2) in acting as representative of the diocese and therefore as plaintiff or defendant in judicial proceedings which involve the rights, prerogatives and property of the diocese.[22] He has his counterpart in the civil society in the person of the prosecuting attorney, district or county attorney, "those sworn ministers of justice whose duty it is to see that the innocent are protected, as well as that the guilty be brought to justice and who must must stand wholly indifferent as between the accused and any private interests." [23] The diocesan promoter not only assumes these duties of the civil prosecutor; but in addition he may be an interested party in all civil judicial proceedings before the diocesan court involving some issue which pertains to the public ecclesiastical good.

It has been said the Promoter is the diocesan prosecuting attorney. This is in full harmony with the general law of the Church. In fact as in all criminal proceedings of the secular courts, the

[21] S. B. Smith, *Elements of Ecclesiastical Law,* II, 132; Lega, *De Judiciis Eccl.,* I, 171; Wernz-Vidal, *Jus Canonicum,* VI, 97, 98; Roberti, *De Processibus,* I, 197; Noval, *De Processibus,* I, 81.

[22] Bouix, *De Judiciis Eccl.,* I, 471; Craisson, *Manuale Juris Canonici,* IV, n. 5770, 107; Roberti, *De Processibus,* I, 197; Augustine, *A Commentary,* VII, 42.

[23] People *vs.* Carr, 64 Mich. 702; People *vs.* Bussey, 82 Mich. 49; People *vs.* Neeley, 130 Pa. St. 199.

State or the Federal Government is a party to the prosecution,[24] so in like manner is the diocese or diocesan government a party to the prosecution of all criminal cases in the diocesan courts.[25] This is but proper. For it is to the interests of the diocese that crime and scandal shall be bridled and that wrongs shall not go unpunished. Were this vindicative justice to remain unexercised, the ecclesiastical authority would soon find itself undermined and ineffectual to the attainment of the divine end for which it was instituted. Indifference, carelessness, error, crime and the resultant scandals are by their very nature subversive of good order and unless they are restrained, punished and censured become stumbling blocks to the proper execution of moral and disciplinary legislation and ultimately, to the salvation of souls for which this legislation was originally enacted. It is true that these abuses might be corrected by popular accusation and episcopal punishments, but the experience of ages has taught the Church as well as civil society that even in the best disposed society, the members are often remiss, negligent and tolerant in their punishment of evils which do not affect them personally. The fear of reprisal or of unpopularity, an exaggerated human respect, the realization of one's own weaknesses, toleration born of long association and a host of other similar reasons all too often deter the average man and woman from seeking out the reparation of the harm done to the social order by scandals and crime. Hence the Church recognizes the necessity of a special officer who in virtue of his office will conscientiously attend to the best interests of the ecclesiastical society and conduct all its criminal proceedings. The added effectiveness of such an appointment cannot be disputed as it places squarely on the shoulders of one individual the tremendous responsibility of safeguarding the discipline and public weal of the Church and souls in his own diocese.[26] The Church further emphasizes the necessity of appointing a Promoter to act as prosecu-

[24] Walker, *American Law*, p. 114.

[25] Canon 1934; Bouix, *De Judiciis Eccl.*, I, 471; Lega, *De Judiciis Eccl.*, I, 172, 173.

[26] Heiner, *De Processu Criminali Ecclesiastico*, p. 19; Bouix, *De Judiciis Eccl.* I, 474, is insistent on this point.

tor and of inviting him to all proceedings of the criminal trial by declaring that the acts of the process are otherwise invalid, null and void.[27]

His other duties to act as plaintiff in the name of the diocese flow from the fact that the diocese is a juridical entity, a moral person and therefore cannot act of itself to insure the protection of the public ecclesiastical good. The Promoter is the official representative of that moral person and must of necessity act in its stead in all litigious proceedings which may involve its rights and welfare.[28]

Bouix, writing at the close of the last century, sums up the office as it existed under the legislation just prior to the Code: [29]

> Ad ipsius officium praecipue pertinet publicum criminum vindictam coram Tribunali ecclesiastico persequi. Ex quo satis patet quanti momenti sit commissum ipsi munus; in quo certo explendo si negligenter sese gesserit atque ex ejus culpa per dioecesim atque in clero libere grassentur vitia et scandala, ipsi coram supremo judice Christo imputabitur collapsae disciplinae, conculcatarum ecclesiasticarum legum et perditorum inde animorum ruina . . . At praeter dictam criminum vindictam publicam, ipsius etiam officii est in judicio agere vel respondere in causis quae bona temporalia, praerogativas et alia jura fisci ecclesiastici respiciunt.

This complete summation affords an idea of the office and the duties it entailed under the old law. How well and how definitely the office had evolved is evident from Bouix's description of it, as practiced in the curias of his own day. It will be seen, as the office is studied, that it has been accepted in all its essential outlines as fixed by the Congregation of Bishops and Regulars. The Code has indeed made some minor changes and given more security and definiteness to the office and its discharge but it may be truly said

[27] Canon 1587; Noval, *De Processibus,* I, 82; Pellegrini, *Praxis Vicariorum,* Pars V, sec. I, n. 19.

[28] Blat, *Commentarium,* IV, 503; Roberti, *De Processibus,* I, 197; Muniz, *Procedimientos,* III, n. 9, 12; Lega, *De Judiciis Eccl.,* IV, n. 526; Bouix, *De Judiciis Eccl.,* I, 474.

[29] Bouix, *De Judiciis Eccl.,* I, 474.

that the Code has canonized the office of *Promotor Fiscalis* and renamed it the Promoter of Justice. Some changes had to be made because of the abandonment of the old popular action and the reform of the inquisitorial procedure. To fill the voids left in the ecclesiastical legislation by these changes the common law amplified the duties of the Promoter, but did not change the essential nature of the office.

The definitions of the office as enunciated by authoritative, contemporary canonists will serve to bear out the truth of this assertion as well as to fix in the mind the nature of the office, the historical background of which the next chapters will attempt to delineate.

Vermeersch in his commentary on Canon 1586 defines the Promoter of Justice as, *sacerdos ab ordinario publice constitutus ut ex officio in causis contentiosis jura ecclesiae vel legis defendat et in criminalibus officium accusatoris publice suscipiat.*[30] He is a public official or agent fostering and protecting the proper administration of justice in the ecclesiastical tribunals.[31] He is the chief auxiliary of the judge in the adjudication of cases involving the public good and will by his suggestions and advice place the judge in a safe position to pass just sentence in the issue.[32] In a broad sense he is the procurator appointed by legitimately constituted authority who in the rôle of plaintiff or defendant will defend or secure the rights of the Church; but in the strict sense he is the prosecutor named by legitimate authority to act in his own name before ecclesiastical tribunals in criminal cases.[33] By joining both these duties together, the Promoter may be described as *persona publica ab Ordinario constituta ut jura legis tueatur, et publici accusatoris munere fungatur seu officialis publicus pro legis et justitiae tutela constitutus.*[34] These definitions of Wernz-Vidal, Noval and A Coronata are nothing more than a re-

[30] Vermeersch-Creusen, *Epitome,* III, n. 43.

[31] Noval, *De Processibus,* I, n. 140, 77.

[32] Ferreres, *Institutiones Canonicae,* II, 239; Wernz-Vidal, *Jus Canonicum,* VI, 131.

[33] Wernz-Vidal, *Jus Canonicum,* VI, 97 ss.

[34] A Coronata, *Institutiones Juris Canonici,* III, n. 1124. *Cf.* Noval, *De Processibus,* I, 77; Augustine, *A Commentary,* VII, 42.

statement of the description of the office given by the Congregation of Bishops and Regulars, *opus est procuratori fiscali pro justitiae et legis tutela.*[35] His main two functions under the old law are still reserved to him and today even as then he is the chief prosecutor in all criminal proceedings and also functions in those contentious cases in which the public good of the diocese has in the judgment of the Ordinary become involved.[36]

In some regions, *v. g.*, in Spain, the practice has been introduced whereby the Promoter of Justice has a part in all trials and in many administrative affairs. He becomes as it were an assessor in the general administration of the affairs of the diocese and enjoys a voice in the settlement of all matters of importance in the diocese. This practice is not only not contrary to the prescriptions of the Code but has its decided advantages; for it enables the Ordinary before settling any major issue to call upon this public official for advice and counsel who in virtue of his office *legis et justitiae tutelam gerentis.*[37] Moreover, this practice is in perfect harmony with the present tendencies noted in modern canonical jurisprudence to extend the duties of the Promoter in all branches of procedural law dealing with questions of interest to the public good.

The Code has, indeed, given the office more security by manifesting the will and mind of the Church that it be established in every diocese and has given more definiteness as to its duties in criminal and contentious cases, the latter of which is a more recent development in the office; but for the most part, it has taken the office of the old law and retained its essential features as developed under the pre-Code legislation and prescribed by the Instruction of 1880. It will suffice for the present if some notion of the nature and necessity of the office has been given so that the historical outline of its early beginnings may be the more easily followed.

[35] Instr. S. C. EE. et RR., 11 Junii, 1880, art. XIII—*A. S. S.*, XIII (1880-), 328.

[36] Canons 1586 and 1934.

[37] Muniz, *Procedimientos*, I, n. 134 118.

PART I

HISTORICAL CONSPECTUS

CHAPTER ONE

THE EARLIEST BEGINNINGS OF THE OFFICE OF THE PROMOTER

ARTICLE I. BEGINNINGS OF THE OFFICE ARE NOT TO BE FOUND IN THE ROMAN LAW OR IN THE DECRETALS

IT is only natural when treating a subject so closely connected with procedure, as this one is, to expect that Roman Law, that fountainhead of most procedural institutions, would afford some light or evidence as to its earliest existence. An examination of the sources, however, discloses that no evidence is to be found of any office bearing the slightest resemblance to the office of our present day prosecutor. Roman Law, indeed, had its procurators and promoters but they resemble the modern promoter in name only. This conclusion is supported by the unanimous consent of all Romanists and canonists. All without exception witness the absolute silence of the Roman Law on the subject.[1]

Nor is this fact surprising when one considers that the Promoter of Justice, as exercised today, was instituted almost exclusively for the prosecution of crime. In Roman Law the procedure was formalistic, the system was accusatory and its civil procedure did not clearly differentiate the private from the public good.[2] The prosecution of crimes among the Romans was entirely in the hands of individual citizens who exercised what the sources term *actio poularis*. An accusation was laid by any private citizen who through-

[1] Mommsen, *Droit Romain Pénal,* II, 16, 17; Sherman, *Roman Law and the Modern World,* II, 484-492; Lega, "De Variis formis processus criminalis," *Jus Pontificium,* 14 (1934), 167, 168; Wernz, *Jus Decretalium,* V, lib. 1, 163ff.; Noval, *De Processibus,* I, 78; Roberti, *De Processibus,* I, 191; Bouix, *De Judiciis Eccl.,* I, 470ff.

[2] Digest 47, 23, *De Popularibus Actionibus;* Esmein, *History of Continental Criminal Procedure,* pp. 1-7.

out the trial bore the burden of the prosecution and were he to default, there would be no criminal trial. One finds two distinct systems of trial in the two periods of Roman history, one which prevailed under the Republic, the other under the Empire, but in both systems the presence of a private accuser was indispensable to the execution of the process. During the Republic criminal jurisdiction was exercised generally with and exceptionally without a jury. The presence or absence of a jury differentiates the two systems.

The jury courts were the *quaestiones perpetuae* over which the magistrate presided as an impartial umpire referring the final decision to the jury. These courts had jurisdiction over practically all crimes. A prosecution brought before any of these courts was called a *judicium publicum.*[3] The guilt or innocence of the accused was decided by a majority vote of the jury.[4]

The procedure of all these criminal jury courts was quite similar. Any Roman citizen or subject desiring anyone to be prosecuted criminally could apply to the presiding judge of the appropriate court for permission to make accusation against the alleged offender.[5] The magistrate upon examining the complaint granted or refused permission to the denunciator to prosecute his charge. In the event that the permission was granted, the accuser made a formal accusation of crime in the presence of the judge and the accused. The magistrate then appointed a day for the trial and the accuser and his friends prosecuted the case before the court. Should the accuser fail to appear, there would be a dismissal of the case. The accuser must appear personally in the court to prosecute his charges, otherwise there was no criminal prosecution.[6]

This system was carried over into the Empire, but finally the new imperial courts without juries became the sole criminal courts of the Empire. The *quaestiones perpetuae* or jury courts disappeared

[3] *Dig.* 48, 1; *Inst.* 4, 18.

[4] Williams, *Droit public romain,* pp. 305, 306.

[5] Esmein, *History of Continental Legal Procedure,* p. 21.

[6] Williams, *Droit public romain,* p. 304; Sherman, *Roman Law and the Modern World,* II, 487.

entirely during the third century A. D.[7] The court of the city prefect and the praetorian prefect together with other criminal courts supplanted the jury trials.[8]

The outlines of the later imperial procedure, however, remained accusatorial in form and retained many of the old procedural forms together with the names.[9] A criminal procedure still commenced by an information or indictment signed by the accuser. The judge is instructed to act impartially,[10] but was permitted to question freely and was permitted to resort to torture in order to wring a confession from the accused.[11] Here is the beginning of the inquisitorial methods in procedure. In addition in order to search out dangerous criminals and to discover crimes, public police officials could institute proceedings.[12] These officials, however, entered the proceedings in the rôle of a private accuser exercising the *actio popularis.* The Romans with their hereditary attachment to formalism never conceived of a public personality who might prosecute in the name of society but adhered to the ancient system of popular accusation to the end.[13]

One does meet titles in the Digest and Code which resemble the Promoter in name and were the titles alone considered, they would seem to foreshadow his office and duties. In Justinian Law one finds such titles as, *De Procuratoribus et Defensoribus, De Officio Caesaris seu Rationalis, De Defensoribus Civitatum.* An examination of the jurisprudence conjoined to these titles demonstrates convincingly that the resemblance is confined entirely to the titles themselves. The first title is concerned wholly and entirely with appointment of private procurators for judicial and extra-judicial matters.[14] The

[7] Mommsen, *Droit pénal romain,* I, pp. 255-257; Esmein, *History of Continental Criminal Procedure,* p. 27, n. 4.

[8] Strachan-Davidson, *Roman Criminal Law,* II, 158, 165.

[9] Sherman, *Roman Law and the Modern World,* II, 491.

[10] *Cod. Theod.* 2, 19, 2.

[11] *Cod. Theod.* 2, 18, 1; *Code* 9, 2, 7; *Dig.* 48, 18, 1, § 1.

[12] *Dig.* 1, 18, 13; *Code* 12, 20, 4; Esmein, *History of Continental Criminal Procedure,* p. 29.

[13] Lega, *Jus Pontificium,* 14 (1934), 167, 168.

[14] *Dig.* III, 3, *De Procuratoribus et Defensoribus.*

second official who is described in the somewhat pretentious terms of the Digest as *quae acta gestaque sunt a procuratore Caesaris, sic ab eo comprobatur atque a Caesare gesta sunt,*[15] was nothing more than a delegate of the emperor for the administration of some particular function which in no way involved the official prosecution of criminal offenses. Likewise, the third title while it reports judicial authority of these officials in matters of minor moment, much after the manner of the present day justices of the peace, it in no way mentions the public duty of prosecuting public offenses and crimes.[16]

In the fourth title which may be mentioned, some Romanists are wont to find the forerunner of the French Procurateurs de Roi whom many canonists recognize as the model after which our own Promoters of Justice were fashioned. This institution was called the *Advocatus Fisci* and owes its origin to the Emperor Hadrian.[17] Every fisc had its advocate in whose responsibility rested the defense of its rights. They administered the fisc of the Provinces to which they were assigned, they sought out its rights and defended those rights against the usurpation by others. In the defect of other accusers they were to pursue the guilty parties.[18] According to the Romanist, D. Serrigny, this last duty was imposed by a constitution of the usurper Maxime at the end of the sixth century, an act which was abolished before his own fall. Sulpitius Severus relates the appointment of Patrinus as the prosecutor of Priscillianus and the condemnation of the latter on the basis of that prosecution.[19] Moreover, the Emperor Trajan advises Pliny that he is not to prosecute the Christians on anonymous complaints.[20]

Despite these exceptional cases the *advocati fisci* were never to reach their full development and become public ministers of justice

[15] *Dig.*, I, 19, *De Officio Procuratoris Caesaris seu Rationalis.*

[16] *Code* 1, 55, *De Defensoribus Civitatum.*

[17] Code II, 9, *De Advocatis Fisci.*

[18] Serrigny, *Droit Admistratif Romain,* lib. II, tit. 1, section VI; Mommsen, *Droit Romain Criminal,* II, 7, ff. *cf. Revue Critique de Lege et de Jus,* XVI, pp. 523 ff.

[19] Sulpitius Severus, *Historiae Sacrae,* p. 430.

[20] Pliny, *Epistles,* X, 98.

as later practiced. The *actio popularis* described above and established under the Republic survived the transformation of the Republic by reason of the Roman's strong prejudice in favor of traditional institutions. This procedure made recourse to and intervention of a public prosecutor entirely unnecessary. These *advocati fisci* did not feel themselves constrained to prosecute *ex officio* or to supply public negligence when popular accusers who could present their causes failed to act. The germ of the modern institution is there, but only the abolition of popular action would allow it to take its full development. The *actio popularis,* however, persisted until after the barbarian invasion.

Hence it may be concluded that one looks in vain among the sources of Roman Law for the public ministry of justice as exercised in modern criminal proceedings. Popular action was the powerful and all sufficient weapon used so effectively by the Romans for the prosecution of delicts and crimes in those early days of procedural development. Indeed, the nebulous beginnings of a public ministry are to be found in the office of the advocates of the fisc; but at no time in its history did it evolve to such an extent that the advocates not only acted as proxy for the fisc in litigious matters but also as its public prosecutor in criminal matters.

Neither is the office to be found in the Decretals or in the writings of later commentators upon them.[21] All that has been said of the Roman Law is equally applicable to the *Corpus Juris Canonici.* The authorities are unanimous in their witness to the silence of the Decretals upon the office and as Roberti pointedly remarks in a footnote,[22] "Instr. S. C. Inquis., a. 1883 (par. 3), *adhuc concedebat actionem popularem pro causis matrimonialibus.*"

This silence is but natural because prior to the ninth century the Church adhered strictly to the Roman procedure of accusation in which no one had the express duty of investigating and prosecut-

[21] Wernz, *Jus Decretalium,* V, lib. 1, 54 ss.; Van Espen, *Omnia Opera,* III, tit. VI, cap. 5; Leurenius, *Forum Ecclesiasticum,* II, quaes. 890, n. 7; Lega, *De Judiciis Eccl.,* I, 171 ss.; Noval, *De Processibus,* I, n. 140, 78, 79; Roberti, *De Processibus,* I, 191 ss.; Bouix, *De Judiciis Eccl.,* I, 470.

[22] Roberti, *De Processibus,* I, 191, n. 3.

ing *ex officio* much less of assisting at private causes.[23] This accusatory procedure persisted until the thirteenth century when it was superseded by the inquisitorial procedure introduced by Innocent III at the Fourth Lateran Council.[24]

The inquisitorial procedure of this period did not require the presence of any other official than the judge to prosecute the causes before it. Nor was any prosecutor appointed by law. His absence was supplied by the *fama* of the crime, the judge, himself, merely establishing the truth or the falsity of the charges which the *fama* had caused to be brought against the defendant. It is only at a much later date, after the procedure had extended itself to many secular courts and to all ecclesiastical courts that the process had perfected itself by supplanting the fiction of the *fama* with an actual accuser, thereby introducing the procedure known as the *inquisitio cum prosequente vel promovente*.[25] And it is not until a still later date that the State or the Church appears as an interested party in the prosecution of crime by demanding the presence of their official prosecutor at all criminal, judicial proceedings.[26]

These being the facts, it may be safely concluded that the Promoter of Justice owes his origin neither to the Roman Law nor the Decretals. His origin postdates both these legal sources and must of necessity be sought in the legal sources, ecclesiastical or civil, of a later date.

Article II. Earliest Evidences of the Office

Before attempting to establish the origin of the Promoter, it might be well at this point to recall the words of Cardinal Lega relative to the early history of the office: *Historia Procuratoris Fiscalis tenebris obvolvitur remotioris antiquitatis et certe in jure canonico initium habet.*[27] The full truth of this statement will be

[23] C. 4, C. II, q. 1 is pseudo-Isidorean but testifies to the practice in the twelfth century; Roberti, *De Processibus,* I, 191, n. 5.

[24] C. 24, X, *de accusationibus,* V, 1.

[25] Durantis, *Speculum Juris,* Book III, pars. I, Inquis., par. Viso, n. 20.

[26] Esmein, *History of Continental Criminal Procedure,* p. 1 ff.

[27] Lega, *De Judiciis Eccl.,* I, 171, footnote 1.

borne out in the pages that follow on the history of the subject; for while canonists agree as to its early existence and exercise, there exists a wide divergence of opinion as to its exact origin and progress. Many canonists and historians accord full credit for the institution to the civil authorities, while still others maintain that it is an ecclesiastical derivation. It is almost impossible with available sources to determine conclusively which society is more responsible for the development of the office and so the writer will content himself with summarizing the findings of various authors as to its earliest existence in the hope that this examination will throw some light on the origins of the office.

It has been observed that office of Promoter in the diocesan curia does not find its origin in the Roman Law. It was, likewise, noted that the Decretals were silent on the office and its existence at that time. One meets a similar silence in the commentators on the Decretals. Yet despite this general silence it seems safe to say that the office has its origin in the Canon Law. The opinion of the late Cardinal Lega cited above and one which he repeated in the recent Juridical Congress held in Rome more than substantiates the belief that he was of this opinion.[28] Noval writing in 1920 says that Lega's opinion grows in favor and accepts it himself.[29] A Coronata after noting the two views as to the early origin of the office maintains that nothing very definite can be discovered and that undoubtedly both societies contributed to the earlier development of the office.[30] Roberti writes that the origin of the office is intimately connected with the process of the inquisition of crime *ex officio*.[31] Vidal, likewise, traces the origin of the office to the accusation of crimes *ex officio*, but following in the footsteps of Wernz assigns the major credit for the development of the office to the civil courts of France.[32] M. Fournier in his remarkable study of the Middle

[28] Lega, "De variis formis processus criminalis," *Jus Pontificium*, 14 (1934), 167-169.

[29] Noval, *De Processibus*, I, 78, 79.

[30] A Coronata, *Inst. J. C.*, III, 36.

[31] Roberti, *De Processibus*, I, n. 119, 191.

[32] Wernz-Vidal, *Jus Canonicum*, VI, 97, 98; Wernz, *Jus Decretalium*, V, lib. 1, 56, 166.

Ages asserts that the ecclesiastical promoters were of a later creation than the civil prosecutors and were copied after the Procurateurs de Roi of the French courts,[33] an opinion which Biener in his study on the inquisitorial procedure seems to adopt.[34] Molitor states that the original of the office cannot be found in Canon Law but grants that it might easily have proceeded from the *inquisitio compromovendi* of Innocent III.[35] He, too, is of the opinion that the major credit for the establishment of the fiscal prosecutor belongs to the courts of France, maintaining that the Church borrowed the office from the courts of France after the *inquisitio cum promovente* had itself given rise to the office in the secular courts. Esmein, a more recent historian on criminal procedure, while crediting the authorities with being the first to employ the procurator as an independent, official prosecutor of criminal offenses leaves no doubt as to the early and remote origin of the office when he writes: "It is into the official inquest that they [Procurateurs de Roi] insinuate themselves through an opening provided for them in the procedure per inquisitionem of the Canon Law."[36] A similar opinion is to be found in Droste's work on criminal procedure, though he certainly errs when he places the date of their introduction as late as the sixteenth century.[37] Lega, notwithstanding, insists that the civil courts did no more towards the establishment and development of the office of the Promoter than the ecclesiastical courts did.[38]

This opinion of Lega appears the better founded, inasmuch as all authorities agree that the *inquisitio ex officio* was the matrix in which all official prosecution of crime had its origin and first development.[39] It wielded a revolutionizing influence on all criminal

[33] Fournier, *Les Officialités au Moyen Age*, pp. 28-31.

[34] Biener, *Beiträge zu der Geschichte des Inquisitions-Processes*, pp. 200, 201.

[35] Molitor, *Über Kanonisches Gerichtsverfahren gegen Kleriker*, pp. 234 ff.

[36] Esmein, *History of Continental Criminal Procedure*, p. 117.

[37] Droste-Messmer, *Canonical Procedure in Criminal and Disciplinary Cases of Clerics*, pp. 65 ff.

[38] Lega, *De Judiciis Eccl.*, I, 173, footnotes.

[39] A. Lawrence Lowell, *Harvard Law Review*, II (1897-98), 185 ff.: Holdsworth, *History of English Law*, Vol. V, *Common Law and Its Rivals*, 158, 159;

procedure. This procedural innovation was seized upon by civil tribunals as better adapted for the attainment of their objectives than the rough compurgation and ordeal of the prevailing common law. The natural development of this inquisitorial procedure gave rise within the Church itself to the procedure of *inquisitio cum promovente,* which was appropriated in like manner by the secular courts. In due time by natural evolution this latter process brought about the introduction of the official prosecutor. And although the civil authorities may have been the first to realize the added effectiveness of such an office and anticipated the Church by creating it as an independent office, the credit for the remote origins and subsequent development must be assigned to Canon Law and the ecclesiastical tribunals. Nor is it at all certain, as it will be seen in treating of the inquisitorial procedure, that there was not already a titular officer in the ecclesiastical tribunals who foreshadowed the office exercised by the civil prosecutor. This official seems to have arisen shortly after the introduction of the inquisitorial procedure by Innocent III.[40] True he owed his origin and existence to custom which did not make him essential to the process and though he did not enjoy legal approbation until long after the successful introduction of the office by the civil authorities, nevertheless, he seems to have been active at the earliest date given for the introduction of the civil prosecutor and was a direct step in that direction. No doubt the successful experiment of the prosecutor in the civil courts and his effective usage in those tribunals encouraged the Church to strengthen his position and define the practice in her own tribunals. But to say that she borrowed the institution entirely from the secular courts is an exaggeration. At least she is equally responsible for its introduction and contributed as much to its development as any secular forum. She beyond all doubt planted the seed of the office in her inquisitorial tribunals which in due course

Pollock-Maitland, *History of English Law,* II, 602, footnote 1, p. 654; Tanon, *Histoire des Tribunaux de l'Inquisition,* p. ii; Esmein, *Histoire de procedure criminelle en France,* pp. 284, 315.

[40] Droste-Messmer, *Canonical Procedure in Disciplinary and Criminal Cases of Clerics,* p. 67, footnote 3.

of time blossomed forth as an independent office as a result of the combined efforts of both institutions, civil and ecclesiastical.

That so wide a divergence of opinion is possible is easily understandable when we consider the condition of society at this period of world history. During the pontificate of Innocent III, the Church was in her zenith, the Papacy was held in high esteem and the closest of union existed between the Church and State. Moreover she was the patroness of all culture and under her supervision and in virtue of her munificence, the revival of the study of Roman Law was made possible. She incorporated the better elements of that ancient system into her own legal systems, perfecting them and adapting them to the conditions in which she found society at the time. Her independent courts guided as they were by the principles of Canon Law became a model for the secular courts and exercised a tremendous influence on their development. One has but to read Esmein's monumental work [41] on European procedure to realize the all pervasive and profitable influence exercised on Continental procedure by the ecclesiastical legislation prior to the Reformation. The Church, herself, did not hesitate to borrow from the secular jurisdictions those improvements which she deemed advantageous to her own mission. Another famous historian writes of this period:

> The Church was able to furnish to the secular courts a lesson and a model in the methods of its ecclesiastical tribunals. By its example it led the way in the substitution, consummated in the 1500's of the inquisitorial procedure for the accusatory system in every country in Europe (a system originally employed for the prosecution of heresy, afterwards for all crimes under the name of *procedure a l'extraordinaire,* the system of the common law in force in royal jurisdictions for the prosecution of crime until 1789). In the latter half of the thirteenth century the influence of Roman Law and procedure which renounced the Germanic tendencies made itself felt and the secular law took its inspiration almost exclusively from these two learned systems.[42]

[41] Esmein, Continental Legal Series, Vol. V, *History of Continental Criminal Procedure.*

[42] Leo, *Histoire de L'Inquisition au Moyen Age,* Book I, cc. IX-XI.

Similarly, Calisse[43] in writing of the Papal States reports: "The States of the Church remained faithful to the principles of Canon Law, slowly coordinating the betterments that were taking place." And Drage,[44] describing Germanic Law at the time of Maximilian I, writes:

> In all these laws the system of public punishment without alternative of fine prevailed exclusively and at the same time the system of public prosecution on the model of the procedure in vogue in the ecclesiastical courts.

Relative to the introduction of the public prosecution of crime, the following statement is found in Esmein's work referred to above:

> We shall see, therefore, a regular official prosecution make its appearance in the 1200's and rapidly develop, simultaneously with the substitution of inquests for old methods of proof. But before studying this movement, it is necessary to explain briefly what was the criminal procedure of the ecclesiastical courts. Its influence in the transformation we are going to describe is undeniable This is not due to the fact that the Church created her own systems in every detail. On the contrary, most of the elements of which it made use were borrowed from secular institutions. It imbued these, however, with a new spirit and lost no time in substantially altering them. It is sometimes said that the inquisitorial procedure of ancient France is merely the result of borrowing from the Church. That as we shall make clear is not entirely true; but it is none the less true that the Church was the first authority which changed from the accusatory to the inquisitorial procedure. And having been the first it naturally furnished a model to France and the neighbouring countries.[45]

Hélie in his authoritative study of criminal procedure writes in a similar vein noting the deep influence of the inquisitorial procedure, as developed in the ecclesiastical courts upon all subsequent official prosecution of crime.[46]

[43] Calisse, *History of Italian Law*, n. 276.

[44] Drage, *Criminal Code of the German Empire*, p. 6.

[45] Esmein, *History of Continental Criminal Procedure*, pp. 78, 79.

[46] Hélie, *Traité de l'instruction criminal*, I, 464; *cf.* Pollock-Maitland, *History of English Law*, II, 654.

These few citations which will be augmented later in speaking of the inquisitorial procedure will serve to show the close interrelation between the ecclesiastical and civil societies. This close interrelation between their various institutions renders it almost impossible to state definitely which society might be more responsible for the creation and full development of certain arms of the law as they exist today and the present subject seems to be one of these institutions. Since all agree that the inquisitorial procedure is the fountainhead of all official prosecution of crime, a short description of its origin, development and spread may afford some light on the subject. First, however, a brief word on the prevailing procedures of the time.

CHAPTER II

THE PROCEDURAL DEVELOPMENTS WHICH GAVE RISE TO THE OFFICE

Article I: Procedure by Accusation

It has already been seen that in Roman Law there was no prosecution of crimes *ex officio*. The only prosecution in practice was the *actio popularis*, by which any individual might become the accuser. This system was taken over to the Canon Law and for many centuries until the twelfth used almost exclusively in the prosecution of crime before the ecclesiastical tribunals. This accusation was *dilatio rei criminis in judicium ad publicam vindictam solemniter facta.*[1] This system implies the accusation by any qualified private individual before the competent judge according to the rules laid down in Canon Law. The accusation must be of a public grave crime and although the private utility of him who has been injured may be the primary end, the secondary end must always be the reparation of the public order which has been violated by the damaging action.[2]

The system was crude and it was not long before difficulties arose from this form of procedure, inasmuch as many heretics availed themselves of it to accuse falsely orthodox bishops of abuses and crimes. So widespread did this practice become of haling ecclesiastics into court on false charges that the first Council of Constantinople was forced to deal with it. In order to remedy the evil and to afford a proper safeguard against future abuses of a similar nature, the Fathers of the Council took the drastic step which the authors term the *poena talionis*. By this the accuser bound himself in writing to prove his charges under penalty of accepting the

[1] Schmalzgrueber, lib. V, tit. I, par. II, n. 21; Reiffenstuel, lib. V, tit. I, par. 1, nn. 5 ss.; Leurenius, lib. V, tit. I, qq. 6, 7.

[2] Schmalzgrueber, lib. V, tit. I, par. II, nn. 22-24.

same punishment the accused would have received had he been found guilty. The Council declared [3] " . . . et accusatione non prius intendere quam in scriptis aequale periculum sibi statuant si quidem in ipsis examinandis accusatum episcopum caluminari convicti fuerint."

This reform despite its good intent and its necessity deterred not only the calumniator but also the sincere Christian from making the necessary accusations.[4] People naturally were hesitant before proffering an act of so serious a nature carrying with it such heavy penalties and reprisals and exposing the complainant to the greatest of dangers in a society where all too often the last word rested in the hands of the privileged nobility and the wealthy.[5] The result was that unless there was a motive of a private nature, *e. g.*, revenge or personal damages, crimes went unpunished.

Under Innocent III (1215) the Church reacted with energy against this crude form of procedure. It brought about the common use of the more practical and effective systems of denunciation and inquisition. Prior to this time both these procedures had been in use but were exercised only as extraordinary procedures. Henceforth, they are to be ordinary procedures and crimes need no longer remain unpunished because of the lack of accusers or the fears which the powerful wrongdoers inspired in them. In fine, Innocent III took the necessary steps and a new procedure becomes effective under the common law of the Church.[6]

Article II. Procedure by Denunciation

Denunciation was *dilatio seu manifestatio criminis superiori facta sine solemnitate*."[7] It is, therefore, the manifestation of a crime

[3] Harduinus, *Acta Conciliorum* I, 811, can. VI.

[4] S. B. Smith, *Elements of Ecclesiastical Law,* II, 145; Reiffenstuel, lib. V, tit. I, nn. 10, 11.

[5] Holdsworth, *History of English Law,* V, 159.

[6] Esmein, *History of Continental Criminal Procedure,* pp. 3-5 incl.; S. B. Smith, *Elements of Ecclesiastical Law,* II, n. 937, 146.

[7] Schmalzgrueber, lib. V, tit. I, nn. 126 ss.; Reiffenstuel, lib. V, tit. I, nn. 58 ss.; Leurenius, lib. V, tit. I, q. 21.

to legitimate authority without assuming the obligation of proving the accusation under the *poena talionis*. Thus it would seem to differ from the preceding system inasmuch as the complainant is not compelled to submit to the obligation of proving the charge. Ordinarily, he submitted the proof to the judge, but it was left to the discretion of the judge whether or not he should act upon the evidence submitted.

The denunciation could be of two kinds, evangelical or judicial. The evangelical had as its objective the fraternal correction of the delinquent by the bishop in the rôle of a fatherly superior rather than as a judge. It was usually employed in the reprimanding of occult offenses but which could be proved by two witnesses. Judicial, on the other hand, was a complaint made to the superior, as a judge, and it sought the reparation of a specific crime through the judicial action of the superior. It had practically all the formalities of the procedure by accusation with the exception of the omission of the *poena talionis* already noted. The charge had to be in writing, giving the names of the judge, the person denouncing, the person denounced as well as the nature of the alleged offense with some indication as to the time, place and circumstances in which it was committed together with the names of witnesses or other substantiating proofs which might be produced at the proper time.[8]

Article III. The Inquisitorial Procedure

A. *Its Origin*

In the harsh and inadequate procedure described in the preceding pages the prosecution of crime was an affair of private individuals. It was only in rare instances that the public authorities could interfere in an effectual manner. Even in the case of capture in the act all the State could do was to seize the culprit and to await the pleasure of the injured party to bring action against him or to obtain the delinquent's consent to the inquest.[9]

This system was manifestly inadequate for the suppression of

[8] Schmalzgrueber, lib. V, tit. I, nn. 152 ss.

[9] Holdsworth, *History of English Law*, V. 59.

the abuses then widespread in the Church. It became essential that a real and effectual prosecution should be devised and the Church laid the foundation for this remedy in her institution of the *processus per inquisitionem* at the end of the twelfth century.[10]

As was already noted, prior to this time the Church adhered strictly to the prosecution by accusation.[11] About the ninth century, however, the Church took a step forward. Ecclesiastical legislation of that century provided that anyone pointed out by popular opinion as a suspect by reason of crime committed might be apprehended. The judge was then free to establish the *mala fama* under which the suspect was laboring. Should the judge find the *mala fama* justified, Canon Law admitted a certain right of action against the *infamatus*. This did not mean that the judge was permitted to introduce witnesses against the accused and condemn him were he convicted, but rather that the *mala fama* once established, the victim was compelled to prove himself innocent. It was difficult to establish the notoriety and as no one had the right to prosecute, the final fate of the prisoner was in his own hands. If he refused to vindicate himself or was unable to exculpate himself, he was convicted and condemned of the offense charged against him.[12]

Hence as early as the ninth century, the Church permitted notorious crimes to be prosecuted without the necessity of an accuser. As a result there arose the legal axiom, *notoria non indigent accusatore*. This system, however, never attained much practical value because of the difficulty in determining what constituted notoriety.[13]

Canon Law at this time did not permit of an official prosecution, properly so called. It rather acquiesced to the popular prejudice of law that the judge should not appear as judge and accuser in the same case, the public prosecutor being as yet unknown. Nicholaus

[10] Lega, *De Judiciis Eccl.*, I, 177, 178; Wernz-Vidal, *Jus Canonicum*, VI, 91; Esmein, *History of Continental Criminal Procedure*, 115 ff.; Holdsworth, *History of English Law*, V, 158, 159.

[11] Fournier, *Les Officialités au Moyen Age*, p. 262 ff.; Wernz-Vidal, *Jus Canonicum*, VI, 98 and footnote 61.

[12] C. 2, X, *De purgatione canonica*, V, 34; c. 2, X, *De purgatione vulgari*, V. 35.

[13] Cc. 15-17, C. II, q. 1; Holdsworth, *History of English Law*, V, 159.

de Tudeschis voices the teaching then prevalent: *Judex non est locus partis . . . non fungitur duplici officio incompassibili quia alius debet esse accusator, alius judex.*[14] This is likewise the teaching of Gratian [15] and Ives of Chartres espouses a similar doctrine.[16]

The apparent weaknesses of such prosecution were remedied by the papal legislation of the late twelfth and early thirteenth centuries. A new form of criminal procedure made its appearance whereby the judge was allowed in proof of ill fame to prosecute the suspected person and could proceed *per inquisitionem.* This process was really an official prosecution by the judge.

It differed from the preceding in which the *infamatus* was forced to exculpate himself in this that the judge may not proceed except on the *infamia praecedente,* but that, once established, the judge may summon, arrest, accuse, cite witnesses to substantiate his charges and in fine condemn the accused if the proof of his guilt warrants such a sentence. It began with a secret inquiry by the judge followed by an interrogation of the accused who was obliged to answer under oath.

This change was brought about by the positive legislation of Innocent III in the year 1189.[17] This innovation gave rise to the standard objection that the process made the judge and accuser one and the same person. This objection was forestalled when the Fourth Lateran Council had recourse to a legal fiction, whereby the *infamia* once established against the suspect took the place of an accuser, the judge remaining impartial.[18] Hostiensis [19] and Nicholaus de Tudeschis very clearly attest to this fact. The latter, commenting on C. 25 X, *de accusatione,* V., 1, writes: *Nota quod in inquisitione judex non tenet hanc partem, sed infamia est loco accusationis seu*

[14] Nicholaus de Tudeschis, *Panormitanus,* lib. V, *De accus., inqui., denun.,* cap. XXV, n. 7.

[15] C. 1, C. IV, q. 4.

[16] Ives of Chartres, Epistles CVIII, CXIX, CCVI—*M. P. L.,* 162, cols., 126, 133, 211, 212.

[17] C. 1, X, *ut ecclesia vel beneficia sine diminutione conferantur,* III, 12; c. 10, X, *De purgatione canonica,* V, 34.

[18] C. 24, X, *de accusatione,* V, 1; cc. 31, 32, X, *de simonia,* V, 3.

[19] Hostiensis, *Summa Aurea,* lib. V, tit., *De Inquisitione,* p. 340.

denuntiationis.[20] Again in commenting upon c. 17, X, *de accusationibus,* V, 1, one reads . . . *de occultis non fit inquisitio ubi non praecessit infamia quia deficit verus et fictus accusator.*[21]

Thus did the Church substitute the inquisitorial procedure for the defective accusatory procedure. The system was far superior for the repression of crime than the preceding systems. It was a salutary departure made by the Church and owes its evil reputation to the tribunal of the Inquisition with which it has been mistakenly identified. It was not, as often has been said, the struggle against heretics which led to its introduction. A special application of it was, indeed, made to heresy in the *inquisitio hereticae pravitatis,* committed to the Franciscans and Dominicans in 1232, but it was the correction of clerical abuses in general that led Innocent III at the Fourth Lateran Council held in 1215 to inaugurate this stronger form of public prosecution.

B. *Notion of the Inquisitorial Procedure*

In what did the inquisitional process of Innocent III consist and how did it function? This procedure is a long detailed process and accordingly only its essential outlines will be given stressing only those features which are necessary for a simple understanding of it.

Inquisition may be defined simply as *criminis vel criminosi per legitimum judicem facta investigatio.*[22] It was of two kinds, general and special, to which occasionally was added a third species called mixed. General inquisition was had when the bishop or a delegated judge as a mere duty of his office conducted an investigation not of any specific person or crime but of the general religious or moral condition of some province or place. It could give rise to the special inquisition if the investigator found evidences of criminal action in the place or monastery. Special *inquisition* took place when the judge either *ex officio* investigated some particular person or crime

[20] Nicholaus de Tudeschis, *Panormitanus,* lib. V, *De accus., inqui., denun.,* cap. XXV, n. 7.

[21] Nicholaus de Tudeschis, *Panormitanus,* lib. V, *De accus., inqui., denun.,* cap. XVII, n. 6.

[22] Reiffenstuel, lib. V, tit. I, nn. 149 ss.; Schmalzgrueber, lib. V, tit. I, n. 172.

by reason of the *mala fama* connected with the person or place or when at the instance of injured parties, he examined the evidences concerned with the guilt of a particular person. This latter procedure was also known as the *inquisitio cum promovente vel prosequente.* That species which was known as mixed, but which the authors classify as general, was the investigation of a specific crime, but not as having been committed by a specific person.[23] The inquisition, especially the general, was called paternal when it had for its objective the correction of abuses after the manner of a solicitous parent; judicial when the superior acted as a judge for the punishment of the delinquent.

A clear concise idea of the process is to be found in the canons themselves of the Fourth Lateran Council held in the year 1215 under Pope Innocent III. Gregory IX embodies these canons in their entirety in his official collection of the decretals. It was this council which under the guidance and direction of Innocent III, an able canonist in his own right, substituted the inquisitorial procedure for the accusatory and molded the former into a strictly judicial process,[24] which was to be employed in the ordinary trials. Its use as an ordinary procedure is ordained in the council, together with the principal rules regulating its exercise.

Canon 6 of the Fourth Lateran Council is reproduced in C. 25, X, *De Accusationibus,* V, 1 and reads as follows:

> Sicut olim a sanctis Patribus noscitur institutum; metropolitani, singulis annis, cum suis suffraganeis, Provincialia non omittant concilia celebrare: in quibus de corrigendis excessibus, et moribus reformandis, praesertim in clero, diliigentem habeant cum Dei timore tractatum: canonicas regulas, maxime quae statutae sunt in hoc generali Concilio, relegentes, ut eas faciant observari, debita poena transgressoribus infligendo. Ut autem id valeat efficacius adimpleri, per singulas dioeceses statuat personas idoneas, providas videlicet et honestas, quae per totum annum, simpliciter et de plano, absque ulla jurisdictione, sollicite investiget, quae correctione vel reformatione sunt digna: et ea fideliter per-

[23] Scaccia, *De Judiciis,* lib. I, cap. LXXXIII, nn. 1 ss.; Durantis, *Speculum,* lib. III, pars I, *De Inquisitione,* Viso, n. 20.

[24] Lega, *De Judiciis Eccl.,* I, 172, and footnotes.

> ferant ad metropolitanum et suffraganeos et alios in concilio subsequente: ut super his et aliis prout utilitati et honestati congruerit, provida deliberatione procedant: et quae statuerint faciant observari: publicaturi ea in episcopalibus synodis annuatim per singulas dioeceses celebrandis. Quisquis autem hoc salutare statutum neglexerit adimplere, a sui executione officii suspendatur.

This was the ***inquisitio generalis*** prescribed by the Council.[25]

Relative to the ***inquisitio specialis*** one finds a similar summary in C. 24, X, *De Accusationibus*, V, 1, and in Canon 8 of the Fourth Lantern.[26]

> Debet, igitur, esse praesens is contra quem facienda est inquisitio, nisi se per contumacian absentaverit; et exponenda sunt ei illa capitula, de quibus fuerit inquirendum, ut facultatem habeat defendendi seipsum. Et non solum dicta, sed etiam ipsa nomina testium sunt ei ut quid et a quo sit dictum appareat, publicanda; necnon exceptiones et replicationes legitimae admittendae, ne per suppressionem nominum infamandi, per exceptionem vero exclusionem, deponendi falsum audacia praebeatur. Ad corrigendos itaque subditorum excessus, tanto diligentius debet praelatus assurgere quanto damnabilius eorum offensas desereret incorrectas. Contra quos, ut de notoriis excessibus taceatur, et si tribus modis possit procedi, per accusationem videlicet, denuntiationem et inquisitionem ipsorum: ut tamen in omnibus diligens adhibeatur cautela, ne forte per leve compendium, ad grave dispendium veniatur; sicut accusationem legitima debet praecedere inscriptio, sic et denuntiationem charitativa monitio, et inquisitionem clamosa insinuatio praevenire: illo semper adhibito moderamine, ut juxta formam judicii, sententiae quoque; forma dictetur.

Here one sees the judge laying aside his rôle of an impartial arbiter and actually conducting an investigation of crime in virtue of his office. The Council empowers him to arrest, cite, produce witnesses, admit or reject proofs, examine the prisoner and should the evidence warrant it condemn the same; for the Council states, ***probatis criminibus gravibus, eum ab administratione removebit.***

[25] Reiffenstuel, lib. V, tit. I, nn. 156-158.

[26] Canon VIII, *De Inquisitionibus*—Harduinus, *Acta Conciliorum*, VII, 26, 27.

At first sight the judge apparently combined the office of judge and prosecutor or accuser, but the Council avoids this unfavorable view of its procedural creation by resorting to a legal fiction. Sensing the ever-present objection of recognized jurisprudence to anything that has the semblance of combining these two independent, important rôles, the legislators provided in Canon 8 of the Council the necessary protection against such a charge or accusation. It personifies, as it were, the *mala fama* and invests it with the rôle of accuser in any given trial. This canon which has been incorporated into the decretals of Gregory IX explains as follows:

> Ex quibus auctoritatibus manifeste comprobatur, quod non solum cum subditus verum etiam cum prelatus excedit, si per clamorem et fama ad aures superioris pervenerit, non quidem a malevolis et maledictis, sed a providis et honestis, nec semel tantum sed saepe (quod clamor innituit et diffimatio manifestat) debet coram ecclesiae senioribus veritatem diligentius perscrutari; ut si rei poposcerit qualitas, canonica destrictio culpam feriat delinquentis; non tantum sit actor et judex, sed quasi fama deferente vel denuntiante clamore officii sui debitum exsequatur.[27]

It was as if the *mala fama* appeared as the interested plaintiff against the accused.[28] Pope Innocent was not over enthusiastic about the *inquisitio mala fama deferente.* He rather favored the *inquisitio cum promovente,* for all too often despite the fiction of the *mala fama* the judge and accuser seemed to be the same person and this was in direct opposition to the popular prejudice which always sharply distinguishes between the two offices.[29]

C. *Development of the Inquisition in the Church*

These simple principles of Innocent III were carried to their full development within the Church by subsequent Popes and canon-

[27] Harduinus, *Acta Conciliorum,* VII, 26.

[28] Hostiensis, *Summa Aurea,* lib. V, tit. *De Inquisitionibus,* p 340; Nicholaus de Tudeschis, *Panormitanus,* lib. V, *De accus., inqui., denun.,* cap. XVII, n. 6, et cap. XXV, n. 7; Molitor, *Über Kanonisches Gerichtsverfahren gegen Kleriker,* p. 183.

[29] Molitor, o. c., p. 183 ff.

ists.[80] Once the *inquisitio* was established in the Church, the judge instead of proceeding of his own accord, *ex officio mero,* could proceed with the inquest upon the denunciation of a private person. This was at first introduced by custom, but later it came to be done as a matter of law. The person who lodged the complaint was naturally vitally interested in the prosecution of the cause. He was entitled to file the accusation but preferred to use the denunciation and thus set in motion the inquisitorial procedure. Technically he was called the *promovens inquisitionem,*[81] and the process itself received the significant title, *inquisitio cum promovente.* The decretals give a set of rules governing it and ascribe to the *promovens* an active part in the procedure.[82]

As a result there arose in the Church a new form of criminal action. The title *inquisitio* was reserved exclusively to the procedure *fama deferente.* Nicholaus de Tudeschis clearly distinguishes between the two procedures in the following statement: *Proprie processus inquisitionis est quando judex facit ex officio puro nemine inquisitionem deferente et impetrante; sed quando fit ad denuntiationem alterius, tunc est proprie processus per viam denunciationis.*[83]

A new organ of ecclesiastical *judicature* was the inevitable outcome of the *processus cum promovente.* This titular officer was nothing more than an official charged with the duty of denouncing offenses to the judge and by that action promoting the process before the judge sitting in the trial. His function is one of progressive growth. Its origin is to be found in the delegation made by the judge in the course of the procedure *per inquisitionem.* When the judge proceeded *ex officio,* he found himself frequently beset with difficult angles in a case and appointed a capable official to act as promoter in a specific case.

The status of this *promotor specialiter delegatus a judice* was not very well defined. Innocent IV testifies that in his time the

[80] Molitor, *Über Kanonisches Gerichtsverfahren gegen Kleriker,* p. 181.

[81] Durantis, *Speculum Juris,* lib. III, pars I, Viso, n. 20.

[82] C. 18, 19, X, *de accusationibus,* V. 1.

[83] Nicholaus de Tudeschis, *Panormitanus,* lib. V, *De accus., inqui., denun.,* cap. XXV, n. 21.

practice had become quite common.[34] Authors sought the basis for it in the decretals on witnesses.[35] At all events he was given the pretentious title *minister inquisitionis.* Hostiensis, however, is careful to note that he does not have the initiative in criminal matters and hence was not a party to the citation, as the process could be conducted without him. Esmein remarks that the same was true of the first civil prosecutors and it is only after a time that they become the exclusive prosecutors of crime.[36] This official was destined, nevertheless, to develop into a permanent titular office. While one does not as yet find any references to the *Promotor Fiscalis,* one does meet enlightening references on this *promotor specialiter delegatus a judice.*[37] Shortly after its introduction towards the end of the thirteenth century (1245-1296), the Procurateurs de Roi of the French Law make their appearance.[38] Esmein, as noted, professes that the procurator of the French Law slipped in to the procedure through the opening provided for him by this *minister inquisitionis.*[39] The French office of prosecutor seems to be only a natural development of the ecclesiastical minister of inquisition. Moreover as early as 1274, one finds a *procurator fiscalis Episcopi Parisiensis.*[40]

D. *Acceptance by Civil Tribunals*

Compurgation and trial by ordeal began to fall into disuse at the beginning of the thirteenth century and in 1215 the latter was given a fatal blow by the Fourth Lateran Council.[41] The wages of battle persisted a little longer because feudal nobility clung to it as a last vestige of their privileges. In France St. Louis IX strove to abolish it and although he was only partially successful, his of-

[34] C. 53, X, *De Testibus,* II, 20.

[35] Hostiensis, lib. II, tit. XX, cap. LIII; C. 53, X, *De Testibus,* II, 20.

[36] Esmein, *History of Continental Criminal Procedure,* p. 294.

[37] Esmein, o. c., p. 88, footnote 2.

[38] Holdsworth, *History of English Law,* V, 158, 159; Wernz, *Jus Decretalium,* V, 166, footnote 18.

[39] Esmein, *History of Continental Criminal Procedure,* pp. 117 ss.

[40] Tanon, *Histoire des Justices des Eglises et Communautés Ecclesiastiques,* p. 341.

[41] Holdsworth, *History of English Law,* V, 158.

ficial disfavor served to weaken the procedure by duel and finally, abolished it altogether. There was no new procedure to supersede the obsolete systems which were dying out and the nation was in need of a judicial system to perfect and supplant the crude inquisition which followed the judicial duels and ordeals. This need was fulfilled by the bold departure made by Innocent III when he set up the inquisitorial procedure to put an end to the scandals that were harassing the Church at the time.

This inquisitorial procedure being in harmony with the spirit of Roman Jurisprudence was gradually adopted by all the continental States, together with the developments brought about in the system by the efforts of Innocent III and his successors to effect reform. The inquisitoral procedure with its *promovens* and its *minister a judice delegatus* was taken over by the State and developed until at last prosecution of crime was carried on almost exclusively by officers of the State.[42] As Holdsworth so well witnesses:

> By the thirteenth century repression of crime had come to be regarded as a matter in which the king is chiefly interested. Therefore it was thought that he could apply the inquest procedure to all cases and it was not long before the two systems, the aprise and the inquest, became merged. The other developments which had occurred in Canon Law soon made their appearance. The private accuser could make use of it by denouncing the accused to the judge. And soon arose a set of public prosecutors in the *procurateurs de roi* of the great nobles.[43]

What has been said of France and its adoption of the inquisitorial procedure as it had developed in the Church is equally applicable to the other countries of Western Europe.[44] Thus in Italy, Albert Grandinus (1300), and his successors to Albert Farranachius (1540) and Julius Clarus (1575)[45] took over the inquisition as

[42] A. Lawrence Lowell, *Harvard Law Review*, II, 197, 198.

[43] Holdsworth, *History of English Law*, V, 158, 159; Biener, *Beiträge zu der Geschichte des Inquisitions-Processes*, p. 96.

[44] Esmein, *Histoire de procedure criminelle en France*, pp. 284, 315; Pollock and Maitland, *History of English Law*, II, 654.

[45] Biener, o. c., pp. 160-165; Holdsworth, o. c., 158, 159.

instituted by Innocent III and organized by his successors with the result that this procedure dominated the criminal systems of the State. In Germany the inquisitorial procedure began with Benedict Carzov (1635).[46] In that country the system was based on Italian jurisprudence, a distinguishing feature of which was the presence of the public prosecutor as plaintiff. These officials were called *promotor fiscalis, procurator fiscalis* or simply *fiscalis,* the names used in ecclesiastical law to designate the same persons. The same officials are found in the secular courts of France in the fourteenth century, and in the courts of Portugal, Spain and England in the fifteenth. Their chief duty was to report on crimes. From France the office found gradual entrance into the Netherlands. In Italy in the sixteenth century the office of *promotor fiscalis* was firmly established in Naples, Milan and Rome.[47] Calisse, a recognized historian on the history of law, writing of the Renaissance period (1100-1789) says:

> The reestablished authority of the state was also expressed through the special magistrates by which the government brought a public action against the accused, that is, supported the charge and whose representatives in many places were called states attorneys (procuratore fiscali) and were the distant ancestors of the public prosecutors of today.[48]

Wherefore this chapter may be summed up thus. The beginnings of a public prosecutor are very obscure, and the evidences of its early existence too scanty to warrant any definite conclusions as to its exact origin and earliest development. It most certainly had its remote origins in the inquisitorial procedure inaugurated by the Church in the Fourth Lateran Council under Innocent III. The gradual development of the process by Pope Innocent and his successors, especially, the illustrious Innocent IV gave birth to entirely new procedural developments, especially, the *minister inquisitionis.* This latter procedure, the *inquisitio cum promovente,* was taken over by the secular courts in its entirety. As the result of a very natural

[46] Molitor, *Über Kanonisches Gerichtsverfahren gegen Kleriker,* p. 232 ff.

[47] Molitor, o. c., p. 232.

[48] Calisse, *A History of Italian Law,* n. 97.

evolution the minister very shortly blossomed forth as an independent office which reached its full development in the French *procurateurs de roi* of the fourteenth century. He was the first real official prosecutor enjoying the right to prosecute *ex officio*. In view of these facts, it seems that it can be safely maintained with the late Cardinal Lega that the Promoter of Justice had his beginning in Canon Law and found his full development by virtue of the combined efforts of both the ecclesiastical and civil tribunals. The inquisitorial procedure was the seed planted in the ecclesiastical courts of the thirteenth century which blossomed forth as the public prosecution of today with its states attorneys and its Promoters of Justice in virtue of the mutual efforts of both societies.

It is time now to pass to the purely historical part of the work and consider the historical vestiges of the Promoter in the *judicature* of the Church. In passing to this phase, let it be borne in mind that no attempt will be made to comment at great length on those links that form the historical background of the subject. The information is too scanty and the sources too unrelated to permit anything like a systematic tracing of the office step by step to its present development. An attempt will be made rather to discover those times and places in the past in which the office enjoyed some standing and, as far as possible, determine the position the official enjoyed in the diocesan curia at such times.

CHAPTER III

THE HISTORICAL VESTIGES OF THE OFFICE OF THE PROMOTER IN THE ECCLESIASTICAL JUDICATURE

ARTICLE I. THE PROMOTER FROM THE XIV TO XVII CENTURIES

The first express mention which is made of the Promoter as a diocesan official is to be found in the official record of the curia in the Archdiocese of Paris. From 1274, one finds a *promotor fiscalis Episcopi Parisiensis.*[1] His duties, however, are obscure and except for the fact that he was an officer in the curia which employed the inquisitorial procedure, little or nothing can be predicated of him. It is significant, however, that he appears at a date so soon after the introduction of the inquisitorial procedure itself.

Early in the fourteenth century the office of the Promoter had become somewhat common in the ecclesiastical courts of France. As early as 1329, Pierre de Cugnéres found a very considerable number of them functioning in the ecclesiastical courts and in 1399, the Archbishop of Sens had four Promoters functioning in his diocese.[2] The official registry of the curia of Cerisy, a town in the department of Manche, under the date of 1314 gives a description of the curia as it existed then. The curia was a complete tribunal and numbered among its officers a *promotor fiscalis.* The curia was to correct, investigate and punish all types of delicts and delinquents which custom and the law had reserved to the Abbot of Cerisy for punishment.[3] In 1327, there appears a Promoter connected with the ecclesiastical inquests in the Diocese of Arras and the rules for the Archdiocese of Rheim, 1329, mention in several places the pro-

[1] Tanon, *Histoire des Justices des Eglises et Communautés Ecclesiastiques de Paris,* p. 341; Esmein, *History of Continental Criminal Procedure,* p. 88.

[2] Fournier, *Les Officialités au Moyen Age,* p. 30.

[3] Registrum curie Cerasiensis, n. 2, referred to by René le Picard, *La Communaute de la Vie Conjugale* (Paris: Recueil Sirey, 1930), Appendix III, pp. 416, 417.

moters or procurators appointed to correct and check any excesses which might be present in the diocese.[4]

Be that as it may, there can be little doubt that the Promoter was functioning in certain dioceses as an independent official in the early part of the fourteenth century. The Council held at Noyon in the year 1344 unquestionably had the office in mind when it wrote chapter sixteen of its reforms into the law:[5]

> . . . quod quamplurimum morum de Dominis temporalibus et judicibus Saecularibus gravem querimoniam receperint, continentem quod nonnulli dictarum curiarum ecclesiasticarum Promotores ac etiam Procuratores, ad excessus citantes eorum homines subditos et Burgenses, varia et diversa crimina et excessus coloribus fictis expositos eisdem ponentibus, non solum in corporibus propriis et scandalo gravi eorundem, damnificant et fatigant; sed etiam gravissimis sumptis et expensis, nobis supplicantes ut vellemus super his providere de remedio opportuno.

The council continues with a caution to ecclesiastical promoters and prosecutors against prosecuting offenders unless they have a just cause and are certain of their guilt both factually and juridically. Thus the council makes a definite reference to promoters and procurators of the ecclesiastical curia who enjoy the express right and duty to cite and prosecute those guilty of public violations of the law and implies from its method of speaking that the institution has been functioning some time and is firmly entrenched in the ecclesiastical judicature at the time of the council.

Shortly after this, a reference and witness may be had which leaves absolutely no room for question, as it definitely refers to this official as the ***Procurator Fiscalis***. The witness is embodied in the acts of the Council of Magdebourg, held according to Mansi in the year 1370, but in the opinion of Hefele about 1390.[6] This Council,

[4] Ordinatio curie Remensis, Arch. adm. de Reims, II, 591—Fournier, *Les Officialités au Moyen Age,* p. 30 in footnotes, 1-3.

[5] Cap. 16—Mansi, XXVI, 2; Hefele-Leclerque, *Histoire de Conciles,* VI, Pars I, 105, 106; Fournier, *Les Officialité au Moyen,* p. 30, n. 2.

[6] Tit. X, *de Officio Delegati Judicis.*—Mansi, XXVI, 574; Hefele-Leclerque, *Histoire des Conciles,* VI, Pars II, 966.

occupied as it was with sorely needed reform of clergy and laity, turns its attention to the thorny problem of those destitute clergy, both secular and religious, whose rights were being wrested away from them by unscrupulous clergy and avaricious and ambitious laymen. To remedy this shameful practice, the Council decreed: . . . *ut clericus cujuslibet civitatis et dioecesis nostrae provinciae habeat unum vel plures procuratores fiscales.* These men without fear and favor were to be in a position to defend the oppressed and destitute clergy and were to seek justice for them even in the highest Courts of Church and State. These *procuratores* shall seek the restitution of all their rights and privileges together with any loss they may have incurred through the unjust privation. The more effectively to attain this end, they are to seek the infliction of the penalties provided in provincial law against the contumacious offenders who refuse to make the proper indemnification for the injuries they have inflicted on these defenseless, innocent persons. The Council, further, provides that in the event the executor is unwilling to execute the sentence, the Ordinary must supply his negligence and see to the execution himself at the instance of the injured party and especially at the request of the *Procurator Fiscalis.* Surely, nothing could be clearer than this decree of the Council. It establishes the procurator as the defender of the poor and oppressed clergy of the diocese, making him an agent of equity and justice in the supervision of the administration of justice in the diocese. It invests him with the special importance of a public personality, whose intervention in a given case is to have special weight with both the court and the executor of judicial sentences.

Benedict XIV, the brilliant Pope and canonist, sheds further light on the early beginnings of our office in his treatise on the canonization of saints. Although he is treating the history of the *Promotor Fidei,*[7] an office to which he himself had been but recently appointed, he necessarily touches upon the present subject as a source from which his own office evolved. The office had been created as an independent office by Pope Clement XI on April 7,

[7] Benedict XIV, *De Servorum Dei Beatificatione et Beatorum Canonizatione,* lib. I, cap. XVIII.

1708 [8] and from Benedict's historical conspectus of it, it is readily apparent that the office of the *Promotor Fidei* is nothing more than the *Procurator Fiscalis* in highly specialized form. He finds the origin of the *Promotor Fidei* as a titular office in the decree of Urban VIII issued January 11, 1631.[9] That Pontiff taking cognizance of the objections being levelled against the practice of using the *Procurator Fiscalis* in solemn cases of canonization decreed: *Promotor Fidei cum sit ad praesens et in postea debet esse de Collegio Advocatorum Consistorialium.* Benedict goes on to observe that although the *Advocatus Fiscalis* is chosen from the same body, the two offices are not necessarly identical and need not be incorporated in the same individual. In fact since they have nothing in common, he believes it preferable that they be given to different officials. In support of his views he quotes one Raphael Fulgasio,[10] a writer of the fifteenth century, who attests to the fact that the *Advocatus Fiscalis* is an older office and one which needs not embody the functions of the *Promotor Fidei.* In further support of his views Benedict cites the opinion of Cardinal de Luca (1614-1683) who deems the separation of the offices highly expedient: *quin immo illa separatio visa est maximopere expediens; . . . vel quia parum decere videbatur, Advocatum Fiscalem, personam plerumque mere laicam et instantem pro punitione delictorum, adhiberi in Beatificationis, et Canonizationis negotio mere ecclesiastico. . . .* The learned jurist, in turn, appeals to the opinions of Aegedius (1374-78) and de Bellemera (1365), auditors of the Roman Rota, whose decisions enjoyed the character of sacred oracles of law in their own day. Bother bitterly inveigh against the use of the criminal prosecutor in canonization processes as unbecoming the dignity and the sacredness of such a process. Bellemera protests: *Et merito cum non videatur aequum citare fiscalem qui in profanis, et criminalibus causis facinorosus accusare solet ut os aperiri possit in his quoque causis, quae sanctissimae sunt et a profanitate longe distantes.*[11]

[8] Benedict XIV, o. c., lib. I, cap. XVIII, n. 6.

[9] Benedict XIV, o. c., cap. XVIII, n. 4.

[10] Benedict XIV, o. c., cap, XVIII, n. 4.

[11] Benedict XIV, o. c., cap. XVIII, n. 5.

Here again in the citations listed by Benedict XIV a clear witness is had to the existence of our office as an independent arm of the ecclesiastical judicature in the courts of the fourteenth century. The citations certify its presence as a well established office which not only cited criminal offenses and prosecuted them, but also strove to safeguard the best interests of the ecclesiastical fisc by occasionally acting as the Promoter of the Faith in canonization processes.

The same brilliant canonist in still another of his works affords additional evidence as to the early existence of the office. Again, it is only in passing that he touches upon the *fiscales* and incidentally, the office which he is discussing is not unlikely one of the reasons why the Promoter did not attain his full development earlier in ecclesiastical history. In his *De Synodo Dioecesana* Benedict is delineating the history of the *testes synodates* down to his own day. These *testes* were to be men of excellent reputation and mature judgment and their duty was to supplement the bishop's supervision of the diocese by sedulously investigating the observance of ecclesiastical law in the diocese and reporting all infractions of the same to the lawful authority. Innocent III [12] in the Fourth Lateran Council provided that a similar office should be instituted for the province and perform like functions in the province. These officials were to enjoy no jurisdiction whatsoever. Their sole duty was to investigate conscientiously the moral and religious condition of the province or diocese, as the case might be, and to report all that was in need of correction to the superiors who had appointed them. The motive which had inspired their office was an ideal one, but the execution of the office was a most embarrasing and distasteful task. As a result conscientious and disinterested priests were unable to withstand the ostracism and suspicion which had become attached to the office and consequently men not well fitted for the task had to be pressed into service. This twofold condition soon brought the office into disfavor and disrepute and finally led to its being discarded altogether. While the office itself ceased to function, its duties, nevertheless, remained as a part of the curial activities. Bishops, for the most part, according to Benedict, added them to the rapidly growing

[12] C. 25, X, *de accusationibus,* V, 1.

duties of the *Procurator Fiscalis*.[13] So once again, the Promoter is to be found as a member of the curia dealing with ecclesiastical discipline and its observance in the diocese to which he has been assigned. In the absence of synodal witnesses, he assumes the added duty of checking the observance of ecclesiastical discipline and of seeking reform and reparation where the ecclesiastical law has been publicly violated or ignored.

The abuses which caused the office of the *testes synodales* to fall into disrepute soon began to make their appearance in the Promoter and the exercise of his office. As early as 1440, Nicholaus de Clemanges[14] bitterly inveighs against the Promoters of his own day for their arbitrary, mercenary and dishonest conduct in the exercise of their office. He gives a striking description of the wide prerogatives which these officials enjoyed. Among other things they were empowered to cite, prosecute and enforce their findings by censures, thereby leaving the avenue wide open for the wholesale mulcting of the innocent and uninformed with which he charges them. Whether or not his charges are true matters little for our present purpose, the fact remains that at the time he wrote his acrimonious attack, there were prosecutors in the diocesan curia who enjoyed the widest of powers in their public ministry of criminal prosecution. Moreover, he is but voicing an attack previously made in the nationalistic-minded Council of Constance on *sceleratos exploratoribus criminum quos promotores appellunt*. In the acts of the Council of Constance, held in 1413, especially in the citations and the execution of the citations against John Hus, Peter de Luna, Jerome of Prague, one finds many direct references made to the *procuratores fiscales* and the *Promotores* who had been employed in the prosecution of these men and their adherents.[15] These attacks were reechoed in the turbulent sessions of the Council of Basel held in 1431. The acts

[13] Benedict XIV, *De Synodo Dioecesana*, I, lib. IV, cap. III, 76-78.

[14] Nicholaus de Clemanges, *De Corrupto Statu Ecclesiae*, cap. XV, n. 1, according to Wernz-Vidal, *Jus Canonicum*, VI, 99, footnote 68; Van Espen, *Omnia Opera II*, Pars III, tit. VI, n. 12, 291.

[15] Concilium Constantiense, Sessio XXIII—Mansi, 27, 1118, 1119; Wernz-Vidal, *Jus Canonicum*, VI, 99; footnote 68; Droste-Messmer, *Canonical Procedure in Disciplinary and Criminal Cases of Clerics*, p. 68, n. 3.

of this Council make reference to the practice of citing and prosecuting through the agency of the *Fiscalis.*

Consequently, there can be little doubt that the Promoter appeared very shortly after the introduction of the inquisitorial procedure by the Fourth Lateran Council. He appeared first simply as the *promovens inquisitionem* and then beginning with the *Procurator Fiscalis Episcopi Parisionsis,* he gradually appears during the fourteenth century as the official, independent prosecutor of the diocesan curia who embodies in himself the powers to cite, prosecute, demand punishments and the execution of these penal judgments. He also appears as the agent of equity to defend the rights and privileges of those who of themselves cannot hope to have their claims enforced in court. Occasionally he appears as the *Promotor Fidei* in the processes of canonization. Custom as early as the beginning of the fourteenth century had entrenched him fairly strongly in the curias of some provinces in the Church if anything may be judged from the conciliar legislation and from the writings both favorable and critical of the period.

Continuing on into the sixteenth century, some very enlightening references to the office are to be seen. It is only quite natural to expect this, as the great Tridentine reform had its inception in this period and while the acts of the Council do not refer to the office, many dioceses found in it a very serviceable agency of reform. The Council did introduce some reforms in criminal procedure by cutting off many frivolous and baseless appeals and introduced a summary procedure to be used against clerics living in concubinage, as well as extended the extra-judicial procedure known as *ex informata conscientia* so that it became a part of the bishop's ordinary power in dealing with offending seculars.[16]

After the Council of Trent, the criminal procedure although amplified and reformed in many special points, remained essentially the same and the inquisitorial *ex officio* procedure was commonly introduced as the ordinary procedure in criminal cases.[17] To this

[16] Wernz, *Jus Decretalium,* V, lib. I, 56; Molitor, *Über Kanonisches Gerichtsverfahren gegen Kleriker,* 209 ss.

[17] Molitor, o. c., 237 ss.

practice was adjoined a more frequent use of the *Promotor Fiscalis,* even though his office enjoyed no basis in the fonts of the common law.[18]

Paul III by the constitution, *Licet ab initio,* issued on July 21, 1542, established a Roman tribunal which he called the *Sacra Congregatio Romanae et Universalis Inquisitionis.*[19] He did this to combat the great apostacy of the sixteenth century and its resultant disastrous effects on the Catholic countries. Paul's successors, especially Sixtus V in his bull *Immensae aeternae* of January 22, 1587, reorganized the tribunal and made further provision for its procedure and competency. It was the first of the Roman Congregations and its personnel included judges, officials, consultors and qualificators. It employed also a fiscal procurator who was at once its official prosecutor and fiscal representative.[20]

Achilli Ratti, our reigning Pontiff, in his scholarly work on the collection of the acts of the Church of Milan from the beginning down to our own day affords a further insight into the office as it was practiced in the sixteenth century in the well organized curia of Milan. In a section entitled, *Pars IV Instructiones Variae,* there is to be found an illuminative chapter on the *Procurator Fiscalis.* This instruction is embodied in a series of instructions on diocesan congregations written by St. Charles Borromeo (1538-84) and it outlines in detail the duties of his own appointee to the office of *Procurator Fiscalis.*[21]

After observing that there should be a *procurator fiscalis* in the curia, to whom he refers as a delegate of the archbishop, St. Charles begins with the famous advice so often cited in the authors: *"Meminerint vero illi se esse promotores veritatis et non debere sub ejus clypeo innocentes opprimere vel alias esse in causis ut quis calumniniis*

[18] Molitor, o. c., 243 ss.; Wernz, *Jus Decretalium,* V, lib. I, 57.

[19] Paul III, *Licet ab initio,—Bullarium Romanum,* VI, n. XLIII, 344-346; *Catholic Encyclopedia,* "Inquisition."

[20] Sixtus V, *Immensae aeternae—Bullarium Romanum,* VIII, n. CXVII, 986, 987.

[21] Achilli Ratti, *Act Eccl. Mediolanense ab Initiis,* II, Pars IV, 1683-86; *cf.* Concilium Mediolanense V, Constitutionum Pars III, tit. XII—Harduinus, *Acta Conciliorum,* X, 1082.

fatigetur." They are to examine all charges before proceeding and shall proceed only after they have established the positive guilt of the parties. He reserved to them the prosecution of all criminal cases, which they will diligently and conscientously execute according to provisions of law. St. Charles continues with an instructive list of cases and duties in which the procurator will serve:

> Ante omnia promovent omni vigilantia causas fidei. Causas inconfessorum et non communicatorum in tempore Paschatis. Causas quae pertinent ad observantiam divini cultus. Causas etiam simoniae, blasphemiae, sodomiae, et concubinatus ad praescripta sacrorum canonum et Constitutiones Pii V. Causas eorum qui incompatabilia beneficia retinunt. Tum eorum qui a beneficiis qui residentiam personalem requirunt absunt. . . . ad illos spectat assistendo causis tueri libertatem ecclesiae ad his qui juspatronatum in his habere contendunt. Illorum officium erit cum sollicitudine promovere causas omnes etiam civiles quae ex officio pertractantur speciatim, pro executione piorum relictorum et bonorum ecclesiasticorum, piorumque locorum usurpatorum recuperatione. Itidem de causis quamlibet spectantibus ad mensem episcopalem jurave spiritualia sive temporalia archiepiscopatus. Itidem de causis ubi de ecclesiastica jurisdictione vel libertate tuenda agitur.

In all these cases the instruction orders him to be present, to cite parties and witnesses, to aid the judge should be desire it in the interrogation of all concerned and generally to prosecute the case to the best of his ability. The instruction adds that he keep a personal record of the whole proceedings together with the sentence and the execution of the sentence. Nothing, however, is said of the invalidity of the process should he be absent. He does not seem at this time to have been a necessary part of the procedure but rather a useful official who makes the handling of the case more systematic and the prosecution far more effective than it would would otherwise be, were the judge, alone, to bear the whole burden of the inquisition.

A few years after the Council of Milan, a provincial Council held in the year 1581 at Rouen in France legislated with a view to effecting the recommended Tridentine reforms in the province, and thereby eliminating some of the abuses and evils which had crept into the provincial law of the region. In its legislation relative to the ecclesiastical jurisdiction the council is emphatic in its delineation of the duties of the *Promotor Fiscalis,* reminding him that he is to confine himself to the rôle of an official plaintiff and is not to usurp the prerogatives of the presiding judge:

> Caveant in posterum promotores excommunicationem et absolutiones decernere, cum hae sunt partes judicum. Procurari enim solum promotores debent, ut sarta tecta conservetur disciplinam ecclesiasticam et tantum accusatoris postulare et requirere, ut in eos qui illam disciplinam violarint, corrupuerint, seu quid vitii et sceleris commiserint.[22]

In a response to the Archbishop of Seville given September 15, 1589, the Sacred Congregation of the Council decided relative to the selection of the Promoter. "*. . . ad Episcopum pertinet electio ac deputatio Promotoris Fiscalis etiam cum is procedere vult contra capitulares capituli exempti.*" [23]

It might be well to observe at this point that, despite all that has been said thus far concerning the office, and notwithstanding the undeniable evidences of its existence in the thirteenth, fourteenth, fifteenth and sixteenth centuries, nothing very universal or absolutely definite can be postulated on the office. The nature of the diocesan fisc and the extent to which the Promoter fostered its best interests had not yet been fixed by law or custom. Each bishop or archbishop entrusted to his particular appointee those specific duties and functions which he adjudged to be a part of the office under discussion. Nor was the practice a universal one. All writers agree that during the sixteenth century the office did grow in prestige and made itself felt in different new fields of ecclesiastical policy, but this is true only of those dioceses and provinces in which the office had already been functioning for some time. Synodal witnesses and in some cases chancellors still exercised many of the duties now

[22] Concilium Rothomagenses, *De ecclesiastica jurisdictione*—Mansi, 34 A, 661.

[23] Pallottini, *Promotor Fiscalis et Procurator,* n. 1.

assigned to the Promoter and it was only after the complete cessation of these practices that he reached his full capacity and development in criminal proceedings. Then, too, many dioceses were slow to adopt the new office, as it was not part of the common law, and adopted it only after the practice and successful experiment of other dioceses had shown it to be a highly serviceable arm of the law.

Article II. The Promoter in the XVII and XVIII Centuries

The seventeenth century finds the fiscal promoter fulfilling still another function in the diocesan curia, one which is now invested in the *defensor vinculi*.[24] In support of this fact, there may be cited the opinions of two canonists before the time of Benedict XIV. Sperelli and De Justis maintain that the *Promotor Fiscalis* should be present to defend the sacramental rights of marriage in certain matrimonial cases.

Sperelli writes: [25]

> Secundum est quod uterque consentiant dissolutione matrimonii citandus est fiscus curiae episcopalis, qui stare debet pro matrimonio ad collusiones et fraudes evitandas.

De Justis voices a similar opinion in the following text:[26]

> . . . propterea in casu quo conjuges concorditer pro dissolutione stent, debet citari promotor fiscalis curiae episcopalis. . . .

Both demand the presence of the *fiscus* who is called an official of the curia, only when the dissolution of the marriage is sought by both parties in order to avoid fraud and collusion.

This is not merely an innovation of these two authors, it was the practice actually followed in many courts. In a petition submitted to the Sacred Congregation of the Council, September 30, 1719, one observes that the question of the validity of the marriage

[24] Lega, *De Judiciis Ecclesiasticis*, I, 137.

[25] Sperelli, *Decisiones Fori Ecclesiastici*, II, dec. 141, n. 68.

[26] De Justis, *De Dispensatione Matrimoniae* (Lucae, 1726), lib. II, cap. XVII, n. 24.

was proposed by the *fiscus* and it involved a declaration of nullity in a matrimonial case.[27] There followed several others, one of which stated that the curia lacked a *fiscus* and so they are referring the whole matter to the Congregation for a solution.[28] Another case cited clearly attests to the practice:[29]

> . . . citato patre Catherinae, et eodem negligente jura prosequi suae filiae, quae est absens, et ignoratur, in quo loco degat, danda esse a Fiscali curiae interrogatoria ex officio.

These cases all involved the invalidity or nullity of marriage and it is possible to cite several others. These few suffice to show very clearly that it was the practice to cite the *fiscus* in some places to appear in defense of the marriage when the party refused or was unable to appear. True the number of indications for the use of the *Procurator Fiscalis* does not tend to prove that the practice was widespread; but they do support the fact that in certain localities, at least, he was employed as the defender of the marriage bond and was entrusted with these cases in view of his general duties to promote the diocesan good and welfare.

In the bulls for the canonization of St. Raymond of Bologna and St. Hyacinth, the *Promotor Fiscalis* in both instances acted as promoter of the faith in the process. In the bulls of St. Raymond's process one finds the significant wording, "*Quae omnia quidem universa, citato Procuratore fiscali, recognita fuerint.*" Similar expressions indicating the practice of citing the *Promotor Fiscalis* are to be found in the records of the canonization processes of SS. Philip Neri, Ignatius, Theresa, Thomas of Villanova, which were published in the years 1609, 1620 and 1621.[30]

[27] Benedict XIV, *Quaestiones Canonicae et Morales,* I, Q. CXX—*Opera Omnia,* XII, 137.

[28] Benedict XIV, *Quaestiones Canonicae et Morales,* I, Q. CCXXVI—*Opera Omnia,* XII, 295.

[29] Benedict XIV, *Quaestiones Canonicae et Morales,* I, Q. CCCLVI—*Opera Omnia,* XII, 463.

[30] Benedict XIV, *De Servorum Dei Beatificatione et Beatorum Canonizatione,* I, cap. XVIII, n. 9.

Further indications as to the usage and practice of the *Promotor Fiscalis* at the beginning of the seventeenth century are to be gleaned from the formula of his appointment used by the Archbishop of Paris:[31]

> Dantes tibi facultatem omnes et singulas causas ad forum nostrum et jurisdictionem nostram Ecclesiasticam et spiritualem spectantes agendi, promovendi, interessendi, et concludendi sententiae et jus super iis a Domino Officiali dictae Nostrae Curiae Ecclesiasticae et spiritualis fori, ipsoque debito executione demandari instandi, Ecclesiasticos et alios subditos nobis delinquentes seu in crimine deprehensos et in culpa, ac alios quos convenerit, citari, evocari, corrigi, puniri, mulctari, sententiari, condemnari, absolvi prout aequitas canonica et Juris ordo postulaverit curandi; et generaliter omnia alia et singula faciendi, gerendi, exercendi, quae ad hujusmodi Procuratoris munus et officium de jure, usu et consuetudine spectat et pertinet.

The statutes for the University of Louvain are almost identical. They grant the Promoter the same prerogatives and empower him to exercise them *in libellando contra excidentes et Statuta Edictave violantes.*[32]

At approximately the same time the Ordinances of the Diocese of Malines demanded an oath of its *Procurator Fiscalis; Neminem citari procurabo ab officio per excessus, nisi credidero illos veros delinquentes et me causam justam habere.*[33] At the same time he pledges, *Excessus non supprimam neque celabo sed cum omni possibili diligentia prosequar; nec disistam, etiam si citatum innocentem putavero nisi id Advocati Fiscali vel Officiali indicavero, ut desuper decernit quod ratio postulabit.*[34]

From these facts one can validly infer that at the beginning of the seventeenth century, the *Procurator Fiscalis* had become a very definite arm of the law and was a definite member of the diocesan judicature at least in certain actions. His duties are clearly out-

[31] Van Espen, *Omnia Opera,* II, Pars III, tit. VI, cap. V, n. 6.
[32] Van Espen, *Omnia Opera,* II, Pars III, tit. VI, cap. V, n. 7.
[33] Van Espen, *Omnia Opera,* II, Pars III, tit. VI, cap. V, n. 16.
[34] Van Espen, l. c., n. 24.

lined in criminal matters by specific curial ordinances and he must take an oath to abide by these statutes and edicts of the curia. The other duties assigned to him by usage and custom are not definitely outlined, as was noted above in speaking of his rôle in the matrimonial procedure of this period, but his official duties as the diocesan prosecutor have become sufficiently definite to have become the subject of fixed and stringent regulations.

During the period under discussion some interesting and instructive responses of the Holy See appear on the subject of the Promoter. Pallottini notes that in a document, S. C. C. in Segobien., it is stated: ***Hinc Promotor Fiscalis ad cujus instantiam Episcopus procedure debet in Causis Capitularium, eligendus est ab Episcopo, non a Capitulo neque a Conjudicibus.***[35] An identical response was given by the same Congregation in the document ***in Calaguritana, die 9 Maii, 1626.***[36] Another response referring to the same subject, ***S. C. C. in una Placentia*** of December 5, 1645, reads: ***Quin imo ad solum Episcopum, absque consilio vel consensu Capituli spectat electio Promotoris Fiscalis.*** A still more instructive response from the same official source comes down in the document, ***S. C. C. in una License, 1 Sept., 1657,*** in which the Sacred Congregation instructs the Promoter to seek the return of a case to his own tribunal in which the parties, having rejected the competence of their own Ordinary, had taken the case to a higher tribunal without the assent or consent of that Ordinary. The Congregation advises the Promoter to take the action whether the case has not yet begun or has already started in the higher court. Still later the Congregation of Bishops and Regulars issued a decree under date of July 2, 1677, in virtue of which lay people can be appointed to the office of ***Promotor Fiscalis*** since the office does not carry with it any ecclesiastical jurisdiction.[39] The decree thus confirms the opinion of those who taught that the ***Promotor Fiscalis*** was an office only

[35] Pallottini, ***Promotor Fiscalis et Procurator,*** n. 2.

[36] Pallottini, ***Promotor Fiscalis et Procurator,*** n. 2.

[37] Pallottini, ***Promotor Fiscalis et Procurator,*** n. 3.

[38] Pallottini, ***Promotor Fiscalis et Procurator,*** n. 5.

[39] ***Analecta Juris Pontificii,*** XIII, n. 31, 44.

in a broad sense and did not carry with it any exercise of the power of jurisdiction.

Towards the close of the century another authoritative witness to the growing practice of the Promoter and his important rôle in the inquisitorial procedure of the ecclesiastical courts of the time is met. It is found in an appendix to the Acts of the Provincial Council of Benevento in the year 1693. The Council fixes the stipend which the Promoter is to receive in connection with his services as the official prosecutor in any given case and it adds that in the event that the *Promotor Fiscalis* comes to a town to investigate a suspect and the suspect is absolved from all crime, the prosecutor may not even ask that his expenses be paid.[40] Here is further evidence of the Promoter as a diocesan public official, whose duty as a member of the curia it is to prosecute officially in the name of the diocese and who is to be reimbursed as often as he exercises that function of his public ministry.

The authors of the period afford some instructive remarks on the office and its functions. Farinaccius [41] in his exhaustive treatise on witnesses, published in 1609, notes that the judge must take cognizance of the objection against the fitness of a witness especially when the *Promotor Fiscalis* takes such action.

Van Espen attests to the progress the office had made in Belgium when he observes:[42]

> Inquisitio, igitur, seu informatio hodie prosequente, ut publici accusatores (fiscales promotores), qui soli moribus hodiernis ad accusandum criminaliter et ad vindictam publicam admittuntur, accusationem instituere, aut contra reum libellum accusationis offerre possunt.

In support of his views he quotes from the ordinances of the dioceses of Malines and Louvain referred to above.

M. Anthony Sabelli, an auditor of the Rota for criminal cases, while not expressly treating the Promoter as an independent office,

[40] Appendix ad Acta Concilii Beneventinae, a. 1693—*Coll. Lac.*, I, 120.

[41] Farinaccius, *De Testibus,* II, par. 54, n. 5.

[42] Van Espen, *Jus Eccl. Universum,* Pars III, tit. VIII, cap. I, n. 23.

has some interesting remarks pertinent to the exercise of the office. In his *Summa Diversorum*, published in 1692, he observes that the [43] "*Procurator Fiscalis cum habet nullum jurisdictionem, nec facultatem deferendi juramentum non potest recipere examen testium et receptum erit nullum, licet emanuerit confessio, quae solum habebitur extrajudicialis.*" He quickly adds, however, that this does not mean that the Promoter may not take any part in the judicial examination of the accused, but rather that he may do so only at the proper time and place outlined by authority and usage for such action and refers to authors whose works are no longer extant for direction and guidance in the matter. Again under the word *Judex* [44] he discusses, in passing, the failure of the Promoter to prosecute in certain cases. He notes there that the Promoter need not heed the denunciations of interested parties unless it is one of those actions that he is bound to prosecute *ex officio*. Should he fail in his duty in these actions, he is bound to make restitution for the damages incurred by the fisc through his failure to act.

Fagnanus (1661), while apparently ignoring the office in his work, gives an incidental reference to its existence. He is treating the question of salary grants to the various members of the diocesan curia in the light of recent instructions on this point from the Sacred Congregation of the Council. In regard to the *Procurator Fiscalis* on this point, he remarks: *Etsi Procuratori Fiscali actu inservienti si ita se habeat consuetudo, assignari potest decima pars ejus quantitatis ex qualibet condemnatione in qua Reus cum Camera se composuerit.*[45] He, thereby, recognizes him as an officer of the fisc to which he is assigned and indirectly testifies to his part in the condemnation proceedings as an *ex officio* representative of the fisc.

Other additional authors and councils might be cited in connection with the subject. These references refer to a public minister who in virtue of his office is charged with different specific func-

[43] Sabelli, *Summa Diversorum*, III, P, 49, n. 11.

[44] Sabelli, *Summa Diversorum*, II, I, p. 41, n. 19.

[45] Fagnanus, *Commentarium in V Libros Decretalium*, lib. V, Pars II, *De Poenis*, cap. II, n. 25.

tions of the prosecution of crime. They are called public ministers and in some instances they are identical with the *Promotor Fiscalis* while in others the identity cannot be established. Only such references have been cited as refer to the *Fiscalis* by name and which afford one an undeniable assurance that they are immediately concerned with the forerunner of our present-day official, the Promoter of Justice. Those selected seem sufficient to establish beyond all doubt the presence of an official, exercising the duties of our Promoter, in many widely scattered curias of the Church and exercising them in view of the fact that he is the *Procurator Fiscalis* of the diocesan curia. His office, it is true, manifests a greater progress in certain jurisdictions than in others, but the fact remains that the office was exercised in widely separated areas in its essential features, as is evidenced by the notice given to it in diocesan regulations, in synods, councils, in the responses of the Holy See and in the practical commentary made on it by the authors of the time. This practice, as would be expected, led to an even more definite practice in the following century.

In view of the gradual growth and development of the office in the seventeenth century and in view of the fact that the various civil societies were at this time occupied with the redrafting and codifying of their civil law, it is little wonder that in the early 1700's a very definite practice arose and is to be found in our own criminal tribunals relative to the usage of the *Promotor Fiscalis* in criminal matters. Van Espen demands his presence as an "actor" in all criminal proceedings. He asserts: [46] *Debentque haec omnia fieri Promotore instante et postulante, ne Judex motu proprio decernendo, sustineat personam judicis et partis.*

So necessary has custom made it to cite the *Procurator Fiscalis* that all judicial acts in criminal trials to which he has not been invited shall be considered null and void and should the sentence be passed as a result of these acts, that sentence will likewise labor under the pain of nullity. This is manifestly evident from the writings of Pellegrini at the very outset of the eighteenth century. After remarking that the bishop should appoint a *Procurator Fiscalis* and

[46] Van Espen, *Tractatus de Recursu ad Principem*, cap. 3, par. 4.

that he, alone, is competent to remove him, he unqualifiedly asserts:[47]

> Est autem, adeo, necessarium in criminalibus ut citetur in omnibus actibus quae fiunt contra Reum, Fiscalis Curiae, ut si feratur sententia contra Reum ipso non citato, sententia erit nulla.

This teaching of Pelligrini is in perfect harmony with the essential nature of a judgment which demands three parties to any judicial action, *i. e.*, the judge, the plantiff and the defendant. In view of this, De Luca writes at approximately the same time;[48]

> Generaliter judicium tale quale est, cujusquamque generis vel speciei, ad sui essentiam tria vulgaria exigit requisita, seu tres pernecesse exigit personas ex quibus illud constitui dicitur nempe, ex Actore, ex Judice, ex Reo, sine quibus judicium non datur, etiam ubi agatur de judiciis criminalibus ex officio seu per acquisitionem absque accusatore, quoniam fiscus in nomine Reipublicae, partes actoris gerere dicitur.

But perhaps the Promoter owes more to Benedict XIII than to any other individual source for his establishment as an independent arm of the Diocesan judicature. Benedict seems to have done much towards the institution of the office for Rome and the Province immediately subject to it. In his chirograph of July 12, 1724,[49] the Sovereign Pontiff established the *Procurator Fiscalis Generalis* for the diocese and Province of Rome. The same provision is enacted in the Council of Rome held in the following year.[50] The immediate reason for its institution was the pressing need in Rome for a criminal prosecutor, who would represent the prosecution in those cases appealed to Rome from their own jurisdictions. Appeals from the sentences and decrees of the bishops of Italy had become an in-

[47] Pellegrini, *Praxis Vicariorum*, Pars IV, sec. I, n. 20, p. 282.

[48] De Luca, *De Judiciis*, disc. I, n. 27—Pierantonelli, *Praxis Fori*, tit. V, n. 2, p. 121; *cf.* also Matthaeucci, *Officialis Curiae Eccl.*, cap. LIV, n. 48.

[49] *Collectio Lacensis*, I, 433.

[50] Tit. XIV, *De Appellationibus—Coll. Lac.*, I, 365.

tolerable burden to the Holy See. Dioceses and religious superiors could not afford to send their own prosecutors to Rome, as heretofore had been the custom. The result was that many criminals scandalously went unchecked, reducing to naught the disciplinary efforts of their own conscientious superiors. Benedict XIII sensed the need of urgent reform and hastened to supply it. His *Promotor Fiscalis* in the future would sit in at every criminal hearing in Rome and after having received the necessary evidence and pertinent documents connected with the case in the lower instance, would conduct the prosecution of the case in the name of the absent bishop or superior.

Then, there is a decree of the Congregation of Bishops and Regulars for April, 1727,[51] which is of assistance in establishing the Promoter as an independent office. The decree expressly forbids the chancellor from incorporating the duties of the Promoter into his own office and functions. In the same year the Sacred Congregation of Bishops and Regulars settled several difficulties which had arisen between the canons of some Church, the name of which does not appear in the response, and the *Procurator Fiscalis* of the curia in that place.[52] This decree is worthy of note because it does not deal with matters of criminal import; but is rather concerned with their duties as canons of the Church and the discharge of those duties.

Further light on the use of the Promoter in other than criminal cases is to be found in the *Mantissima Decisionum* of the S. R. Rota by Cardinal De Luca. The decision [53] was given in a case involving a property dispute between two parishes. The party which had received the adverse decision appealed the case to the Rota and that tribunal disallowed the appeal which had been based upon the invalidity of the first sentence. The Rota decision in the case reads in part:

> Nec eadem possessio potest de ulla invaliditate redarguere, dum judex processit servatis servandis, citato procuratore fiscali, qui legitime comparet pro defensione libertatis ecclesiae.

[51] *Analecta Juris Pontificii,* XIII, n. 33, 44.

[52] *Fontes,* no. 1843.

[53] *Mantissima Decisionum S. R. R.* (1734), IV, lib. XV, dec. 7, n. 1.

Here is a duty of the Promoter which has found its way into the New Code of Canon Law.

The Sacred Congregation of the Council [54] in a response, dated January 14, 1758, shows the Promoter exercising his office in another non-criminal proceeding. The Congregation is dealing with the matter of according some stipend to the *Synodales Examinatores* in return for their services to the diocese. The *Procurator Fiscalis* of the diocese in question had successfully maintained that the immemorial custom of the various Spanish dioceses which had permitted the practice of remunerating the *Synodales Examinatores* justified the practice in his own diocese notwithstanding the Tridentine legislation to the contrary. The Congregation does not uphold the argument, but rather reverses his opinion by recalling the constant teaching of the Congregation which might be summed up in one of the responses which it cites in answer to the case presented, *Non licere synodalibus examinatoribus quidquam accipere.* Despite this adverse sentence, here is the Promoter acting as an agent of equity, trying to preserve both the spirit of the law and the seemingly justifiable request of the examiners that they be permitted to benefit by the ancient custom which allowed them some nominal return for their work. This feature of the office has developed continually and is still being amplified in the present day canonical jurisprudence of the Rota and the Signatura.

Towards the last quarter of the eighteenth century, there appeared an excellent comparative study of the prevailing Canon Law and the so-called Gallican Liberties. Its author, an advocate in the royal courts of France, shows himself remarkably conversant with the prevailing Canon Law and its sources. Among other subjects which the author treats is the office of the *Promotor Fiscalis* in the ecclesiastical *Officialité* and in so doing gives an excellent description of the office as it was practiced in the curias of France in his own day. He describes the Promoter as an ecclesiastical officer who exercises the public ministry in the ecclesiastical tribunals.[55] The

[54] Lingen-Reuss, *Causae Selectae,* n. 459, p. 778.

[55] Louis de Hericourt, *Les Lois Ecclesiastiques* (Paris, 1771), E, II, 36, p. 201.

Promoters are to the *Officialité* what the Gens des Rois are to the secular tribunals and the fiscal promoter to the Justices des Seigneurs. It is their duty to see to it that the judicial order is observed in the ecclesiastical tribunals, to bring charges against delinquent clerics and to maintain and defend the rights, privileges and immunities of the Church. They are to be held responsible for the conservation and preservation of ecclesiastical discipline in a diocese and accordingly are bound to demand an accounting of all those who violate or offend against that discipline by unbecoming or criminal conduct. Since these offenses admit of no compromise, the Promoter must defend the common ecclesiastical public order by prosecuting the defendant in his rôle of principal, official plantiff in criminal proceedings before the diocesan courts.[56] Moreover, as often as the matter under consideration pertains to the competence of the ecclesiastical courts, the Promoter of the diocesan curia will vindicate to that court the right to try the case even though the delinquent cleric has renounced his *privelegium fori* and has petitioned the civil authorities to try the case.[57] While it is not necessary that the Promoters be in sacred orders, it is advisable that only those who are in sacred orders be appointed to the office since it is not fitting that a layman should be the official plantiff in the criminal cases against clerics.[58] And finally, the Promoter enjoys an official standing only in the *Officialité* for which he has been appointed and will not be recognized in that official capacity in a superior instance.[59]

In these few citations one sees that the office had come to a fairly high development in the ecclesiastical courts in France at the end of the eighteenth century.

Thus during the seventeenth and eighteenth centuries, the office of the Promoter was rapidly spreading throughout the Church despite the havoc wrought in the administration of justice by the up-

[56] de Hericourt, *Les Lois Ecclesiastiques,* E, XIII, 11, p. 274; E, XXI, 3, 4, p. 342.

[57] de Hericourt, *Les Lois Ecclesiastiques,* E, XIX, 10 and 30, pp. 310, 317.

[58] de Hericourt, *Les Lois Ecclesiastiques,* E, II, 37, p. 201.

[59] de Hericourt, *Les Lois Ecclesiastiques,* E, XXV, 31, p. 397.

heavals that were taking place in the civil societies during the period. He was found acting as the defender of the marriage bond in certain matrimonial causes, as the *Promotor Fidei* in causes of canonization, as the diocesan prosecutor in criminal matters, as the official representative of the diocesan curia in the adjudication of contentious cases involving the public good of the diocese, and finally as an agent of equity *pro legis et justitiae tutela*. His rôle of the defender of the marriage bond ceased when Benedict XIV created the independent office of the *defensor vinculi* in 1741. So, too, he is no longer cited as the official investigator of the proofs submitted in the causes of canonization after Clement XI had instituted the office of the *Promotor Fidei* as an entirely distinct office of the Roman Curia. But as the criminal prosecutor and the interested representative of the diocese in certain contentious and in all criminal cases, he remains and waxes strong. By the beginning of the eighteenth century, the custom of employing him in criminal procedure had become so constant that the authors did not hesitate to demand his citation for the validity of all criminal proceedings. This was the first really definite impress made by the office on the common law. Prior to this time his status depended solely on the good judgment of the bishop and it was entirely up to the bishop whether or not he was to be cited; but from the beginning of this century the authors very definitely demand his presence, a principle which grew more and more insistent with the progress of time and reached its crowning point in Canon 1934 of the Code. Wherefore this period can be correctly concluded with the statements found in Cardinal Lega:

> In jure ecclesiastico, quia ex jure communi ejus officium non designatur, constans non est disciplina neque universalis sed certe apud curias melius ordinatas, officium Procuratoris fiscalis sedulo constitutum fuit et late exercetur.[60] Quum sub saeculo decimo sexto et decimo septimo passim apud curias Ecclesiasticas invaluerit mos instituendi Procuratorem Fiscalem, ejus officium magis extendi coepit, adeo ut evaserit custos et vindex legis, quasi censor justitiae judicialis, invigilans tum judicem tum partes contendentes

[60] Lega, *De Judiciis Ecclesiasticis,* I, 174, n. 1.

> etiam in causis mere civilibus, in medium proferendo suas animadversiones vel contra partium allegationes vel judicis agendi rationem.[61]

Article III. The Promoter in the XIX Century

In the nineteenth century after the French Revolution in many regions, even where heretofore well ordered tribunals had existed, the canonical procedure in criminal trials had fallen into desuetude.[62] Nevertheless the Holy See constantly promoted reform of the ecclesiastical tribunals and procedure through the responses of her congregations especially that of the Congregation of Bishops and Regulars and by the reform of her own laws in the Papal States where Gregory XVI effected a full reform. As a consequence of this reform, it is in this century that one witnesses the first, general, strictly canonical legislation relative to our subject. In its course the Promoter at length wins the legal approbation he had heretofore lacked and becomes for the first time a regularly, canonically established officer of the diocesan curia. The longstanding custom, the practice of widely separated curias, the gradual development of forensic methods within the Church added to the urgent desire voiced by the Fathers of the Vatican Council for a new procedure which would be better adapted to modern exigencies made itself felt and led to a reform of existing procedure. This new reform appropriately enough embodied within itself some very definite provisions regarding the establishment and exercise of the office of the Promoter, thereby affixing official sanction to the prevailing custom and no longer leaving *it entirely dependent upon* the pleasure and will of the individual Ordinary.[63]

But first a few words on the practice in the early part of the nineteenth century. This period saw a very definite tendency towards the establishment and increased usage in the Church of a public ministry in the various departments of ecclesiastical discipline. As

[61] Lega, *De Judiciis Ecclesiasticis,* I, n. 139.

[62] Wernz, *Jus Decretalium,* V, lib. II, p. 57; Peries, *La Procedure Moderne,* pp. 349 ff.

[63] Laemmer, *Institutiones,* p. 242.

one turns the pages of conciliar legislation or glances through the pronouncements made by the Holy See on matters referred to its congregation and tribunals for solution, one readily notes the steady growth of this concept of a public ministry in the diocesan curia. These public ministers are mentioned in connection with the protection of doctrine and morals in the diocese, with the observance of disciplinary legislation, with the punishment of abuses and infractions of diocesan legislation and with the general supervision of justice. Relative to those various departments entrusted to the public ministers, note will be taken only of such functions as are entrusted to the *Procurator Fiscalis* of the diocesan curia and reference will be made only to such pronouncements as legislate and interpret his duties for him in that official capacity.

Turning first to the pronouncements of the Holy See on the office, some very valuable contributions to the evolution of the office and its exercise are to be found. For example on June 30, 1826, the Sacred Congregation of Bishops and Regulars decided that once the judicial process had been published, the Promoter could add no more conclusions and that the right to prescribe a new inquiry belonged to the tribunal alone.[64] The Congregation, S. Immunitas, on June 30, 1835, ruled that the Promoter could be a layman inasmuch as that official exercises no jurisdiction.[65] Then the Sacred Congregation of Bishops and Regulars on January 15, 1835, decreed that when an appeal has been forwarded to Rome, the *Procurator Generalis Fisci* shall represent the diocesan tribunal from which the appeal was taken.[66] Under the date of December 25, 1844, a case involving parochial concursus was discussed before the same congregation. It seems that some injustice had taken place in the concursus and the Archbishop of Benevento referred the whole matter to the Congregation for solution and for advice on the remedial measures to be taken. The petition of the Archbishop to the Congregation closes with the significant words: [67]

[64] *Analecta Juris Pontifiicii,* XIII, tit. VI, n. 37, 44.

[65] *Analecta Juris Pontificii,* XIII, n. 33, 44.

[66] Bizzari, *Collectanea S. C. EE. et RR.*, p. 164.

[67] Lingen-Reuss, *Causae Selectae,* n. 455, p. 774.

> Promotor fiscalis hujus meae curiae cui terminum decem dierum assignavi ad deducendum quidquid in Domino censerit, non contradicit rehabilitationi petitae a Sacerdote Angelo R. Quatenus vero EE. VV. placeat eundem sacerdotem ad beneficium parochiale rehabilitare, nullum idcirco scandalum oritur quoniam communis sententia est, eum in hac re deceptum fuisse solitis astutiis.

Here is a duty that becomes quite common to the Promoter.

The Council of Tours held in the year 1853 makes a very definite reference to the Promoter. It states that in the prosecution of crime the Promoter should be a priest, *Officium Promotoris, vero, nisi presbytero vel saltem in sacris ordinibus constituto in posterum committatur.*[68]

A few years later, in 1869, the Second Provincial Council held in Quito, Ecquador, provided for the appointment of several *Promotores Fiscales.* The council instructed each diocese to set up diocesan congregations after the fashion of those which the Council had set up for the Province. One of these Congregations bore the title of the Congregation for Faith and Morals. The *Promotor Fiscalis* was to be an important member of this congregation. It was his duty to denounce before the Congregation any books or pamphlets brought to his attention which might be harmful to the true religion or to Catholic morals. The matter was thereupon referred to the metropolitan congregation of the same name and its official promoter handled the prosecution of the offensive literature and its propagators.[69]

Finally in various manners and in widely separated areas, the office of the *Promotor Fiscalis* became a specific part of the ecclesiastical judicature. This took place on June 11, 1880, in virtue of an Instruction of the Sacred Congregation of Bishops and Regulars.[70] The title of this instruction was, *Pro ecclesiasticis curiis quoad modum procedendi oeconomice in causis disciplinaribus et criminalibus clericorum.* The summary procedure, thus established

[68] Can. XIX—Mansi, 34 A, 849.

[69] Decr. II—*Coll. Lac.*, VI, 433.

[70] Instr. S. C. EE. et RR.. 11 Junii, 1880—*A. S. S.*, XIII (1880-) 325.

by the Congregation, was the answer of the Holy See to repeated and insistent pleas of the bishops of the world for a more practical method of procedure in these cases. Like so many other institutions in the Church it was the result of a normal and gradual evolution which incorporated within itself those improvements of ecclesiastical procedure, which practice and experience had vindicated as being practical, useful and at the same time in harmony with the general spirit of Canon Law.

The Instruction itself gives us the reason for the publication of the new procedural regulations, *ut formas magis oeconomicas adhibere valeant in exercitio suae disciplinaris jurisdictionis super clericos. Ecclesia, ubique impeditur quoniam externam explicit suam actionem super materias et personas ecclesiasticas.*[71]

Article XIII of this Instruction provides expressly for the presence of the Promoter in every well regulated curia: *Unicuique curiae opus est Procuratori Fiscali pro justitiae et legis tutela.* Articles XXXIII, XXXIV and XXXV outline his duties in this capacity. The duties remain the same as those relegated to him by the immemorial custom of certain dioceses. He remains the official accuser and prosecutor of the diocesan curia.

Further provision for the office and an indication of its nature and duties are to be found in the *Lex Propria Santae Romana Rotae et Signatura Apostolicae* published on June 29, 1908,[72] and in the *Regulae Servandae apud Sanctam Romanam Rotam,* published on August 4, 1910.[73] The constitutions of both tribunals provide for the appointment of a Promoter. The *Regulae Servandae* makes provision for the Rotal Promoter both in the contentious cases involving the public good and in criminal cases. The regulations providing for his appearance in these procedures are set forth in paragraphs 39-42 and in paragraph 108.[74] These documents pertain rather to the commentary and will be discussed in their proper place.

For our own country on July 20, 1878, the Sacred Congregation

[71] S. C. EE. et RR., 11 Junii, 1880—*A. S. S.*, XIII (1880-), 325.

[72] *A. A. S.*, I (1909), 20.

[73] *A. A. S.*, II (1910), 783.

[74] *A. A. S.*, II (1910), 798, 799 and 819.

de Propaganda Fide under whose jurisdiction the country was at the time published a procedure to be used in this country for disciplinary and criminal cases involving clerics. It is interesting to note that while the instruction provides that some one be appointed in each case to fulfill a rôle exactly similar to that played by the Promoter, it in no way provides for the appointment of a permanent prosecutor and is silent on the office of the *Procurator Fiscalis*. The procedure, however, was shortlived. It gave rise to a great deal of confusion and doubt. Many questions were referred to the Congregation for solution. To remedy this defect and to eliminate some of the doubt and the confusion, the Propaganda extended the Instruction of the Congregation of Bishops and Regulars of June 11, 1880, to the United States. The decree *Cum Magnopere,* by which this extension was affected was published in 1883.[75] The Instruction employed practically the same wording relative to the office of the Promoter as the former instruction had: *In qualibet Curia Episcopali, procurator Fiscalis constituatur, ut lege et justitiae satisfiat.*

In compliance with the express wish of the Holy See, the Third Plenary Council of Baltimore held in 1884 established and defined the office, as it was to be practiced in the curias of this country, as follows: [76]

> Procurator Fiscalis (qui etiam Promotor et Advocatus Fiscalis nominatur) ab Episcopo constituatur, "ut justitiae et legi satisfiat" (A. III). Generale igitur ejus officium est, justitiam et legem tueri, ne violentur; si vero violatae sint, vindicare. Itaque quando earum violationem quoque modo compererit, apud Episcopum instabit, ut inquisitio instituatur, et si opus fuerit, judicialiter in inquisitum procedatur.

What is true of the Third Plenary Council of Baltimore may be equally applied to the various provinces and the dioceses throughout the Catholic world, as often as they legislated after the issuance of the Instruction of 1880. They had awaited the publication of this process and they lost no time in incorporating its various provisions

[75] *Collectanea de S. C. de Prop. Fide,* n. 1586, 169.

[76] *Acta et Decreta Plen. Con. Balto.,* III, n. 301.

and enactments into their own synodal or provincial legislation. Even a most superficial perusal of the acts of these councils held after the publication of the Instruction of 1880 invariably discloses some provision for the institution of the *procurator fiscalis* as a permanent official in the diocesan curia.

Even though one grants the contentions of certain authors[77] that there was no absolute necessity on the part of the bishop to employ a Promoter in all disciplinary and criminal trials involving clerics, one can hardly deny the obligation of appointing him and employing him in those procedures had become a practical necessity, which was universally recognized by the bishops of the world. Despite the fact that the Instruction was permissive and not preceptive in its intent and purpose, Lega could correctly conclude in his work published at the turn of the century,[78] *Hodie ex receptis moribus actio vere judicialis solet relinqui Procuratori Fiscali.* The reason for this is very evident from the remarks made on the office by Bouix, one of the more prominent canonists of the last century:[79]

> Nisi constituatur in qualibet episcopali curia Promotor Fiscalis, plurima orirentur incommoda; nec possint causae criminalis servatis ordinarii judicii formas (quas in certis dumtaxit casibus non autem semper omittere licet) regulariter expedit.

Similarly Peries, commenting on the new Instruction shortly after its publication, declares that it is no longer possible for bishops to evade the obligation of appointing a permanent diocesan prosecutor in view of the insistence of the Holy See so often expressed and now authoritatively set forth in the present Instruction. He says the negligence of bishops in this regard is unintelligible and inexcusable.[80]

[77] Wernz-Vidal, *Jus Canonicum,* VI, 100, n. 73; Molitor, *Über Kanonisches Gerichtsverfahren gegen Kleriker,* 234 ss.

[78] Lega, *De Judiciis Ecclesiasticis,* I, 184.

[79] Bouix, *De Judiciis Ecclesiasticis,* I, Pars 2a, 475.

[80] Peries, "Le Procurateur Fiscalis ou Promoteur," *Revue des Sciences Ecclesiastiques,* 75 (1897), 339.

In the latter part of the nineteenth century, another right and duty was added to the office of the Promoter. This right was to accuse marriages invalid by reason of an impediment *publici juris*. Under the pre-Code legislation in cases of impediments *publici juris* any Catholic had the right to act as plaintiff in attacking the marriage and the Promoter could also act *ex officio* whenever there had been a denunciation and a widespread rumor of the invalidity of the marriage. His action, however, was limited to cases of impediments *publici juris* and he might not institute proceedings *ex officio* in cases of impediments *juris privati* except in cases where the fact of invalidity was notorious.[81] The present law has amplified the duties of the Promoter in this matter by abolishing the right of others than the parties and the Promoter of Justice to attack the marriage.[82]

Thus by custom, by usage, by various decrees and instructions of the sacred congregations, by the teaching of authors the office of the Promoter of Justice has been erected, his privileges and his obligations, his rights and duties defined. These the Code of Canon Law further defines and complements in some thirty canons of the present legislation. There the work of the Promoter is minutely described and if the office is exercised after the intention of the Code, it is an important one. It will be the purpose of the remaining pages of this work to comment upon these various functions of the office as outlined in the text of the Code and endeavor to give a proper appreciation of the office.

[81] Instructio Austriaca, 4 Maii, 1855, n. 118; Gasparri, *De Matrimonio* (1904), II, n. 1478, 402; *cf. Coll. Lac.*, V, 1301; S. B. Smith, *The Marriage Process*, p. 195; Wernz, *Jus Decretalium*, IV, Pars 2, n. 216, pp. 5, 6; Bassibey, *Procedure Matrimoniale*, par. 188.

[82] Canon 1971.

PART II

COMMENTARY ON THE LEGISLATION OF THE CODE

CHAPTER IV

SOME GENERAL NOTIONS IN CONNECTION WITH THE OFFICE OF THE PROMOTER OF JUSTICE

Article I. The Appointment of the Promoter of Justice

The appointment of the Promoter of Justice according to Canon 1589 [1] belongs to the Ordinary. The Code of Canon Law includes under the title of "ordinaries" all residential bishops, abbots nullius, prelates nullius and their vicars general; also administrators apostolic, as well as all those who succeed them according to the provisions of the law.[2]

The common law regards all these officials as "local ordinaries." [3] The enumeration of the Code, however, does not include the major superiors of clerical exempt congregations or Orders under the term of "local ordinary."

The words, Ordinarii est . . . , of Canon 1589 are quite clear. All residential bishops, abbots or prelates nullius, vicars, prefects or administrators apostolic are empowered by law to elect the Promoter of Justice for their own territory, as prescribed by Canon 1586.

What of the powers of the vicar general and of the cognate office in missionary districts of the vicar delegate in this matter? Can they appoint the Promoter of Justice in their respective territories?

The vicar general is apparently permitted by law to appoint a Promoter. A strict interpretation of the prevailing legislation certainly permits him to make the appointment. Nor does he seem to need a special mandate to exercise this right as he is an Ordinary in the sense of the law [4] and Canon 1589 nor any other canon in the Code places any restriction upon his power in this matter.

1 "Ordinarii est promotorem justitiae . . . eligere."

2 Canon 198, § 1.

3 Canon 198, § 2.

4 Canons 368, 198, § 1, " . . . eorumque Vicarius Generalis . . . "

This opinion seems to be warranted and an examination in the light of the legislation of the Code, it seems, would permit the inference and approve its validity.

Commentators on the Code have taken only slight notice of the question. It is easily understandable, when one considers the number of details which naturally arise in any work dealing with processes. One can hardly expect to find an exhaustive treatment of every fine point in procedure in the Fourth Book which is replete with difficulties of an important nature.

Vermeersch [5] would permit the vicar general to appoint a Promoter without the need of any special mandate from the bishop as often as the official incumbent is not actually present in the tribunal. In support of his opinion he cites Cardinal Lega [6] who, likewise, admits that the vicar general may appoint a Promoter to expedite judicial business when the official appointed by the bishop is absent from the curia. He adds, however, that the vicar general may not afterwards ignore the regular appointee of the bishop nor remove him from office. Hence they would at least permit the vicar general to appoint a Promoter for the expediting of the business at hand.

A Coronata, on the contrary, demands and expressly requires that the vicar general and the *Officialis* have a special mandate from the bishop before they proceed to the appointment of a Promoter.[7] In support of his opinion he quotes the commentary made on this point by Wernz-Vidal, which, likewise, permits the vicar general to appoint a Promoter only in the event that he has a special mandate from the bishop to that effect.[8]

In the case of the *Officialis* this is quite understandable, as he possesses ordinary jurisdiction only in judicial matters whereas the present question pertains to administrative affairs. Moreover, the fact that he enjoys ordinary jurisdiction as a judge, does not constitute him an Ordinary in the legal sense of the term as it is em-

[5] Vermeersch-Creusen, *Epitome,* III, n. 43, 20.

[6] Lega, *De Judiciis Eccl.*, I, n. 140; *cf.* also Bouix, *De Judiciis Eccl.*, I, 472.

[7] A Coronata, *Institutiones Juris Canonici,* III, n. 1124, 37.

[8] Wernz-Vidal, *Jus Canonicum,* VI, n. 114, 101.

ployed in Canon 198 and therefore he is not included in the term Ordinary used in Canon 1589. Consequently, he may not appoint a Promoter without a special mandate from the bishop.

There is only one exception to this rule and that is the case of a judge delegated by the Holy See to try a particular case. If the mandate of his appointment does not require him specifically to use the officials of the diocesan curia, his delegation gives him discretionary powers to use either the officials of the regularly constituted tribunals or to choose others, whom he may deem better fitted for the execution of the commission entrusted to him. The rescript of his appointment will determine his powers in these matters.[9]

The same reasoning does not apply to the vicar general. The lack of the power in the *Officialis* to appoint a Promoter without a special mandate does not affect the merits of the present question in the least. The bishop is perfectly free to delegate his ordinary power to others in whole or in part as he sees fit.[10]

Vidal[11] bases his reason for the limitation placed on the vicar general's power in this matter upon the doctrine of Benedict XIV,[12] which restricts the power of the vicar general relative to those matters *quae sunt merae liberalitatis et gratiae, vel speciem habent alienationis*. Vidal concludes from this that the vicar general needs a special mandate for the free conferring of an office or a benefice and as the appointment of the Promoter is an act of free nomination to a diocesan office, the vicar general must have a special mandate.[13]

It is difficult to see where the Code and the present law demands this mandate. It certainly cannot be argued from the fact that the Code in Canon 152 requires a mandate: for Canon 152 is speaking solely of ecclesiastical offices in the strict sense of the term. This is further confirmed by Canon 145 which states that *in jure* ecclesiastical office is always to be understood in the strict sense unless the text and context manifestly show that it is to be taken otherwise.

[9] Lega, *De Judiciis Eccl.*, I, 177.

[10] Canons 198, § 1; 199, § 1.

[11] Wernz-Vidal, *Jus Canonicum*, VI, 101, n. 75.

[12] Benedict XIV, *De Synodo Dioecesana*, II, 8, n. 2.

[13] Bouix, *De Judiciis Eccl.*, I, 472, uses the same intrinsic argument.

Canon 145 defines an ecclesiasical office in a strict sense of the term. There an ecclesiastical office is defined as one which must in some way participate in the power of orders and jurisdiction. The office under consideration does not carry with it the exercise of any jurisdiction.[14] The Promoter is nothing more than an official of the diocesan curia to whom the defense of the rights of the Church in criminal proceedings and in certain contentious cases is entrusted.[15] His rôle is simply that of an official plaintiff or defendant in those judicial cases involving the public welfare of the diocese. Nor may it be argued that, since he is numbered among the officials of the diocesan curia,[16] his is an office in the strict sense. The canon which follows demonstrates that some of the offices enumerated in Canon 363, § 2, are not offices in the strict sense or in the legal meaning of the word. Were these offices in the strict sense of the word there would be absolutely no need for the additional prescriptions of Canon 364, § 1; for Canon 159 had already provided that appointment to ecclesiastical offices should always be made in writing.

Therefore, it would seem that the restriction placed by Vidal on the right of the vicar general in this instance can find no basis in prevailing law. The restriction of Canon 152 on the power of the vicar general to appoint to ecclesiastical offices refers only to those offices which are such in the strict sense of the term, that is, enjoying either the power of orders or jurisdiction, and should not be extended to other offices unless the law itself expressly makes that extension.

Whether or not it would be prudent for the vicar general to exercise his power independently of the bishop is a different question. Notwithstanding the fact that he has the power from the law, he would seldom, if ever, be justified in exercising it without consulting his bishop. After all, the Promoter is a member of the diocesan curia, the members of which according to Canon 363, § 1, either rule the diocese in the name of the bishop or assist him in the general administration of diocesan affairs. These officials are the tried and

[14] Wernz-Vidal, *Jus Canonicum,* VI, 101, n. 77; A Coronata, *Inst. J. C.* III, n. 1124, 36; Roberti, *De Processibus,* I, 194.

[15] Canon 1586.

[16] Canon 363, § 2; *Jus Pontificium,* 14 (1934), 308.

worthy members of his private cabinet on whom he relies a great deal in the discharge of his own obligations and, therefore, it would be imprudent and perhaps unjust for the vicar general to appoint a Promoter without being advised to do so by the bishop, both because the Promoter is an important, permanent official personally attached to the bishop's household and curia, and also because the vicar general in the exercise of his office is bound to act in accordance with the desires and will of his Ordinary and should cooperate with him in the closest of harmony in the administration of the affairs of the diocese, taking the proper precaution that his actions will not be the occasion of acts contrary to the will and mind of the bishop.[17] Normally the presumption will be that the bishop wishes personally to fill any vacancies that may occur in his official household and the vicar general should respect this presumption.

Most authors simply state that the members of the diocesan curia should be appointed by the bishop in writing. They content themselves with this general statement, ignoring the wording of the particular canon, governing the appointment of the Promoter and the *defensor vinculi.* They state that the appointment belongs to the Ordinary.[18]

It seems certain, therefore, that the vicar general may both licitly and validly appoint the Promoter of Justice at least for one or several cases when the official incumbent of the office is not present in the curia.[19] The necessity of exercising this prerogative might well arise in various ways. One might easily have the case where the exception of suspicion has been accepted against the Promoter, thus preventing him from acting in the present case and the bishop is away.[20] Or as it may easily happen the offices of the defender and the Promoter have been invested in the same person and the case before the diocesan tribunal demands the services of both officials,

[17] Canon 369, § 2.

[18] Wernz-Vidal, *Jus Canonicum,* II, 675; Chelodi, *Jus de Personis,* 327, Vermeersch-Creusen, *Epitome,* I, n. 432, 2.

[19] Vermeersch-Creusen, *Epitome,* III, n. 43, 20; Lega, *De Judiciis Eccl.,* I, 177.

[20] Canon 1613, §§ 1, 2.

the one to accuse, the other to defend the marriage, an occurrence which might take place in the absence of the bishop. Should the vicar general exercise his ordinary jurisdiction and appoint a Promoter, no certain objection could be raised against the validity or liceity of the appointment made by the vicar general. In virtue of Canons 1589 and 198, § 1, he would certainly have acted validly as he is an Ordinary in the legal sense of the Code and has the power to exercise the ordinary jurisdiction attached to his office by the law itself.

The vast majority of the authors are silent on this fact and their silence is due rather to the moral impossibility of treating all the details that arise in the treatment of procedural law than to any positive disagreement.[21]

Does this prerogative also apply to the vicar delegate who exercises in a missionary territory an office somewhat similar to that of the vicar general? The answer is in the negative.

Vicars and prefects apostolic may and should appoint a vicar delegate[22] with the right of succession. The general law grants to this official practically all the spiritual and temporal jurisdiction which the Code gives to the vicar general, leading some authors to call him a quasi-vicar general.[23]

This does not give the vicar delegate the power to appoint the Promoter of Justice in the absence of a special mandate from the Ordinary. The basic reason for the vicar general's right in the matter is to be found in the fact that he is an Ordinary in the sense of Canon 198 and Canon 1589 places no limiting clause on the exercise of this ordinary power in the appointment of the Promoter of Justice.

The vicar delegate while similar to the vicar general in many respects is essentially different from him. He does not constitute one person with the prefect or vicar apostolic in the eyes of the law, nor

[21] Roberti, *De Processibus,* I, 198, Noval, *De Processibus,* I, 83.

[22] Epist. S. C. P. F., 8 Dec. 1919—*A. A. S.,* XII (1920), 120; *Periodica,* X (1922), 199.

[23] Vermeersch-Creusen, *Epitome,* I, 253; Vermeersch, *Periodica,* IX (1921), (24).

does he lose his jurisdiction simultaneously with the cessation of the jurisdiction in the prefect or vicar apostolic.[24]

The vicar general is an Ordinary in the sense of the law only because he constitutes one person with the bishop and is, as it were, the *alter ego* of the bishop. The vicar delegate, on the other hand, is not one person with the vicar or prefect and is not, therefore, an Ordinary in the legal sense of the term.[25] He becomes an Ordinary upon succession to the office of vicar or prefect apostolic but not prior to that moment.[26]

It may be validly concluded that since he is not an Ordinary, he is not included among those empowered by Canon 1589 to appoint a Promoter of Justice.

The Promoter of Justice may be appointed by the vicar capitular or administrator, as he is more popularly called, though he may not be removed by him. The law itself expressly places this last restriction upon the powers of the administrator or vicar capitular.[27]

In the event that the office becomes vacant during the *interregnum* and in the term of the administrator, he can appoint a new incumbent to the office. The vicar capitular is an Ordinary in the legal sense of the term and is enumerated in Canon 198 among those who enjoy ordinary jurisdiction in the administrative affairs of the diocese.[28] He, therefore, has the power to fill the office in virtue of Canon 1589, § 1. This is confirmed by the parallel case described in Canon 1573, § 7, where the *Officialis* who has been appointed administrator is instructed to appoint his successor in the office of the *Officialis*.

Moreover, he has the obligation to appoint one. The Code in reference to the office unqualifiedly asserts: "*Constituatur in dioecesi promotor justitiae et defensor vinculi. . . .*" [29] This clearly evinces

[24] Vermeersch-Creusen, *Epitome*, I, 253; Vermeersch, *Periodica*, IX (1921), (25).

[25] Canon 198.

[26] *Jus Pontificium*, III (1923), 145.

[27] Canon 1590, § 1.

[28] Canon 198, § 1: " . . . itemque ii qui praedictis deficientibus interim ex juris prescripto aut ex probatis constitutionibus succedunt in regimine. . . ."

[29] Canon 1586.

the will of the Holy See to have a Promoter of Justice in every diocesan curia.[80] This rule was in force before the Code and was officially set forth in the Instruction of the Sacred Congregation of Bishops and Regulars, published on June 11, 1880.[81]

In missionary countries there is also the office of pro-vicar or pro-prefect. The law commands that the vicar or the prefect apostolic appoint these officers shortly after their own entrance into office.[82] The pro-vicar and the pro-perfect enjoy only delegated powers during the actual incumbency of the vicar or prefect apostolic; but succeed the latter whenever their jurisdiction is impeded or expires from any reason whatsoever.[83] Hence the pro-prefect and the pro-vicar upon cessation from office of vicar or prefect apostolic, as the case may be, enjoy ordinary jurisdiction until such time as the Holy See makes provisions for the appointment of a new vicar or prefect apostolic. Consequently, both the pro-vicar and the pro-prefect upon assuming the government of the vicariate or prefecture may validly appoint a Promoter of Justice in virtue of Canon 1589, since they are Ordinaries in the sense of Canon 198.

The appointment of the Promoter of Justice should be in writing.[84] The writing is not for validity but it serves as an effective precaution and is unassailable and undeniable proof of the validity of the appointment to office. This precaution may prove of invaluable assistance as the whole validity or invalidity of a canonical process may rest upon the proof of the validity of the Promoter's appointment.

The Promoter while owing his appointment to the Ordinary must, while actively engaged in the court, accord reverence, respect and obedience to the trial judge and is subject to his rulings and counsel.[85]

[80] A Coronata, *Inst. J. C.,* III, n. 1124, 36; Roberti, *De Processibus,* I, 193.

[81] N. XIII—*A. S. S.,* XIII (1880), 328; Bouix, *De Judiciis Eccl.,* I, 475; Lega, *De Judiciis Eccl.,* I, 184; S. B. Smith, *Elements of Ecclesiastical Law,* II, 133.

[82] Canon 309, § 1.

[83] Canon 309, § 2.

[84] Canon 364, § 1; Vermeersch-Creusen, *Epitome,* I, 282.

[85] Canon 1640, § 2; A Coronata, *Inst. J. C.,* III, n. 1161, 72.

The judge not only has the right and the duty to inflict such penalties as the decorum of the court and the effective administration of justice demand, but also can condemn the Promoter to pay any damages or make amends for any loss occasioned by a remissive exercise of his office.[86]

Article II. The Tenure of Office of the Promoter of Justice

The bishop may appoint the incumbent to the office of the Promoter of Justice permanently or he may appoint him for one or more cases.[87] These conditions will be specified at the time the appointment is made as well as any reservations, limiting the power of the Promoter, which the Ordinary may deem necessary to make.

The necessity for appointing a Promoter for individual cases might easily arise even in a well organized diocese which already has a permanent appointee in the office. The regular incumbent might be ill or away on a legitimate leave of absence. Again, he might be related to one of the parties to the trial or may have previously served the party in some capacity which would exclude him from acting in the present case. Or as might easily happen in some dioceses, one person exercises both the office of the Promoter and the defender of the bond and the cases before the matrimonial court require the services of both officials, the one to accuse the marriage, the other to defend the bond. The appointment of the special Promoter naturally ends with the completion of the case or cases for which he was appointed.

It is the mind of the Code, however, that at least one person should be appointed permanently and that there should be a stable office of the Promoter in the diocesan curia. In the event that the Promoter is appointed permanently to his office *ad universitatem causarum,* his appointment may be terminated by removal by the bishop, resignation and, of course, his own inability to execute the specific requirments of his office.

The bishop may remove him for just cause.[88] The Code pre-

[86] Canon 1625, § 1; Noval, *De Processibus,* I, 131.
[87] Canon 1588, § 2; Noval, *De Processibus,* I, 82.
[88] Canon 1590, § 2.

scribes that the bishop should have some good reason for his removal. A good reason implies something more than the mere pleasure of the bishop; for removal entails in many instances a loss of prestige. Should the bishop remove him without reason, the removal would, indeed, be valid, but it would be illicit and in the event that the removal carried with it some personal injury to his character or good repute, the Promoter could take recourse to the Congregaton of the Council against the bishop's decree of removal. In the removal the bishop can proceed without any recourse to canonical procedure.

As was pointed out above when speaking of the respect due to the *Officialis* on the part of the Promoter, the *Officialis* is empowered to remove the Promoter from office as often as the maintenance of proper court discipline and the exact administration of justice may warrant so severe a punishment.[89] May the vicar general remove the Promoter from office without a special mandate of the bishop? Again it will be a question as to what extent the vicar general is empowered to appoint and to act relative to those offices which are not such in the strict sense of the term. As was indicated above, there seems to be no restriction in the prevailing law on the faculty of the vicar general to appoint a promoter, but does this also empower the vicar general to remove him? When the removal takes on the nature of a penalty, the vicar general may not do so, inasmuch as the Code expressly limits the power of the vicar general relative to the infliction of penalties. Canon 2220, § 2, definitely demands that the vicar general possess the special mandate of the bishop before he can inflict penalties. If the vicar general, on the other hand, had exercised his faculty in appointing the Promoter and now wishes to remove him for purely administrative reasons, it is difficult to see what would prevent him from taking such action independently of any special mandate; for all restrictions in the Code apply to offices understood in the strict sense of the term. It would perhaps be imprudent for the vicar general to act in this manner without previously consulting his bishop, whose wishes are to be a norm of conduct for himself and the exercise of his office. Should the Promoter have been appointed by the bishop, himself, it would seem that Canon 369,

[89] Canon 1625, §§ 1, 3.

§ 2, would demand that the vicar general refer the case of removal to the bishop, himself, and allow him to signify at least informally his own wishes in the matter. A great deal of the power of the vicar general in these matters will be determined in the general policy outlined by the bishop for his curia. Where the law makes no express provision on the subject, the vicar general will usually find his powers definitely described and delineated in the policy of the diocesan curia and will regulate his actions according to that policy which is usually a traditional one.

The power of the vicar capitular or administrator, on the other hand, is expressly restricted in this instance. If the See were to become vacant through the death, transfer or incapacity of the bishop in any form, the Promoter appointed *ad universitatem causarum* continues in office and may not be removed by the vicar capitular.[40]

The apostolic administrator may remove the Promoter as often as that administrator enjoys a permanent appointment; for he becomes the "Local Ordinary" free from the restrictions placed upon the other ordinary administrators mentioned in the Code. He may not be removed by the temporarily appointed administrator who in all things is, practically, the counterpart of the vicar capitular. The temporary administrator is the substitute for the vicar capitular and labors under all the restrictions and disabilities placed by the Code upon the latter.[41]

If the office of the Promoter, for any reason, become vacant during the *interregnum*, the administrator and the vicar capitular have unrestricted authority to appoint one should the need for such action arise. Such action would not entail any violation of the rule laid down in Canon 436; [42] for he is not introducing any permanent change in the diocesan affairs, since the officials appointed by the administrator need the confirmation of the incoming prelate, who, therefore, can licitly refuse the approbation and make his own appointments.[43]

[40] Canon 1590, § 1.

[41] Canons 1590, 315, §§ 1, 2, n. 1; Noval, *De Processibus,* I, n. 148, 83.

[42] "Sede vacante, nihil innovetur."

[43] Canon 1590, § 1: ". . . adveniente autem novo Praelato, indigent confirmatione."

Normally, during the *interregnum,* the Promoter will continue in office until the new bishop takes possession of his See. But whether the Promoter was an officer in the cabinet of the preceding bishop or was appointed by the vicar capitular during the *interregnum,* he needs the confirmation of the new Ordinary upon his advent into office.[44]

However, this does not mean that with the arrival of the new bishop, the Promoter automatically ceases from his office. He remains in office until such time as he learns of the new Ordinary's failure to confirm his appointment; [45] for in using the word "indigent" the legislator imposes the obligation on the bishop of either confirming them in their offices or of removing them.

The opinion of Noval seems to be more in harmony with the general teaching of the Code on the revocation of jurisdiction and the removal from office.[46] According to this teaching, the one holding office or enjoying jurisdiction does not lose that office until such time as the revocation or removal has been clearly and directly intimated to him and only upon the receipt of this information does the revocation become effective. While the Promoter does not exercise jurisdiction and it is certain that his is not an office in the legal sense of the term, there is a striking parallel between his office and that of other offices enjoying jurisdiction at least in its effects. There are cases which require his intervention and presence for their valid execution. The same reasons which are present for the safeguarding the validity of the actions of the judge or confessor are to be found in the appointment of the Promoter of Justice. If the teaching of Noval is not accepted, the whole trial of a case or series of cases might be declared null because the Promoter had not received notice of his failure to obtain the confirmation of the incoming prelate. The opposite opinion does not seem to be valid reasoning, nor does it carry with it sufficient weight to challenge the validity

[44] Canon 1590, § 1.

[45] Noval, *De Processibus,* I, 83; Roberti, *De Processibus,* I, 199; A Coronata, *Institutiones J. C.,* III, 38 thinks differently.

[46] Canons 371, 207, 192, § 3, n. 2; Ayrinhac, *General Legislation,* 367; Chelodi, *Jus de Personis,* n. 149, 253; Vermeersch-Creusen, *Epitome,* I, 200; Ojetti, *Commentarium,* II, 138.

of a trial which had employed a Promoter, whose express confirmation had not been received from the new bishop.

Moreover, Canon 20 will support this contention; for although the law does not expressly treat this question, it does demand in the parallel questions of office and jurisdiction that the denial of confirmation as regards either be fully intimated to the interested incumbent of the office in question. Consequently, if the new bishop is dissatisfied with the incumbents he finds in the offices of the diocese upon his arrival, he may remove them; but that removal does not become effective until he has informed the officials themselves of that fact. Then, too, the failure of the new bishop to act may be justly interpreted an an implicit approval.

So much for the cessation from office for extrinsic reasons. There remains for consideration the intrinsic causes which may remove the Promoter from the office he holds.

The Promoter ceases from office by incurring excommunication, suspension from office or by falling under personal interdict. All these penalties prohibit the placing of legitimate acts and the administration of the office he holds.[47] Acts performed in violation of these penalties are illicit if done before a declaratory or condemnatory sentence, invalid if they are placed after such sentences.[48]

Finally, the Promoter is free to resign his office. He should have just cause, which need not be grave, *i. e.*, advanced age, pressure of parochial duties, etc. He should observe the formalities laid down in the Code to insure intimation of the renunciation to the proper superior from whom he received the office.[49] Any of the causes enumerated in Canon 188 would naturally carry with them a loss of office, were the Promoter to be guilty of them as they imply a tacit renunciation of office.

Article III. The Personal Requirements of the Promoter of Justice

The Code of Canon Law enumerates a certain number of qualifications which should be found in the Promoter of Justice. They

[47] Canons 2256, 2263, 2279, 2275.

[48] Canons 2264, 2283, 2275.

[49] Canons 184-187.

are certain attributes which should characterize the appointee to that office and stamp him as fit and capable of exercising the duties and obligations which the office entails.[50]

The first requirement is priestly orders. The prevailing law in the Code requires that the official incumbent of the office be a diocesan priest. Under the pre-Code legislation this requirement was not insisted upon; for as the office exercised no jurisdiction, it was commonly thought that the Promoter might be a layman.[51] Though the law itself before the code did not require the Promoter to be a priest, much of the teaching before the Code indicates that the appointment of a priest or at least of a person in major orders was preferable both because of the importance of the office and the nature of the cases and duties it entailed.[52] The Code places its official stamp of approval on this preference and now makes it a necessary requirement for appointment to the office.

The second requirement flows as a natural corrollary from the nature of the office itself; for one could hardly prosecute the cause of justice or undertake the safeguarding of the public welfare unless he, himself, were possessed of probity of life and a knowledge of the law.[53] The Code is even more precise in its requirements for it demands integrity of reputation and a doctorate in Canon Law or proportionate knowledge. And as befits the office, it requires prudence and a disinterested zeal for justice. This means that the Promoter must not only be of good habits, but must also enjoy a spotless reputation. It suffices, however, that the repute be negative inasmuch as it has never been challenged or discredited.[54] That the Code

[50] Canon 1589, § 1.

[51] Droste-Messmer, *Canonical Procedure in Disciplinary and Criminal Cases of Clerics*, 65; S. C. EE. et RR., July 2, 1677—*Analecta Juris Pontificii*, XIII, n. 31, 44; S. C. Immunitas, June 30, 1832—*Analecta Juris Pontificii*, XIII, n. 33, 44; Lega, *De Judiciis Eccl.*, I, 178.

[52] Council of Tours, decr. II—*Coll. Lac.*, VI, 433, Achilles Ratti, *Acta Eccl. Mediolanense*, II, Pars IV, 1683-86; Third Plenary Council of Baltimore, n. 300; Hericourt, *Les Lois Ecclesiastiques*, E, II, 37, 201; Lega, *De Judiciis Eccl.*, I, 178; Droste-Messmer, o. c., 65, footnote 3.

[53] Lega, *De Judiciis Eccl.*, I, 178; Pellegrini, *Praxis Vicariorum*, Pars IV, sec. 1, n. 19.

[54] Noval, *De Processibus*, I, 83.

should require a certain degree of knowledge is only natural, when one considers the important duties the Promoter must be prepared to perform. The Code mentions the degree of the doctorate of Canon Law, but does not insist absolutely upon it. It recognizes the fact that many excellent diocesan officials have acquired the necessary knowledge and technique from their own private studies in Canon Law and moral theology together with a practice in its application over a period of time. Such men have made excellent officers in the curia and the Code recognizes them as competent. The prudence and zeal for justice, which should characterize the Promoter in the delicate issues he must necessarily handle, ought not to be based merely on negative facts. These virtues and their presence in the appointee should not be the subject of a *priori* judgment on the part of the Ordinary, but should have marked the life of the nominee up to the time of his appointment. His past performances and his strong character in the presence of an issue should be the solid grounds upon which the bishop now entrusts to him the prosecution of the public diocesan interests and welfare.[55]

In addition to these specific requirements demanded by the law, the Code requires that the Promoter be free from the exception of suspicion in the individual cases in which he may be called upon to act. This simply means that the Promoter should see to it that his participation in any given case will not give rise to the fear or belief that justice may not be administered in a disinterested manner. Should there be any solid reason to suspect that the Promoter might be prejudiced or biased either in favor of or against the parties to the trial, the Promoter should of his own initiative abstain from acting in the procedure and not await the taking of an exception to his presence in the trial.[56] In the question of suspicion he is bound by the same regulations as the judge and his associate members of the judiciary.[57]

The reason behind this wise legislation is self-evident; for the Promoter, the defensor, and the judge are essential elements in the

[55] Noval, *De Processibus,* I, 83; Bouix, *De Judiciis Eccl.,* I, 474.

[56] Canon 1613; A Coronata, *Inst. J. C.,* III, 54.

[57] Canon 1613, § 2; Roberti, *De Processibus,* I, 248; Noval, *De Processibus,* I, 118; Muniz, *Procedimientos Eccl.,* III, 121 ss.

administration of justice. The proper and effective administration of justice demands that they execute their respective rôles without bias or prejudice to the parties seeking the services of the tribunal. The parties have a right to expect a disinterested prosecution of their cases and the public good demands that they should be accorded that right. Should the Promoter feel the party might have grounds to suspect his independence of feeling, it is much more opportune to withdraw of his own volition than to be made the object of an exception of suspicion or refusal.[58]

The natural law and equity would suggest to the Promoter apart from all positive law that he must abstain from performing prejudicial actions in the exercise of his office. He exercises a natural influence upon the court, which unless disinterestedly employed works to injustice in some form or other.

As a result, all positive law excludes judges and other essential members of the tribunal, whenever there is a presumption of suspicion, *i.e.*, prejudice in some form or other. They list certain circumstances which are adjudged by the common law to be such that the official may be considered unfit and therefore should withdraw from any active part in the case, even before exception has been taken to him. There are other circumstances which respect a determined case or the peculiar relations of the officials to the parties in the case, which can give rise to a well founded fear that the perfect equilibrium of judgment and will, so essential to the fair and proper administration of justice, will be upset or unbalanced one way or the other.

The Code in Canon 1613 enumerates the causes which should restrain the Promoter from acting, even before any exception has been lodged against him.

The Promoter is bound to withdraw from a case as often as he is related to one of the principals by consanguinity or affinity in any degree in the direct line and within the first or second degree in the collateral line. He is, likewise, bound to desist from the action as often as he has acted in the capacity of an administrator or guardian to one of the parties before the court. This prohibition

[58] Roberti, *De Processibus*, I, n. 156, § 1, 248.

is not confined to the present moment, but rather includes the past and so if the Promoter in the past acted in either of these capacities towards one of the parties to the trial, even though he may no longer exercise the legal relationship, he would still come under the prohibition of Canon 1613. The reason for this exclusion lies in the fact that the bond of affection growing out of such relationship is presumed to continue even though the legal relationship itself has ceased.[59]

The Promoter is also excluded if he is connected by the bonds of intimate friendship with any of the parties to the trial. The same rule holds if the Promoter harbors any ill feeling towards a party to the trial. The ill-will must be really objective and not simply an absence of friendly feelings towards the party. It should be based on past performances which show that the Promoter was injured by the party or himself manifested a positive antipathy or committed a serious act against the party.[60]

Neither may the Promoter act in a case where he is likely to suffer a great loss or to acquire a great gain or in a case in which he has previously acted as either advocate or procurator for one of the parties involved.[61] The reasons for these exclusions are self-evident and need no explanation.

All authors admit that acts placed in violation of these prohibitions would be at most illicit. The canon contains no invalidating clause and so in virtue of Canon 11, it must be considered as a simple prohibition.[62]

Some canonists insist that the enumeration of Canon 1613 is exhaustive and exclusive.[63] This is difficult to understand, since there are other circumstances listed in the Code which give rise to an exception of suspicion. Moreover, all these causes have their

[59] Noval, *De Processibus,* I, 118, says this presumption yields easily to contrary proof.

[60] Noval, *De Processibus,* I, 118, 119.

[61] Roberti, *De Processibus,* I, 249; Muniz, *Procedimientos,* III, 147; Augustine, *A Commentary,* VII, 64.

[62] A Coronata, *Inst. J. C.,* III, 54; Augustine, *A Commentary,* VII, 64; Roberti, *De Processibus,* I, 248.

[63] Roberti, *De Processibus,* I, 248.

origin in natural equity [64] and certainly it cannot be said that the catalogue of reasons set forth in Canon 1613, § 1, exhausts the causes which might prove prejudicial to justice. Any good reason, prompting a party or the judge to believe that the Promoter will not be dispassionate or disinterested in the exercise of his rôle, would be justifiable grounds for raising and admitting the exception of suspicion. The preferable opinion seems to be that this enumeration is only demonstrative.[65]

The opinion of Roberti might be understood when viewed from another angle. Canon 1613, §§ 1, 2, imposes an obligation on the judge and the Promoter to withdraw from a case in which any of the listed causes are present.[66] The obligation to withdraw even before any objection is placed is not imposed by any other canon in the Code. In this sense the catalogue of circumstances listed in the canon is taxative; for in the event that circumstances other than those listed in this canon were present, there would be no obligation for the Promoter to withdraw of his own initiative or at best the obligation would be doubtful and therefore not binding.[67] There is nothing in this explanation which would prevent a party from taking exception to any cause which might preoccupy the mind of the Promoter against the party.[68]

It does not suffice to take exception to the Promoter on one of the grounds mentioned; the presence of these causes must be established to the satisfaction of the court. The allegation does not require a great deal of proof. It is easily proved because the presumption already exists, but the proof must be strong enough to convince the court.

The exception to the Promoter will always be heard by the presiding judge of a collegiate tribunal or by the single presiding

[64] Wernz-Vidal, *Jus Canonicum,* VI, 126.

[65] A Coronata, *Inst. J. C.*, III, 54; Muniz, *Procedimientos,* III, 121 ss., 112, n. 3.

[66] Canon 1613, § 1: ". . . ne suscipiat causam . . ."; § 2, ". . . ab officio suo abstinere debet . . . "

[67] Roberti, *De Processibus,* I, 248.

[68] The opinion of Roberti, I, 248, however, embraces both the list and the obligation and is wider than the one explained.

judge if the case is one which requires only the presence of one judge.[69]

The Promoter may not act in a case in which he appears as a witness, as Canon 1757, § 3, n. 1, expressly excludes him. It is also evident that the Promoter cannot exercise the two incompatible offices of Promoter and notary [70] or auditor in the same case.[71] This is to protect as far as possible the perfect balance of judgment against any prejudicial dispensation of justice.

As an additional safeguard against any miscarriage of justice, we have in a somewhat similar vein the prohibition of Canon 1624. The canon forbids the acceptance of any gifts or favors by the judge or other officials intimately connected with the trial.[72] The prohibition of the canon is absolute and does away with the pre-Code legislation which permitted the acceptance of small tokens as cigars, food, etc. The stringent new rule is quite appropriate, as it guards against the danger of the slightest coloring to justice in a case.

Although the two offices of the Promoter and the defender of the marriage bond are different and independent, they are not normally incompatible and can be held by the same person. After all the defender is nothing more than a highly specialized Promoter. The law expressly permits the multiplication of offices of the Promoter and the defender in dioceses where the volume of cases is not too great.[73] In general, the duties of the two offices are of the same nature; they both foster and protect the public good though in different ways. The Promoter urges the execution of the law and is perfectly free in his conclusions, while the *defensor vinculi* in virtue of his office must always stand for the validity of the marriage bond. The legislator presupposes that the parties in all these cases attack the marriage bond and therefore *pro legis tutela* the defender, as the public minister, should always act in the defense

[69] Canon 1614, § 3; Roberti, *De Processibus,* I, 251.

[70] S. C. EE. et RR., April, 1727—Wernz-Vidal, *Jus Canonicum,* VI, 101, n. 76.

[71] Roberti, *De Processibus,* I, 195.

[72] Noval, *De Processibus,* I, 130.

[73] Canon 1588, § 1.

of the bond. But the public good can also demand that the nullity of a marriage be declared and in those cases unless the parties themselves urge the nullity, the Promoter of Justice should urge the same, *i.e.*, cases in which the parties are culpable causes of public impediments. In these cases it is hardly fitting that the two offices be exercised by the same diocesan official,[74] who would be compelled to open the trial by attacking the validity of the marriage in his capacity of the Promoter of Justice [75] and also obliged to defend the validity of the same marriage in virtue of his duties as the defender of the bond.[76] The Ordinary knowing well the needs of the diocese will construct this section of his curia accordingly, keeping at the same time before his mind the will of the Church as expressed in the Code.[77]

It would not be permissible for the vicar general, however, to also hold the office of the Promoter. The vicar general and the Ordinary constitute one person, the local Ordinary, in the eyes of the law.[78] The law always held that the Promoter of Justice should be a person entirely distinct from the Ordinary or bishop. The vicar general should not hold the office of the Promoter nor appoint himself as such, should the opportunity present itself; for then he would act as judge and prosecutor in the same case, a contingency the slightest possible semblance of which is always avoided by the common law. Moreover, the express exception made in Canon 1588, § 1, permitting the same person to hold the offices of the Promoter and the *defensor vinculi* is a clear indication of the will of the legislator, showing his displeasure to the multiple holding of offices, where the office of the Promoter is concerned.

Article IV. Preliminary Formalities

There are certain formalities that the Promoter must observe before entering upon his term of office.

[74] Lega, *De Judiciis Eccl.*, IV, 496; Roberti *De Processibus*, I, 196; Muniz, *Procedimientos*, III, 12, n. 9; Canon 156, §§ 1, 2.

[75] Canon 1971, § 1, n. 2.

[76] Canon 1968.

[77] Canon 1586.

[78] Vermeersch-Creusen, *Epitome*, I, 253.

The Promoter of Justice appointed permanently to a stable office and for all cases which the exercise of the office may involve is obliged to take an oath of office before actually participating in any of the duties of his office.[79] This oath was always a requirement of the law and is taken to insure fidelity in the fulfillment of the office to which he has been recently appointed. He swears to uphold the public ecclesiastical good by a fearless, unbiased interpretation, execution and application of the law. His office is a grave one which if properly carried out brooks no respect of persons and nothing which bears the slightest semblance to self interests. By his oath the Promoter affirms that the exercise of his office will be as dispassionate and disinterested as is humanly possible.

As indicated, this requirement is one of longstanding. It was required by custom at each and every trial. As the office developed, custom and the doctors required that it be taken only upon induction into office.[80] This last provision has been incorporated into the law, has become a requirement of the positive law and the Promoter is now required to take the oath only once and that upon entering into office.[81]

This obligation of the Promoter to take the oath is now set forth in two places in the Code, since it is found in both Canon 364 and Canon 1621. This does not mean that the Promoter must elicit two oaths. If the Promoter has taken the oath upon his appointment to the curia, that oath suffices. Canon 1621 is simply supplementary, explaining that the oath need only be taken once at the beginning of the term of office when the appointee has been named permanently to the office for all cases.

The bishop may include an oath of secrecy should he so desire it.[82] Such action might be fittingly taken in view of the delicate, personal issues which fall within the scope of the Promoter's activity.

The oath is taken before the Ordinary who appointed him, his vicar general or any other priest delegated by the Ordinary to

[79] Canons 363, § 2, 364, § 2.

[80] Pellegrini, *Praxis Vicariorum,* Pars IV, sec. 1, n. 20; Lega, *De Judiciis Eccl.,* I, 178.

[81] Canon 1621, § 1.

[82] Canons 1623, 364, § 2, n. 3.

accept it.[83] If the Promoter has been appointed only for individual cases or as the necessity arises, he must take the oath as often as he appears as a party to a trial.

With regard to the form of the oath, it simply follows the essential form laid down in the Code. It must begin with the invocation of the Divine name, the Promoter, since he is a priest, touching the region of his heart in accordance with the ancient custom.[84] The wording of the body of the oath is left to the judgment of the individual Ordinary, who has the obligation of administering it.

Besides the oath of office the Promoter must also make a profession of faith in accordance with the rules laid down in the *Motu Proprio* of Pius X, *Sacrorum Antistitum.*[85] This special general law is still in force and imposes a twofold obligation. The appointee must not only make a profession of faith according to the formula of Pope Pius IV with the Tridentine additions; but he must also take the oath against modernism.[86] The Profession of Faith and the taking of the Oath must be made personally before the Ordinary or his delegate.[87]

This last obligation does not derive from the Code. It derives from the special general law enacted by Pius X. The law has not been rescinded by the Code and binds the Promoter of Justice until such time as it is expressly revoked by the Holy See.[88]

Article V. The Cases in Which the Promoter of Justice Must Intervene

The duties of the diocesan Promoter of Justice under the common law are set forth in general language in Canon 1586. There it is stated in general terms that his duties will consist in the defense of the rights of the Church by judicial procedure in both criminal

83 Canon 364, § 2, n. 1; Noval, *De Processibus,* I, 126.

84 Canon 1622, § 1.

85 September 1, 1910, Pars IV—*Fontes,* III, n. 869, 783.

86 *Motu Proprio,* Pius X, *Sacrorum Antistitum,* September 1, 1915, *Fontes,* n. 869.

87 S. C. Consist., *Declar.,* September 25, 1910—*Fontes,* n. 2075; Canon 1407.

88 S. C. S. Off., 22 March, 1918—*A. A. S.,* X (1918), 136; Vermeersch-Creusen, *Epitome,* II, 460.

and contentious proceedings. In both these proceedings the Promoter will appear as plaintiff or defendant according as he has to vindicate the rights of the Church or to defend the same rights.[89] While the duty of the Promoter of Justice to intervene in cases involving the public good is an institute flowing from the public ecclesiastical law, the diocesan Promoter, unlike the cognate office in most secular principalities, is not a representative of the executive power who supervises the administration of justice in the tribunals of the realm. The supervision of justice and its administration in the diocese pertains to the bishop, the Promoter merely defends that justice in the tribunals by appearing in the rôle of official plaintiff or defendant as often as that intervention is adjudged to be necessary. He is always an active party to the trial and only in this capacity does he exercise his office.[90]

His duties consist in the safeguarding of ecclesiastical law and its observance together with the prosecution of crime. Personal knowledge of crime will mean that he must take action against it. Should the notification of crime be brought to him, he must investigate the information, act as guardian of the law, and at once begin proceedings with a view to correcting or punishing the delinquents. The position of the Promoter in the ecclesiastical plan of things might be likened to the position held by the State attorney in our own American system of government. He is the diocesan attorney general who may be summoned by the bishop to appear in either criminal or contentious cases which are deemed of sufficient importance to demand this special treatment. He may of his own initiative appear in certain criminal cases, but, as will be seen, should not do so without notifying his Ordinary of his proposed action.

His intervention in criminal cases is absolutely necessary, as all criminal action is now reserved exclusively to him. No formal criminal[91] trial can be held without him and the process will be

[89] Bouix, *De Judiciis,* I, 472; Muniz, *Procedimientos Eccl.,* III, 11; I, 118.

[90] Cocchi, *De Processibus,* 56; Roberti, *De Processibus,* I, 195; A Coronata, *Inst. Juris Canonici,* III, 57 ff.

[91] Canon 1934; Chelodi, *Jus Poenale,* 145; Augustine, *A Commentary,* VII, 43.

held absolutely invalid, were anyone other than the Promoter, including the bishop, himself, to prefer criminal action against a delinquent and prosecute the case. This criminal action embraces the whole procedure of a criminal trial. The Promoter, alone, will draw up the bill of complaint or accusation, demand the citation of the accused, establish the person before the court as the guilty party, marshall the proofs, present them to the court, and defend them against the exceptions of the defense, and finally ask for a sentence and its execution against the defendant.[92]

However, it is not only the delicts repressed by the penal laws which compromise the best interests of any society; for the public good may find itself endangered in contentious cases.[93] Under the pre-Code legislation the Promoter was occasionally called upon to give his opinions in a case introduced by the parties and in some instances to introduce the case himself. His presence was not considered necessary in each case as a superior interest was vested in the judge;[94] besides, according to the jurisprudence of the Congregation of the Council, the interests of the Church were sufficiently protected by its natural representative, the parish priest.[95] There were cases, however, in which the public welfare was jeopardizd and no person was designated to defend its interests and the parish priest was not in position to act in these cases. To whom could this mission be attributed other than the Promoter of Justice? One sees appearing in the Code a discipline which the law of the Code has explicitly canonized by expressly recognizing to the Promoter of Justice the right to attack the validity of a marriage invalid by reason of a public impediment [96] and basing this right of official intervention upon the necessity of protecting the public good. An even clearer indication and evidence of the advance of canonical jurisprudence relative to the intervention of the Promoter in contentious cases is to be found in a comparison be-

[92] Noval, *De Processibus,* I, 502.

[93] Canons 1586, 1619.

[94] *Regulae Servandae in judiciis apud S. R. R. Tribunal,* par. 108, nn. 2, 3.

[95] *S. C. C., "Santanderien,"* 24 November, 1906—*A. S. S.,* XL (1907), 37.

[96] Canon 1971.

tween the rules of the Roman Rota published in 1910 and the most recent norms of the Rota, edited in 1934.[97]

The Code in prescribing his intervention in certain contentious cases involving the public good has amplified and extended the duties of the Promoter of Justice in the diocesan curia. As a consequence, under the prevailing jurisprudence it is the office and the duty of the Promoter of Justice as a public person to see to it that the interests of justice are served, that the common good is protected and that the faithful of the diocese are protected as far as possible from whatever is or will become a source of scandal.[98] There are cases scattered throughout the Code which call for the intervention of the Promoter. Generally, this necessity arises only when the case under consideration involves the public good and the Ordinary discerns that the proper protection of the common good demands his intervention in the adjudication of the case.[99] The basis of this intervention is to be found in the nature of the ecclesiastical common good. The Church has for its objective the sanctification of souls and the eternal salvation of its members through the use of the necessary means placed at her disposal by her Divine Founder. Among these means is the common ecclesiastical moral order consisting in the free exercise of one's right as a member of the Church, the practice of virtues, the immunity from dangers to virtue and sanctification as well as the removal of these obstacles, especially scandal, thereby, safeguarding the individual members of the faithful in their use of the means of salvation and in their efforts to escape its pitfalls. The preservation and conservation of this external ecclesiastical order will at times demand the presence of the Promoter of Justice, its chief representative in the diocesan curia. The writer has no intention of identifying the notions of public order and public good as so many do, because the two notions, while they coincide in large part, are not coextensive. The public order is, so to speak, the proper arrangement of

[97] *Regulae Servandae . . . S. R. R. Tribunal—A. A. S.,* II (1910), 783; *Normae S. R. R. Tribunalis—A. A. S.,* XXVI (1934), 449.

[98] Blat, *Commentarium,* IV, 503; Noval, *De Processibus,* I, 569.

[99] Canon 1586.

institutions and the orderly organization of rules which are indispensable to the exercise and function of any society. The public good, such as the Canon Law understands it, enjoys a wider extension and can find itself concerned in private affairs as often as the occasion should require it. These private affairs from their nature do not directly concern the public good, but by reason of present circumstances indirectly do touch upon that public good, as for example, a civil suit between two pastors which may scandalize the whole neighborhood. Hence the public ecclesiastical good which is really synonymous with the general welfare and the salvation of the faithful [100] includes not only a defense of the public ecclesiastical order, but also an intervention into private affairs as often as these affairs may affect the common welfare. An examination of the circumstances in the case will determine whether or not the public good is involved and the results of this examination will determine whether or not the intervention of the Promoter of Justice is demanded in the process in virtue of his office under the prevailing jurisprudence.[101]

While the intervention of the Promoter of Justice in all formal criminal trials is unquestionably required for the validity of the process, the necessity of his intervention into the process in contentious cases involving the public good is not so clear. While Canon 1586 clearly defines the duties of the defender of the bond and the necessity of his intervention into all cases involving the bond of marriage and of sacred orders, it does not definitely establish the necessity of intervention on the part of the Promoter of Justice in the remaining contentious cases involving the public good. One would be led to believe by the language of the canon that the necessity of intervention on the part of the Promoter must depend entirely upon the judgment of the Ordinary and according as the Ordinary adjudged this intervention to be necessary or not, the validity of the subsequent trial would depend. In other words, from the wording of the canon the presence of the Promoter of Justice in contentious cases would seem to be accidental and entirely dependent upon the discretion of the Ordinary.

[100] Noval, *De Processibus*, I, 123; Lega, *De Delictis et Poenis*, 2 ed., 21.
[101] Canon 1586.

Such, however, is not the case. There are certain contentious cases which involve the public good and therefore require the intervention of the Promoter of Justice as a necessary party to the process; [102] while there are many others in which the public good may find itself concerned not as the basis of the main issue in the trial, but by reason of the presence of special circumstances such as the dignity of the person, the notoriety of the event, the damage experienced by third persons who are defenseless, the scandal caused to the faithful, etc. It is this last fact which justifies the whole tenor of Canon 1586. In order to safeguard the public good which might be compromised in a case, the canon prescribes the presence of the Promoter of Justice. But since the estimation of the danger to the common good or to put it more exactly of the possibility of danger to the public good does not pertain to a judicial analysis, but rather presupposes an examination of the whole affair in its concrete reality, it is to the Ordinary that the decision appertains and not to the judge. The parties and the Promoter can only influence or dispose him to consider the case as pertaining to the common good.[103]

The fact that there are cases which pertain to the public good and therefore necessitate the intervention of the Promoter of Justice is very clearly set forth in the recent rules of the Rota. After declaring that the intervention of the Promoter into a case will generally depend upon the invitation of the Ponens in the case, they state that there are cases in which the Promoter will intervene in virtue of his office independently of any invitation of the Ponens. They give a demonstrative list of these cases which is as follows: the cases of impediments to the valid contraction of matrimony, cases involving the existence of pious foundations, the rights of the Church, cases of *juspatronatus* denying the freedom of ecclesiastical authorities to appoint the incumbent, the separation causes of

[102] Canon 1971; cc. 1, 2, X, *de officio judicis,* I, 32; Roberti, *De Processibus,* I, 197; Noval, *De Processibus,* I, 123; *Normae S. R. R. Tribunalis,* art. 27—*A. A. S.,* XXVI (1934), 457; Ferreres, *Institutiones,* II, 239.

[103] Roberti, *De Processibus,* I, 198; Augustine, *A Commentary,* VII, 42; *Normae S. R. R. Tribunalis—Jus Pontificum,* 14 (1934), 308.

consorts.[104] As often as the Promoter intervenes in any of these causes, his intervention is presumed to be necessary to the process.[105] Even though one were to grant the contention made by C. Bernardini in his commentary on these new norms of the Rota that this distinction between cases which by their nature pertain to the public good and those which accidentally effect the public good is too obscure to be of much practical value,[106] it shows an advance in the jurisprudence of the Rota relative to the office of its Promoter and is a reminder to the Ponens that he must take certain permanent exigencies of the public good into consideration in determining whether or not the Promoter has a right to participate in the case.

The authors enumerate a number of cases in which the presence of the Promoter seems to be necessary. It should be noted, however, an attempt to enumerate even in general facts which besides delicts respect the public good would be meaningless and perhaps rash since in most instances the connection with the public good depends upon circumstances.[107] It might be of assistance, however, to call to mind some of these cases which by their very nature pertain to the public good, and in which therefore the Ordinary should employ the Promoter of Justice, since these cases pertain precisely to his office which is to sustain the part of plaintiff for the public good and to suggest to the judge in his capacity as a public person those things which pertain to the defense of the public good.[108]

The office and duty of the Promoter of Justice as a public person to see to it that the common good is protected and that the faithful are protected as far as possible from whatever is or will become a source of scandal [109] makes him a necessary party to many contentious trials. The public good may demand that certain marriages or ordinations be declared null which cannot be attacked

[104] *Normae S. R. R. Tribunalis,* arts. 26, 27—*A. A. S.,* XXVI (1934), 457.

[105] *Normae S. R. R. Tribunalis,* art. 26, 2—*A. A. S.,* XXVI (1934), 457.

[106] Bernardini, *Apollinaris,* 7 (1934), 438.

[107] Noval, *De Processibus,* I, 123.

[108] Wernz-Vidal, *Jus Canonicum,* VI, 131; Ferreres, *Inst.,* II, 239.

[109] Blat, *Commentarium,* IV, 503; Noval, *De Processibus,* I, 569.

other than through the Promoter of Justice.[110] Again, it may be a question of the defense of the rights of minors or juridicial persons enjoying the rights of minors, *e. g.*, the diocese, *mensa episcopalis,* parishes, charitable institutions, etc. These persons enjoy the favor of the law and it is the duty of the Promoter to see to it that no damage or injustice befall them either in their spiritual rights or in their temporalities.[111] Still again, the public good is necessarily involved in the defense of certain procedural questions such as the declaration of nullity of a sentence previously pronounced by the court or the defense of a sentence through the pronouncement of which an affair has become a *res judicata;* for it is to the best interests of a society that judicial proceedings should not be interminably drawn out and that the sentence of its courts should be respected as firm and just.[112] The Promoter of Justice must also be heard in the recourse taken against the rejection by the court of the introductory *libellus* in all cases save those entrusted to the defender of the bond and in the granting of free legal services.[113] The Promoter of Justice is fittingly assigned to both these cases to see that the guarantees of full justice supplied by the Code are accorded to the petitioner, since justice demands that no plaintiff or defendant should suffer from a lack of defense of his rights; for if that necessary legal representation is not given, it impugns the good name of the Church and becomes a scandal to the faithful.[114]

These cases quoted from the authors suffice to show that there are cases in which the public good is involved not merely acci-

[110] Canon 1971; Blat, *Commentarium,* IV, 503; Lega, *De Judiciis Eccl.,* IV, 496; Roberti, *De Processibus,* I, 197; Noval, *De Processibus,* I, 123; Muniz, *Procedimientos Eccl.,* III, 12.

[111] Roberti, *De Processibus,* I, 197; Wernz-Vidal, *Jus Canonicum,* VI, 102, 131; Muniz, *Procedimientos,* III, 11, n. 2; A' Coronata, *Institutiones J. C.,* III, 57.

[112] Canon 1903; Roberti, *De Processibus,* I, 197; "Acta summatim relata," *Periodica,* XI (1922), 199; *S. R. R.,* 20 June, 1922, *S. R. Rotae Decisiones seu Sentent.,* 14 (1922), 191, 198 and 43, 65; Bouscaren, *Canon Law Digest,* p. 760; Muniz, *Procedimientos,* III, 427, n. 1; A Coronata, *Institutiones J. C.,* III, 338.

[113] Canons 1709, § 3; 1914, § 2; Roberti, *De Processibus,* I, 198.

[114] Noval, *De Processibus,* I, 123, 282.

dentally but as a primary issue. These authors reiterate their contentions in commenting upon Canon 1619 which discusses the obligation of judges to supply defects of the plaintiff or the defendant as often as they are hearing cases which involve the public good. In commenting upon this duty of the judge, the authors advise that he need not be too concerned about it since this duty precisely pertains to the intervention of the Promoter of Justice who sustains the rôle of official plaintiff for the public good and who ought to suggest to the judge all those things which are necessary for the defense of that common ecclesiastical good. They enumerate as cases involving the public good matrimonial trials, criminal causes, procedural questions, the causes of minors and juridical persons.[115]

These examples enumerated from the current jurisprudence of the Rota and of the authors, which claims the Promoter to be a necessary party in these cases, are not given here with a view to maintain that the absence of the Promoter would invalidate these proceedings, but rather to demonstrate that there are cases which by their very nature demand the intervention of the Promoter of Justice to protect the interests of the public good and to show that the intervention of the Promoter is not something merely accidental in all contentious cases. Canon 1586, as indicated, is less firm and definite on the duties of the Promoter than on those of the defender of the bond whose duties are expressly stated there. The latter is to be cited in all cases involving the validity of the marriage bond or of the bond of sacred orders. The Promoter is constituted for all criminal cases and for all cases in which the public good has in the judgment of the Ordinary been jeopardized, or called into question or is in danger of being compromised.[116] From this text it is evident that the public good can find itself involved in a private affair by reason of circumstances and when this is the case the Promoter of Justice should be present to defend the interests of the diocesan fisc; but this does not mean that the public good is never involved in a case except by reason of circumstances, so that the Promoter

[115] Noval, *De Processibus,* I, 123; Wernz-Vidal, *Jus Canonicum,* VI, 131; Ferreres, *Institutiones,* II, 239.

[116] Canon 1586.

would be called into the case accidentally and not as a normal procedure. This is contrary to the whole notion of public order and public good. The redaction of the canon is not a decisive objection. The expression, "in the judgment of the Ordinary," simply signifies that the evaluation of the case in the light of the public good pertains to the Ordinary; the Promoter accordingly will only attempt to convince the Ordinary that the case is of interest to the public welfare of souls in the diocese. This does not mean that the Ordinary can dispense with certain imperative rules in making the decision. One must agree that the examination is governed by certain permanent exigencies of the public good which the Ordinary has no right to sacrifice and upon which the Promoter of Justice is bound in virtue of his office to insist. The Promoter would not be fulfilling the mandate of his office, unless he insisted upon these permanent exigencies of the common good, nor is he justified in leaving their evaluation entirely to some one else.[117] The Ordinary, however, as the supreme judge of the diocese, has the final decision as to whether or not a case is to be considered as affecting the public good and both the Promoter and the parties should abide by this decision of the Ordinary without further argument.[118] As for the other expression used in the canon, *in discrimen vocari potest,* does it imply that the danger is ever anything but a possibility? The Code could certainly have said that the Promoter was constituted for all cases in which the public good is jeopardized or can be compromised; but would that theoretical precision have added anything to the canon? Hardly, for certainly if the presence of the Promoter is required for those cases in which the public good might possibly be involved, there is all the more reasons for his intervention in those cases in which the danger is not only a possibility but also a certainty, as in the cases enumerated in the preceding paragraphs.

Although this intervention of the Promoter seems to be a normal procedure in some cases and the necessary result of an examination of circumstances in others, his presence will never be essential to

[117] Ferreres, *Institutiones,* II, 239; *Normae S. R. R. Tribunalis* (1934), art. 27, 28, 30—*A. A. S.,* XXVI (1934), 457.

[118] Noval, *De Processibus,* I, 81.

the case and under the pain of invalidity of the process save in those contentious cases in the adjudication of which the Ordinary feels his intervention is necessary to protect public good and interests. While his presence in criminal trials as the plaintiff is absolutely essential to the validity of the process,[119] his presence in contentious cases, even though apparently necessary from the very nature of the case and its essential connection with the public good, will depend entirely upon the judgment of the Ordinary. Wherefore if the Ordinary knowingly and prudently remains inactive, after the Promoter has satisfied his obligation by trying to incline the Ordinary to consider the case as involving the public good, the contentious case, technically at least, ought not in any manner whatsoever be considered as pertaining to the public good and therefore requiring the intervention of the Promoter of Justice.[120] It is the Ordinary who will determine the opportuneness of the Promoter's intervention and should he decide that the defense of the public good requires the Promoter's presence in a given case, he becomes a necessary party to the trial and should be cited to the proceedings under pain of invalidity but not otherwise.

In fine, then the Promoter must take part before the diocesan tribunal in all formal criminal trials and in all contentious cases in which the Ordinary has adjudged the public good to be involved or to be in danger of being compromised.

There are certain places in the Code where the law prescribes that Ordinary or the judge, as the case may be, consult the Promoter and hear his official opinion in the matter.[121] These various instances will be pointed out in the course of the commentary. It will suffice for the present to say that the common and the more authoritative interpretation of Canon 105, n. 1, requires that the Promoter be consulted or heard as often as the ablative absolute is used in connection with the exercise of his office and that the bishop or the judge who disregards this condition placed by the

[119] Canon 1934.

[120] *Jus Pontificium,* 14 (1934), 308; Roberti, *De Processibus,* I, 198; Augustine, *A Commentary,* VII, 43; Noval, *De Processibus,* I, 81.

[121] Canons 1688, § 2; 1709, § 3; 1786, 1793, § 2, 1956, 1957, etc.

law upon the exercise of their own authority acts invalidly, thereby rendering their own decrees and sentences in a given case invalid. This question and the authorities who propose both sides of the question will be discussed in full in a later article.

In all these cases the sanction of the law is the same. Whenever the presence of the Promoter is required by law, he must be properly cited to the sessions of the trial or the entire *acta* of the process are invalid, unless he happened to be present at the trial even though he was not cited.[122] It should be borne in mind that the citation is for each truly judicial act, *i.e.*, rejection of *libellus*, examination of witnesses, joinder of issue, etc. The warning or citation for each strictly judicial act should be made to the Promoter personally.[123] In the event that the Promoter was not cited and was not present, the acts are invalid and should be declared such. They can be validated by repeating the acts before the same judge before whom they were originally performed by the application of the norm found in Canon 1679. The Promoter whose duty it is to protect the law against the nullity of actions should take the necessary steps to instance this repetition and revalidation of the acts and only in the event that he fails to perform this duty should the judge himself *ex officio* urge the action. Should the Promoter have been summoned but was absent from some sessions of the trial, the minutes are valid but should be submitted to the examination of the Promoter, so that he may correct or supplement them if he deems such action necessary. This he may do either orally or in writing.[124]

Some canonists interpret this to mean that if the Promoter has been legitimately cited, he need not appear at the sessions of the trial; but merely approve them afterwards to insure validity to the acts. They argue that this examination of the *acta* suffices; for the actual presence of the Promoter at the sessions of the trial does not itself constitute a procedural act, nor is it required by the positive prescriptions of the Code under pain of invalidity.[125] They contend

[122] Canon 1587, § 1; Pellegrini, *Praxis Vicariorum*, Pars. IV, Sec. 1, n. 20.

[123] Noval, *De Processibus*, I, 82.

[124] Canon 1587, §§ 1, 2.

[125] Canon 1680; Noval, *De Processibus*, I, 82; Roberti, *De Processibus*, I, 195; Vermeersch-Creusen, *Epitome*, III, 19.

that simply because the Code uses the words, *aliquibus actibus,* it may not be argued that the acts of the trial are invalid, if the Promoter should absent himself from all the sessions of the trial.

The reasoning of Noval, accepted by the other canonists quoted, seems to be sound. The fact that the Code uses the words, *aliquibus actibus,* does not militate against the opinion in the slightest. The eminent canonist is not placing a broad construction on the words referred; but is simply arguing that neither this canon nor Canon 1680 demands the actual presence of the Promoter under pain of invalidity. The fact that the Code says that if he were absent from some acts, the trial is valid if he was cited, does not warrant the conclusion that the trial is invalid if he were not present at all after citation. To argue thus seems to draw more from the premises than is warranted by the text of the canon.[126]

No doubt the Code prefers the actual presence of the Promoter at certain sessions of the trial especially at the hearings of the parties and the examination of witnesses, as is evidenced by the privileges accorded by the common law to the Promoter in these sessions of the trial, as well as the fact that the Code prescribes the actuary to note his presence or absence from the sessions of the trial and to record the same in the *acta.* The Promoter would certainly be failing in his duty were he to absent himself entirely from the proceedings and the trial judge would be acting imprudently to tolerate such action on his part. All this is undeniably true, but that is far different from saying that *acta* themselves would be invalid despite all later approval and to say that the present canon implies such a teaching.

The question is purely a theoretical one; for the Promoter in virtue of his office should have as his objective the expediting of judicial business to the best interests of the public good in the diocese which he represents. This expediting of judicial business is more effectively accomplished when he is actually present at the proceedings. No study, no matter how careful, of the minutes of a trial can prove an adequate substitute for actual presence at the

[126] Augustine, *A Commentary,* VII, 42, and Dolan, *Defensor Vinculi,* 36, think otherwise.

proceedings where the Promoter may weigh well the value of the defenses made from actual observation of the reactions of the plaintiff or defendant, as the case may be, with whom he is actively engaged in a judicial controversy. All canonists, Noval included, will urge the Promoter to be present at all proceedings, if he is to render a full service in the office with which the Ordinary has honored him.

CHAPTER V

THE PROMOTER OF JUSTICE IN CRIMINAL PROCEEDINGS

ARTICLE I. THE RIGHT OF ACCUSATION IN A FORMAL CRIMINAL PROCESS

EVERY criminal procedure involves three essential points—the accusation, the trial, and the sentence. Without anyone of these the whole procedure would be invalid.

The first and most necessary step is the accusation; for where there is no accuser, there is no accused. This accusation is a judicial accusation and the law draws a marked distinction between it and simple accusation, which may more properly be termed denunciation. The civil law calls this action by which legal action or procedure is taken against the accused an "indictment" and reserves it to the civil prosecutor appointed according to the provisions of the civil law. The Canon Law, likewise, reserves the official action insuring the trial of the accused to the diocesan prosecutor, the Promoter of Justice, and does this to the exclusion of all other persons even of the Local Ordinary.[1] In virtue of this reservation a judicial accusation of crime can be lodged only by that official who acts as the Promoter of Justice in the diocesan curia. Were the vicar general, the dean or any other ecclesiastic to lodge this accusation, it would be of no consequence and were the proceedings carried out on the strength of such accusation, they would be null and void and the sentence of the court unenforcible.

Thus the Code goes a step further than the former law and abolishes popular action altogether in criminal matters. Under the prevailing discipline the Promoter of Justice has become so vital a factor in the prosecution of crime that he alone can lodge the

[1] Canon 1934: "Actio seu accusatio criminalis uni promotori justitiae, ceteris omnibus exclusis, reservatur."

criminal action corresponding to the indictment of the civil courts.[2]

This criminal action which is reserved to the Promoter may be defined as the right to accuse a delinquent or to prosecute a crime before the diocesan courts in order to obtain the infliction of a penalty or the declaration to the effect that the penalty has already been incurred by the defendant and should be observed by him.[3] This action carries with it several rights and duties which will be enlarged upon in their proper place. It entitles him to present the *libellus* to the judge according to the rules of Canons 1954 and 1955. He has the duty to present to the court the proofs and evidence which have been uncovered either in the acts of the inquisition or from his own investigation, *e.g.*, affidavits, witnesses, instruments, heresay, etc. It authorizes him to take exceptions not only to the person and defenses of the accused but also to the personnel of the court should the administration of justice demand such action. He may produce rebuttal evidence and sum up his own case after he has read the defenses of the accused and his counsel. It is his duty to demand the sentence against the accused and to attack it if it is certainly unjust or null.[4]

As was noted above, the popular accusation has been abolished and the right of the Promoter is exclusive. Should he fail or be remiss in the exercise of his office, the Ordinary is bound to supply this negligence or failure to act by removing him and naming a new Promoter. The accusation of crime pertains to the common good and the Ordinary is not exempt from the care of that good by his appointment of the Promoter: for the bishop never ceases to be the chief promoter of justice in his own diocese.[5]

The exclusion of Canon 1934 permits of no exception and therefore includes within its ambit the complainant and all the more so the one making a denunciation. The reason for this exclusion ought not to be sought in the fact that the faithful of our own day are less

[2] Canon 1934; S. R. Rota, 2 Dec., 1922, n. 3—*S. R. Rotae, Decisiones seu Sentent.*, XIV (1922), 329.

[3] Canon 1702; Noval, *De Processibus*, I, 271, A Coronata, *Institutiones J. C.*, III, 381.

[4] Noval, *De Processibus*, I, 501, 502; Roberti, *De Processibus*, I, 197.

[5] Canon 1625, § 3; Noval, *De Processibus*, I, n. 140, 78.

strenuous or solicitous in their efforts to promote the common good, but rather in the positive action of the Church, limiting the right of judicial accusation which it had formerly conceded to all the faithful as being more in harmony with the accepted customs of the time. At the present time there is no such necessity and both Church and State agree that the common good is more effectively served and preserved by the modern system of criminal proceedure, which affords a more effective guarantee of protection to the suspect. This makes more effectively for the rehabilitation of the delinquent, the reparation of the crime and its disastrous effects upon the social order.[6]

This should not be interpreted to mean that the faithful have no part in the prosecution of crime under the prevailing ecclesiastical law. Though they are excluded from acting as plaintiffs in criminal judicial proceedings, they still have the right and in some cases the duty to denounce the offender to the authorities. Occasionally their own personal interests will dictate this denunciation, as, for example, when the complainant has suffered defamation of character or some other personal injury as a result of the actions of the accused. Or again, it may be a suit for damages growing out of a delict or other criminal actions. In both these instances, the denunciation of a delict based on private interest is called a *querela* or complaint.[7]

The public spiritual good, on the other hand, may demand that the scandal of certain actions be removed and repaired as they are proving harmful to the faith and morals of individual members of the faithful. It can also take the form of a public service to third parties who are either unaware of the damages they have suffered at the hands of the unsuspected delinquent or who are unable to defend themselves.[8]

The denunciation should be put in writing and signed by the party making it, but it may be made orally in the presence of the Ordinary, the chancellor, the rural dean or a pastor who, in turn,

[6] Noval, *De Processibus,* I, 502.

[7] Canon 1938, § 1.

[8] Canon 1935.

should commit it to writing.[9] The denunciator should attach reasons, proofs and arguments to his denunciation which will enable the Promoter to determine whether or not there is a basis for criminal action. It is not the simple denunciation of crime which will move the Promoter to take action, but it is rather the substantiation of the charges as set forth in the denunciation which will enable him to choose a course of action which will do justice to all concerned in the affair. The honor of the Church and of the clerical state, the good character of the priesthood so indispensable to any beneficial labor for the salvation of souls, the full confidence in the priest so necessary to those confided to his care are the high considerations which should guide the Promoter in his acceptance of private complaints and denunciations. He must be exceedingly discreet, careful and circumspect in his every official action against a suspect. It often happens, as the Sacred Congregation of Bishops and Regulars wrote to the Bishop of Elba, that a cleric is "all too often prosecuted by inimical parties who accuse for their own ends." [10]

Since the one making the denunciation forms one person, as it were, with the Promoter, the latter is entitled to demand the assistance of the denunciator in gathering the evidence and in establishing the guilt of the accused.[11]

The Code, before entering into an explanation of the points peculiar to the prevailing criminal proceedure, adds a very pertinent remark relative to damage or libel suits growing out of injurious actions and defamation of character which are of a criminal nature. It is emphasized there that while the duty of criminal accusation lies entirely with the Promoter, he will never of his own initiative prosecute criminally except in cases in which the members of the clerical or religious state are the victims or the perpetrators of the defamatory or injurious actions.[12]

[9] Canon 1936.

[10] 19 April, 1858—*A. J. P.*, XX, 166.

[11] Canon 1937; *Regulae Servandae* . . . S. R. R., par. 41, n. 1—*A. A. S.*, II (1910), 799; Augustine, *A Commentary,* VII, 364.

[12] Canon 1938, § 2.

All damage or libel suits of a private or personal character, although based upon criminal actions of the accused, necessarily require a previous warrant or complaint of the party who believes himself injured;[13] otherwise no criminal action by the Promoter may follow. Upon acceptance of the warrant the Promoter will adjudge the proper course to be adopted and his introductory bill in the case will fix the limits of the cause beyond which the tribunal is not free to go. The Rota decisions for 1922 record the reversal of a lower tribunal which had acted in a case of defamation. The Promoter of the lower tribunal had received no warrant relative to the defamation and since it was not a case of defamation provided for in Canon 1938, § 2, he did not include it in his bill of complaint in accordance with the first paragraph of the same canon. He confined his bill of complaint entirely to the charge of excess taxes which he could of his own initiative accuse. The tribunal in the course of the action discovered that there had also been defamation of character and in virtue of Canon 2355 punished the defendant. The Rota in its decision upheld the action of the Promoter who had acted correctly in view of the present canon and reversed the decision of the tribunal relative to the defamation.[14]

This is the practice in every civilized court of justice based on the presumption that the damage or defamation concerns only the private good and interests. However, since the clerical or religious state is a privileged one in the Church and since injury or defamation committed against one of its members reflects upon and affects the whole state, especially if the member who is injured holds some office or dignity in the Church, it is but logical to permit the bringing of criminal action against the delinquent by the Promoter of Justice. This rule also applies whether seculars or religious have defamed or injured lay persons or another of their own class.[15] In the event that the latter case should come before the diocesan courts and it should involve two priests who exercise the

[13] Canon 1938, § 1: "*Actio injuriarum* may be for real or personal damages."

[14] S. R. Rota, 2 Dec., 1922—*S. R. R. Decisiones seu Sentent.*, XIV (1922), 329.

[15] Canon 1938, § 2; *S. R. R. Decisiones seu Sentent.*, Dec. XXXVI, n. 4, XIV (1922), 329; Noval, *De Processibus*, I, n. 769, 505.

pastoral care of souls, the Promoter may intervene and insist in virtue of Canon 2355 that both plaintiff and defendant be removed from their parochial duties in as much as their actions now being reviewed by the court have rendered their services useless, if not harmful, to their respective parishes.[16]

Consequently, with the publication of the Code the action *diffamari* of the old law has lost all its force. This follows as a corollary of the changed system of accusation, the popular accusations of the old law being completely abrogated and the criminal action being reserved to the Promoter of Justice. Canon 1937 reserves to him exclusively the criminal actions resulting from injuries and defamation, always presupposing, however, the warrants of the injured parties as a *conditio sine qua non* when the case involves injuries or defamation of a private character. If the harm is done by a cleric or a religious,[17] the Promoter may institute the *actio injuriarum* of his own initiative. In fine, the one who believes himself injured may file a complaint or warrant with the Ordinary or the Promoter, but would never under the present legislation be permitted to establish before the courts the criminal responsibility upon which his warrant is based. Nor is the Promoter competent to do so, unless there has been a previous warrant filed with him or the libel is of a public character since it involves privileged persons.[18]

Article II. Various Types of Procedure

Under the pre-Code legislation one finds four common types of procedure employed in the diocesan tribunals to expedite criminal cases. Each one of them had its own characteristic note differentiating it from the others.

1. If the person proposing the accusation was a person distinct from the judge but a private person, the form of judgment was called *private accusatorial.*

[16] S. R. Rota, 2 Junii, 1924—*S. R. R. Decisiones seu Sentent.*, XVI (1924), 185.

[17] Canon 1938, § 2.

[18] *Coram Lega,* Dec. XXXI, p. 367, n. 1.

2. If, however, the accuser was a person distinct from the judge but a public personality, *i. e.*, one appointed by public authority to accuse crimes, and prosecute them before the diocesan courts without any previous investigation on the part of the bishop, the process was termed *public accusatorial.* It was public because it was prosecuted before the courts by a public appointee called the *Promotor Fiscalis.*

3. If, on the other hand, the crime was brought to the attention of the court by reason of reputation or rumor or by a person who merely denounces the delict without undertaking the proof, and the judge, himself, examines the evidences of criminal guilt and the defenses of the accused, there is had what was popularly known as the *inquisitorial procedure.*

4. And finally, if the delict was known from reputation, heresay or from denunciation either by the *Promotor Fiscalis* or a private individual, the Instruction of 1880 prescribed that in most cases a secret investigation should be made into the available evidences of crime and that a report relative to the findings of the investigation be remitted to the superior who ordered the inquisition. That superior was to proceed with the prosecution only if the investigation disclosed certain, or, at least, probable basis for criminal action. In the event that this was verified, the public prosecutor was empowered to present a formal criminal accusation and a criminal trial in the strict sense ensued. This form of procedure was known as the *mixed procedure,* because it combined the two elements of accusation and inquisition in a single process.

The Code of Canon Law has introduced some radical changes into this judicial system for the treatment of criminal cases. The purely inquisitorial procedure has fallen into disuse outside the Holy Office.[19] The legislator by his silence has implicitly revoked the simple inquisitorial procedure.[20] The system of private accusation and what was practically its equivalent, judicial denunciation, had become ineffective and are now expressly suppressed by the Code.[21]

[19] Noval, *De Processibus,* I, 490.

[20] Canon 6, n. 6.

[21] Canon 1934.

The third procedure, the public accusatorial, has been amplified and clarified by the Code. The fourth and last process and the one most recently introduced had become the object of much misunderstanding. Consequently the legislator sets forth in the common law clearly and precisely the specific actions which constitute the period of the inquisition and those which pertain entirely to the accusatorial period of the proceedure, as well as the exact conditions under which the mixed procedure must be employed.

Another very notable change introduced by the Code in criminal proceedings is the obligation imposed upon the Ordinary to substitute judicial correction for criminal trial as often as the defendant confesses and the fault with which he is charged admits of that correction.[22] The result is that criminal trials are much less frequent than they were before the Code. One should not overlook another very striking innovation by which the law restricts criminal trials absolutely to delicts factually public, a change which also tends to lessen the number of criminal trials.

Hence it is evident that only two criminal procedures survive the transformation wrought by the Code in the matter of criminal prosecution. The two that remain are the public accusatorial procedure and the mixed procedure. In the latter procedure the two forms of inquisition and accusation are harmoniously blended together into a single process, are coordinated and are both conducted under the supervision of public authority.

Not all authors speak of a twofold method of proceeding in criminal matters even after the Code. Many authors do describe the twofold manner of procedure, outlining both the public accusatorial and the mixed procedure.[23] Others speak only of the mixed procedure.[24] Still others without any mention of special forms simply explain or comment on the text of the Code as Woywod, Haring, Augustine and Eichman. From this it ought not to be deduced that

[22] Canon 1947.

[23] Wernz-Vidal, *Jus Canonicum,* VI, 667; Muniz, *Procedimientos Eccl.,* III, nn. 548, 469; Vermeersch-Creusen, *Epitome,* III, 115; Noval, *De Processibus,* I, 491.

[24] Claeys, Bouuaert-Simenon, *Manuale Juris Canonici,* nn. 1169 ff.

the authors do not agree in their teaching but rather, at most, that they have not adopted a common terminology. Be that as it may, as Muniz and Vidal observe,[25] both the form of the mixed procedure and of the accusatorial method may be reduced to the single form of public accusation, for without the presence to the public accuser a criminal process may not be held under the prevailing law.

One should note carefully that accusation is always an essential element in the mixed process and is not confined to the public accusatorial system.

Article III. The Promoter of Justice in the Mixed Procedure

Under the law prior to the Code, the Promoter exercised almost complete active supervision of that inquest which was known as the *inquisitio specialissima.* It was a true judicial act in which the Promoter appeared as the actual plaintiff and accuser. He presented the bill of accusation, demanded the citation of the accused, marshalled the proofs for the prosecution, and moved the condemnation of the accused. Not infrequently he usurped the prerogatives reserved in all law to the judge alone. He was the dominant figure in the inquisition and one finds the authors cautioning him against this illegal usurpation of the rights and duties of the judge.[26] This type of inquisition bears a marked resemblance to our present accusatorial procedure, likewise instituted and conducted by the Promoter.[27]

With the advent of the Instruction of 1880 a new process made its appearance, new in the sense that it combined the best features of the inquest and the accusatorial procedure. It was called the mixed process because it opened with an inquiry for the information of the court and continued on to a judicial accusation of crime

[25] Muniz, *Procedimientos Eccl.,* III, 469; Wernz-Vidal, *Jus Canonicum,* VI, 667.

[26] Lega, *De Judiciis Eccl.,* IV, nn. 141, 142, 202, n. (1); 167 (1); Pellegrini, *Praxis Vicariorum,* Pars IV, sec. 1.

[27] Noval, *De Processibus,* I, n. 770, 506.

only when the investigation disclosed sufficient grounds for the taking of such action.[28]

The chief service rendered by this instruction was a better differentiation of the offices of the Promoter and the trial judge.[29] It circumscribed somewhat the prerogatives and functions accorded to the Promoter by custom and particular law[30] by insisting upon and clearly outlining the position the trial judge was to occupy in the proceedings. The instruction left the Promoter an important rôle in the preliminary investigation. Since the informative process was a strictly judicial act, the judge could not take any steps whatever without the intervention of the Promoter or, at least, without citing him. Were he to do so, the act would be null and void. It was the right and duty of the Promoter to draw up the charges, and petition that the informative process be undertaken. It was also his duty to present the witnesses, documents and other proofs to the auditor who presided over this hearing even though the delinquent had not yet been cited. In a word, he was the active plaintiff both in the preliminary stages of the trial and in the subsequent actual criminal trial.[31]

The inquisition, on the other hand, provided for in the present law, though still a judicial act, excludes the action of the Promoter, as is evidenced by the grudging exception made to its strict secrecy in Canon 1945, which permits the inquisitor to consult the Promoter as often as he is faced with a difficulty in the procedure. It is the only reference made to the Promoter relative to the preliminary inquisition of the present law and then the presence of the Promoter is only by way of exception.

Under the present system the inquisition is conducted along judicial lines although it does not follow the strict procedure laid

[28] Instr. S. C. EE. et RR., 11 Junii, 1880, nn. 10 ff.; Instr. S. C. S. Off., 6 augusti, 1897, n. 3—Coll. S. C. de Prop. Fide, nn. 1534, 1977; Droste-Messmer, *Canonical Procedure in Criminal and Disciplinary Cases of Clerics*, p. 53.

[29] Lega, *De Judiciis Eccl.*, IV, 203.

[30] Lega, *De Judiciis Eccl.*, IV, 167, n. 1.

[31] Lega, *De Judiciis Eccl.*, IV, 203, 204; S. B. Smith, *New Procedure in Criminal and Disciplinary Causes of Ecclesiastics*, 77 ff.

down for a judicial trial in view of the nature of the object with which it deals. Similar to the inquisition of the Instruction of 1880, it has for its object the investigating of probable grounds for penal action. As often as certain knowledge is not had either of the delict or the party responsible for the delict, the Code obliges the bishop to use the mixed procedure. Rash and precipitous criminal charges jeopardize the good name, character and welfare of the accused and often carry gravely injurious consequences with them, giving the party unjustly accused the the right to seek damages against the diocese.[32] In order to avoid such distasteful and embittering consequences the law safeguards both the bishop and the suspect by requiring this previous, secret investigation into the probable basis of crime.[33] Consequently a previous inquisition must be held as often as the delict is based on knowledge derived from reports, rumor, heresay, observaton by the Ordnary, damage suits, denunciations of private persons, etc., as long as the source of knowledge does not carry with it moral certitude both as to the delict and the moral responsibility for the delict.[34]

The secret inquisition is usually conducted by one of the synodal judges, though the Ordinary is free to delegate any prudent priest, who is called an inquisitor. The inquisitor is a delegate chosen for a single case. He has the same obligations as the judge in any ordinary trial but may not act as the judge in the subsequent criminal trial should the evidence uncovered in the inquisition warrant these criminal proceedings.[35]

The inquisitor should not proceed with his investigation until the Ordinary has adjudged that the materials on hand are sufficient to institute a formal inquiry. Once advised by the bishop that the evidence is sufficient, the inquisition may begin. It must be con-

[32] S. C. EE. et RR., 23 julii, 1830—*A. J. P.*, XX, 460; Wernz, *Jus Decretalium*, V, lib. 2, n. 823, 64.

[33] Canon 1939, § 1; Instr. S. C. EE. et RR., 11 Junii, 1880, art. 15—*A. S. S.*, XIII (1880), 328; Chelodi, *Jus Poenale*, 157.

[34] Canon 1939, § 1.

[35] Canons 1941, 1621-24; Noval, I, 511, says the last mentioned prohibition is only "ad liceitatem," but Augustine, VII, 369, holds it is "ad validitatem." The former opinion seems the more preferable.

ducted with the utmost secrecy and caution so that no rumor of crime is permitted to get abroad and the good name of no one, delinquent, accomplice or other parties involved, is compromised. The inquisitor will examine witnesses acquainted with the accused and the accusers as far as the secret nature of the examination will permit him. He may examine the instruments in the case and endeavor to weigh their value. In all these things he will follow the general rules laid down in the Code, although he is free from all the formalities connected with the public and solemn summons in ordinary procedure.[36]

After the acts of the inquisition are closed or the finding is complete in the judgment of the inquisitor, all the available sources of information having been exhausted, the inquisitor will formulate his opinion, which the law calls a vote. This vote along with the evidences uncovered in the hearings must be forwarded to the Ordinary or to the *Officialis* empowered to receive it in virtue of a special mandate from the Ordinary for the present case. They, in turn, must examine all the proofs and the findings of the court of inquisition.[37]

The examination of the acts leaves the Ordinary or the specially empowered *Officialis* one of three courses of action, and he must issue a decree in accordance with the conclusions of this examination.[38]

If the denunciation, suspicion, rumor, ill repute, etc., appears to be groundless, the decree declaring that it is so is incorporated into the acts of the inquisition and placed in the diocesan archives.[39]

If the evidences are insufficient to justify criminal prosecution, they are placed in the diocesan archives and the suspect is placed under vigilance or called in for question about his behavior and, if necessary, he is given an admonition according to the rule laid down in Canon 2307.[40]

[36] Canons 1943, 1944, 1774, 1775, 1819-1824.
[37] Canon 1946.
[38] Canon 1946, § 2.
[39] Canon 1946, § 2, n. 1.
[40] Canon 1946, § 2, n. 2.

If the evidence gathered in the inquisition is conclusive or, at least, probable and sufficient for criminal prosecution, the delinquent is summoned into court.[41] Should the delinquent "freely and considerately" plead guilty to the charge,[42] the bishop may give him a canonical rebuke or correction if the crime is one that admits such procedure.

Canon 1948 excludes judicial correction as often as the charge before the court involves any of the cases enumerated. It is excluded:

1. In all causes, even though confessed, in which the crime is one which is punishable by excommunication especially reserved or most especially reserved to the Holy See, or one which is punishable by privation of benefice, infamy, deposition or degradation.

2. In all crimes which require only a declaratory sentence for the enforcing of a censure or vindicative penalty already incurred.

3. Whenever the Ordinary deems a judicial correction is insufficient to repair the scandal given and to restore justice. This last limitation on the right to substitute judicial correction for criminal proceedings is left entirely to the prudent judgment of the Ordinary.

Aside from these cases, judicial correction can be employed twice but no oftener. If the second rebuke proves fruitless or inefficacious in restraining and deterring the delinquent from committing crime again, criminal procedure must be applied and the recalcitrant must accept his punishment according to the rigor of the due process of law.[43] The same is true even though the correction took place in the midst of proceedings on a previous occasion.

Judicial correction may be employed in all cases save those mentioned in Canons 1948, 1949 at any moment in the trial in which the defendant confesses. The application of the correction suspends the trial and the action of the Promoter as long as the contrite defendant behaves himself.[44]

Should the Ordinary decree the prosecution of the accused, from

[41] The sufficiency of the evidence will be based upon the rules laid down in Canons 1789-1791, 1812-1818, 1750-1753.

[42] Canons 1751, 1947.

[43] Canons 1949, 1954.

[44] Canon 1950.

this point to the end of the trial the mixed procedure is identical with the accusatorial procedure which is being discussed separately, in as much as the Code permits its use independently of the previous inquisition in certain cases and under certain conditions. This process and the duties of the Promoter in it will be treated in the following article.

It has already been noted that the common law in no way provides for the official presence of the Promoter at any of the sessions of this preliminary inquisition, nor in the substitution of judicial correction for criminal action. Moreover the law gives him no right to be present at the proceedings. In Canon 1945 which makes the sole reference to any part the Promoter might have in these proceedings, permission is granted to the judge as often as he encounters some difficulty in the proceedings to invite the Promoter to be present and to disclose the acts of the investigation to him. This reference to the presence of the Promoter in the proceedings is merely incidental to the question of the guarded secrecy of the inquisition and is strictly permissive in its intent. His appearance in these proceedings will be contingent upon the invitation of the inquisitor, and his part in the proceedings will be within the limits placed upon his intervention by the invitation tendered by the judge. The Promoter will be present and will assist only in those points upon which the inquisitor feels he may be of assistance and no more.[45]

The inquisitor may require the assistance of the Promoter at any moment of the inquisition up to its conclusion and show him the acts of the trial thus far completed. This sole exception to the strict secrecy of the trial is only fitting. The inquisitor may well fall into some difficulty in directing the inquisition, as he is not accustomed to procedure in criminal matters. The office of the Promoter, however, demands that he be versed at least in the theory regulating these matters and, if he has had the practice in the same, his value is just so much enhanced.

Moreover the inquisitor in conducting the informative process does not intend to collect proofs so that vindicative measures may be taken against a suspect, whose guilt is not at all evident, rather

[45] Canon 1945; Muniz, *Procedimientos Eccl.*, III, n. 566, 482.

he is trying to satisfy the demands of justice by endeavoring to arrive at the objective truth in a case. The Promoter of Justice has a similar duty in the diocesan curia, since it is his duty not only to take action against a delinquent in order to protect the public good, but also to see that justice is administered to the suspect whenever there is the slightest doubt about his guilt. The Promoter has the duty of getting at the objective truth in a case and of abstaining from any action that may prove prejudicial to the suspect or defendant in a case. In view of these facts the law relaxes the secrecy with which it surrounds the inquisition and rightly admits the Promoter to act as an assessor in order to obtain as far as possible the objective truth about the guilt of the suspect.[46]

The intervention of the Promoter of Justice into the inquisition will be only for single difficulties. It will not be so pronounced that he seems to prepare and conduct the inquisition. This would be foreign to the purpose of the inquisition and to the spirit of the law which models its legislation in the present matter upon that system prevailing in the civil courts, a system which sharply distinguishes between the three officials necessary to complete the mixed process. First, these should be the inquisitor whose action is not precisely to prepare for a criminal trial (such action pertains to the Promoter), but rather to arrive at the objective truth of the charges based upon an examination of available evidence, so that he may judge whether the suspect is to be held for further judicial proceedings or is to be dismissed without further embarrassment. Secondly, there should be the Promoter who will act as the official accuser in the criminal trial proper, and finally, the judge who is to pass definitive sentence upon the evidence submitted to the court in the criminal trial.[47] Were the Promoter by his intervention to dominate the entire inquisition, he would be acting contrary to this wise ordination of the legislator and would be upsetting this well devised method of administering unbiased justice,

[46] Canon 1945; A Coronata, *Inst. J. C.*, III, 393; Augustine, *A Commentary*, VII, 372; Chelodi, *Jus Poenale*, 158; Noval, *De Processibus*, I, 517.

[47] Canon 1941, § 3; Lega, *De Judiciis Eccl.*, IV, nn. 114, 167, 168; Vermeersch-Creusen, *Epitome*, III, 119; Noval, *De Processibus*, I, 517.

for he would be usurping the rôle intended by the legislator for the inquisitor who alone and personally is to evaluate the objective facts revealed in the course of the inquisition.

It would be a desirable thing for the inquisitor upon his appointment to confer with the Promoter and with his assistance and under his guidance roughly outline the entire inquisition, fixing the tentative limits of the inquisition from the information already on hand, examining the pros and cons of the case as well as framing the interrogatories at least in their principal points. Such a conference would enable the Promoter to point out the probable difficulties which might arise in the course of the inquest, and to discuss with the inquisitor the practical results of such an inquest, making clear to him the type of proof that is necessary to establish probable or certain crime together with the action that is to be taken should the inquisition disclose such evidence. This prior consultation will enable the inquisitor to derive invaluable information drawn from the studies and practical experience of the Promoter in criminal matters.[48]

Besides his preliminary discussion with the Promoter before the opening of the case, the common law permits the judge, as already stated, to invite the Promoter to attend the proceedings at any moment up to their conclusion. The Code names the Promoter as a sort of official assessor or counselor whom the inquisitor may consult at any stage of the proceedings as often as he deems it useful or necessary. He may also show him a transcript of the proceedings for the purpose of obtaining his advice. Muniz[49] sees no objection in inviting the Promoter to be present at the examination of witnesses in the event that the inquisitor feels it would be advantageous in obtaining the end for which the inquisition was undertaken. The inquisitor is the sole judge of the necessity or advantage of the Promoter's intervention and, unless invited, the latter may not voice his advice or opinions.

The inquisitor will do well to seek the advice of the Promoter

[48] Muniz, *Procedimientos Eccl.*, III, n. 556, 482, strongly advises this preliminary discussion with the Promoter.

[49] Muniz, *Procedimientos Eccl.*, III, 482 and n. 1.

as often as he has some difficulty or doubt. Such action on his part will safeguard the best interests of justice in many instances. Not infrequently the knowledge of a specific crime will influence even the best disposed judge. The inquisitor since he hears the case without any contradiction of plaintiff or defendant, without any systematized or well presented allegations and denials, is in danger of being influenced one way or another, but the chief danger is that the bias will work to the disadvantage of the suspect. The chief quality in the inquisitor is absolute freedom from any prejudicial notions. He should consider only the objective truth of the facts before him, attempting to do full justice to both the public interests of the common good and the private interests of the defendant. Consequently, in the face of doubt he will do well to confer with the Promoter whose duty it is to see that the defendant is accorded full justice and that the public good be served. In the circumstances described the Promoter can see more clearly the various contingencies in the case, and from his personal experience give the inquisitor a disinterested and objective solution of the difficulty or doubt. At any event the intervention of the Promoter should prove a balancing influence in all questions of difficulties or doubts.

The inquisitor is free to avail himself of the services of the Promoter of Justice and the latter is bound by his office to render the desired services.[50]

The inquisition concluded, the inquisitor will submit the acts of the sessions together with his decision to the Ordinary. The Ordinary, in turn, will pursue the action he considers advisable in the case. In the event that judicial correction is not permitted or he feels that is is insufficient or inefficacious, he will order the acts of the inquisition to be delivered to the Promoter who upon reception of them will immediately prepare the *libellus* of accusation. The handing over of the acts to the Promoter is an implicit approval of the Ordinary to the prosecution of the accused by the Promoter as the only means of satisfying the public good.

[50] Canon 1945; Wernz-Vidal, *Jus Canonicum,* VI, 678.

Article IV: The Promoter of Justice and the Purely Accusatorial Procedure

The mode of proceeding by public accusation [51] is barely recognized by the Code and may be deduced only indirectly from Canon 1939, which permits this manner of procedure without any previous denunciation or inquisition, as often as it is a question of the prosecution of a notorious or absolutely certain delict which does not admit of judicial correction.[52] Otherwise, even in cases of notorious delicts, the judicial correction may precede the criminal proceedings unless the Ordinary discerns that such rebuke would be insufficient or inefficacious.[53] Yet even in these cases the public accusatorial procedure must await the decision of the Ordinary as to whether the correction is to be used.

Noval [54] seems to admit of two cases in which the Promoter may proceed by way of public accusation, namely, the cases of notorious and entirely certain delicts mentioned in Canon 1939 and the cases of those delicts which are excluded from the use of judicial correction prescribed in Canon 1947, but the case of Canon 1947 does not seem to be distinct from the case mentioned in Canon 1939. Canon 1947 seems to be a restriction upon Canon 1939, so that even when the delict or crime is notorious, the judicial correction must be used, if there is place for it, before criminal action is proposed by the Promoter. Consequently, criminal action may be taken by the Promoter in the form of the public accusatorial procedure only when it is a question of the prosecution of a crime which is notorious or absolutely certain and which does not admit the use of judicial correction.[55] In all other cases the mixed procedure with its prior secret investigation and its subsequent public accusation must be used.[56]

[51] Canon 1934.

[52] Canons 1947-1953.

[53] Canon 1947; A Coronata, *Inst. J. C.*, III, 380 and n. 3.

[54] Noval, *De Processibus*, I, n. 749, 491.

[55] Canons 1939 and 1947.

[56] Canons 1939, 1947, ss., 1935.

Wherefore as often as the Promoter has knowledge from any source of a public delict, which is notorious in fact or, at least, certain, and the delict is not one of those which admits of judicial correction, he has not only the right to act of his own initiative against the delinquent, but he has also the duty to do so. In the circumstances described, the Promoter is technically free to introduce the cause in the diocesan tribunal without any previous inquisition by the courts. The opinion of Vermeersch-Creusen permitting the Promoter to exercise this prerogative of introducing criminal causes without resorting to any prior inquisition in cases where only serious probability of crime is had [57] does not appear to be canonically sound. Such crime, no doubt, affords sufficient grounds for the institution of an inquisition, but it can hardly form the basis of a purely accusatorial procedure on the part of the Promoter.[58]

When is a crime notorious in fact or sufficiently certain? A crime is notorious in fact when it is publicly known and has been committed in such circumstances that it cannot be concealed by any artifice and cannot be excused by any legal assumption or circumstantial evidence.[59] From the definitions given in the common law, it would seem that the public character of a crime refers to the knowledge of the fact itself of crime, whereas the notion of notoriety carries with it not only the knowledge of a public fact but also the knowledge of that public fact as a delict in which the moral responsibility of the delinquent is so certain that *non ulla possit ter giversatione celari.*[60] The second clause, *nullo juris suffragio excusari,* refers to this imputability which may be lessened by the extenuating circumstances recorded in Canons 2201-2206. Hence, not only the fact itself of the crime must be certain or notorious but also its criminal character.[61] Thus, for example, the killing of man

[57] Vermeersch-Creusen, *Epitome,* III, 116.

[58] Compare this opinion with Canons 1939, 1947 ff., 1955.

[59] Canon 2197, n. 3.

[60] Sole, *De Delictis et Poenis,* n. 11, 6-8.

[61] Reiffenstuel, lib. V, tit. I, n. 265; Hollweck, *Die kirchlichen Strafgesitze* (1899), 68.

might take place in the presence of several witnesses who may not be sure whether or not the killing was murder or self-defense. In that event one has a crime that is public, but it is not notorious in fact. If, on the other hand, the witnesses were certain of the murderous intent of the assailant and there were no excusing circumstances, one has a crime notorious in fact. It is this element of inexcusability or of the knowledge of the criminal character of the evil act which distinguishes a public crime from one that is notorious. The Code manifestly lays stress on the divulgation with regard to public crimes and emphasizes the criminal character as being known and inexcusable in crimes notorious in fact.[62]

Therefore, before the Promoter institutes a public accusatorial procedure, he must have before him certain knowledge of a deed which is public and the criminal character of which is unquestionable, *i. e.*, the deed must be known as a crime and cannot be excused. He must have certain knowledge not only of the objective fact of crime but also of the subjective guilt of the delinquent or, at least, he must have in his possession evidences which point with certainty to the suspect whom he accuses as the culpable cause of the delict. Furthermore, it must be one of those delicts in which the Code does not permit judicial correction.[63] These elements being present the Promoter must institute proceedings by making a judicial accusation of crime against the delinquent or at least this is true, were one to consider only the strict wording of the Code.[64]

While canonists who treat the question are unanimous in agreeing that the Promoter is perfectly within his rights were he to take such independent action, the same canonists without exception maintain that he should confer with the Ordinary before taking any positive steps to introduce the issue in the diocesan courts. He should present the Ordinary with the evidences of crime and seek his advice, for while the right and duty of accusing and prosecuting the defendant of a criminal trial is his by law, he does not exercise this duty absolutely independently of the supervision

[62] Augustine, *A Commentary,* VIII, 17.

[63] Canon 1948.

[64] Canons 1934, 1955.

of the Ordinary.[65] The reason for this restriction lies in the very nature of the office of the bishop and derives from the fact that a bishop in his diocese has the principal right and obligation to decide and determine what means are most conducive to the attainment of the end of the Church, the salvation of souls and the public welfare of the ecclesiastical society. It is his judgment in the light of the supernatural end of the Church which will determine whether paternal methods or judicial procedure are to be employed and which is the more opportune in a given specific instance.[66] Even when the crime is notorious, judicial correction should be employed if it is at all possible.[67] The Ordinary not the Promoter of Justice is the sole judge as to whether the correction is prudent and satisfactory. Even in those notorious cases in which judicial correction is excluded by the positive law, the nature of the Church as a spiritual society demands that the Ordinary alone decide whether a delict, which the Promoter alleges to be notorious, is really such, for many delicts are called notorious which are not such.[68] Furthermore, it certainly is the right of the Ordinary to determine whether the delinquent is to be haled before the court immediately or whether it might not be opportune and perhaps even necessary to defer the accusation for some time. Hence even if the accused has already been brought before the tribunal or if the Promoter has requested that such action be taken, the *Officialis* will do well to inform the Ordinary of the facts in the case and await his decision on what action is to be taken.[69] It goes without saying that the decision of the Ordinary prevails and the *Officialis* will act accordingly. In fine, the Promoter of Justice should never

[65] Wernz-Vidal, *Jus Canonicum,* VI, 102 and n. 78; Noval, *De Processibus,* I, 519; A Coronata, *Institutiones J. C.,* III, n. 1465, 396.

[66] Instr. S. C. EE. et RR., 11 Junii, 1880, art. 33-35, "Conscientiae et prudentiae Ordinarii horum remediorum incumbat applicatio juxta praescriptiones canonum et casuum adjunctorum gravitatem"; Canons 1946-1954.

[67] Canons 1946-1954; A Coronata, *Institutiones J. C.,* III, 380, and n. 3.

[68] Noval, *De Processibus,* I, 311, 312.

[69] Noval, *De Processibus,* I, 520; A Coronata, *Institutiones J. C.,* III, 396; Wernz-Vidal, *Jus Canonicum,* VI, 682; Roberti, *De Processibus,* I, 163, 164.

lodge a formal accusation without the knowledge and approbation of the bishop.[70]

In view of these facts the Promoter will prepare a twofold *libellus* whenever he is engaged in a public accusatorial procedure, one which the authors call the material *libellus*,[71] the other the formal *libellus* which will mark the opening of the formal criminal trial. The material *libellus* is addressed to the Ordinary unless the vicar general or the *Officialis* is empowered to receive it. The material *libellus* is nothing more than a denunciation of crime made *ex officio* by the Promoter and is merely a step preparatory to the formal introduction of a criminal cause. It corresponds to the denunciation prescribed in Canon 1936, whereby private persons can and ought to make the denunciation. The formal *libellus*, on the other hand, is always addressed to the judge and is drawn up according to the rules laid down in the first part of the Fourth Book of the Code.

In preparing the material *libellus* the Promoter will merely indicate in a general way the delict with which he charges the delinquent and the proofs and evidence of his guilt. Although he need not give a detailed account of the delict and the responsibility for it, the Promoter should clearly and definitely establish three things in his material *libellus*. He should note, first of all, whether the delict is notorious or only public and that the delict is absolutely certain both objectively and subjectively to be of a criminal character. Secondly, he should set forth in summary fashion the evidences at his disposal which substantiate both the notorious character of the delict and its certainty. Lastly, it should petition the *Constitutio rei*. It would certainly suffice for the Promoter to write:

> Accuso N. N. Vicarium Cooperatorem N. N. de delictis adulterii, non residentiae, et impedimenti oppositi ecclesiasticae jurisdictioni. Primum est notorium utpote con-

[70] Roberti, *De Processibus*, I, 196, 197; Droste-Messmer, *Canonical Procedure in Disciplinary and Criminal Cases of Clerics*, p. 50.

[71] This practice is based upon Canons 1934 and 1955; the material *libellus* will be in virtue of Canon 1934 and the formal *libellus* in virtue of Canon 1955; Noval, *De Processibus*, n. 800, I, 531.

> fessum coram tribunali civili civitatis N.; alterum est saltem omnino certum, ut patet ex monitionibus ipsi rite factis die . . . et die . . .; tertium est publicum et omnino certum, quippe quod probatur quampluribus testibus de visu et auditu inter quos N. N. sacerdos domiciliatus . . . N., N. et N., necnon testes de auditu auditus N., N. et N.; qui omnes promptissimi sunt veritati exhibendae.[72]

The Ordinary or the specially empowered *Officialis* will examine the material *libellus* and decide upon the course of action to be taken. He will refuse to proceed further, or order the defendant to appear for judicial correction, or will order the continuation of the prosecution of the accused.

In any event the Promoter must await the decree of the Ordinary before instituting the formal process for the prosecution of the delinquent.[73]

Once he has received the precept of the Ordinary decreeing the prosecution of the accused, the Promoter will immediately prepare the formal *libellus* for presentation to the ecclesiastical court. This formal bill should set forth six things based on the knowledge which the Promoter has in the case and upon the conclusions he has drawn from that knowledge.

The formal *libellus* will open with the name of the judge or at least of the tribunal to whom he presents the *libellus.*

It will clearly indicate the qualified crime with which the defendant is accused and the penalties demanded by the Promoter. It will state the occasion and date of crime, thereby, giving the defendant a fair opportunty to prepare his defense.

It will clearly and definitely set forth the name, surname and office of the defendant against whom the official accusation is levelled.

[72] This example of a material *libellus* is to be found in Noval, *De Processibus,* I, 533.

[73] As A Coronata, *Institutiones J. C.,* III, 405, footnote 2 observes, this is not a command of the positive law but such action is more in harmony with the general nature of the bishop's office as outlined in the law. Wernz-Vidal, *Jus Canonicum,* VI, 682; Chelodi, *Jus Poenale,* n. 122, 164; Muniz, *Procedimientos Eccl.,* III, 507, all admit the independence of action on the part of the Promoter but they all teach that in practice there should be a precept from the bishop before the promoter takes any *ex officio* action against a delinquent.

It will give a compendium of the proofs by which the Promoter intends to establish the juridical basis of his accusation of crime. It will therefore set forth the laws, general or particular, which the defendant is alleged to have violated and which prove his contentions that the actions of the defendant constitute a true delict.

In support of these allegations of law, he will briefly outline the various constituent facts which coalesce to make the delict, giving the names of witnesses, depositions, documents, proofs taken from the previous inquest, etc., which establish the participation of the defendant in these various facts.

It will give the various circumstances which increase or decrease the guilt of the accused.

It will close with a petition requesting the services of the court in the examination of the accused according to the attached interrogatories, the citing and examination of witnesses at the proper time and asking the court to apply the penalties provided in the law to the defendant.

The entire *libellus* will be signed by the Promoter and will note the month, day and year on which it was presented to the court as well as the place of residence of the Promoter. This last requirement will be important if the Promoter is appointed for individual cases according as the necessity arises.[74]

Noval in his commentary on the fourth book gives an example of the criminal *libellus* which may serve to clarify the above requirements, which are to be found in a formal *libellus*. It reads:

> *Pono* vel assero;—1. N., Vicarius cooperator paroeciae N., die . . . mensis . . ., in foro secus paroecialem Ecclesiam sito, pluribus astantibus dixit se fustibus coacturum esse retrocedere per eandem viam Oeconomum ab Episcopo nominatum. Super hoc exhibeo testes N. N. N. et N.—2. Die . . . nemo aperuit ianuas domus Paroecialis Oeconomo pluries ad tintinnabulum pulsanti et tandem imminente iam nocte ad domum N. confugienti. Super hoc exhibeo testes N. N. N. et N.—3. Item Oeconomus sequenti mane Sacrarium Ecclesiae petenti [petens] audivit sibi intimari parochi vetitum celebrandi ibi missam.—4. Facta hactenus recensita constituunt verum delictum, quod juxta c. 2337 consistit in de-

[74] A Coronata, *Institutiones J. C.*, III, 406.

liberata voluntate impediendi exercitium iurisdictionis ecclesiasticae.—5. Die praedicta, quando Oeconomus ad tintinnabulum pulsabat, Vicarius erat domi, et quidem clauso ab ipsomet ostio, contra consuetudinem; quod ostendit participationem ejus in delicto.—6. Oeconomus, ante nominationem ab Episcopo factam erat Vicario amicissimus; hoc autem constituit *circumstantiam aggravantem* delictum: prohibitio celebrandi Oeconomo per administros ecclesiae intimata induit *circumstantiam scandali.*—7. Attentis his circumstantiis et dispositione praedicti Canonis 2334 N. meretur poenam suspensionis praeter praeceptum degendi per mensem in aliqua domo religiosa.—8. Peto ut super positionibus *facti* examinentur tum reus iuxta interrogatorium hic annexum, tum testes in eis designati iuxta interrogatoria opportune exhibenda.[75]

Article V. The Promoter in the First Stages of the Criminal Trial

Since there are some things in the opening stages of a criminal trial which are peculiar to that process, they will be discussed presently, whereas the discussion of the duties of the Promoter in the body of the trial will be treated in a later article. The reason for this division is that the duties of the Promoter in the remaining stages of the contentious and criminal trials coincide for the most part and hence may be discussed together, noting whatever slight changes that are necessitated by the nature of the criminal process.[76]

A. *The Promoter and the Presentation of the Formal Libellus*

The *libellus* is a plea or original writ setting forth the statement of the case to the competent judge, petitioning him to admit the cause and to grant the redress requested.[77] Every formal trial must open with the presentation of this original writ by the plaintiff who may be appearing in his own behalf or cumulatively with others, or officially in virtue of his office.[78]

[75] Noval, *De Processibus,* I, 533, 534.

[76] Canon 1959; A Coronata, *Institutiones J. C.,* III, 410; Muniz, *Procedimientos Eccl.,* III, n. 631, points out the minor differences between the two procedures in the probatory period of the trial.

[77] Augustine, *A Commentary,* VII, 160.

[78] A Coronata, *Institutiones J. C.,* III, 76.

This requirement of the common law is also verified in criminal proceedings. Criminal trials in general proceed along the same lines as the contentious cases with Promoter of Justice acting as the plaintiff and the accused in the rôle of the defendant.[79] Hence, unless it is stated otherwise in the law, the same rules of judicial procedure apply to both criminal and contentious proceedings.[80]

It is the Promoter of Justice of the diocesan curia who will act as the plaintiff in all judicial criminal proceedings before the diocesan courts. As noted above, the official incumbent of this office is the only one competent to prosecute the charges.[81] It will be his duty, therefore, to prepare and present the *libellus* to the judge in all cases of criminal prosecution.[82] This *libellus* is called the formal *libellus* to distinguish it from the material *libellus* described above. As was noted then, the presentation of the formal *libellus* marks the opening of the criminal trial proper.

The Promoter should present the statement of his case against the accused in writing, but if he is legitimately impeded from doing so, he, no doubt, as other plaintiffs, enjoys the right to make the petition orally in the presence of the judge and the notary.[83]

The *libellus* will contain all those six points which were enumerated in the previous article on the duty of the Promoter in the public accusatorial procedure. There is no necessity to repeat those points here, but there does remain the question as to the form of the *libellus* and its acceptance by the court.

As to form, the *libellus* must necessarily be presented in the form required by the law for contentious cases.[84] The Promoter should take care to observe all the requirements of the common law as to form under pain of the possible rejection of his *libellus* by the judge.

Upon reception of the *libellus* the *Officialis* will determine his own competence to act in the matter and if competent he will, as soon as

[79] Canon 1955; Wernz, *Jus Decretalium,* V, 136.

[80] Canon 1959; Wernz-Vidal, *Jus Canonicum,* VI, 687.

[81] Canon 1934.

[82] Canon 1955.

[83] Canon 1707.

[84] Canon 1955; *Cf.* Benedetti, *Ordo Judicialis,* p. 17 ff.

possible, admit or reject the *libellus*. Should he reject the *libellus*, the *Officialis* must give the reasons for his action to the Promoter.[85]

The *Officialis* need not accept the *libellus* of the Promoter as it stands. He can and should reject it as often as there are manifest defects in the bill.[86] He will demand that the Promoter amend or correct his bill by eliminating the defects which he has pointed out in the decree of rejection. Thus it may happen that the *libellus* of the Promoter contains the name of a witness who is incapable of testifying in ecclesiastical courts, or, one of the facts with which the defendant is charged has been stated in an obscure manner, or, again, the questions which have been submitted by the Promoter for the examination of the defendant may offend against the rules on questioning. When any one of these or similar defects are present in the bill, the Promoter should correct the bill and submit it again to the judge in its corrected form.[87]

While Canon 1955 orders the Promoter to submit the *libellus* of accusation to the *Officialis* according to the norms laid down in the first Section of the Fourth Book,[88] the right of the *Officialis* to reject the *libellus* is not the same as it is in contentious cases. Canon 1709, indeed, states that the *Officialis* may reject the *libellus* entirely as destitute of legal grounds for judicial contention; but the same conditions are not had in criminal causes as are had in contentious cases to which this canon apparently must be confined.

When the *libellus* is presented to the *Officialis* in contentious proceedings, the *libellus* itself is the sole source by which the court may learn the nature of the cause and the basis for its adjudication. Consequently, his examination of it will determine whether or not the case is to be admitted or rejected. On the contrary, when the Promoter of Justice presents his *libellus* of accusation, the substance of the accusation has already been carefully examined and weighed, for as was noted in the preceding articles, the Ordinary has already

[85] Canons 1609, 1611, 1709, §§ 1, 2.

[86] Noval, *De Processibus,* I, 546; Roberti, *De Processibus,* I, 430.

[87] Augustine, *A Commentary,* VII, 161.

[88] Canon 1955, " . . . conficere . . . libellum . . . secundum normas in Sectione Prima statutas."

examined the case thoroughly and has decreed that criminal proceedings are in order and are opportune. In both the mixed and the accusatorial procedure when the Promoter has presented his *libellus,* the Ordinary has already signified that all the means of avoiding a criminal prosecution have been exhausted and that the only avenue left for a reasonable defense of the public good is the present proceedings which he has authorized the Promoter to undertake in virtue of his office.

Now it is self-evident that the bishop and the *Officialis* constitute a single tribunal [89] and that the *Officialis* and the members of the tribunal have the right to examine the *libellus.*[90] Since the bishop has made a previous examination of the substance of the bill of accusation and has admitted the prosecution of the accusation to the diocesan courts, nothing remains for the *Officialis* except to admit the *libellus* and confine his examination to the form of the *libellus* which, if it is defective, he may reject and require the Promoter to submit it again in a corrected form.[91]

Hence the *Officialis* may not change or reject what the Ordinary has already admitted and accepted as the substance of the accusation. He can inquire and judge those things which the Ordinary has not yet considered, such as the form of the *libellus* and such cause for rejection as could arise only at the time of the presentation or after that moment, *e. g.*, absolute incompetence is discovered after the inception of the trial. Even in this latter case it would be more prudent and more in harmony with the proper administration of justice in a diocese for the *Officialis* to notify the Ordinary of his grounds for rejection before defining this of his own initiative. Such action will enable the Ordinary and the Promoter to rectify the defect and provide a new manner of dealing with the defendant who apparently has shown himself worthy only of the judicial application of penalties.[92]

[89] Canon 1573, § 2.

[90] Canon 1709, § 1.

[91] Roberti, "De reiectione libelli in processu criminali," *Consultationes J. C.*, I, 251.

[92] Roberti, *Consultationes J. C.*, I, 251.

B. *The Promoter of Justice and the Constitutio Rei and the Litis Contestatio*

Just as in the contentious case the citation of the defendant follows the acceptance of the *libellus* by the court,[93] the criminal trial also opens with the citation of the accused who is ordered to appear in court and to reply to the bill of accusation proposed by the Promoter of Justice.[94] It is the *libellus* of the Promoter and its acceptance by the court which prompts the court to cite the accused and to demand from him an answer to the interrogatories composed by the Promoter and presented at the time of the *libellus.*

In the event that the criminal trial also involves a suit for civil damages, inasmuch as the criminal proceedings have been occasioned by the warrant of a private person seeking damages growing out of the delict committed by the defendant, this party will also be cited and will be associated with the Promoter at this first hearing of the accused which is held in order to fix the limits of the *litis contestatio.* The party thus cited will look after and protect his own interests in the case. Should the party suffering the damages, however, be a moral person, the Ordinary may name the administrator or another procurator to represent the moral person, although he is perfectly free to entrust the claims of that person to the Promoter of Justice, who in that event will incorporate the civil claims in his *libellus* of accusation and will prosecute the two claims simultaneously. Hence his *libellus* will not only set forth the criminal charges, but it will also demand damages from the defendant and the Promoter will see to it that these claims for damages are incorporated into the formula of doubts regulating the trial.[95] Should this claim for damages arise after the trial has opened, the Promoter or the third party, as the case may be, will enter the incidental cause known as the *interventus tertii* and the declaration of damages will be discerned in the final sentence.[96]

This formal citation of the accused by the judge and his exami-

[93] Canon 1711.

[94] Wernz-Vidal, *Jus Canonicum,* VI, n. 733. 687.

[95] Wernz-Vidal, *Jus Canonicum,* VI, 688, n. 2.

[96] Canons 1852, 1853; A Coronata, *Institutiones J. C.,* III, 407.

nation according to the interrogatory prepared by the Promoter give rise to a step peculiar to the criminal trial and known to the authors as the *constitutio rei.* This procedural step derives its name from the customary words of the old law with which it was wont to open, *Constitutus N. personaliter coram Rvmo. N.*[97]

The defendant will appear or not appear in answer to the citation of the court and his appearance or non-appearance will govern the subsequent actions of the Promoter in the trial.

Should the defendant appear, he will be given a first hearing at which the judge will question him as to the general facts concerning himself, his office, place of residence, etc. This general preliminary questioning concluded, the judge will read to the accused the assertions of fact and the penalties demanded by the Promoter. He will then proceed to question the defendant on these facts according to the interrogatories prepared by the Promoter.[98]

The interrogatories to be prepared by the Promoter always present difficulties to the canonists. Ecclesiastical legislation always favors the defendant and makes him the privileged party in the formal criminal trial. The Promoter may not use any means, physical or moral, to procure the confession of the accused to any point in his indictment. Hence his interrogatories must be prepared with the greatest of care. The special questions must be relevant to the issue, yet no leading questions may be asked. Even when the questions relate to particular circumstances or details in the *libellus,* the questions must not be phrased in such a way that the accused is forced unavoidably to commit himself on the crime with which he is charged. The Promoter should carefully avoid passing quickly from one point to another, only to return to one of them unexpectedly; this manner of questioning is mere trickery and only a snare to the innocent and therefore unbefitting the ecclesiastical forum. In addition, his questions should be short and simple and no question include things that are to be asked separately. It is only logical to begin with the more general matter and gradually come to the more spe-

[97] Pellegrini, *Praxis Vicariorum,* Pars IV, sec. IX, n. 27.

[98] Wernz-Vidal, *Jus Canonicum,* VI, 688; Noval, *De Processibus,* I, 527, 535.

cial and more important points, which give serious indication of crime.[99]

Should the Promoter offend against any of the general rules laid down in Canons 1742-1746 and 1775, the presiding judge should return the *libellus* to him to be corrected before making it known to the defendant.[100]

The defendant is permitted in this first hearing to give his own version of the facts in the case and he must be heard relative to any exceptions he may wish to make. The Promoter will oppose these exceptions, whether dilatory or peremptory, as often as he feels they are unfounded and are proposed simply for the sake of obstructing justice.[101]

The *litis contestatio* will be formulated as a result of this questioning of the judge and the replies of the defendant. The issue in pleading (*litis contestatio*) is a determination of the object of the judicial controversy and of the proofs to be adduced in the course of the pleading. In contentious proceedings this assigning of the object for judicial controversy will result from the petition of the plaintiff and the denial or contradiction by the defendant of the plaintiff's demands, coupled with the manifestation of the intention of prosecuting the cause before the judge.[102] Wherefore, if the defendant confesses or denies but cedes his right to the plaintiff, no joinder of issue is had and the result is no trial.

This definition of the issue in pleading does not adequately cover the notion of the *litis contestatio* as it is had in criminal trials, for, although the defendant confesses, the trial itself may proceed, since the public good can demand that the truth relative to the commission of a delict and its responsible author be established judicially so that the defendant may be punished by judicial sentence.[103] The prevailing discipline speaks only of the suspension or deferring of criminal proceedings in the face of a judicial con-

[99] Canon 1775: This question will be treated more fully in connection with the examination of the parties and witnesses.

[100] Noval, *De Processibus,* I, 534.

[101] Vermeersch-Creusen, *Epitome,* III, 116; Noval, *De Processibus,* I, 502.

[102] Canon 1726; Augustine, *A Commentary,* VII, 174.

[103] Lea, *De Judiciis Eccl.,* IV, n. 198, 267.

fession in a case in which judicial correction may be employed.[104] This suspension is contingent upon the defendant's subsequent good behavior and should he lapse from his good conduct, the Promoter would not only be justified in renewing the criminal proceedings, but would have a duty to do so and this despite the fact that there had been a confession of crime.[105]

Hence, in criminal proceedings notwithstanding the confession of the delinquent which every criminal trial has for its objective, there may still be a necessity to fix the terms of the issue in the trial relative to the following points: (a) the delict committed; (b) the person of the defendant and the relative degree of imputability for the crime ascribed to him; (c) the penalties prescribed in the law for the criminal actions involved in the trial.[106]

The formula of doubts which will embody these three points and constitute the issue in pleading will also form the object of the probatory period of the trial. It will regulate and guide the entire subsequent proceedings. The formula is drawn up by agreement between the Promoter and the defendant or his legal representatives under the active direction of the judge, who, since criminal proceedings pertain by their very nature to the public good, will exercise a vigilant supervision over the outlining of the formula of doubts. In the event of disagreement between the Promoter and the defendant, the judge will formulate the doubts by judicial decree.[107]

It may be noted here that the Promoter can modify his charges or specifications after the preliminary hearing of the accused. The law permits him to alter them up until the *litis contestatio* [108] and he should change them, if he wishes to present the specifications in accordance with the additional knowledge gleaned at the first hearing. In this event, the changes made in the original *libellus* must be communicated to the defendant through the agency of the

[104] Canon 1950.

[105] Canons 1586, 1934.

[106] Noval, *De Processibus*, I, 536.

[107] Canon 1729, §§ 2, 3; Wernz-Vidal, *Jus Canonicum*, VI, 688; Augustine, *A Commentary*, VII, 176.

[108] Canon 1731, § 1.

court, so that the accused may make his categorical replies to the corrected specifications.

These counts or specifications should be submitted by the Promoter in writing. The judge has the right and duty to accept them or reject them according to the prescriptions of the law. Once they have been properly presented and accepted by the judge to be filed in the acts of the trial, they may not be changed by the Promoter without grave cause and a judicial order of the court.[109]

These *capituli* or counts must be drawn up properly by the Promoter. They must pertain to the crime charged or otherwise, the defendant need not answer them. They must be clear, not vague or obscure and if they are equivocal, the accused has the right to ask for an explanation before he gives his categorical reply. These specifications should contain only one item. They should state facts and should not propound questions of law. They should be made assertively and not interrogatively. Finally, they should not be captious, that is, framed in such a way that no matter how the defendant answers, he will ensnare or entrap himself into damaging admissions.[110]

Once the *litis contestatio* has been reached, the Promoter may not change his conclusions set forth in the *libellus* and the formula of doubts without a new decree of the judge who should also hear the defendant's reaction before granting the petition of the Promoter.[111] It is well to note that in this instance the Code uses the word "change." The term "correction" was used in reference to the emendation of the *libellus* upon the judge finding it unsatisfactory.[112] A change then means a substantial alteration of the charges made by the Promoter; but as the text notes, it is not to be considered a change if the Promoter limits or alters the mode of proof; or if less is asked either in the substantial demand or in the accessories; if certain facts alleged in the *libellus* are made clearer

[109] Canon 1729, §§ 2, 4.

[110] Reiffenstuel, lib. II, tit. 18, n. 206; Leurenius, *Forum Ecclesiasticum*, II, tit. 20, q. 644.

[111] Canon 1731, n. 1.

[112] Canon 1709, § 2.

or corrected provided that the point at issue remains the same; if instead of the restitution of a thing, the money is asked. These are all corrections and not changes and the Promoter may make them of his own initiative.[113]

He may not, however, make substantial changes as such action would be unfair to the defendant, since it would render a practical defense of his rights impossible or at least highly difficult, nor would there be any equality between the rights of the Promoter and the accused.[114] The only exception would be, were the Promoter in the course of the proceedings to discover reasons, heretofore unknown, which established the innocence of the defendant relative to some of the points in the accusation. He can and should withdraw those points against which the certain proof of innocence militates; for he appears in the trial in the interests of justice and must seek justice to the common good and, consequently, to the defendant. He appears as a prosecutor, not as a persecutor, and all suppression of evidence favorable to the defendant is unworthy of the office he holds.[115]

The new norms of the Rota published in 1934 give the Promoter wide discretionary powers in prosecuting criminal causes before that tribunal. The Rota empowers its Promoter to withdraw the charges entirely, if they appear groundless or insufficient to him.[116] The Code permits the diocesan Promoter no such liberty and freedom of action and rightly so. The Promoter in prosecuting a cause before the diocesan tribunals does so in virtue of a mandate from the Ordinary, who considered the present proceedings to be the only solution of the problem presented by the defendant and hence, should the Promoter feel that the charges brought by him are groundless or of insufficient importance in the face of the contradictory proof brought by the defendant, he must refer his opinion to the Ordinary and await the decision of the latter before

[113] Canon 1731, n. 1.

[114] S. C. EE. et RR., 30 Junii, 1826—Wernz-Vidal, *Jus Canonicum,* VI, 102, n. 80.

[115] Droste-Messmer, *Canonical Procedure in Disciplinary and Criminal Cases of Clerics,* p. 68; Wernz-Vidal, *Jus Canonicum,* VI, 102 and n. 80.

[116] *Normae S. R. R. Tribunalis,* art. 25, § 2—*A. A. S.,* XXVI (1934), 457.

abandoning the charges he has caused to be brought against the defendant.[117]

Should the Promoter, however, realize after the defense of the accused has begun that his case for the prosecution has not been adequately presented and has not been instructed in such a way as to be apt to move the convictions of the court and obtain the judicial verdict which he feels to be justice in the case, a new instruction of the case may not be undertaken by the Promoter without the decree of the judge. There is nothing to prevent the Promoter from seeking the decree of the judge, permitting him to supplement the petition and the presentation of his case. The weighty reasons required by the law will be easily founded in the public good because of which the case was first instituted.[118]

Another effect of the *litis contestatio* will be the determining by the judge of the terms for the presentation of proofs. Canon 1731, n. 2, imposes a precept upon the judge to determine these terms, because the parties have now acquired a right to establish their claims by proofs.[119] In contentious cases the term for the presentation of evidence and proof will be common to both parties; but in criminal proceedings, as both Bouix and Noval point out, the period for the presentation of proof is not common to both parties. This is evidenced by the practice and procedural regulations current in the ordinary ecclesiastical courts.[120] The first term is assigned to the Promoter to substantiate his assertions and accusations; the second to the defendant to disprove and contradict the charges and conclusions of the Promoter. The Promoter will observe the terms laid down by the judge or, if they prove unsatisfactory to him, he may ask that they be lengthened or shortened according to the exigencies present in the case. The judge will grant his petition or deny it after hearing the reasons for the request and the reactions of the defendant who is entitled to be

[117] C. Bernardini, *Apollinaris*, 7 (1934), 438.

[118] Wernz-Vidal, *Jus Canonicum*, VI, n. 116, 102.

[119] Noval, *De Processibus*, I, 296.

[120] Noval, *De Processibus*, I, 296; Bouix, *De Judiciis Eccl.*, II, cap. IV, par. IV, n. 2.

heard on his right for adequate time for his defense or for the speedy settlement of the case.[121]

A third element which may affect the presentation of the case by the Promoter is the fact that after the *litis contestatio* the good faith of the defendant in his possession of any object legally ceases. Prior to the joinder of issue the defendant, though guilty, may claim good faith; but after that moment he is not only bound to restitution of the article asked by the Promoter; but also a satisfaction for any losses or damage suffered by the thing or right in his possession after the *litis contestatio* may be demanded by the Promoter.[122]

C. Contumacy in Criminal Trials

Thus far the first meeting between the Promoter and the defendant has been considered in the light of the defendant's appearance in the court room. It may happen that the defendant who has been duly summoned will not appear in the court on the day and at the hour named in the citation for the first hearing in his cause. Should this be the case, the defendant may be declared in contempt of court and punished according to the provisions of the law.[123]

Before the defendant may be declared in contempt of court, the common law demands that two conditions be verified. It must be certified that the summons was lawfully issued[124] and that it reached the defendant or would have reached him had he not wilfully taken means to avoid the service of the summons by the court.[125] The report of the courier, who is frequently used in criminal cases, or the signed receipt which is returned to the sender of registered mail or the depositions of two witnesses that the summons was served or would have been served had not the defendant deliberately gone into hiding; or had he not refused to accept it; or had he not by his own activities and through the agency of his friends thwarted the efforts of the court to reach him by courier or

[121] Canon 1731, n. 2.
[122] Canon 1731, n. 3.
[123] Canons 1842-1851.
[124] Canons 1711 ff.
[125] Canon 1843, § 1, n. 1.

mail. Secondly, the defendant must have failed to excuse his absence or in the event that he attempted to excuse himself, the reasons alleged by him for his absence do not reasonably justify that absence.[126] Any just reason for non-appearance may be alleged by the defendant at any moment in the proceedings to purge himself from contumacy and receive full judicial attention to his defenses.[127] It must be evident to the judge, however, that the accused is prevented from appearing by the presence of a just cause such as infirmity, sickness, pressure of outside interests, death or sickness in his family, or public facts such as internal disorders in the community in which he resides.[128]

In any event, if the accused neither appears nor offers a reasonable excuse for his absence, the Promoter should demand that the judge declare the defendant to be in contempt of court and that the subsequent stages of the process are in order.[129] The public good demands that the trial be undertaken and the satisfaction of that public good demands that the trial already begun be carried through to its logical conclusion, the final sentence. The defendant by his willful absence is presumed to have renounced his rights of defense and to have thrown himself upon the justice and mercy of the court, abandoning the just settlement of his case to the tribunal.[130]

The judge in criminal proceedings not only can, but should threaten the defendant with ecclesiastical penalties in order to break his contumacy. While the plaintiff in the contentious proceedings may not demand the application of these penalties, the Promoter of Justice can in the interests of the public good demand that the judge exercise the power given to him in Canon 1845.[131] Should the judge use the power granted him in the law and issue a second summons threatening penalties and it can be proved that the defendant received this summons but maliciously ignored it, the

[126] Canon 1843, § 1, n. 2.

[127] Canon 1846.

[128] A Coronata, *Institutiones J. C.*, III, 280; Roberti, *De Processibus,* II, 131.

[129] Canon 1844, § 1.

[130] Canon 1844, § 1; Wernz-Vidal, *Jus Canonicum,* VI, 507.

[131] Canon 1934; Noval, *De Processibus,* I, 392.

Promoter may ask the application of these penalties over and above those already petitioned in his *libellus*. The proof is easily established by the testimony of a courier or the receipt slip of a registered letter.[132]

Upon the motion of the Promoter, the judge will declare the defendant to be in contempt of court whenever the two conditions laid down in Canon 1843 are verified. The process will continue to the final sentence and to the execution of that sentence, provided the judge observes all the rest of the rules prescribed for a judicial process.[133] This means that the proceedings are regular and are conducted along the lines of the general rules governing trial procedure with the sole omission of the parts which the defendant would exercise were he present. Therefore, the interrogatories for the examination of the defendant and his witnesses, the confrontation of proofs and the exchange of defenses are omitted.[134] This rule of Canon 1844 will mean that the defendant will have an advocate present at the proceedings [135] who will see to it that the Promoter substantiates his accusations with proof, but who will not present any set defenses since the defendant has forfeited his right to them by his obstinacy [136] and is deemed to have abandoned the adjudication of his cause to the justice of the court.

Contumacy, as has been said, may take place at this first summons, but it may also take place at any moment during the trial. In either case the willful disobedience of the defendant does not establish his guilt and the Promoter is not freed from the duty of proving that guilt. The Promoter must establish to the satisfaction of the court that a delict was committed, that the accused is morally responsible for the delict with which he is charged, and that the penalties requested in his *libellus* are those approved of in the law. The Promoter must establish these points with sufficient

[132] Augustine, *A Commentary*, VII, 291.

[133] Canon 1844: " . . . procedere servatis servandis . . . "

[134] *Regulae Servandae . . . S. R. R. Tribunal*, § 126, n. 6—*A. A. S.*, II (1910), 793; Augustine, *A Commentary*, VII, 290; Droste-Messmer, *Canonical Procedure in Disciplinary and Criminal Cases of Clerics*, p. 37.

[135] Canon 1655, § I; Noval, *De Processibus*, I, 391.

[136] A Coronata, *Institutiones J. C.*, III, n. 1475, 499.

force to produce moral certitude in the mind of the judge as to the guilt of the accused; otherwise, the judge must observe the axiom of law ***actore non probante, reus absolvitur,*** and insure that justice is done even to the absent defendant.[137]

If the defendant purges himself of contumacy to the satisfaction of the judge, he may appear in court and present his proofs and defenses. He must be heard and the Promoter must answer his counterclaims and defenses.[138]

If the defendant appears in court only after the final sentence has been pronounced, the only redress open to him is the ***restitutio in integrum*** and he must ask for that within three months from the date of the notification of the sentence of the court.[139] Under the present law a sentence which is not appealed within ten days useful (***utile***) time becomes a ***res judicata*** unless it is a question of the state of persons; criminal proceedings are not included in the latter class and hence should the defendant fail to appeal, the case becomes a ***res judicata.***[140] The public good demands that the sentence passed be presumed as just and that it be executed. Should the defendant receding from contumacy petition for a ***restitutio in integrum,*** it would be the duty of the Promoter of Justice as the defender of the public good to defend the sentence of the court against the petition for the extraordinary remedy made by the condemned party.[141]

The canons to be used in contempt procedures also speak of the contumacy of the actor in judicial proceedings; but since the Promoter, the actor in all criminal trials, is an official, he cannot be declared in contempt. The holder of the office, however, may be punished and forced to act if he is negligent in the exercise of his duties.[142]

[137] Canon 1869; Roberti, *De Processibus,* II, 132.

[138] Canon 1846; Wernz-Vidal, *Jus Canonicum,* VI, 506, 507.

[139] Canon 1847; A Coronata, *Institutiones J. C.,* III, 283, 284.

[140] Canon 1902; Noval, *De Processibus,* I, 444.

[141] Roberti, *De Processibus,* I, 197.

[142] Canon 1625, §§ 1, 3; Roberti, *De Processibus,* I, 195; Chelodi, *Jus Poenale,* p. 155, n. 4.

D. *The Promoter and the Provisional Remedies of Canons 1956 and 1957*

Canons 1956 and 1957 provide for special remedies which may be adopted to protect the dignity of the priesthood and to insure a fair procedure. Canon 1956 provides that if a crime is of a more serious nature and the Ordinary is of the opinion that the faithful would be scandalized, were the accused cleric to exercise his sacred ministry or perform the spiritual functions which may be attached to any office he holds, he may after having heard the advice of the Promoter forbid the accused to exercise his sacred ministry or spiritual offices and even the public reception of Holy Communion. This prohibition is not of a penal character; it is rather an administrative privation provided by the law as often as the scandal warrants its application.[143]

The canon clearly states that it is the Ordinary and not the judge who has the right to inflict this prohibition, for it is an administrative remedy and it is to the Ordinary and not to the judge that the care of souls for which this remedy was provided is committed.[144] As often, therefore, as the summons has been duly served (it makes no difference whether the defendant has appeared or is in contempt of court), the Promoter of his own initiative shall suggest the application of the remedy either directly to the Ordinary or indirectly to him through the agency of the judge as often as the conditions laid down in the canon are verified in the case.[145]

It should be noted that the use of this remedy is confined to the more serious crimes and that there must be scandal or a well-founded fear of it. Certainly listed among such crimes would be those which do not admit the use of judicial correction.[146] It should also be remarked that the prohibition affects only the spiritual functions and the public administration or reception of the sacraments, indicating that neither the administration of the temporalities nor

[143] Canons 1956, 2222, § 2.

[144] Vermeersch-Creusen, *Epitome,* III, 122.

[145] Muniz, *Procedimientos Eccl.,* III, 521; A Coronata, *Institutiones J. C.,* III, 407.

[146] Canons 1848, 1849; Noval, *De Processibus,* I, 537.

the private reception are forbidden.[147] A pious office, referred to in the canon, in the mind of the Code seems to include any office in pious associations of laymen canonically erected or formed into sodalities.[148]

The authors demand that the Ordinary consult both the defendant and the Promoter of Justice before inflicting the penalty as there is always a danger of harming the rights of the defendant.[149] The Promoter, it would seem from the wording of the canon, should be consulted by the Ordinary if the prohibition is to be valid. Vermeersch-Creusen deny this necessity of consultation,[150] but they give no reasons for their view, contenting themselves with a mere assertion of the opinion. In giving this opinion, they are only being consistent with their commentary on Canon 105 where they argue chiefly from the consequences of the opposite opinion that as often as the Code demands that the Ordinary seek the advice of some one or other, the Ordinary acts illicitly without it and not invalidly.[151] Their argumentation does seem to enjoy a strong canonical basis. They argue chiefly from the consequences which might follow from adopting the opposite opinion. Such argument is valid for the enactment of legislation but not for the interpretation of already existing legislation. The common opinion in explaining Canon 105 maintains that the word *audito* of the canon has the same force as that part of the canon which speaks of the necessity of consent for valid action on the part of the Ordinary, as often as the law commands that he obtain consent for some action or other. The authors who maintain this view declare that as often as the Code demands that advice be sought by using the ablative absolute *audito Promotore, parocho,* etc., that advice must be sought if the subsequent action of the Ordinary is to be valid.[152] The present

[147] Canon 1957; Augustine, *A Commentary,* VII, 384.

[148] A Coronata, *Institutiones J. C.,* III, 407; Noval, *De Processibus,* I, 537.

[149] Noval, *De Processibus,* I, 537.

[150] Vermeersch-Creusen, *Epitome,* III, 122.

[151] Vermeersch-Creusen, *Epitome,* I, 151, 152.

[152] Leitner, *Handbuch des kath. Kirchenrechts,* I, §§ 12, 77; Maroto, *Inst. Juris Canonici,* I, n. 471, 555; Ferreres, *Institutiones,* I, n. 229; Ojetti, *Jus Pontificium,* 7 (1927), 13 ff., and *Commentarium,* II, 186 ff; Chelodi, *Jus De Personis,* 180, et alii.

canon simply states that the Ordinary may inflict the penalty *audito Promotore* and if this phrase is to be understood in the light of Canons 105, n. 1, and 1587, it would seem that the seeking of the advice of the Promoter is an essential condition for the validity of the prohibition.[153]

Canon 1957, on the other hand, places an effective weapon in the hands of the tribunal itself in order to insure a just trial. Justice and the public order require that the witnesses should not be intimidated or bribed. Hence if a judge fears that this might be done, he should consult the Promoter and issue a decree ordering the defendant to leave his town or parish for the time being and reside in a place assigned to him by the tribunal, remaining there under vigilance. It need hardly be remarked that the Promoter of Justice should invoke the application of this provisional remedy to the accused as often as there is a probability of the use of these unfair and unjust practices by the defendant in the trial.[154]

The Promoter, however, may not invoke the use of these remedies unless the defendant has been duly summoned and has appeared at the first hearing of the trial or has been declared in contempt by the judge because of his failure to heed the summons of the court. Needless to say, the Promoter may invoke the application of these remedies at any stage of the trial whenever the conditions laid down in the two canons are verified by the defendant's conduct.[155]

The reason why the remedies may not be applied before the citation of the defendant is because these remedies are restrictions on his rights which prejudice his defense and he should be heard in his own defense against their infliction.[156] Moreover, the provisions of Canon 1958 protect the reputation of the accused so that the judge may not act against him from any preconceived notions of guilt. The Promoter and the judge should always guard against unnecessarily harming the reputation of the accused and should not apply the remedies without having a definite basis for such action.

[153] A Coronata, *Institutiones J. C.*, III, 408.

[154] Muniz, *Procedimientos Eccl.*, III, 522.

[155] Canon 1958.

[156] Noval, *De Processibus,* I, 537.

As above, the valid application of this remedy by the judge would seem to require the intervention of the Promoter. The canon uses the same ablative absolute, *audito Promotore,* and hence for the valid imposition of the remedies the tribunal would be required to consult the Promoter or at least to cite him for consultation.[157] The citation of the Promoter to appear satisfies the requirement of the law and, should he not appear, the judge may proceed of his own initiative to apply the sanctions of the law.[158] In a collegiate tribunal majority vote of the tribunal over and above the citation to the Promoter would be required for the validity of the decree imposing the remedies of the law.[159]

E. *The Period of the Trial for the Presentation of Proof*

As was previously remarked, the judge upon accepting the *litis contestatio* and the formula of doubts, which it crystalizes, will assign by a judicial decree a term of time for the presentation of the proof by the prosecution and the defense.[160] It must be borne in mind that the probatory period is not common to both parties as it is in the contentious proceedings. In criminal cases two distinct periods are assigned, the first to the Promoter, to establish his accusations, the second to the defendant to present his defenses.[161]

The Promoter having accepted the terms laid down in the judicial decree will proceed to instruct his case by proof. The procedure to be followed by the Promoter in this point will differ slightly according as the trial thus far has proceeded according to the purely accusatorial or along the lines of the mixed procedure.

If the process is purely accusatorial, the proofs to be presented will not have been formally collected by anyone prior to the present

[157] Canon 1957.

[158] Canons 105, 1587; A Coronata, *Institutiones J. C.*, III, 409.

[159] Canon 1577, § 1.

[160] Canon 1731, n. 2.

[161] This rule of procedure is not derived from the positive common law but from the practice of criminal tribunals and is based upon the nature of a criminal trial. Noval, *De Processibus,* I, 296; Muniz, *Procedimientos Eccl.,* III, 526; Bouix, *De Judiciis Eccl.,* II, cap. IV, par. IV, n. 2; Pellegrini, *Praxis Vicariorum,* Pars 2, sec. 2, subs. 3, n. 1.

proceedings; but since the crime charged to the accused is presupposed to be notorious and certain, the Promoter of Justice will have collected in the course of his extrajudicial investigation of the crime a definite amount of proof to substantiate his accusation and will have already presented it to the Ordinary in a summary fashion in his material *libellus* and to the *Officialis* in his formal *libellus*. Once the *litis contestatio* has been settled the Promoter will formally draw up and perfect these proofs, setting them forth in approved legal fashion. He will (1) with the permission of the judge obtain all the documents related to the case and deposit them in the chancery; (2) he will prepare, elaborate upon and present to the court the arguments he has adduced from the documents in his possession; (3) he will present to the judge well prepared interrogatories along the lines of which he wishes the judge to examine the witnesses whom he will present in the course of the trial; (4) he will petition the judge to cite the witnesses and to interrogate them according to the interrogatories admitted into the trial; (5) he will be present at the examination of the witnesses for the prosecution and for the defense and will suggest any new questions which their testimony may occasion.[162]

If the trial thus far has proceeded along the lines of a mixed procedure, the greater part of the proofs will have been already assembled in the previous inquisition and will have been delivered to the Promoter of Justice in virtue of the Ordinary's decree.[163] These proofs consisting mainly of the testimony of witnesses and the replies of the defendant on the occasion of judicial correction and taken, as they were, before the formal accusation by the Promoter are not valid proofs in the criminal proceedings until they are legitimated by the defendant, at least in the sense that he is given ample opportunity to either acknowledge their probatory value or to impugn their value as valid evidence.[164] Hence, after the *litis contestatio* the Promoter of Justice will communicate to the

[162] Noval, *De Processibus,* I, 539.

[163] Canon 1954.

[164] Wernz-Vidal, *Jus Canonicum,* VI, 688; A Coronata, *Institutiones J. C.,* III, 410; Muniz, *Procedimientos Eccl.,* III, 527, 528.

defendant or his advocate by means of the court an account of all the minutes of the inquisitorial process. He will render the defendant an account (1) of all the arguments based on documents and copies of the entire documents unless there exists a just reason for the suppression of some points contained in them; [165] (2) a literal transcript of all the testimony taken in the inquisition; (3) the names of the witnesses who testified in the inquisition. It is within the discretionary powers of the judge upon motion of the Promoter to withhold these names until the final publication of the cause; but these names should not be kept from the defendant without grave necessity, nor should this be easily imagined.[166]

Hence if the Promoter desires to submit the minutes and acts of the inquisition as proof, they must be made known to the accused who must be given a fair opportunity to legalize the proofs; otherwise, the proofs gathered in the inquisition are not valid proofs in the trial. This legalization of proof is expressly demanded by Canon 1861, § 2, under pain of nullity to the process.[167]

This legalizing of proof by the defendant offers no great difficulty, since for the most part it is concerned with the testimony of witnesses and experts.[168] This legalizing of proof may be accomplished in a twofold manner.

The first method is by the declaration of the defendant. After the evidence collected in the inquisition has been communicated in any way by the Promoter to the defendant, the latter is asked whether he is satisfied with the witnesses, their method of examination, their testimony in the previous inquisition. If he states that he has no objection to the introduction of these proofs into the trial and is willing to permit the evidence collected in the inquisition to be used in the present proceedings, the testimony becomes

[165] Canon 1823.

[166] Wernz-Vidal, *Jus Canonicum*, VI, 690 and n. 6; S. B. Smith, *New Procedure in Criminal and Disciplinary Causes of Ecclesiastics*, 145, 146.

[167] Muniz, *Procedimientos Eccl.*, III, 528; Noval, *De Processibus*, I, 539; A Coronata, *Institutiones J. C.*, III, 410; Wernz-Vidal, *Jus Canonicum*, VI, 690.

[168] Muniz, *Procedimientos Eccl.*, III, n. 617, 521, notes that the prevailing law is silent upon the notion of legalizing and legitimatizing proofs.

legalized by this declaration of the defendant, that is, by a legal fiction the evidence is regarded as having been taken after the *litis contestatio* and therefore *jam constituto et citato reo* and consequently, as having the same legal value as proof of guilt as though the witnesses had been examined after the *litis contestatio.* In other words, the above declaration of the accused gives the evidence the force of legal proof and exempts the Promoter from the obligation of introducing it and establishing it again. Relative to this legitimation of proof by the accused it must be always borne in mind that even where the defendant has made this waiver, he, nevertheless, retains the full right to object both against the persons and the testimony of the witnesses as well as the authenticity of the documents used in the inquisition. By his declaration the defendant simply declares that though the witnesses were examined prior to his own citation, he is willing to look upon them as though they had been examined after the *litis contestatio* and not that he considers their person or testimony unobjectionable and without reproach. On the contrary, he retains the right to attack the testimony indirectly by attacking the manner in which it was taken or by producing his own witnesses who will establish a contradictory fact or he may attack the evidence directly by showing that it is obscure, contradictory, inconsistent, malicious, etc.[169] This method of legalizing proof is more in harmony with the general tenor of the laws governing judicial procedure, as evidenced in Canon 1786.

The second method of legalizing the proofs of the inquisition is self-evident. It is done through the repetition of all the evidence taken in the inquisition. The defendant can demand that the witnesses be cited by the judge and be re-examined according to the interrogatories of the Promoter of Justice and to the question lists prepared by himself. This repetition of testimony must take place as often as the defendant refuses to legalize the proofs of the inquest by a waiver. The reason is always the same, namely, that

[169] Wernz-Vidal, *Jus Canonicum,* VI, 690; Muniz, *Procedimientos Eccl.,* III, n. 617, 528; A Coronata, *Institutiones J. C.,* III, 410; Bouix, *De Judiciis Eccl.,* II, 218.

otherwise the evidence has no legal value as proof of the guilt of the accused. No evidence has legal value unless it is produced in court after the citation of the accused. Now all the witnesses who were examined in the inquisition were produced and examined before the citation of the accused. Consequently these witnesses, no matter how many, prove nothing against the accused unless they are examined over again or the accused waives his right to have them repeat their testimony.[170]

This communication of proofs to the defendant coupled with his right to attack their probatory value by the presentation of new or contradictory proof might be called the *legitimatio processus inquisitivi,* and is considered to have taken place at that moment, when the defendant waives his right to demand the re-examination of the witnesses or demands their re-examination according to the interrogatories prepared by the Promoter of Justice and to those presented by himself.[171]

The criminal trial from this point on follows the lines of contentious trials and the rules for both are almost identical. They both employ the same manner of introducing and judging proofs and they both enjoy the same methods of redress against the sentence passed. Hence, there is no necessity of discussing separately the duties of the Promoter in the remaining stages of the criminal trial. These duties will be discussed in a later article in which any slight peculiarities pertaining to the criminal procedure will be noted.

[170] Canon 1730; Instr. S. C. EE. et RR., 11 junii, 1880, art. XIX—*A. S. S.*, XIII (1880), 329; Muniz, *Procedimientos Eccl.*, III, 529; A Coronata, *Institutiones J. C.*, III, 410; *cf.* Canon 1730 for exceptional cases in which the witnesses may be heard with permission of the court before the citation of the accused.

[171] Noval, *De Processibus,* I, 539.

CHAPTER VI

THE PROMOTER OF JUSTICE AND MATRIMONIAL PROCEEDINGS

ARTICLE I. THE PROMOTER OF JUSTICE AND HIS RIGHT TO ACCUSE INVALID MARRIAGES

Canon 1971

1. Habiles ad accusandum sunt:
n. 1. Conjuges in omnibus casibus separationis et nullitatis, nisi ipsi fuerint impedimenti causa.
n. 2. Promotori Justitiae in impedimentis natura sua publicis.

2. Reliqui omnes etsi consanguinei non habent jus matrimonia accusandi, sed tantummodo nullitatem matrimonii Ordinario vel promotori justitiae denuntiandi.

Canon 1970 clearly states that a collegiate tribunal, otherwise competent, may examine and define matrimonial causes involving the question of the validity of the marriage bond only upon one condition, namely, that a regular accusation or a legitimately made petition precede the action of the tribunal. This action must be made by a person physically distinct from the judges comprising the tribunal; otherwise the said tribunal may not even consider the question. This prior accusation or petition is absolutely essential to the tribunal's exercise of its right and duty to examine the marital status of the parties involved in the cause before it.[1]

The accusation of marriage is the proposal of a legal action before a competent court in order to prevent the contracting of a marriage or to declare a marriage already contracted null and void or to obtain a separation *a mensa et a toro*.[2] It presupposes in the

[1] Canon 1970; Noval, *De Processibus*, I, 568.

[2] Cappello, *De Sacramentis*, III, n. 878, 994; A Coronata, *Institutiones J. C.*, III, 422.

accuser a legitimate right to appear in court and to prosecute the cause, since the one who proposes an action becomes the actor in the process and assumes all the obligations which pertain to the plaintiff in a trial. From this it is evident that accusation is a strictly judicial act.[3]

It can readily be seen that this accusation differs radically from the denunciation of an invalid union. The latter is only a manifestation made to legitimate authority concerning any fact pertaining to the public good and which in the interests of the public welfare should be made known to the proper authorities. The one making the denunciation does not introduce the process nor take part in it, although indirectly he may be the occasion of it. Denunciation indeed prepares the way for judicial action and opens the way for inquiry, but is itself an extrajudicial act. Relative to the present subject the denunciation is nothing more than a report made to the Ordinary or the Promoter of Justice, disclosing the grounds upon which the validity of the marriage might be impugned and attacked. Denunciation does not propose legal action, but only furnishes the Promoter and the Ordinary with a knowledge of the legal grounds upon which the former might act if a process is deemed opportune.[4] This denunciation merely serves to promote an extrajudicial investigation into the probable grounds of invalidity of the marriage denounced, an investigation the Promoter is always bound to make before he undertakes the official accusation of any marriage.[5]

This accusation also differs from the petition which is made according to the prescriptions of the law, asking that in view of the presence of certain conditions a valid union be dissolved, *e. g.*, petition *super matrimonio rato et non consummato*. The petition gives rise to a procedural action, but the action is not the vindication of one's rights; it is rather the request of a dispensation to be granted on the basis of conditions and causes verified in the process.

[3] Roberti, "De jure accusandi matrimonium," *Apollinaris*, III (1930), 249.

[4] Cappello, *De Sacramentis*, III, 994; A Coronata, *Institutiones J. C.*, III, 422.

[5] Cappello, *De Sacramentis*, III, 994; A Coronata, *Institutiones J. C.*, III, 422; Pasquale Vito, *Palestro del Clero*, IX (1930), 385.

Since the parties alone have the right to seek such dispensations, these actions are removed entirely from the ambit of the rights and duites of the Promoter of Justice.[6]

Canon 1970 introduces a change in the law relative to the accusation of marriages. Before the Code in virtue of an instruction of the Holy Office the tribunal could proceed of its own initiative to an investigation into a rumor which questioned the validity of a marriage. In the event that the rumor proved to be well founded, the court, again, of its own initiative could proceed to an examination of the validity of the marriage and should the proofs of invalidity warrant it declare the marriage invalid without the intervention of any accuser:

> . . . ex officio etiam inquisitio fieri potest et quandoque debet, quando praesertim contra alicujus matrimonii validitatem simplex denuntiatio facta fuerint, aut fama, fundamentum veritatis prae se ferens, de alicujus impedimenti existentia divulgata sit.[7]

This inquisitorial procedure of the old law has been abrogated just as it has been in criminal procedure. This is confirmed by Canon 1971 which states specifically those persons who are at liberty to lodge a legal accusation against a marriage before the ecclesiastical tribunals. The canon makes no mention whatsoever of the inquisitorial procedure of the old law and at the same time reserves all official accusation of marriage to the Promoter of Justice exclusively.[8] Hence, in virtue of Canon 6, n. 6, the matrimonial procedure *ex mero officio,* as outlined in the Instruction of the Holy Office of June 20, 1883, has been abrogated since the aforementioned instruction in no way limited the right of official accusation to the Promoter of Justice.[9]

Another radical curtailment of the right of accusation of marriages was introduced by the present legislation. The law before

[6] Canon 1973; S. C. de Sacr., 7 maii, 1923, *Regulae Servandae . . . Super Matrimonio Rato et non Consummato,* cap. II, n. 5—*A. A. S.,* XV (1923), 389.

[7] Instr. ad Ep. Rituum Orient., 20 junii, 1883, n. 3—*Fontes,* n. 1076.

[8] Canon 1971, § 1, n. 2.

[9] Noval, *De Processibus,* I, 568.

the Code permitted any Catholic to accuse a marriage invalid by reason of an impediment of a public nature. Popular action was permitted in matrimonial cases as long as the impediment invalidating the marriage was one of public law as distinct from those of private law.[10] The right of Catholics other than the parties is now restricted to the extrajudicial denunciation of the invalid union to the Ordinary or the Promoter.[11] As a consequence, the distinction of the old law between impediments of public law and private law no longer holds at least in the sense in which it was then admitted; but it is retained in the sense that any Catholic even under the present law may denounce a marriage null because of the existence of a public impediment and thus afford the Promoter of Justice an opportunity to accuse the marriage.[12]

Canon 1971 supplements and completes these rules on the accusation and its necessity by accurately defining and determining those who enjoy the right to accuse marriages under the present law. The canon is at pains to enumerate precisely and exactly the persons who can attack the marital status. It allows of accusation against the marriage solely by the following: (a) The married parties themselves can accuse the marriage in all cases of separation and nullity unless they themselves are the cause of the impediment;[13] (b) The Promoter of Justice may attack the marriage whenever the contract is rendered invalid by impediments which are *of their nature public;*[14] (c) all other persons have no right to appear in the matrimonial courts of the diocese as plaintiffs or petitioners but enjoy only the right to denounce the invalid marriage to legitimate authority, *i. e.,* the Promoter of Justice, who will investigate the probability of the invalidity and, if justice demands it, will as plaintiff or petitioner bring it before the matrimonial court.[15]

[10] C. 6, X, *qui matrimonium accus. potest.* IV, 18; C. 7, X, *de cognatione spirituali,* IV, 11; Instr. S. Officii, 20 junii, 1883, Pars I, tit. 1, n. 3—*Fontes,* n. 1076; S. R. Rota, Decision, June 27, 1916—*A. A. S.,* IX (1917), 242.

[11] Canon 1971, § 2; Cappello, *De Sacramentis,* III, 995.

[12] Gasparri, *De Matrimonio* (1932), II, 292; G. Oesterle, *Jus Pontificium,* 12 (1932), 142.

[13] Canon 1971, § 1, n. 1.

[14] Canon 1971, § 1, n. 2.

[15] Canon 1971, § 2.

This canon is of the utmost importance, since it is the opening portal to the examination and definition of all formal matrimonial causes and, as such, is the cornerstone upon which the whole validity of a matrimonial process rests. If the plaintiff before the court does not enjoy the legal right of standing in court, the process and the sentence which is based upon it may be rendered invalid and if neither party enjoyed this right, the sentence of the court is irrevocably invalid and must be so declared.[16] The importance of the canon is readily attested to by the number of responses edited by the Pontifical Commission in reference to its interpretation. A study of these official responses is absolutely indispensable in order to appreciate and establish the rights and duties of the Promoter of Justice relative to the accusation of invalid marriages before his own diocesan tribunal.

The married parties, of course, are always free to accuse a marriage which has been rendered null by the presence of an impediment, whether that impediment be public of its nature or only *de facto* public, *i. e.,* whenever the marriage has been rendered invalid by an impediment which can be proved in court; provided always that they themselves are not the cause of the impediment and the invalidity of the marriage. This statement of the law seems clear enough, but it has been in the past the source of widespread difference of opinion on the part of authors and the tribunals.

Before the Code the term "impediment" was commonly understood to mean any circumstance which would render a marriage invalid whether it was in relation to the person, the consent or the form. Therefore the authors of the old law speak indiscriminately of the impediments of consanguinity, of fear, of clandestinity, etc.[17]

The Code, however, uses the term "impediment" in a strict sense to designate only personal circumstances which invalidate and prohibit marriage (1067-1080) and not those which proceed from a vitiated consent (1081-1093) or from the lack of proper form (1094-1103).

[16] Canons 1892, n. 2; 1971, § 1, n. 1.

[17] Roberti, "Animadversiones," *Apollinaris,* III (1930), 55; Cappello, "De jure accusandi matrimonium," *Periodica,* 16 (1927), 228 ff.

The authentic interpretation of the canon, given by the Pontifical Commission on March 12, 1929,[18] extends the interpretation of the term "impediment" to include also impediments, improperly so called and enumerated in Canons 1081-1103. In virtue of this decision the term "impediment" of Canon 1971 embraces besides the impediments properly so called (1067-1080) the lack of consent, error, conditional consent, ignorance, fear, the lack of canonical form of marriage, etc. Concerning the last mentioned there is no special difficulty as to procedure, for if the Catholic was married without the presence of an authorized priest and later a declaration of nullity of such a marriage is sought, no canonical trial is required but merely an investigation of the facts and the decision of the Ordinary that the proper form had not been observed and that there was no necessity for its omission.[19]

The authentic interpretation of March 12, 1929 on Canon 1971 was far reaching in its effects upon the practice of tribunals. It places the official seal of approval upon the teaching of those canonists who maintained that the term "impediment" was to be understood in the wide sense as including the impediments improperly so called and that the present legislation had retained the meaning given to the term in the old law.[20] Were the term "impediment" to be understood in the strict sense, it would militate against the very principles of morality and justice so clearly taught down through the centuries by the practice of the Church.

As a consequence of this interpretation, under the prevailing discipline, not only parties who were the culpable cause of an impediment understood in the strict sense, but also all those parties who are the culpable cause of the impediments considered in the wide sense by which the consent or form are substantially vitiated or lacking are interdicted from accusing those marriages before the matrimonial tribunals of the Church. Therefore, if only one party is the responsible cause of the impediment, the innocent party

[18] Ad V—*A. A. S.*, XXI (1929), 171.

[19] Pont. Comm. for Interpret., October 16, 1919—*A. A. S.*, XI (1919), 479.

[20] Cappello, *De Sacramentis*, III, 995; Noval, *De Processibus*, I, 569; Vermeersch-Creusen, *Epitome*, III, 129.

retains his or her right to accuse the marriage and always retains that right no matter how long after the invalid contraction of marriage he or she may care to exercise it. If both parties are the guilty cause of the impediment, neither may exercise the right to act as plaintiff or petitioner before the diocesan courts.[21]

It seems also of service to consider the meaning of the clause, contained in the canon and referred to in the response of the Pontifical Committee, "unless they are the cause of the impediment," which carries with it the disqualification and disability to act as plaintiff or petitioner, for if the parties themselves are capable of petitioning for the declaration of invalidity, there will be frequently no necessity of intervention upon the part of the Promoter of Justice in the matrimonial trial.

Is this disqualification contained in the clause, "unless they themselves were the cause of the impediment," a sanction of the law to protect the public good or does it partake of the nature of a strict penalty? If it were a penalty, ignorance and all the other excusing causes which diminish or remove the imputability would excuse entirely from the disqualification of Canon 1971, § 1, n. 1. If it were not a penalty, such would not be the case since ignorance does not excuse from laws which carry with them disabilities.[22]

Roberti [23] and Creusen maintained that the privation was not a strict penalty, whereas Noval and Gasparri held that it has the nature of a penalty and therefore is subject to all the excusing causes of penalties.[24] The Pontifical Committee in a recent reply to a query on this point seems to place the seal of official approval upon this opinion of Gasparri and Noval. The Committee was asked:

[21] Canon 1971, § 1, n. 1; Pont. Comm. for Interpret., 12 martii, 1929, ad V—*A. A. S.*, XXI (1929), 171; A Coronata, *Institutiones J. C.*, III, 423; "De matrimonii accusatione," *Jus Pontificium*, XIII (1933), 187.

[22] Canon 16, § 1.

[23] Roberti, "Animadversiones," *Apollinaris*, III (1930), 57 and "De jure accusandi matri.," *Apollinaris*, VI (1933), pp. 441 ff.; Creusen, "Jus matrimonium accusandi," *Nouvelle Revue Theologique*, 60 (1933), 733.

[24] Noval, *De Processibus*, I, 569; Gasparri, *De Matrimonio* (1932), II, 292.

I. An ad normam canonis 1971, § 1, n. 1 habilis sit ad accusandum matrimonium conjux qui metum et coactionem passus sit?

II. An ad normam ejusdem canonis 1971, § 1, n. 1 habilis sit ad accusandum matrimonium etiam conjux qui fuerit causa culpabilis sive impedimenti sive nullitatis matrimonii?

III. An causa impedimenti honesta et licita a conjuge apposita abstet quominus conjux habilis sit ad accusandum matrimonium vi norma 1971, § 1, n. 1.

Resp. ad I, Affirmative, ad II, Negative, ad III, Negative.[25]

The answer to the first query makes clear what is meant by the culpable cause of nullity. The second and third replies introduce a new and important distinction in regard to matrimonial causes. They ask in effect whether the disqualification applies only to the culpable cause or also to the inculpable cause (*causa honesta et licita*). The response clearly indicates that the privation of the right of pleading is a strict penalty and therefore should not be inflicted except on the strictly guilty parties.

But does the phrase "the culpable cause of the impediment" extend this far? Does it mean that the parties who were to blame for the invalidity of the marriage, for example, by knowing that they had an impediment and nevertheless attempted to contract the marriage, or does it refer solely to impediments like crime, force and fear, conditions against the essence of matrimony, abduction, etc. If the clause of Canon 1971 includes all who knowingly contracted marriage with a diriment impediment, the rule would be easy to understand, but not all commentators agree on this interpretation of the canon. It seems reasonable to say that the Church does not permit the party who knowingly concealed a diriment impediment and yet attempted to contract a marriage to attack that marriage in her matrimonial courts.[26] Cardinal Gasparri, on the other

[25] *A. A. S.*, XXV (1933), 345.

[26] A. Toso, "De jure accusandi matrimonium," *Jus Pontificium*, XIII (1933), 188; Creusen, "Jus accusandi matrimonium," *Nouvelle Revue Theologique*, 60 (1933), 733; Schaaf, *The American Ecclesiastical Review*, XCI (1934), 78.

hand, insists that even though Catholics attempt to contract and yet knowingly fail to obtain a dispensation from a diriment impediment, they are not to be deprived of the right of accusing the marriage. He denies the analogy to the preceding cases of crime, force and fear, etc., since in the case contemplated by him the parties are not themselves the cause of the impediment.[27] Certainly parties seem to be the culpable causes of the invalidity of the marriage, as often as they contracted, concealing a diriment impediment.[28] However, in practice it will be for the tribunal to decide whether the parties in such cases are to be permitted to attack the marriage or whether the accusation will be entrusted to the Promoter of Justice in virtue of the disability contained in Canon 1971, § 1, n. 1.

Hence, it may be concluded that Catholics whenever their marriages are invalid because of the presence of an impediment, understood either in the strict sense of the term or in the wide sense, may attack the marriage, as often as this invalidity is demonstrable in the court and they themselves have not been the active culpable causes of the invalidating impediments.

Although the Catholic party who is the culpable cause of the impediment should be repelled *ex officio* from attacking the marriage he has invalidly contracted, the invalid marriage still remains. But if it is invalid in virtue of an impediment either of divine or ecclesiastical law, it ought either to be convalidated, if that is possible, or to be declared null. The salvation of souls, which is the supreme law of the Church, and the public good will demand that such procedure be followed, for as soon as the party who knowingly contracted the invalid marriage realizes it is null, he has no right to exercise his marital rights and he cannot celebrate a new marriage. The parties can, it is true, the obstacle being removed, renew their marital consent but, as it often happens, they now entertain anything but marital affection for one another. More-

[27] Gasparri, *De Matrimonio* (1932), II, 292.

[28] Schulte, *Eheprozesz,* 82; Creusen, *Nouvelle Revue Theologique,* 60 (1933), 733 and Graziani, *Il Diritto Ecclesiastico,* XLVI (1933), 114-126 oppose this opinion of Gasparri.

over, while these impediments are often occult by their nature, they may and frequently do become factually public with consequent scandal to the faithful. The public good demands that this scandal be removed whenever possible by a declaration of nullity, as often as all hope of reconciliation and convalidation is absent.[29]

What remedies are still open to the parties who have forfeited their rights of accusation by their detestable and sinful action of placing an impediment to the validity of their marriage or in which the innocent party refuses to relieve the intolerable situation by exercising his or her right recognized by the law? There are only two remedies recognized under the prevailing jurisprudence to which the parties can have recourse.

The first is self-evident. A dispensation from the prohibitive law may be sought from the Holy See or a rescript of favor may be sought from the same source, petitioning the restoration of the right to act as plaintiff in judicial proceedings.[30] An analogous case is had when the petitioner for the dispensation *super matrimonio rato et non consummato* has avoided the consummation through the practice of onanism and is now sincerely contrite about it.[31] The Ordinary may follow the same procedure for the preceding case in order to obtain from the Holy See the restoration of the right to plead, but it will be entirely unnecessary in view of the prevailing jurisprudence.

The second remedy is to be found in Canon 1971, § 1, n. 2, which permits the Promoter of Justice to attack the marriage which has been rendered invalid by the presence of *an impediment by nature public*. As often as the marriage is rendered invalid by *an impediment of its nature public* the Promoter of Justice has the

[29] Blat, *Commentarium,* IV, 503; Noval, *De Processibus,* I, 569; "De jure accusandi matri.," *Jus Pontificium,* XIII (1933), 188; Creusen, "De jure denuntiandi nullitatem matrimonii," *Revue Nouvelle Theologique,* 57 (1930), 521.

[30] A Coronata, *Institutiones J. C.,* III, 423; Cappello, "De jure accusandi matrimonium," *Periodica,* 16 (1927), 239.*

[31] S. C. de Sacr., 7 maii, 1923, Regulae Servandae . . . 1923, n. 11—*A. A. S.,* XV (1923), 394.

right and *per se* the duty to attack the invalid marriage.[32] Prudence and an evaluation of the circumstances present in the individual case will determine whether or not the Promoter will exercise this duty independently of any denunciation on the part of the consorts. At any rate, he has a cumulative right with them to attack the marriage as often as the impediment is *by nature public*.

The Code of Canon Law nowhere defines what is meant by an impediment *by its nature public*. Commentators explain the clause in various ways and according to their definitions they extend or limit the right of the Promoter in this regard.

Canon 1037 explains the difference between public and occult impediments, but it is entirely silent upon the classification of impediments *by their nature public*. In fact the only mention made of this type of impediment is in the present canon.

Canon 1037 defines a public impediment as one which may be proved in the external forum. The idea of public prescinds from the knowledge of it in the community. Hence, if a fact is by its nature occult, as affinity or consanguinity growing out of illicit carnal relations, but it can be proved by a document, the impediment is to be considered public even though it may not be known to the community.[33] Something more than this proof in the external forum must be required for the impediment *of its nature public*. Evidently the term, of its nature public, suggests that the fact which the impediment involves is public, *e. g.*, the conferring of sacred orders, profession of solemn vows or that the fact upon which the impediment is based is one of public record, *e. g.*, age, consanguinity, a prior marriage recorded by the State or in the ordinary matrimonial record of the parish. According to Canon 1813, § 1, n. 4, ecclesiastical records of baptism, marriage, death, orders, solemn profession, etc., are public records. A matter which is of public record is considered *public of its very nature* even though accidentally it may not be known to the public.[34] Impedi-

[32] Cappello, *De Sacramentis,* III, 996.

[33] Gasparri, *De Matrimonio* (1932), I, 126.

[34] Chelodi, *Jus Matrimoniale,* 35, n. 1; Cappello, *De Sacramentis,* III, 238; Blat, *Commentarium,* IV, 502; A Coronata, *Institutiones J. C.,* III, 424.

ments of this class are age, affinity, consanguinity arising from legitimate blood relationship, bond of former marriage, spiritual and legal relationship, public honesty, sacred orders, religious professions. Relative to public honesty it should be noted that this applies even though the impediment arises from an invalid marriage contracted with proper form or in exceptional cases in the presence of two witnesses.[85]

The phrase "public by nature" is used in contradistinction to the phrase "by nature occult." The latter owes its origin to a fact which is commonly and in ordinary circumstances occult and can be established only by the parties themselves as, for example, the impediments of crime, blood relationship arising out of illicit carnal relations, error occasioned by willful fraud, and, in general, any and all of the impediments understood in the wide sense of the term.[86]

Per accidens, it can happen that an impediment by nature public can become occult and one by nature occult can become *de facto* public. To keep one of the examples given, the fact of consanguinity arising from licit relations may occasionally be unknown or at least incapable of proof and the impediment of crime which is normally occult can be known and provable in the external forum. Accordingly, one is obliged by the terms of Canon 1037 to classify as public, all impediments, whether public by their nature or public only in fact, whose existence can be established in the external forum and as occult, all those which cannot be proved in the external forum even though they may be by their very nature public.[87]

With these distinctions in mind, one may proceed to examine the rights and duties of the Promoter of Justice relative to the accusation of marriages and while Canon 1037 apparently abolishes the classification of impediments by their nature public, it does not relieve one entirely from understanding the distinctions of the

[85] De Smet, *Tractatus theologicus canonicus De sponsalibus et matrimonio* (4 ed.) 410, nn. 1, 2; Wernz-Vidal, *Jus Canonicum,* V, 167.

[86] A Coronata, *Institutiones J. C.,* III, 424; Wernz-Vidal, *Jus Canonicum,* V, n. 147, V, 167 ff; Haring, *Grundzüge des Kath. Kirchenrechtes,* II, 898; Chelodi, *Jus Matrimoniale,* 192.

[87] Cappello, *De Sacramentis,* III, 240; Chelodi, *Jus Matrimoniale,* n. 35; Pont. Comm. for Intepret., July 25, 1932, ad II—*A. A. S.,* XXIV (1932), 284.

past, for in one place in the Code the law retains the pre-code distinctions *de natura sua publicis* and it is in the present canon which deals with the rights of the Promoter of Justice to impugn the marriage when it has been rendered invalid by such impediments.

The phrase "public by its nature" has led to varying interpretations by the authors. Some have retained the strict legal sense it had in the old law, while others with a view to providing an adequate defense of the public good have given the term a wider interpretation; but all the earlier commentators on the Code without exception restrict the right of the Promoter to attack *ex officio* a marriage to impediments of their nature public. This right is curtailed or extended according to the interpretation of the phrase *natura sua publicis* adopted by the individual authors.

Those commentators who adopt the strict, pre-Code definition, as given above, deny the right of the Promoter of Justice to attack marriages other than those which have been rendered invalid by an impediment *of its nature public* understood in the full strict sense of the term. The party or the parties who have not been the culpable cause of the impediment are the only ones competent to attack a marriage rendered invalid by an impediment by nature occult. Nor may they, according to this opinion, denounce the invalidity of the marriage to the Promoter despite the fact that the impediment may be factually public. This first opinion excludes the right of the Promoter to attack the invalidity in such cases as those of crime and impotency even though the impediment is notorious. In a word, as often as the impediment is by nature occult and this opinion includes all the impediments understood in a wide sense in this classification, the Promoter of Justice may not attack the validity of the marriage either of his own initiative or upon the denunciation of the culpable parties. The only remedy which this opinion recognizes to them is a recourse to the Holy See by the aggrieved party, petitioning the restoration of the right to act as plaintiff in the matrimonial procedure before the diocesan courts.[38]

[38] A Coronata, *Institutiones J. C.*, III, 425; De Smet, *Tractatus theologicus canonicus De sponsalibus et matrimonio* (4 ed.), n. 465, 410; Vermeersch-Creusen, *Epitome*, III, 129; Haring, "Jus accusandi matrimonium," *Consulta-*

These canonists contend that the enumeration of Canon 1971 is exclusive and that the Promoter of Justice cannot institute proceedings in any case where the impediment is not *of its nature public,* even though he may have received a denunciation of the impediment from the parties in accordance with Canon 1971, § 2. They insist that the clear meaning of the canon is to limit the power of the Promoter of Justice to act as an accuser to cases of impediments by their nature public. They maintain that what the legislator has clearly expressed there is no reason to change.[39]

The second group of canonists give a wider significance to the phrase, "by nature public." They would include among the impediments by their nature public certain causes of impotence and crime which are notorious, as often as these have been denounced by the parties or by some member of the faithful. Upon denunciation of an impediment of crime or impotency which is notorious, the Promoter of Justice would be empowered to attack the validity of the marriage.[40] Although this class of authors permit the addition of one or both of these cases to the list of impediments by their nature public, they do not go beyond that. They, likewise, maintain that with the possible exception of the two named impediments and then only provided they are notorious, the Promoter of Justice may not even in the presence of a denunciation of an otherwise public impediment attack the marriage, if it has been rendered invalid by an impediment by its nature occult. [41] They, like the preceding opinion, include in this latter class all the impediments taken in a wide sense.

If the views of these canonists were correct, no one could attack the marriage when the impediment is not public by its na-

tiones J. C., I, 263, and *Apollinaris,* VI (1933), 243; Hilling, "Die ihrer Natur nach offentlichen und geheimen Ehehindernisse," *Afk KR.*, CII (1922), 14.

[39] Vermeersch-Creusen, *Epitome,* III, 129; Payen, *De Matrimonio,* n. 1691; Haring, "Jus accusandi matrimonium," *Apollinaris,* VI (1933), 243; Triebs, *Kanonisches Eherecht,* n. 515; A Coronata, *Institutiones J. C.*, III, 424.

[40] Gasparri, *Tractatus Canonicus de Matrimonio* (1904), n. 1478, ex Instr. Austriaca, § 118; Wernz-Vidal, *Jus Canonicum,* V, 834, n. 38; Augustine, *A Commentary,* V, 419.

[41] Wernz-Vidal, *Jus Canonicum,* V, n. 698, 834.

ture, understood in the pre-Code sense of the term, and the parties are deprived of exercising their right or the innocent party is unwilling to exercise it. Dr. Haring, one of the exponents of this view which maintains that the enumeration of Canon 1971 is taxative and exclusive and that the Promoter of Justice cannot institute proceedings in any case in which the impediment or defect is not of its nature public even though he has received a denunciation from the parties in accordance with the provision of Canon 1971, § 2, endeavors to escape this impasse by saying that while the parties may not formally plead against the marriage, they or the Promoter of Justice may apply to the court for a decision on the fact of the existence of the impediment. He claims that such a plea is not an accusation of marriage, inasmuch as a trial on the fact of an impediment is not the same as a process instituted to determine the validity of the marriage and that the favorable decision as to the existence of the impediment in virtue of Canons 1813, § 1, n. 3, and 2197, n. 2, makes the impediment public by nature and, therefore, renders the Promoter competent to attack the validity of the marriage.[42] This solution seems to be a quibble. It seems as though canonists generally would consider the trial on the fact of an impediment and the trial on the invalidity of a marriage on the same level and would therefore reject Dr. Haring's distinctions as a sophistry. At any rate, it does not seem to afford a satisfactory explanation of the problem and has not been adopted by any of the contemporary canonical writers in the knowledge of the writer.

A third interpretation of the phrase, *natura sua publicis,* is to be found in the writings of Noval [43] and seems to have been accepted by Muniz.[44] Noval in certain circumstances would include within the scope of the Promoter's activity not only the impediments properly so called (1067-80) but also the lack of the conditions prescribed by the natural or the ecclesiastical law (1071-94). He

[42] Haring, "Jus accusandi matrimonium," *Apollinaris,* VI (1933), 243 and *Consultationes Juris Canonici,* I, 262, 263.

[43] Noval, *De Processibus,* I, 569.

[44] Muniz, *Procedimientos Eccl.,* III, 35 and n. 2.

defines impediments by their nature public as those impediments by their nature manifest in view of the manifest character of the fact with which they are bound up and gives as examples of these facts the prior bond, the lack of baptism, and solemn profession on which the impediments of ligamen, disparity of cult and solemn vows are based. Thus far, he is in accord with the preceding opinions. He then proceeds, however, to identify this notion of an impediment by its nature public with those impediments which, although by nature occult, are *de facto* public and therefore capable of proof in the external forum on the grounds that this public knowledge concerning it is either already certain to be or at least will regularly in the course of events be divulged with consequent scandal. In such cases the very knowledge of the invalid marriage may be adjudged to be scandalous or, at least, it may be safely concluded that the scandal will necessarily arise and be prejudicial to the public good.[45]

In effect, the great canonist identifies the notion of an impediment by its nature public with an impediment which can be proved in the external forum and the knowledge of which is certain either from the very nature of things or is certain regularly to carry scandal with it. Having thus satisfied the objections that he knew would otherwise arise, he maintains that the Promoter of Justice, as the legitimate authority entrusted with the protection of the public good, is empowered to accuse the marriages and thereby, remove the scandal which is always prejudicial to the common ecclesiastical good. He recognizes the right and duty of the Promoter to accuse these marriages which may become a source of scandal and accuse them independently of any denunciations from the parties or others. He says that there are not lacking authentic responses to particular cases which support his opinion in this matter.

This opinion has its merits and is more in harmony with the general notion of the public good and the office of the Promoter to whose care its defense is entrusted, but fails to take into account the positive wording of Canon 1971, § 1, n. 2. Noval simply dis-

[45] Noval, *De Processibus*, I, 569; Sangmeister, *Force and Fear*, 182, 183.

penses with all consideration of the pre-Code legislation on the nature of an impediment by its nature public and defines such impediments to his own satisfaction.[46] The wording of Canon 1971, § 1, n. 2 does not leave one entirely free from these interpretations of the old law relative to the nature of impediments of their nature public.[47] He mentions the existence of particular authentic responses which justify his extensive interpretation of the phrase *de natura suis,* but does not give any indication as where they might be found. Were this the case, does it not seem strange that despite the fact Noval wrote in 1920, his opinion has not been adopted in any of the subsequent canonical literature on the problem, much of which will be referred to, to justify or at least to offer a reasonable basis for the intervention of the Promoter not only of his own initiative, as he permits it, but even in the face of a denunciation by reliable parties. His opinion while well intended appears to be founded upon arguments which are still forthcoming.

Somewhat analagous to this opinion is the opinion of those canonists who would permit the Promoter of Justice to accuse an invalid marriage of his own initiative and independently of all denunciation by the aggrieved parties, as often as the invalidating impediment is *de facto* public in the sense of Canon 1037.[48] They base their argument upon the fact that the nullity of marriage always pertains to the public good and that after it becomes public, it is of interest to the public good to declare the invalidity because of the scandal which is generally attendant upon such public knowledge of the invalidity. Since the Promoter of Justice is the legitimately established authority for the defense of the public good, he is empowered, as often as the impediment which invalidates the marriage

[46] Vermeersch-Creusen, *Epitome,* III, 129; A Coronata, *Institutiones J. C.,* III, 424, 425 and 425, n. 1.

[47] Cappello, "De jure accusandi matrimonium," *Periodica,* 16 (1927), 228* ff; G. Oesterle, *Jus Pontificium,* 12 (1932), 142, 143; Haring, "Jus accusandi matrimonium," *Apollinaris,* VI (1933), 243; Hilling, *Afk KR.,* CII (1922). 14 ff.

[48] Roberti, "De jure accusandi matrimonium," *Apollinaris,* III (1930), 250; *Il Monitore Ecclesiastico,* Serie V, Vol. V (1933), 271; Stocchiero, *Il Matrimonio in Italia* (2 ed.), 96; De Becker, *De Matrimonio* (1931), 275.

is *de facto* public, to attack the marriage in the matrimonial courts independently of any denunciation of the marriage.[49]

In favor of this opinion it might be said that it solves the difficulty of providing for the accusation of marriages in all cases. It, however, identifies the words *vi muneris sui* used by the Pontifical Committee in its response dated July 17, 1933[50] with the words *ex officio* and overlooks the fact that the response appeals to a canon on denunciation to vindicate the exercise of the right to the Promoter. It is true that the word *ex officio* in the Code is usually contrasted to *ad instantiam partis.* It may be pointed out, however, that *ex officio* does not exclude the denunciation of the parties. It certainly did not in the Instruction of the Holy Office for 1883.[51] An official proceeds *ex officio* when he acts not as an individual but in virtue of his official capacity. In the present question these canonists are using responses given relative to the right of the Promoter to act in cases in which the parties or others have made a reliable denunciation of the invalid marriage to cases in which no denunciation was forthcoming. The earlier authors, quoted in this opinion as Roberti, simply identify the impediments by nature public with impediments public in fact. Were this the solution of the question, why did Canon 1971, § 1, n. 2 not content itself with saying that the Promoter of Justice enjoyed the right cumulatively with the parties to attack the marriage in all cases in which the marriage was invalid because of the presence of public impediments, instead of specifically restricting the duties of the Promoter of Justice to impediments which are *natura sua publicis?*

While it seems that the Promoter of Justice enjoys the right to attack these marriages rendered invalid by the presence of a public impediment in the event of a reliable denunciation from the parties or others, the extensive interpretation given by some authors to this right whereby the Promoter may in the presence of a simply

[49] "De matrimonii accusatione," *Il Monitore Ecclesiastico,* Serie V, Vol. V (1933), 271; Creusen, "De jure denuntiandi nullitatem matri.," *Nouvelle Revue Theologique,* 57 (1930), 521 and "De jure accusandi matri.," 56 (1929), 685 ff.

[50] Ad IV—*A. A. S.,* XXV (1933), 345.

[51] Instr. S. O., 20 junii, 1883, pars. 1, tit. 1, n. 3—*Fontes,* n. 1076.

public impediment without any previous denunciation attack the validity of the marriage does not seem to be justified by the tenor of the canon nor the responses made up it.[52]

Wherefore it seems to be a valid conclusion to state that the Promoter of Justice of his own initiative has the right and *per se* the duty to attack the validity of the marriages of Catholics solely when the impediment to a valid marriage is public by its nature. This last phrase is to be understood in the sense of the pre-Code legislation as demanding something more than the mere possibility of proof in the external forum or the mere fact of publicity with attendant scandal. The impediment must be one of those which is bound up in a fact which in itself is public and which were enumerated at the outset of this article.

The exercise of the right and duty to attack such marriages will depend upon the findings resultant from the Promoter's extrajudicial investigation into the invalid marriage. Were this investigation to disclose that his action would occasion further scandal inasmuch as the parties would not accept and have no desire for an ecclesiastical decree of nullity, the Promoter would be obliged to desist from making an accusation which he would be otherwise competent to make, since it is presupposed that the impediment is by nature public, for the very basis of the Promoter's right of action is the removal of a scandal which is prejudicial to the public good.

While the Promoter of Justice does not seem to be empowered by the law to attack of his own initiative marriages which have been rendered invalid by impediments of their nature occult, it does not follow that the competence of the Promoter in the accusation of invalid marriages is therefore limited to the powers given him in Canon 1971, § 1, n. 2. The opinion of those canonists who espouse the first and the second opinions and hold that Canon 1971, § 1, n. 2 is exclusive and taxatively determines and defines the com-

[52] G. Oesterle, *Jus Pontificium,* 12 (1932), 142, 143; "De jure matrimonium accusandi," *Jus Pontificium,* 9 (1929), 108; Haring, "De jure accusandi matrimonium," *Consultationes Juris Canonici,* I, 263; A. Toso, "De matrimonii accusatione," *Jus Pontificium,* XIII (1933), 187; Gasparri, *De Matrimonio* (1932), II, 292. "Ein komplitizieter Eheprozesz," *Th. Pr. QS,* LXXXV (1932), 809, 810.

petence of the Promoter in all matrimonial causes does not seem to be warranted in the light of recent contributions to canonical literature. These later decisions of the Pontifical Committee and the writings of the authors commenting upon them certainly justify the intervention of the Promoter of Justice in matrimonial causes, other than those involving the invalidity of marriages on the grounds of impediments by their nature public and it is a consideration of this intervention which forms the basis for the third remedy at the disposal of parties who have forfeited their rights of accusation by being the culpable causes of the invalidity of their marriage.

As often as the parties are the culpable cause of the impediments rendering their marriage invalid and the impediment is not of its nature public, there is only one remedy left and that is to denounce the impediment to the Promoter of Justice, who thereby becomes competent to attack the marriage. Despite the fact that it was held that he might not of his own initiative attack such marriages as are not rendered invalid by an impediment of its nature public, in view of recent decisions of the Pontifical Committee on the matter, it is sufficiently certain that he may attack marriages rendered invalid by a public impediment, as often as he receives a reliable denunciation of their invalidity.

Canon 1971, § 2 indicates that all persons who know of the invalidity of a marriage and can substantiate this knowledge of the invalidity in the external forum may denounce this marriage to the Ordinary or the Promoter of Justice. After the Pontifical Committee had announced on March 13, 1929 that the term "impediment" used in Canon 1971 was to be understood in a wide sense [53] and that the parties who were the culpable cause of an impediment even in this wide sense were to be absolutely excluded from accusing the marriages, a doubt arose as to whether these parties were to be permitted to use the faculty of denunciation permitted in paragraph 2 of Canon 1971. The doubt owes its origin undoubtedly to those opinions of certain old canonists who in commenting upon the legislation before the Code regularly laid down the same requirements for denunciation which had already been laid down for accusa-

[53] *A. A. S.*, XXI (1929), 170.

tions.[54] Such doctrine can no longer be maintained in virtue of the prevailing notions and definitions of denunciation and accusation set forth by modern canonists and noted at the outset of this article. The authentic interpretation given by the Committee affirms these notions. The parties who were the culpable cause of the impediment in so far as it relates to the private good are deprived of the right of accusing the marriage as a penalty for their fraud. But the public good can demand that the matrimonial process be instituted and the promotion of that public good is entrusted by the prevailing law to the Promoter of Justice.[55] However, all are bound to cooperate with that public personage in order that he may rightly fulfill his office in the ecclesiastical community. Wherefore, all are generally commanded to denounce facts of this kind to the proper authorities. Nor are the married parties themselves excluded since the right of denunciation exists for the defense of the public good, not the private good, and this is expressly stated by the Pontifical Commission in its authentic response dated February 17, 1930, and published in the *Acta* for that year.[56]

Since the parties are thus empowered to denounce their invalid unions to the Promoter of Justice in virtue of Canon 1971, § 2, this procedure naturally gives rise to the question as to what title or from what reason of action does the Promoter of Justice derive the right to accept such a denunciation and institute an action against the invalidity of the marriage. By what title does he accept the action, and, once he accepts it, by what reason does he elect to act or refuse to act as plaintiff in the case? This difficulty was put to the Pontifical Commission in the following query, *An vi Canonis 1971, § 2 promotor justitiae vi muneris sui agit in judicio?* The answer was in the affirmative.[57] Wherefore the Pontifical Committee replies that the Promoter of Justice performs all these du-

[54] Reiffenstuel, lib. V, tit. 1, par. II, n. 85; Lega, *De Judiciis Eccl.*, III, n. 135.

[55] Canons 1971, § 1, n. 2, and 1586.

[56] *A. A. S.*, XXII (1930), 196.

[57] Pont. Comm. for Interpet. 17 julii, 1933, ad IV—*A. A. S.*, XXV (1933), 345.

ties *vi muneris sui,* that is, in virtue of the fact that it is his duty to foster and protect the public good in the judicial forum.[58] In other words the duty of the Promoter in matrimonial causes is not changed; he acts in these causes only in the interests of the public good and only in the defense of that common good.

The meaning of the response of the Pontifical Commission to this fourth query is then that, when the Promoter of Justice receives a denunciation of an invalid marriage, he can institute the proceedings for a matrimonial trial and act as plaintiff in that trial in virtue of his office. The phrase *agere in judicio* is that used frequently in the Code to signify acting as plaintiff in a judicial trial.[59] In this case it is the same as *accusare matrimonium.* As it had already been decided that the parties to a marriage may bring the denunciation even in cases of impediments of their nature occult, it follows that the Promoter of Justice can institute proceedings against the validity of a marriage even in a case of a marriage invalid by reason of an impediment by its nature occult, as long as the invalidity shall have been denounced to him. This was the interpretation put on the canon by some canonists even prior to the response of the Pontifical Commission.[60] Their interpretation of Canon 1971 maintained that the Promoter of Justice can institute proceedings of his own initiative in all cases of impediments by their nature public, but in all other cases he can act only upon the receipt of a denunciation. It would appear in any case that his competence is not limited to impediments by their nature public and that the statement of Canon 1971, § 1, n. 2 is not taxative or exclusive.

But it may be asked why did the Pontifical Committee employ the words *vi Canonis 1971, §1, n. 2,* in its decision; why appeal to a

[58] Canon 1586; Gasparri, *De Matrimonio* (1932), II, 292; Roberti, "De jure matri. accusandi," *Apollinaris,* VI (1933). 444; A. Toso, "De matri. accusatione," *Jus Pontificium,* 13 (1933), 187; "De matri. accusatione," *Il monitore Ecclesiastico,* Serie V, Vol. V (1933), 271.

[59] Canon 1646.

[60] Gasparri, *De Matrimonio* (1932), II, 292; G. Oesterle, *Jus Pontificium,* 12 (1932), 142; *Jus Pontificium,* 9 (1929), 108; Creusen, "Jus accusandi matrimonium," *Nouvelle Revue Theologique,* 60 (1933), 733, accepts this view.

canon dealing with denunciation to authorize a procedure without denunciation? And also it may be asked why did Canon 1971, § 1, n. 2 not content itself with saying that the Promoter was competent to introduce all causes in which the impediment to validity was public? Why did the same canon specify that he could institute proceedings only when the invalidity results from impediments by nature public?

The problem is not an easy one and no satisfactory explanation is forthcoming as yet.[61] It was seen that Noval solved the problem to his own satisfaction, but that there seemed to be no sound canonical basis upon which to accept his opinion, and, that, despite the fact that it offers the easiest solution of the problem, it has not been accepted by the recent writers in their efforts to explain the present question. Dr. Haring offered a suggestion, but it did not seem to be a satisfactory solution of the problem. Roberti and the last mentioned canonists do not take into account either the wording of the Canon 1971 or the conditions set forth in the responses of the Pontifical Commission.

The best approach to the problem of interpreting Canon 1971 seems to be from the standpoint of previous legislation upon the subject.[62] The pre-Code legislation in the accusation of marriages made a distinction between impediments which some canonists described as *juris privati* and *juris publici,*[63] while others used the expressions *natura sua publica* and *natura sua occulta* to express the same distinction.[64] This latter terminology has been adopted by

[61] Roberti, "De jure matri. accusandi," *Apollinaris,* V (1933), 444; Creusen, "Jus accusandi matri.," *Nouvelle Revue Theologique,* 60 (1933), 733; G. Oesterle, *Jus Pontificium,* 12 (1932), 142, 143; P. B. Melcon, "Anotaciones," *Religion y Cultura,* 27 (1934), 230 ff; Haring, "De jure accusandi matrimonium," *Apollinaris,* VI (1933), 243.

[62] Browne, "Recent decisions of the Commission for Interpretation of the Code"—*Irish Ecclesiastical Record,* LXIX (1933), 525-532.

[63] S. B. Smith, *The Marriage Process,* n. 193, p. 60; Wernz-Vidal, *Jus Canonicum,* V, 834; Wernz, *Jus Decretalium,* IV, pars 2, n. 216, 5.

[64] Gasparri, *De Matrimonio* (1904), I, n. 252, and *De Matrimonio* (1932), I, 126, 127; Feije, *De Impedimentis et Dispensationibus Matrimonialibus* (1895), n. 97.

the Code. The right to accuse marriages was given to the parties exclusively in the matter of invalidity arising out of impediments of private law (impotence, crime, force and fear, conditional consent, etc.). In the case of impediments of public law any Catholic had the right to act as plaintiff. The Promoter of Justice could also act *ex officio* when there was a denunciation or a widespread rumor. He was, however, limited to cases of impediments of public law and could not institute proceedings of his own initiative in cases where the marriage was invalidated by impediments of private law except in cases of certain impediments where the invalidity was notorious.[65]

The new law contained in Canon 1971 has abolished the right of others than the parties and the Promoter of Justice to accuse the marriage; henceforth, they can merely report the invalidity to the Odinary or the Promoter of Justice.[66] This means that the right of accusation which accrued to any Catholic party before the Code, whenever a marriage was rendered invalid by an impediment of public law is now reserved to the Promoter of Justice. As the purpose of Canon 1971 is not to restrict, but rather to extend the functions of the Promoter of Justice, it follows that paragraph 1 must not be taken as an exclusive enumeration of the cases in which the Promoter of Justice is competent to act. Paragraph 2 of the same canon is a clear though indirect proof that the faculties which he enjoyed under the old law to proceed *ex officio* whenever there was a denunciation have not been abrogated by the Code. The recent decision of the Pontifical Commission has carried this amplification of the duties of the Promoter a step farther. It means that the old rule, whereby the Promoter of Justice could act only *ex officio* solely in cases of impediments *publici juris* does not henceforth hold, at least, as often as there has been a previous reliable denunciation.[67]

[65] Instructio Austriaca, 4 maii, 1855, par. 118, *cf.* Gasparri, *De Matrimonio* (1904), II, n. 1478, 402; S. B. Smith, *The Marriage Process,* 195; Wernz, *Jus Decretalium,* IV, pars 2, n. 216, 5, 6; Bassibey, *Procedure Matrimoniale Generale,* 188.

[66] Canon 1972, § 2.

[67] Pont. Comm. for Interpret., 17 julii, 1933, ad IV—*A. A. S.*, XXV (1933), 345; *cf.* all the authors quoted above in reference to this decision of the Pontifical Commission with the exception of Haring.

It seems reasonable, therefore, that the exception for notorious cases of impotency and crime likewise holds.

In view of these facts it may be concluded that when the impediment is not by nature public in the strict sense of that term, the Promoter is competent to institute proceedings whenever there is a reliable denunciation and in the case of crime or impotency whenever the impediments are notorious. Such a consideration of the nature and conditions of the matrimonial procedure will show that under these limits the Promoter of Justice enjoys all the power and competence his office requires.

Instances where the matrimonial procedure was instituted *ex officio* by the Promoter, even in cases where the marriage was invalid because of impediments public by nature, have been exceedingly rare in the past. Bassibey [68] could find only three instances in the entire records of the Congregation of the Council. One may safely forecast cases of impediments by their nature occult (force and fear, conditions, impotence, error, crime, etc.) where the Promoter of Justice might be called upon to intervene without a previous notification or cooperation of the parties will be very rare. In practice, if neither party takes any steps to denounce the marriage, it would indicate that they have no desire for a trial and would not appear in court to give evidence. Yet it is particularly in these cases that the evidence and cooperation of the parties is indispensable and that the notoriety of fact is least likely to occur. In such impediments the greatest of care would be required of the Promoter to determine whether the invalidity was notorious and causing real scandal.[69] If the parties in question do not seek or would not accept the verdict of the ecclesiastical courts, the proceedings for a decree of nullity instituted *ex officio* by the Promoter would not remove the scandal, but perhaps would augment it. Therefore, proceedings in cases where the marriage has been rendered invalid by impediments of their nature occult as a rule will not be initiated by the Promoter of Justice, unless he has some assurance that the parties desire a decision and will abide by it. This assurance may be had normally only from

[68] *Procedure Matrimoniale Generale,* § 191.

[69] Gasparri, *De Matrimonio* (1932), I, n. 209.

the actions taken by the parties themselves who through themselves or through others have brought the invalidity of the marriage to the attention of the matrimonial court by means of a reliable denunciation.

The problems involved in the exercise of the functions of the office of the Promoter of Justice in matrimonial causes are not so much of competence and jurisdiction as of prudence, and, when the law has given him authority to act in occult cases and the party has made a denunciation, it may be urged that he has all the authority that is required to institute the proceedings. The recent interpretations of Canon 1971 by the Pontifical Committee together with the doctrinal commentary made upon them by authoritative contemporary canonists afford a reasonable basis of action for the intervention of the Promoter of Justice in these causes and in virtue of his office he may accept the denunciations of occult cases and proceed to seek a declaration of nullity, as often as the invalid marriage has become a scandal to the salvation of the parties and to the faithful who know of the invalidity. The best interests of the ecclesiastical society demand that the government of that society take cognizance of the public invalidity of the marriage and she empowers the Promoter, the public defender in the diocesan curia, to correct the situation and remove the scandal giving him at the same time all the competence and jurisdiction he needs to undo the harm brought on by the sinful action of the culpable, but now contrite, parties to a marriage.

Article II. The Duty of the Promoter of Justice to Act in Matrimonial Proceedings

Thus far the action of the Promoter of Justice in matrimonial causes has been considered as a right. It was concluded that the enumeration of Canon 1971, § 1, n. 2 was not taxative and exclusive and that the Promoter of Justice had the right not only to accuse marriages which had been rendered invalid by impediments *natura sua publicis* as understood in its strict sense, but also had the right to institute proceedings against the validity of a marriage which had been invalidated by impediments by their nature occult, as often as the parties or others have denounced the marriages to him. The question arises as to what is the duty and obligation of the Promoter relative to these invalid marriages. What official cognizance must he take of marriages that have been rendered invalid by impediments by their nature public and of the denunciations made to him when the marriage is invalid in virtue of a simple public impediment?

It need hardly be remarked that as often as the Ordinary adjudges the declaration of nullity to be of interest to the public good, the Promoter of Justice in his official capacity as plaintiff for that public good should seek the declaration of nullity before the diocesan tribunal. The bishop is the official in any diocese who determines what cases involve the public good and in the present question the Promoter is bound to cooperate with the bishop.[70]

What, however, should be the attitude of a Promoter in those cases in which the law and the Ordinary leave the solution of the question to his own prudence and good judgment?

Relative to marriages which have been rendered invalid by impediments of their nature public, the Promoter *per se* has the duty of denouncing these marriages to the diocesan tribunal and seeking a declaration of their nullity or their convalidation, if that is possible. Personal knowledge of the invalidity of a marriage which has been rendered such by reason of an impediment by its nature public would mean that the Promoter of Justice in virtue of his office must seek the convalidation of that marriage or, if that is not possible either because of the nature of the impediment or the obstinacy of the parties, he should seek a declaration of nullity. The nature of the office of the Promoter of Justice in these matters is identical with the one he exercises in criminal matters; he is the public personage entrusted with the defense of the public good and the public invalidity of marriage is always or is regularly prejudicial to the salvation of souls and the public ecclesiastical good.[71]

[70] Canon 1586; G. Oesterle, *Jus Pontificium,* 12 (1932), 142, 143; Roberti, *De Processibus,* I, 198.

[71] Cappello, *De Sacramentis,* III, 996; Toso, "De matrimonii accusatione," *Jus Pontificium,* 13 (1933), 188; Blat, *Commentarium,* IV, 503; Vermeersch-Creusen, *Epitome,* III, 129; De Becker, *De Matrimonio* (1931), p. 275; Roberti, "Animadversiones," *Apollinaris,* III (1930), 57.

While the Promoter *per se* has the clear duty in these cases, *per accidens* he is excused from acting, nay more, he should desist from taking action to accuse these marriages as often as the public good would suffer by the taking of such action. Since the duty of the Promoter in matrimonial causes is the same as it is in other contentious cases, he should not initiate or participate in the proceedings unless they redound to the benefit of the public good.[72] The only way he can decide whether or not the judicial examination of an invalid marriage would accrue to the public good is by making an extrajudicial investigation into the invalid marriage, whenever there has been no previous denunciation by the parties or others at the instance of the parties. He does not seem to be justified in proceeding otherwise.[73] Were this previous investigation to disclose that the parties have no desire to change their present modes of life and would not abide by the decision of an ecclesiastical court, but would nevertheless persist in their present invalid union, what could be possibly gained by having the Promoter exercise the right clearly given him in Canon 1971, § 1, n. 2? Would not such a procedure tend to increase rather than remove the scandal which his action is primarily intended to remove? Since the impediment is presupposed to be its nature public, he no doubt could establish the invalidity of the marriage, but such an action would be an empty and in some instances a harmful service to the public good when the parties refuse to abide by the decision of the ecclesiastical courts. Prudence, therefore, will guide the Promoter in these cases and the instances in which he will be called upon to exercise his office apart from the denunciation of the marriage will be exceedingly rare. The circumstances in any given case will determine the extent of his obligation.

Relative to the acceptance of denunciations and the action to be taken upon them, the obligation of the Promoter is more definite. Since Canon 1971, § 2, gives the faithful the right to denounce the invalid marriages and since the Pontifical Commission has clearly

[72] Roberti, *Apollinaris,* VI (1933), 444; Blat, *Commentarium,* IV, 503.

[73] Roberti, "De jure accusandi matri.," *Apollinaris,* III (1930), 250; Pasquale Vito, *Palestro Del Clero,* IX (1930), 385; A Coronata, *Institutiones J. C.*, III, 422, n. 7; Blat, *Commentarium,* IV, 503.

taught that the parties enjoy the same right, the Promoter of Justice has the right and the duty to accept these denunciations.[74] Frequently both classes of denunciators have a grave duty in justice or charity to denounce the invalid union,[75] and since the law recognizes their right to do so, the Promoter and the Ordinary have a corresponding duty of making it possible for them to exercise their right by accepting the denunciation, for where the law confers a right on a party it is incumbent upon him who makes the exercise of that right possible to cooperate with that party.[76]

This mere denunciation, however, will not in itself oblige the Promoter to act. The denunciation must be reliable and must manifest a possibility of establishing the invalidity of the marriage in the external forum.[77] It should set forth an accurate description of the case, giving all the necessary details of the impediment involved and indicating the available proof by noting the witnesses or documents which may be used as a basis for the accusation in the formal trial.

As often as the denunciation has these qualities, the Promoter, since the denunciation is directed to protect the public good and not the private good of the parties, must weigh the value of the denunciation and determine whether or not to act as plaintiff in the case. The Pontifical Commission declares that he does this in virtue of his office, that is, in virtue of the fact that it is his duty to foster and protect the public good in the judicial forum.[78] Wherefore if the arguments brought against the validity of the marriage are groundless, in virtue of his office he should reject the denunciation and seek the reconciliation of the parties; if, however, the arguments are grave and the impediment is an ecclesiastical one and is remediable, he will use his office to try to effect a convalidation and

[74] Noval, *De Processibus,* I, 570.

[75] Vermeersch-Creusen, *Epitome,* III, 129; Roberti, "De jure accusandi matri.," *Apollinaris,* III (1930), 250.

[76] Noval, *De Processibus,* I, 570; Gasparri, *De Matrimonio* (1932), II, 292.

[77] Instr. S. O., 20 junii, 1883, Pars I, tit. I, n. 3—*Fontes,* n. 1076.

[78] Pont. Comm. for Interpret., 17 julii, 1933 ad IV—*A. A. S.,* XXV (1933), 345; Canon 1586; Blat, *Commentarium,* IV, 503.

persuade the couple to remain together after the convalidation, and only in the event that the convalidation is out of the question as the impediment is not remediable or there is no hope of reconciliation, will he by reason of his office introduce the cause of nullity, if the public good demands it.[79]

The Promoter of Justice is to use his own discretion as to whether or not the declaration of nullity pertains to the public good. When the denunciation is made by third parties, the Promoter will have to determine whether there is scandal and whether or not an official action on his part will effectively remove the scandal. Some authors say that as often as the parties themselves denounce the marriage and afford sufficient proof of nullity, the Promoter of Justice should accuse the marriage.[80] Roberti, however, states that the whole judgment as to the benefit accruing to the public good rests with the Promoter; but that he can seldom abstain from instituting the process whenever the invalidity is *de facto* public.[81] Practically then, whenever there is a reliable denunciation made either by the parties themselves or at their instance which sets forth a satisfactory proof of nullity and in which there is no hope of reconciliation, the Promoter of Justice will be bound to institute the proceedings since the denunciation will invariably establish the impediment as *de facto* public and, hence, regularly attendant with scandal. It may be concluded, therefore, that the Promoter of Justice will be obliged by his office to act as plaintiff and seek out justice in these cases in the interest of the common good. Nor may it be alleged that the Church is thereby placing a premium upon dishonest behavior of her children by placing at their disposal a ready-made accuser, for in so providing for the accusation of such marriages, she is merely showing a necessary consideration for pub-

[79] Toso, "De matri. accusatione," *Jus Pontificium*, 13 (1933), 188; Creusen, "De jure denuntiandi nullitatem matri.," *Nouvelle Revue Theologique*, 57 (1930) 521; Noval, *De Processibus*, I, 570; Cappello, *De Sacramentis*, III, 995.

[80] Gasparri, *De Matrimonio* (1932), II, 292; Noval, *De Processibus*, I, 570; Chelodi, *Jus Matrimoniale*, 192; Creusen, "Jus accusandi matrimonium," *Nouvelle Revue Theologique*, 60 (1933), 733.

[81] Roberti, *Apollinaris*, III (1930), 250 and *Apollinaris*, VI (1933), 444; *cf.* also P. B. Melcon, *Religion y Cultura*, 27 (1934), 230 ff.

lic morality and welfare and the benefit to the individual is only incidental.[82]

This exercise of the right and duty to act as plaintiff has a further practical application other than that already discussed. There are cases in which the parties have already been admitted into the court and it is only discovered in the course of the proceedings that they have not come into the court with clean hands and that both parties or at least the plaintiff in the trial has been the culpable cause of the impediment which rendered the marriage invalid. In the former case there is nothing to do but to legitimate the process and the proofs thus far submitted by having the Promoter of Justice reintroduce the cause by presenting a new introductory *libellus*; otherwise, the final definitive sentence in the trial will be *ipso jure* invalid since it has been pronounced in a cause in which neither party enjoyed the right of standing in court.[83] In the latter instance where the plaintiff alone is disqualified, the innocent party may attack the marriage, but if that party has been declared in contempt or refuses to exercise the right of attacking the marriage, it devolves upon the Promoter of Justice to attack the marriage, since the invalidity is public and the public good and the ends of justice can be served in no other way than by the official action of that officer of the diocesan curia intended for that purpose, the Promoter of Justice.[84]

Another contingency that can arise is the contumacy of the legitimately admitted plaintiff to the trial. It might happen that the innocent party has begun proceedings with a view to seeking a declaration of nullity and then drops the proceedings for some cause other than the reconcilation and convalidation of the prevailing union. When there are reasonable grounds to believe the marriage invalid, the Promoter of Justice may step into the case and should do so to fill the rôle of the absent plaintiff, since the spiritual

[82] Creusen, "De jure denuntiandi nulli. matri.," *Nouvelle Revue Theologique*, 57 (1930), 521; P. B. Melcon, "Anotaciones," *Religion y Cultura*, 27 (1934), 230 ff.

[83] Canons 1892, § 1, n. 2; 1971, § 1, n. 1; A Coronata, *Institutiones J. C.*, III, 423.

[84] Roberti, "De jure accusandi matri.," *Apollinaris*, III (1930), 55 ff.

welfare of the defendant and the public good demand that the tribunal pass judgment upon the allegedly invalid marriage.[85] He simply continues the case from the point in the trial where the contempt occured.

As often as the Promoter of Justice in the interests of the public good introduces one of these proceedings, it will be his duty to act as the principal litigant in the trial. He will prepare the *libellus* and will perform all the duties of a plaintiff in contentious proceedings, which duties will be outlined in a later article. And in the event that the sentence in the matrimonial trial is unfavorable and he does not believe the sentence sufficiently protects the public good, he will appeal from his diocesan court and interpose that appeal within the legal period fixed for such action.[86] The actual prosecution of the appeal before the higher court will be prosecuted by the respective officer of the appellate tribunal, since the Promoter has no standing outside the tribunal for which he was appointed.[87]

A similar rule will also hold in the event that the Promoter obtains a decree of nullity in the first instance. The defender of the bond will automatically appeal from this first sentence of nullity, but it is not the Promoter of the lower court who will be the plaintiff before the appellate tribunal in the prosecution of the appeal; it will be the incumbent of the same office in the higher court who will be cited to prosecute the case. This Promoter must be cited for the validity of the appellate trial in order that the interests of the public good may not be unprotected. He will represent the Promoter of the first instance and act as plaintiff.[88]

Article III. The Promoter of Justice and the Matrimonial Causes of Non-Catholics

In the year 1928 the Holy Office in the solution of a doubt declared that non-Catholics were no longer competent to act as plaint-

[85] Canon 1850, 2; Suprema Signatura, Recursus, 15 martii, 1921—*A. A. S.*, XIII (1921), 271.

[86] Canon 1879; Augustine, *A Commentary*, VII, 318.

[87] Suprema Signatura, Recursus, 15 martii, 1921—*A. A. S.*, XIII (1921), 271.

[88] V. Dalpiaz, *Apollinaris*, VIII (1935), 139, 140.

iff or petitioner in our matrimonial courts and based that exclusion upon the prohibition found in Canon 87 which rules that those who are not in communion with the Church are not free to exercise those rights which baptism confers upon members of the Church.[89] If, then, a Catholic desires to marry a non-Catholic or is already married to a non-Catholic who has been previously married and divorced, does this reply of the Holy Office mean that the Catholic party may not bring the non-Catholic's matrimonial cause to the attention of the diocesan matrimonial courts short of a faculty conceded by the Congregation itself?

If the impediment comes under those classified in Canon 1990, there is no difficulty, for the prohibition extends only to acting as plaintiff in a formal trial and hence the bishop may pronounce on the invalidity of the first marriage independently of any recourse to Rome.[90] If, however, the impediment does not come under the cases enumerated in Canon 1990, the case would require a formal trial in the diocesan courts. This will also be true as often as the proof for the existence of the impediments under 1990 is so difficult as to require that it be remanded to the diocesan tribunal for examination in accordance with the provisions of Canon 1992. It is relative to these causes requiring a formal trial that it may be asked: Is there any way in which the validity of the marriage between two non-Catholics may be passed upon in the diocesan courts without having recourse to the Holy See?

It may prove of assistance in the answering of this question to give the historical background of the problem.

Before the Code, the diocesan court was competent to pass judgment on these cases in order to establish the free state of the non-Catholic party whom the Catholic desired to marry, or had already married and is now desirous of convalidating the marriage. This was expressly declared in a rescript of the Holy Office published on January 23, 1903:

[89] Congr. S. O., 27 Jan., 1928—*A. A. S.*, XX (1928), 75.

[90] Gasparri, *De Matrimonio* (1932), II, p. 293; Park, "Competence of Ordinary in a case under Canon 1990," *The American Ecclestiastical Review*, LXXXVI (1932), 88-93.

> . . . Quando agitur de matrimonio mixto contrahendo cum haeretico separato per divortii sententiam tribunalis civili ab haeretica erit Episcopus domicilii partis catholicae ad quem spectat judicare an contrahentes gaudeant status libertate.[91]

As late as 1925, bishops were referred by the Holy Office to this rescript of 1903 for competence in such matters.[92] The diocesan tribunals exercised the right independently of any recourse to the Holy See.

The first indication one has of any change in policy relative to these matters is to be found in a private rescript of the Holy Office, published in the same year 1925. The rescript bears the date of April 8th and was addressed to the Bishop of Freiburg, who published it in a diocesan newspaper from which it found its way into the *Periodica*. Vermeersch in reprinting it notes that it never appeared in the *Acta*. The rescript is as follows:

> In Congregatione Generali S. R. Et U. Inquisitionis, propositis sequentibus dubiis ab A. T. expositis, utrum nempe;
>
> 1. Tribunal ecclesiasticum judicare possit de validitate matrimonii duorum acatholicorum, instante parte acatholica quae nempe cum Catholica contrahere vult, aut parte Catholica acatholico nupturiente aut utraque, aut solo Promotore justitiae?
>
> 2. Quod tribunal competens sit ejusmodi causae, an loci in quo matrimonium celebratum est, vel domicilii aut quasi-domicilii partis acatholici vel catholicae instantis?
>
> Emi. et Rmi. Patres una mecum Inquisitoris Generalis respondendum mandarunt:
>
> Ad 1. Recurrendum in singulis casibus.
>
> Ad 2. Ut in Collectanea de Propaganda Fide (II, n. 2170) (June 23, 1903).

[91] *Fontes*, n. 1266.

[92] J. Haring, "Kodex und Älteres Recht," *L. Q. S.*, LXXIX (1926), 829; *Jus Pontificium*, VI (1926), 159-161; De Becker, *Ephemerides Theol. Lovaniensis*, I, (1924) 36 ff.

Quam E. morum Patrium resolutionem S.mus approbare dignatus est.

Et fausta cuncta atque felicia Tibi a Domino apprecor.

A. T. Revmae addictissimus.

R. Card. Merry del Val.

Illmo. et Revmo. D. Archiepiscopo Friburgen.[93]

Yet, as late as 1927, one finds the dean of the Rota vindicating the right of that tribunal to pass upon, examine, and define the matrimonial causes of non-Catholics. The dean of the Rota on the occasion of his allocution which marked the opening of the juridical year for that tribunal turns his attention to the recently decided Marconi-O'Brien case and declares that the Rota had acted in accordance with the principles laid down in Canon 1960 in pronouncing sentence in that much discussed case. He noted that though many non-Catholics do not look upon marriage as a sacrament and leave to the State the adjudication of the causes pertaining to its validity, that does not prevent the ecclesiastical tribunals from accepting the case when the non-Catholic directs a petition to the proper ecclesiastical authorities and thereby recognizes the competence of the Church in such matters. He continues by saying that the Church should not refuse the petition since it tends to ward off spiritual harm or damage which Canon 1654 expressly states to be sufficient reason for admitting the excommunicated. The fact that such action should prove distasteful to the co-religionists of the non-Catholic parties is nothing new, but is to be expected. At no time does he admit that the Rota does not enjoy competence to hear these cases independently of the Holy Office.[94]

Shortly afterwards, comes the official response of the Holy Office of January 27, 1928, which authentically settles the matter and forbids non-Catholics to be admitted in the matrimonial courts as plaintiffs in accordance with the doctrine set forth in Canon 87. In the event that special circumstances seem to demand their admission as plaintiffs, recourse must be made in each individual case to

[93] Vermeersch, *Periodica,* XIV (1925), 166; Vermeersch, "Annotationes," *Periodica,* XVII, XVIII (1928-1929), 54; *Afk. KR.*, CVII (1927), 569-574.

[94] *A. A. S.*, XIX (1927), 354.

the Holy Office for the necessary permission to admit such a procedure. This important response of the Holy Office appears in the *Acta* for 1928 and reads: [95]

Suprema S. C. S. Officii

De Competentia In Causis Matrimonialibus Mixtis

Dubia

Propositis Supremae huic Sacrae Congregatione Sancti Officii sequentibus dubiis:

I. Utrum in causis matrimonialibus *acatholicus*, sive baptizatus sive non baptizatus, *actoris* partes agere potest.

II. Utrum in quibuslibet causis matrimonialibus inter partem catholicam et partem acatholicam, sive baptizatam sive non baptizatam, quocumque modo ad Sanctam Sedem delatis, Suprema Sancta Congregatio Sancti Officii exclusivam competentiam habeat.

Feria Quarta, die 18 januarii, 1928.

E. mi ac Rev.imi D.ni Cardinales rebus fidei et morum tutandis praepositi, praehabito RR. DD. Consultorum voto, respondendum decreverunt:

Ad. I. *Negative*, seu standum Codici I. C., praesertim Can. 87. Siquidem autem speciales occurrant rationes ad admittendos acatholicos ut *actores* in huiusmodi causis, recurrendum ad Supremam Sacram Congregationem Sancti Officii in singulis casibus.

Ad II. *Affirmative*, habita praesertim ratione Can. 247, § 3, salvo prescripto Can. 1557, § 1, n. 1.

Et feria V, die 26 eiusdem mensis et anni Ss.mus D. N. D. Pius divina Providentia Pp. XI in audientia R. P. D. Assessori Sancti Officii impertita, relatam E.morum Patrum resolutionem approbavit, confirmavit et publicari mandavit.

Datum Romae, ex aedibus S. Officii, die 27 Ianuarii, 1928.

ALOISIUS CASTELLANO,
Supremae S. C. Sancti Officii Notarius.

[95] *A. A. S.*, XX (1928), 75.

It is clear that this response of the Holy Office abrogates the former procedure published in 1903, so that Ordinaries may no longer admit the non-Catholic party as a plaintiff in the diocesan courts. This restriction relative to non-Catholic plaintiffs is to apply to all marriage causes; the Holy Office does not seem to contemplate any formal matrimonial process involving the validity of the bond of a non-Catholic marriage as exempt from its response except by a faculty granted by itself. In fact, so anxious is the Holy Office that non-Catholic plaintiffs be excluded from instituting actions in the diocesan matrimonial courts that it is said to be unwilling to grant permissions to accept the petitions dealing with the marriages of non-Catholics in which the plaintiff is a non-Catholic party unless such a one is first converted.[96] This rule of the Holy Office applies to every judicial procedure and is interpreted so strictly as not to admit of any exceptions.

Is this to be interpreted then to mean that there is no way of bringing such cases before the diocesan matrimonial courts save by recurring to the Holy See for the faculty in each one?

Notwithstanding the declaration of 1928, opinion is divided upon this question. There are some canonists who maintain that the prohibition of the Holy Office is absolute and that no non-Catholic matrimonial cause whatever may be introduced into the diocesan courts without an express permission of that Congregation; others are equally insistent that the non-Catholic marriage may be brought to the attention of the diocesan tribunal either as a connected cause or through the intervention of the Promoter of Justice and the tribunal thereby becomes competent to examine the matter. The latter view would restrict the decree of the Holy Office to the non-Catholic acting as plaintiff before the courts and maintains that both the connected cause and the action of the Promoter of Justice are licit and canonical procedures in the expediting of the issue and are not affected by the official response of 1928.

Prescinding from the question as to whether or not the non-Catholic marriage may be considered as a legitimate incidental cause to the determination of the Catholic's freedom to marry, the

96 " . . . Oratrix convertatur et postea iterum recurrat . . . "—S. C. S. Officii, 17 julii, 1928—*L. Q. S.*, LXXXIII (1929), 788.

intervention of the Promoter of Justice in these cases solely will be considered.

The answer is bound up in three authentic replies of the Pontifical Commission on the proper interpretation of Canon 1971. These authentic replies were considered in the preceding article, but may be briefly and profitably recalled here. The first declared that the term "impediment" of Canon 1971, § 1, n. 1 was to be understood to embrace not only the diriment impediments properly so called, but also all those obstacles to a valid marriage which might be called impediments in a broad sense, so that if one was responsible for the invalidity of his marriage on account of either, he should be barred from attacking that marriage.[97] The first declaration was the cause of much disquietude, for, on one hand, in many cases such fault was so manifest that the parties bringing suit or at least the party seeking freedom from the marriage could not be admitted to bring suit, and, on the other hand, if the apparent meaning of Canon 1971, § 1, n. 2 was to be observed, the Promoter of Justice would not be capable of receiving the denunciations of invalidity and entering suits for the parties. The result would be that there would be no means of relieving the plight of these unfortunate Catholics. However, the Pontifical Commission removed this impasse. In virtue of two declarations[98] the Catholic who forfeited his or her right to seek the declaration of nullity is permitted to denounce the invalid union to the Promoter of Justice, and the latter in virtue of Canon 1971, § 2 may enter the suit of nullity even though the impediment is not by its nature public. He, as was seen previously, is not bound to enter the suit in every instance but the exception in which he will not do so is very rare.[99] The Church realizes the plight of the guilty party bound in this invalid union, and, guided by the supreme law of the Church, *Salus animarum suprema lex,* she places at his disposal a possible redress while main-

[97] Pont. Comm. for Interpret., 12 martii, 1929, ad V—*A. A. S.*, XXI (1929), 171.

[98] 17 feb., 1930, ad VI—*A. A. S.*, XXII (1930), 196; 17 julii, 1933, ad IV—*A. A. S.*, XXV (1933), 345.

[99] Roberti, *Apollinaris,* III (1930), 248-250.

taining at the same time the principle enunciated in Canon 1971, § 1, n. 1. She authorizes the Promoter of Justice upon a reliable report of the guilty party to institute the suit for nullity and to act as the plaintiff in his stead.

Those who deny the right of the Promoter of Justice to enter a suit of nullity, when it is a question of a non-Catholic marriage, would restrict this right conferred by the interpretations of the Pontifical Commission to the Catholic parties of an invalid marriage and to Catholic marriages. They contend that the Pontifical Committee had in mind only Catholic marriages and Catholic denunciators. Hence the Catholic cannot legtimately raise the question of invalidity, since he is disbarred by Canon 1971, § 2 from entering the suit, as he is not one of the parties to the invalid marriage, and he may not denounce the invalidity to the Promoter of Justice since his power to file a suit is directly intended for the exclusive benefit of Catholics.[100]

This opinion seems to be based upon the supposition that the Church in authorizing the Promoter of Justice to act in these cases is solicitous for the salvation of her subjects. They are her own children despite the fact that they may have fallen from her grace by contracting an invalid union and so she is willing to help them by empowering the Promoter of Justice to relieve their plight. This is not to be construed to mean that she has no solicitude of non-Catholics or others outside her fold. She entertains the deepest solicitude for their welfare even though they be separated from her, but her primary interest in them is that they be converted and receive the true faith. As long as they refuse to recognize her as the divinely constituted guardian of truth and justice and as the one entrusted with the duty and authority to guide souls in the affairs of salvation, she cannot pass judgment upon their marriage difficulties. It would be interpreted as a form of proselytizing altogether unworthy of her.[101] Nor may one draw a parallel between

[100] Roberti, "Animadversiones," *Apollinaris,* III (1930), 58; Toso, "De accusatione matrimonii," *Jus Pontificium,* XIII (1933), 187, 188; Schaaf, *American Ecclesiastical Review,* XCI (1934), 79, 80.

[101] Schaaf, "Diocesan tribunal lacks competence over marriages between non-Catholics," *American Ecclesiastical Review,* XCI (1934), 79, 80.

the unfaithful Catholic and the non-Catholic plaintiff. Unfaithful though the Catholic may have been in deliberately contracting an invalid marriage, he never fully rejected the Church or her authority. The baptized non-Catholic, on the other hand, denies the divine authority of the Church by refusing submission to her. Even though he be in good faith, he may not exercise his rights acquired in valid baptism because heresy and separation from the communion with the true Church offers an obstacle to their legitimate exercise, an obstacle that can be removed only by conversion.[102] That is why Canon 87 and the decree of the Holy Office for 1928 deprive them of the exercise of their rights. As for the unbaptized, they lack the first essential for the exercise of ecclesiastical jurisdiction. But might it not be argued that the Catholic who is living in civil marriage with the non-Catholic deserves some consideration? Does not his or her position, often a difficult one, warrant an examination by the Church of the non-Catholic's previous marriage so that they may be given an opportunity to return to the practice of his or her faith?

The case of such a person is, indeed, pitiful but the party has only himself or herself to blame for such a situation. There are causes in which the Church claims and exercises jurisdiction over matters pertaining to non-Catholics. Marriage cases, however, in which she does exercise her jurisdiction are always those in which she exercises her power directly and immediately upon the Catholic party and upon the non-Catholic party only indirectly and on account of the relation to the Catholic. But in the case under discussion it is not the case of the Catholic which is to be immediately and directly examined, but one in which the non-Catholics alone are concerned and in which the Catholic has no direct interest. It is, therefore, fitting that the Church should not permit the question of the validity of a marriage between two non-Catholics to be brought before her courts as an ordinary procedure, not even when the case might open the way for a Catholic to contract a valid marriage with

[102] Roberti, *Consultationes Juris Canonici,* I, 253; *Periodica,* XVI (1927), 141, footnote 1.

a non-Catholic or to convalidate the marriage with one of the non-Catholics involved in the cause.[103]

Nor may it be objected that the non-Catholic, by having the Catholic party denounce his first invalid marriage to the Promoter of Justice, thereby, recognizes the competence of the Church to authoritatively settle the question of his former marriage, since it is to be justly feared that his action is dictated by expediency and that he will ignore the decision of the court and refuse its verdict in the event of an unfavorable decision.[104]

In view of these truths, the first opinion contends that the Holy Office in its solution of a doubt under the date of January 27, 1928 proscribes entirely the introduction of a formal cause treating the invalidity of a non-Catholic marriage. The question may not be raised by the non-Catholic since the Holy Office denies him a standing in court by the present decree. The Catholic cannot raise the question, as he is debarred by Canon 1971, § 2 from entering the suit since he is not a party to the disputed marriage which is to form the object of the judicial examination. At most, he could denounce the invalidity to the Promoter of Justice, but according to this first opinion he is also interdicted from bringing the suit, notwithstanding the declarations of the Pontifical Committee clarifying his powers in this regard. His authority is restricted by the proponents of this first view to Catholic marriages and Catholic denunciators of the same.

Practically all the authors who treat the authentic interpretations of the rights and duties of the Promoter of Justice to receive denunciations and institute proceedings seem to limit their discussion of the matter to Catholic marriages denounced by a Catholic party to them. This in itself does not prove that they exclude the non-Catholics, but it may be legitimately interpreted, and is thus taken by the exponents of the first view, to mean that that official does not receive the denunciations from anyone relative to invalid marriages contracted by two non-Catholics.

[103] Woywod, *The Homiletic and Pastoral Review,* 33 (1933), 1282, 1283. 1283.

[104] Vermeersch, "Annotationes," *Periodica,* XVII-XVIII (1928, 1929), 55.

Some canonists expressly exclude these causes from the competence of the Promoter of Justice in virtue of the response of the Holy Office for 1928. A. Toso,[105] writing in the *Jus Pontificium,* expressly excludes them as does Roberti in a similar article in the *Apollinaris.*[106] Both assert that the opposite view is no longer tenable in view of the cited response of the Holy Office. Relative to Roberti, however, it should be remarked that this opinion referred to here is in direct contradiction to an earlier and equally emphatic opinion given by him in connection with his commentary on the decision of 1928, in which he deemed it permissible for the non-Catholic to denounce his invalid marriage to the Promoter of Justice, who, in turn, could *ex officio* act as plaintiff in the proceedings for the declaration of nullity.[107] Nor does he give any reason for his change of opinion since he passes over the first opinion without any reference to it, contenting himself with the simple statement that it need hardly be remarked that the Promoter is incompetent in the matter. Vermeersch in his remarks upon the decree of 1928 implies that the action of the Promoter of Justice is to be excluded in these cases, since he unites the decree of 1928 with an earlier reply of the same congregation to the Archbishop of Freiburg in 1925, in which the action of the Promoter of Justice is expressly interdicted and recourse to the Holy Office commanded in every instance.[108] He quotes the same private response to the Archbishop of Freiburg against the dean of the Rota who had defended the right of that tribunal to define the cases of non-Catholics by appealing to Canons 1960 and 1654. Fr. Vermeersch calls the attention of the dean to the fact that Canon 1654 applies to excommunicated persons and not to those who are members of an heretical sect and that in the latter cases the Holy Office alone is competent, to which congregation recourse must be made in every instance for competence. He uses the private rescript of 1925 to the Arch-

[105] A. Toso, "De accusatione matrimonii, *Jus Pontificium,* XIII (1933), 187, 188.

[106] Roberti, "Animadversiones," *Apollinaris,* III (1930), 58.

[107] Roberti, "Animadversiones," *Apollinaris,* I (1928), 217.

[108] Vermeersch, "Annotationes," *Peridodica,* XVII, XVIII (1928, 1929), 54, 55.

bishop of Freiburg to vindicate his interpretation of Canon 1654 and the necessity of recourse in individual cases.[109] Creusen, likewise, in his commentary on the declaration of 1928 seems to deny the right of the non-Catholic party to take action in any way before the diocesan courts other than in virtue of a faculty granted by the Holy Office itself. He, too, cites the rescript to the Archbishop of Freiburg in support of his view that there is no other alternative for the non-Catholic party despite the presence of special circumstances which would seem to militate for a more considerate and immediate treatment of the case.[110]

A recent writer in *The Ecclesiastical Review* expressly treating this subject grants that the arguments drawn from authority and the fitness of things are not in themselves cogent enough to destroy the probability of the opposite opinion which permits the Promoter of Justice to act in these cases. He says that the final settlement of the question must come from the Holy See. He appeals to the authority of two papal documents which, he claims, definitely settles the question.[111] The two documents to which he appeals are the two rescripts addressed to the Bishop of Berlin. The rescripts are the following: [112]

Suprema Sacra Congregatio
Sancti Officii
Num. de Protoc. 2824/31

ex aedibus S.Officii
die 30 Novembris, 1931.

Excellentia Revma.

Die 6 Septembris nuper elapsi Excellentia Tua Revma. a S. Officio petebat utrum recepta denunciatione nullitatis matrimonii acatholicis celebrati, a catholico facta qui cum parte acatholica illegitime convivit, Ordinarius vel Promotor Justitiae actionem instituere possit, ita ut tribunal ordinarium jam causam, servatis prescriptionibus juris,

109 Vermeersch, *Periodica,* XVII, XVIII (1928, 1929), 55, 56.

110 Creusen, *Nouvelle Revue Theologique,* 55 (1928), 450.

111 Schaaf, *American Ecclesiastical Review,* XCI (1934), 81 ff.

112 *Amtsblatt des Bischoflichen Ordinariats Berlin* (1932), p. 3, (1931), p. 124; reprinted in *Archiv. fur Katholisches Kirchenrecht,* CXII (1932), 154, 155; *Apollinaris,* VII (1934), 279, 280.

cognoscere et definire valeat. Cui petitioni haec Suprema Sacra Congregatio respondendum mandavit:

Recurrendum in singulis casibus.

Maximan meam observantiam Tibi obtestor.

ac permaneo,

Excellentiae Tuae Revmae

Addictissimus

D Card. Sbarreti

Episcopus Sabinensis et Mandebosis

Secretarius.

Exc. mo et Remvo Domino
Dno. Christiano Schreiber
Episcopo Berolinen.

Sacra Congregatio
De Sacramentis
5002/31

Relatis in hac S. Congregatione litteris Ordinario Berolinensis quibus postulat utrum praehabita denuntiatione nullitatis matrimonii juxta Can. 1971, parag 2, Promoter justitiae vel Ordinarius jus habeant actionem instituendi et an tribunal ordinarium in causa indigeat venia S. Sedis ad causam instruendam eodem S. C., attentis expositis, in Congressu diei 30 Octobris, 1931, rescribendum censuit; Rmus Ordinarius in excipienda denuntiatione nullitatis matrimonii et in causa introducenda, se gerat ad normam decisionis Commissionis Pontificae datae sub die 17 Februarii, 1930, absque venia S. Sedis, nisi agatur de causis S. Officio reservatis juxta decretum ejusdem S. Officii diei 27 Januarii, 1928.

Datum Romae, die 3 Novembris, 1931.

M. Card. Lega
Eppus Tusculan. Praef.
D. Jorio, Secr.

Ill. mo ac R. mo
Ordinario Berolinensi.

The argument built upon the rescripts may be summarized as follows: The first rescript emanated from the Holy Office. The case which it contemplates is identical with the one under consideration; the Catholic is already living with the non-Catholic and, as the phrase implies, in civil marriage; the marriage cannot be rectified until the question of the non-Catholic's prevous marriage has been cleared up. Despite a denunciation to the Ordinary or the Promoter of Justice of the nullity of the non-Catholic's previous marriage, the Holy Office denies the right of the Promoter of Justice to enter the case and institute proceedings and requires that each case be referred to itself.

The rescript of the Congregation of the Sacraments supplements that of the Holy Office. The question is not so explicit as that in the rescript of the Holy Office. Nevertheless, the answer has the same effect, for there is no prohibition against introducing causes regarding the validity of a marriage except that of the declaration of the Holy Office of January 27, 1928. The Congregation of the Sacraments grasped the import of the query and excluded all cases which come under the terms of that decree of the Holy Office from those which the Promoter of Justice could introduce into the matrimonial courts of the diocese without the permission of the Holy Office.

Since both rescripts are general in their import, as is evidenced by the generic terms used in them, they should be considered to enjoy general force. There is nothing in them to indicate that they were intended for particular causes nor do they suggest that they were issued in view of some peculiar conditions existing in the diocese of Berlin. While they cannot be considered as being *per modum legis exhibitae,* they can be employed to settle the question since they indicate the *praxis curiae* which, in the absence of positive law, will be considered as binding in virtue of Canon 20. These two rescripts are in perfect conformity with the rule laid down in the decree of the Holy Office for 1928. Both rescripts recognize the fact that the Holy Office has reserved all causes involving the invalidity of non-Catholic marriages to itself and that the Promoter of Justice is excluded from instituting the procedure in these cases without the permission of the Holy Office. Hence, one has here a *praxis curiae* which makes it uncanonical for the Promoter of Justice to introduce a cause which involves the nullity of a marriage between two non-Catholics even after the denunciation of the marriage of the non-

Catholic party, as long as the interested party remains a non-Catholic.[113]

Those authors, on the other hand, who defend the opposite view maintain that the Catholic party in virtue of the responses of the Pontifical Committee may denounce the invalid marriage of the non-Catholic party to the Promoter of Justice.[114] They do not limit the action of the Promoter of Justice to Catholic parties nor do they find any objection in the decree of 1928 to the practice of denouncing the invalid non-Catholic marriage to the Promoter of Justice, thereby empowering him to attack it as the plaintiff in the cause. They would limit the ruling of the Holy Office to the prohibition of acting as plaintiff in a formal process and since in circumstances described by them, it is the Promoter of Justice who acts as the plaintiff, there can be no objection on that score.

Dr. Haring describes a case that is identical with the one under discussion; the non-Catholic girl has already contracted an invalid marriage with a Catholic and now wishes to contract marriage with another Catholic. He unqualifiedly asserts that though the Protestant girl may not attack the marriage in the rôle of plaintiff, she may denounce the marriage to the Promoter of Justice, who in virtue of Canon 1971, § 2 may accept the case and prosecute the plea of nullity without any recourse to the Holy Office whatsoever.[115] The editor of *Il Monitore Ecclesiastico* describes a similar situation in which the Catholic is desirous of marrying a non-Catholic already bound in a previous non-Catholic marriage and the solution is identical.[116]

The writer in the *Jus Pontificium* asserts that the response of the Pontifical Commission for March 12, 1929, forbidding the exercise of the right of pleading to the party who is responsible for the

[113] Schaaf, *American Ecclesiastical Review,* XCI (1934), 83, 84.

[114] "De jure accusandi matrimonium," *Jus Pontificium,* 9 (1929), 108; *Jus Pontificium,* 8 (1928), 234: Haring, "Wer ist Akatholisch in Sinne des Kanonischen Rechtes," *L. Q. S.,* LXXXIV (1931), 790, 791; Ayrinhac-Lydon, *Marriage Legislation,* pp. 357, 358; *Il Monitore Ecclesiastico,* Annotazioni, Series 4, T. 10 (1928), 67.

[115] Haring, *L. Q. S.,* LXXXIV (1931), 790, 791.

[116] "Annotazione," *Il Monitore Ecclesiastico,* Series 4, T. 10 (1928), 67.

impediment even in a wide sense, is connected with the previous response of the Holy Office denying the right of the non-Catholic party to act as plaintiff in formal matrimonial processes. Nevertheless, he maintains that the non-Catholic party himself or the Catholic party desiring to enter marriage with the non-Catholic already bound in a previous non-Catholic marriage may denounce the invalidity to the Promoter of Justice who, in turn, may accept the denunciation and act as plaintiff in the formal trial, should the grounds for invalidity warrant such *ex officio* action on his part.[117]

Hence, it is evident that these writers restrict the prohibition of the Holy Office to the actual acting as plaintiff in the matrimonial trial. Since the law contains a restriction on the rights of individuals, it is to be interpreted in its strictest sense, and all that the Holy Office mentions in its response is the action as plaintiff in a formal process.[118]

Nor may the rescripts addressed to the Bishop of Berlin, the one of the Holy Office, and the other of the Congregation of the Sacraments, be objected to this view, for even granting that they do treat an abstract case or class of cases, they remain private rescripts and as such oblige only those for whom they were given.[119] When rescripts are addressed to particular persons, as these two are, both being addressed to the Bishop of Berlin, it may be well suspected that they were given by the official interpreter in view of particular conditions omitted in the rescript but perhaps explained in the petition.[120] This is forcibly brought home when one considers that the rescript to the Archbishop of Freiburg was published at a time when both the parties and the Promoter of Justice were still permitted to introduce the cause of nullity of non-Catholic marriages. It was not until three years later that the faculty was withdrawn by the Holy Office, since one finds the Rota a year later de-

117 *Jus Pontificium,* 9 (1929), 108; *Jus Pontificium,* 8 (1928), 234.

118 Canon 19; S. C. S. Officii, 18 januarii, 1928, ad I—*A. A. S.*, XX (1928). 17.

119 Canon 17, § 3.

120 Michiels, *Normae Generales,* I, 388, 389; Van Hove, *De Legibus Eccl.,* 255.

ciding the Marconi-O'Brien cases in which both the principals were non-Catholics. Might not one logically infer from this that the petition to the Holy Office contained an exposition of facts which made it advisable for the Holy Office to exclude not only the parties but also the Promoter of Justice from accusing the non-Catholic marriage and to demand a recourse to itself in every instance? The rescript to the Archbishop in this matter is identical with the later one to the Bishop of Berlin on the same subject; it mentions no particular local conditions and uses generic terms, and yet the Holy Office advises at a time when every non-Catholic had the right to denounce his marriage [121] that the Archbishop of Freiburg should have recourse to Rome in every instance. The only possible conclusion is that Protestanism in the Archdiocese of Freiburg presented a special problem which made it advisable for the Holy Office in that particular region to withdraw the faculty already recognized by itself in its rescript of 1903, which permitted both the party and the Promoter to attack the marriage before the diocesan courts. Hence the fact that the rescripts are silent on particular conditions and that they employ generic language does not prove that they were not given in view of particular local conditions prevailing in Germany, which made it inadvisable to permit the Promoter of Justice to attack the validity of non-Catholic marriages before the diocesan tribunals of Berlin without first obtaining the permission of the Holy Office in each case.

Furthermore, the two above mentioned rescripts were never published in the *Acta Apostolicae Sedis*. Both were published in the local diocesan papers from which they found their way into the unofficial canonical reviews of the day. Hence they may not be said to have been published or exhibited *per modum legis*, a condition required by the law itself even though the interpretation is only declaratory.[122] Both were published by private authority and in

[121] Hilling, "Die Entscheidung des Hl Offizums Vom 18 januarii, 1928, über seine Kompetenz in Ehesacher," *Afk. KR.* CVIII (1928), 537-549; *Jus Pontificium,* "Consultationes," VI (1926), 159-161; J. Haring, "Kodex und Älteres Recht," *L. Q. S.*, LXXIX (1926), 829.

[122] Canon 17, § 2.

private organs of the press, and such publication of the acts of the Holy See is not considered *per modum legis exhibitae.* They indeed offer to others a safe norm of acting, but are not to be considered even as much as an invitation on the part of the Holy See to conform to the rule laid down in the response of the individual congregation. The fact that the Congregation has not seen fit to publish its response in the *Acta* seems in itself to be an indication that the Holy See did not wish to settle the issue definitively.[123]

The particular declarations which the Sacred Congregation give in doubtful matters or decisions which they pronounce in administrative affairs bind only the parties for whom they were given, even though their import be general in character.[124] The two rescripts under consideration are particular in their inscriptions and in their method of publication, and, although they deal with an abstract principle of law, they bind only those for whom they were given.[125]

Relative to the argument that these two rescripts, when joined to the response of the Holy Office for 1928 constitute a *praxis curiae,* and, as such, in the absence of positive law in the matter supplement the law and make the exclusion of the Promoter of Justice from these cases obligatory, it seems to be based upon an unwarranted assumption as to what constitutes the *praxis curiae* described in Canon 20 of the Code. Even though one were to grant that the rescripts were supplementary in their nature and not corrective of Canon 1971 and the subsequent responses of the Pontifical Committee on that canon, as they might well seem to be, there would still be room for doubt that they constitute a *praxis curiae,* binding on others outside the Diocese of Berlin. One might well hesitate to consider the two particular private rescripts, both privately published, as a positive, obligatory indication of the *praxis* of the Roman Curia in a matter as common and as universal as the one under consideration. One might well point to them as a norm of safe act-

[123] Canon 17, § 2; Vermeersch, "De Vi rescriptorum S.S. Congregationum," *Periodica,* IX (1921), p. 3; Michiels, *Normae Generales,* I, 398, 399; A. Brems, *Jus Pontificium,* May, 1935, p. 190; Van Hove, *De Legibus Eccl.,* pp. 333, 334.

[124] Van Hove, *De Legibus Eccl.,* p. 334.

[125] Vermeersch, *Periodica,* IX (1921), p. 3; A. Brems, *Jus Pontificium,* May, 1935, p. 190; Van Hove, *De Legibus Eccl.,* p. 334.

ing but to give them the force of law on the assumption that they constitute the *praxis curiae* is somewhat of an exaggeration, an exaggeration which Van Hove points out was quite common under the pre-Code legislation.[126]

The authors have not as yet established an exact, determined standard by which one may determine when a practical settlement of a case has become the *praxis curiae*. Opinion is widely divided upon the exact requisites which must be present before one can consider that the practical solution of a given case constitutes a *praxis curiae* binding upon all inferior ecclesiastical tribunals in the absence of positive legislation.

By far and away the more common and probable opinion demands that before the *praxis* should be considered binding, these decisions of the Roman Curiae should be sufficiently numerous and of such a nature that they indicate a constant practice on the part of the Roman Congregations or, at least, a fixed attitude of the same Congregations relative to the proper manner of expediting an issue. This opinion, in fine, requires a *jus consuetudinarium* in the solution of a case which should closely approximate the conditions laid down in the Code for the valid introduction of an obligation by custom.[127] Canon 20 clearly indicates that particular decisions do not constitute such a *praxis* and that the words of the canon taken in their obvious sense are to be understood of a constant mode of acting in the same case and hence a custom. Neither the element of time nor the element of *frequenter repetitae decisiones similes* in the same matter demanded by the authors who hold this opinion can be verified in the present question.

There is, however, a more recent opinion sponsored by Michiels which does not require that the *praxis* conform to the rules laid down for custom in order to induce a valid obligation. Quoting

[126] Van Hove, *De Legibus Eccl.*, p. 334.

[127] Vermeersch-Creusen, *Epitome*, I, n. 99, 91, and n. 109, 98; Maroto, *Inst. J. C.*, I, n. 343, 414, 415 and n. 367, 433; De Meester, *Inst. J. C.*, I, nn. 277, 281, p. 197; Wernz, *Jus Decretalium*, I, n. 187, 281 ff and n. 146, 178; Ojetti, *Commentarium* I, 153; Van Hove, *De Legibus Eccl.*, p. 336; Toso, *Commentaria Minora*, p. 56.

D'Angelo in his support, he says that in his opinion one or other rescript of the Holy See is sufficient to indicate a *praxis curiae* binding upon the lower tribunals.[128] In the absence of positive law, such a rescript or two rescripts would constitute a jurisprudence which the lower tribunals would not be free to set aside. It is interesting to note that he prefaces his opinions with the terms *credimus et opinamur,* confessions that his own opinion is by no means certain in view of the weight of authority in favor of the above opinion.

He does, however, insist that the rescript be *authentice proposita* in order to exercise this binding force on the lower tribunals. Can one say that the two rescripts in question fulfill the requirement of *authentice proposita* found in the milder opinion? Authors who treat the subject always require that the rescripts at least be published in the official commentary of the Holy See before they can be considered as authentically published or proposed and, therefore, even as inviting others to conform to the norm laid down in the response settling an issue or a doubt.[129] Van Hove understands by the term authentically published, as used in Michiels, publication in the *Acta Apostolicae Sedis.*[130]

The Sacred Congregation of Rites in a reply to a query stated that the various decrees and rescripts sent out by the Prefects of the various Congregations are authentic if they are *proprie seu formiter editae.*[131] This *formiter edita* of the response gave rise to further doubts and the question as to its meaning was settled in a later response, which stated that the *formiter edita* of the first response simply meant that the rescript would be considered authentic if it was included in the official collection of the Congregation of Rites.[132]

Moreover in the Papal Constitution *Promulgandi,* 4 Sept., 1908, the Holy Father decreed the following: [133]

[128] Michiels, *Normae Generales,* I, 475, 476; S. D'Angelo, *De Conceptu Aequitatis,* p. 29.

[129] Vermeersch, *Periodica,* IX (1921), 2, 3; Van Hove, *De Legibus Eccl.,* p. 336; A. Brems, *Jus Pontificium,* May, 1935, pp. 186-190.

[130] Van Hove, *De Legibus Eccl.,* p. 334, n. 1.

[131] S. R. C. decr. auth., n. 2916.

[132] S. C. R. decr. auth., n. 3023.

[133] *A. A. S.,* I (1909), 6.

> Edicimus ut . . . Commentarium officiale de Apostolicae Sedis actis edatur Vaticanis typis. Volumus autem Constitutiones pontificias leges, decreta, aliaque tum Romanorum Pontificium, tum Sacrarum Congregationum et Officiorum scita, in eo commentario de mandato Prelati a secretis . . . inserta et in vulgo edita, hac una eaque unica ratione legitime promulgata habere, quotiens promulgatione sit opus, nec aliter fuerit a S. Sede provisum. Volumus praeterea in idem commentarium cetera S. Sedis acta referri quae ad communem cognitionem videantur utilia, quantum ipsorum natura certe sinat . . .

Thus it seems that the Holy See understands by "authentically proposed" that the rescript appear in the official commentary or in the official *collectanea* of a Congregation. Vermeersch's conclusion that responses which do not appear in the *Acta* cannot enjoy force of law seems to be justified. He says that the Congregation by its action seems unwilling to settle definitely a doubt.[134]

Should one then attribute to two particular rescripts addressed to the same bishop and published by him in a diocesan newspaper the force of law by considering them *authentice proposita?* Hardly, and until such time as the Holy See sees fit to indicate the *praxis* of the Roman Curia by publishing an authentic general rescript on the subject in the *Acta Apostolicae Sedis,* one may not conclude that the *praxis* of the Holy See in handling these matters is the same in all cases referred to it and that the general and constant attitude of the Holy See is to deny competence to the Promoter of Justice in the expediting of non-Catholic matrimonial causes. Such indeed may be the practice of the Holy See, and the defection of Roberti from his former opinion without any explanation would seem to indicate it. But until such time as the Roman Congregations in an official manner indicate that the practice of the Holy See is to reserve all formal trials dealing with the invalidity of non-Catholic marriages to itself, and thereby forbids the practice of employing the Promoter of Justice to institute the proceedings in these causes of nullity, one can at best say that the two rescripts to the Bishop of Berlin indicate a safe norm of acting, a conclusion for which there is no need

[134] Vermeersch, *Periodica,* IX (1921), 3.

of any rescript. One certainly has here a *dubium juris* which it is not within the power of any private, particular rescript to solve, and until such time as the practice is expressly interdicted by the Holy See in one of its official organs, the Promoter of Justice may introduce the causes of nullity in formal trials of non-Catholic marriages and the procedure may not be considered uncanonical. The *dubium juris* still persists and the diocesan curia is within its rights, if it wishes to take advantage of the *dubium* and continue the practice of introducing the cause of nullity in non-Catholic marriages through the official action of the Promoter of Justice. The final settlement of the question has yet to come from the Holy See and the final solution still rests with its Congregations.

Article IV. The Promoter of Justice and the Causes for Separation

The Catholic Church in her legislation expressly declares that married people are bound to live together unless they have a just cause for separation.[135] This conjugal cohabitation implies a community of dwelling place, of board, of bed or bed-chamber, at least habitually and as far as circumstances permit. This obligation flows from the secondary end of marriage, since the mutual help and the mutual rights and duties which the marriage state has conferred on husband and wife require a mutual common life for their fulfillment.[136]

This cohabitation, however, is not so essential that the bond of marriage cannot exist without it or that separation may never become legitimate. The cohabitation pertains to the integrity of marriage and not to its essense and therefore can be suspended or ended entirely for a just or weighty cause.[137] Serious reasons will be required because separation is not the normal condition of married life and may lead to serious disorders in the moral and public order.

[135] Canon 1128.

[136] Cappello, *De Sacramentis,* III, 929.

[137] Gasparri, *De Matrimonio* (1932), I, 15, 16; II, 243; Cappello, *De Sacramentis,* III, n. 823, 929.

The Council of Trent declared against Protestant teaching that temporary or permanent separation was permitted for a just cause.[138] The cause, however, must be a serious one which the ecclesiastical judge would recognize as canonical and would justify him in pronouncing a sentence of separation.[139] This also obtains when the Catholic has married a non-Catholic with a proper dispensation and the latter gives cause for separation.

The Church recognizes only one cause which would permit the parties to separate of their own authority independently of any authority invested in the bishop or the diocesan curia and that is adultery committed by one of the parties and not condoned or compensated by the other party. This sin of adultery must fulfill all the conditions laid down in the law itself before it may be considered just grounds for separation.[140] If the crime of adultery fulfills all the conditions laid down in the law and is both certain and notorious, the innocent party can discontinue the cohabitation of his or her own authority. This right of separation is granted by the law itself and since the adultery is both certain and notorious, the sentence of an ecclesiatstical judge is superfluous.[141] If, however, the fact of adultery is certain but occult or cannot be sufficiently proved, the innocent party in his or her conscience is free to leave the guilty party but because of the dangers to which both parties may be exposed, were private separation to be permitted upon such uncertain grounds, the ecclesiastical judge should compel the innocent party to resume cohabitation in the event that the dismissed party should enter an action *de spolio* to force the innocent party to take him or her back.[142]

The Code enumerates other causes for separation besides adultery, such causes, for example, as the other party joins a non-Catholic sect; or gives the children to be educated in a non-Catholic religion; or leads a criminal life; or gravely endangers the bodily or

[138] Sess. XXIV, can. 8, de sacr. matri.

[139] Augustine, *A Commentary,* V, 370.

[140] Canon 1129.

[141] Canon 1130.

[142] Gasparri, *De Matrimonio* (1932), II, 246.

spiritual welfare of the other spouse; or renders the marital life intolerable by acts of cruelty.[143]

Whenever such a cause is proved by facts and witnesses, the innocent party may freely depart and invoke the assistance of the ecclesiastical courts. However, paragraph 2 of the same canon states that when the reasons which prompted the separation cease, the marital relations must be resumed. Only after the ecclesiastical court has rendered a decision in favor of the separation either for a limited time or indefinitely is the innocent party free from the duty of cohabitation. If the Ordinary should command a resumption of cohabitation, or if the decree of separation was given for a limited time only, the married life must be resumed. It is therefore always safer to invoke the authority of the Ordinary in these cases, and since the Church vindicates to herself exclusive competence in causes of separation *a mensa et a toro* of the baptized, pastors and confessors who advise this relief as a last resort should direct the parties to propose a petition to the Ordinary or the ecclsiastical judge.[144] The Third Plenary Council of Baltimore forbids recourse to the civil courts without consulting the Ordinary. This recourse will often be necessary in order to obtain a judgment relative to the civil effects of matrimony such as alimony, legitimate support, etc.[145]

The cause of separation may be examined and defined either according to the rules of the ordinary judicial process or administratively.[146] The latter is more conformable to the nature of the cause and the authentic response of the Pontifical Committee implies that the administrative and not the judicial procedure will be the normal procedure in these cases.[147]

The judicial forms of the ordinary process should be observed as often as it is requested by the parties, or is required by the mandate of the bishop either as a general practice, or because of the difficult

[143] Canon 1131.

[144] Canon 1960; Noldin, *De Sacramentis*, III, 774; Cappello, *De Sacramentis*, III, 940.

[145] *Concilii Plenarii III Baltimorensis Acta et Decreta*, nn. 126, 127.

[146] Pont. Comm. for Interpret., 25 junii, 1932, ad I—*A. A. S.*, XXIV (1932), 284.

[147] Cappello, *De Sacramentis*, III, n. 831, 938.

nature of the case before him, or wherever there exists an agreement between the civil authorities and the eccesiastical authorities as to the proper regulation of these causes in order to safeguard the civil effects of the same. The parties are always free to prosecute their rights in any matter by invoking the ministry of the ecclesiastical judge, for every right is guaranteed and protected by a corresponding action in the ecclesiastical courts, unless it is expressly stated to the contrary.[148] Consequently, the judge made not deny the services of the court as often as either or both the parties or only one request it in a suit for separation.[149] The judicial procedure will also be observed as often as the Ordinary adjudges from the circumstances of the persons and the matters involved that the cause cannot be properly handled in an administrative manner, or, as often as there has been an agreement between the civil authorities and the Holy See requiring a judicial sentence as a necessary condition for obtaining the civil effects of separation.[150]

Now in all cases in which the validity of the bond forms the object of judicial procedure or as often as there is an administrative procedure dealing with the dissolution of an already existing valid marriage bond, the law requires that the defender of the bond be present to protect the sanctity of the marriage bond.[151] No such provision is made by the law for the protection of the unity of conjugal life against the evils of unwarranted and selfish separations. The defender of the bond is appointed solely for intervention in those cases which involve the validity of the marriage bond; the remaining issues pertaining to the defense of the public good are entrusted to the Promoter of Justice.[152] As a consequence, it is not surprising that the recent trend in canonical jurisprudence to extend and amplify the duties of the Promoter of Justice has introduced a practice whereby the Promoter is brought into these causes as a protective measure against unjustifiable separations.

148 Canon 1687.

149 Canon 1960.

150 Cappello, *De Sacramentis*, III, 939.

151 Canon 1586; Regulae Servandae . . . a. 1923 a S. C. de discipl. Sacr. propositae, n. 27—*A. A. S.*, XV (1923), 396.

152 Canon 1586; Roberti, *De Processibus*, I, 196-198.

One readily sees the reason for this practice when he considers that the Promoter of Justice has been appointed to defend the interests of the common good, as often as there is a possibility that the actions taken by the faithful may be of such a nature as to jeopardize or impair the common good. Surely, if his office demands that he protect the public good in those causes in which the public good is involved only as a possibility, how much more should this be true in those causes in which the danger to the public good is a reality and a certainty? If the Promoter has the right to intervene and demand a separation in those cases in which the public nullity of the marriage interdicts the right of the parties to cohabitation, has he not the same right and duty to oppose the separation when the law of cohabitation is being flouted and transgressed for frivolous reasons and in many instances without any reasonable cause whatsoever?

When one considers, on one hand, the manifold benefits that accrue to the civil and ecclesiastical societies from a righteous observance of the law of cohabitation and, on the other hand, the many evils which derive to the same societies from the non-observance of the same law, he cannot but conclude that the law flows from the very essence of the public order and forms, as it were, one of the cornerstones upon which the ecclesiastical moral order is raised. The non-observance of the law of cohabitation is fraught with moral dangers not only to the parties themselves, but also with danger of scandals to the ecclesiastical society at large occasioned by the subsequent conduct of the separated parties.[153] René Le Picard in a recent work gives a full presentation of this argument that cohabitation is an obligation flowing from the public order and as a practical conclusion he maintains that these causes require the presence of the Promoter of Justice, the natural representative of the public order in the diocesan curia.[154] A similar conclusion is to be found in Muniz's practical commentary on the Fourth Book and

[153] Cappello, *De Sacramentis,* III, 940.

[154] Picard, *La Communauté De La Vie Conjugale* (1930), cap. III, par. 7, 42-67.

he bases the reason for the Promoter's intervention in these causes upon identical grounds.[155]

Cardinal Lega, then Dean of the Roma Rota, in his redaction of a decision on a cause of separation tried before his tribunal, gives a summary of the jurisprudence evolved by the Roman Pontiffs, the Holy Office and the Congregation of the Council on the duty of the marital cohabitation which clearly established it as an obligation flowing from the public order.[156] The Cardinal in his capacity as presiding judge for the hearing of the case cited the Promoter of Justice to be present at the proceedings to defend the duty of cohabitation.[157]

Still later in 1925 one finds that in the list of the causes examined by the Rota the cause *Alexandrina Armenorum* which had for its object a separation a *mensa et a toro*. It will be noted in the report of the decision that the Promoter of Justice of the Rota was expressly cited to be present at the examination of the cause.[158]

Consequently when the new norms of the Rota were published in 1934, one is not surprised to find the causes for separation listed among the cases which pertain to the office of the Promoter of Justice and require his presence.[159] The causes of separation are listed among those causes in which the exigencies of the public good demand that the trial judge cite the Promoter, and the latter is reminded that he has a duty in virtue of his office to intervene in these causes even though he is not cited, and, that should he intervene, the judge is to consider the intervention as necessary.[160]

Thus, while the practice of our ordinary diocesan tribunals does not require the presence of the Promoter of Justice in the settlement of the causes for separation and there is no express requirement of the sort in the general positive law of the Church, there is a growing tendency in the canonical jurisprudence to interject his presence into

[155] Muniz, *Procedimientos Eccl.*, II, n. 523, 650, 651.

[156] *S. R. Rotae Decisiones seu Sententiae*, II (1910), dec. XXIV, 238-247.

[157] Picard, *La Communauté De La Vie Conjugale*, p. 224.

[158] *A. A. S.*, XVIII (1926), 97.

[159] *Normae S. R. R. Tribunalis*, art. 27—*A. A. S.*, XXVI (1934), 457.

[160] *Normae S. R. R. Tribunalis*, art. 27, pars. 1, 2—*A. A. S.*, XXVI (1934), 457.

these proceedings involving separation. This tendency is in perfect harmony with the nature of the cause and the nature of the office of the Promoter of Justice and might well be introduced into the Church as a universal practice in a time like the present when our Catholic people are being infected with the pernicious philosophies of modern sociologists and are being influenced by the alarming growth in the laxity of civil laws on marriage and divorce. This duty of the Promoter may, as others which he exercises in contentious cases, grow out of the struggle which the Church will necessarily have to make in the defense of the serious obligation of conjugal unity and indissolubility of the marriage life. Practically every duty which the Promoter exercises in contentious cases is a recent development of canonical jurisprudence and the present one noted in the prevailing canonical jurisprudence may in the near future become one of legal obligation for him.

CHAPTER VII

THE PROMOTER OF JUSTICE IN OTHER CONTENTIOUS PROCEEDINGS

ARTICLE I. THE PROMOTER OF JUSTICE AND MORAL PERSONS

THE canonical personality or the capacity to acquire and exercise rights in the Church, which by divine ordinance accompanies the individual human nature and the reception of baptism, may also be conferred by public ecclesiastical authority upon corporate bodies and institutions which thus obtain many prerogatives normally reserved to individual rational beings. The law calls such persons moral or juridical persons as distinct from physical and individual persons.[1]

As often as collegiate or non-collegiate bodies enjoy the status of moral persons they are favored in ecclesiastical law. The common law assimilates them to minors and extends to them the same protection as it does to persons under age, because, no doubt, the interests of these institutions are liable to be neglected or misadministered by their administrators, and, even in the case of moral collegiate persons what concerns the body does not usually receive the same consideration and attention as that which touches the individuals directly.[2] In view of this favor of the law, which in itself is a direct consequence of the fact that all these persons directly or indirectly contribute to the common good, all authors without exception teach that, not only the procurator whom the law provides, but also the Promoter of Justice has the duty to see to it that no harm or injury befalls such persons, either as a result of the negligence, or inability

[1] Canon 99; Cavagnis, *Institutiones Juris Publici Eccl.*, 2a, n. 344; The Code calls these persons by various names, *i. e., persona moralis, persona juridicum, ens juridicum.* For further information on ecclesiastical moral persons confer, Gillet, *La Personalité Juridique en droit Ecclesiastique,* 232, 233; Cavagnis, o. c., 2a, nn. 344, ss; Wernz-Vidal, *Jus Canonicum,* II, 26 ss.; Maroto, *Inst. J. C.,* I, nn. 458 ss.

[2] Canons 100, § 3; 1687, § 1; 1688, § 2; Ayrinhac, *General Legislation,* 216.

of their legal representatives, or of the deception and fraud practiced by third parties. Consequently, as often as the rights of moral persons have been usurped or impaired in any way, he will be present in the civil process to demand such reparation as is possible in the case, to assist the judge by advice and suggestion in the settlement of all problems occasioned by the contentious proceedings to which the moral person is a party. The authors unanimously include the forensic defense of the rights of moral persons and their vindication among the duties which the Promoter of Justice must exercise in the pursuance of his office.[3]

The jurisprudence of the Roman Tribunals teaches a similar duty to be incumbent upon their Promoters. The recent rules of the Roman Rota number the contentious proceedings involving moral persons as among the cases which by nature pertain to the duty of the Promoter of Justice. He is to be present at all judicial proceedings at which one of the parties or both are moral persons and is to do this in virtue of the office he holds.[4] The Apostolic Signatura in a decision on a case appealed to it from the Rota is most explicit in relation to the Promoter's duty in this regard. It describes him as the natural defender of the rights of moral persons who is to vindicate these rights everywhere. He is to exercise the same care and vigilance over the affairs of these persons in judicial proceedings that the Ordinary does in extrajudicial matters. In the judicial forum the duty devolves upon him to see that they are given the full protection of the law, and, in the event that their representative for any reason is declared in contempt of court, he is to take up the proceedings and vindicate the rights of the moral person itself, and will do this in virtue of the provision of Canon 1850, that he is to substitute himself for the absent plaintiff as often as the public good demands such action.[5]

[3] Wernz-Vidal, *Jus Canonicum,* VI, 131; A Coronata, *Institutiones J. C.,* III, 57; Ferreres *Inst.,* II, 239; Noval, *De Processibus,* I, 81, 123; Blat, *Commentarium,* IV, 61; Muniz, *Procedimientos Eccl.,* III, 11 and n. 2; Roberti, *De Processibus,* I, 198.

[4] *Normae S. R. R. Tribunalis,* arts. 27, 38—*A. A. S.,* XXVI (1934), 457.

[5] Signatura Apostolica, "Tergestina," Recursus, 15 March, 1921—*A. A. S.,* XIII (1921), 269-273.

As often as the moral person appears in the court as plaintiff or defendant in judicial proceedings, the Promoter will confine his attention and efforts to those parts of the trial which affect the moral person strictly and directly, prescinding entirely from all private questions which may exist in the case. He appears in these cases in the interests of public good and hence his sole reason for intervention will be concerning the issues which touch the public moral person as such.[6] He acts in these proceedings as a disinterested third party save in these issues which directly affect the rights and prerogatives of the moral person itself. In the vindication of these rights he will exercise an active intervention in the formulation of the *litis contestatio*, the citing of witnesses, in the preparation of interrogatories, in the presentation of new questions which the answers of the parties or the witnesses at whose examination he may be present may suggest, in the citation of additional witnesses, in fine, in aiding and abetting the judge in his duty to protect the rights of these persons who before the law enjoy the status of minors, thereby placing him in a safe position to pass just judgment upon the case before him, and should the evidence warrant it, the Promoter will seek *ex officio* a restitution of the moral person into its original state as it was before the matter, which occupies the attention of the court, transpired.[7] In a word he will do all in his power, always within the bounds of truth and justice, however, to protect the rights and the privileges of these moral persons against injury and impairment, thereby guaranteeing the favor which the law expressly grants these persons in judicial matters.[8]

While the office and the rôle which the Promoter ordinarily exercises in these proceedings is an objective one, and, to quote the words of the Signatura and the Rota, a collateral one, it can happen that the Promoter of Justice will occupy the rôle of plaintiff for the moral person. It was already mentioned above in passing

[6] *Normae S. R. R. Tribunalis*, art. 28—*A. A. S.*, XXVI (1934), 457; Suprema Signatura, "Tergestina," Recursus—*A. A. S.*, XIII (1921), 272.

[7] Canons 1745, § 1; 1759, § 2; 1687, § 1; 1688, § 2; 1773, § 2; Wernz-Vidal, *Jus Canonicum*, VI, 131; Ferreres, *Inst.*, II, 239.

[8] *Normae S. R. R. Tribunalis*, art. 28—*A. A. S.*, XXVI (1934), 457.

that the Signatura numbers among the cases in which the Promoter will supply the absence of a plaintiff declared in contempt of court the class of cases under consideration, *v. g.*, contentious proceedings involving moral persons, and will do this in accordance with the rule set forth in Canon 1850, § 2. It may also happen that the Promoter in prosecuting criminal charges against the rectors, administrators or procurators of these persons may be entrusted with the rôle of procurator for the moral person in its suit for recovery of damages. He will never assume this duty unless the Ordinary assigns it to him because as often as the negligence happens outside the curia, the provision to supply it rests not with the Promoter of Justice but with the Ordinary.[9] In the event that the investigation into the delict of the person in charge of the moral person discloses damages to the latter, the Ordinary may entrust the prosecution for civil damages to the Promoter who will prosecute both claims before the diocesan courts; otherwise, the procurator appointed by the Ordinary will appear and propose his own claims for damages against the defendant, and the sentence will define both claims.[10]

Since the Promoter is the natural defender of the rights of the Episcopal Curia and the *mensa episcopalis*,[11] he may appear in the judicial proceedings in a twofold rôle relative to these moral persons. He may appear as the vindicator of its rights as far as the public good is concerned, and therefore in a collateral rôle as an auxiliary to the judge in the just and equitable settlement of its rights, or, again, he may appear before the court as the official procurator for the diocesan curia or the *mensa episcopalis*. Whenever he appears before the court in the latter rôle he may not enjoy any of the prerogatives of his office as Promoter of Justice. He may not act as procurator for a cause and adhere entirely to one of the parties and at the same time exercise the rôle of the Promoter of Justice

[9] Canon 1653, 5; Signatura Apostolica, Recursus, 15 March, 1921—*A. A. S.*, XIII (1921), 272.

[10] Wernz-Vidal, *Jus Canonicum*, VI, 688, n. 2.

[11] Muniz, *Procedimientos Eccl.*, III, 11, n. 2; Roberti, *De Processibus*, II, 181.

in the same case, as would be verified in the case under consideration.[12] Canon 1613, § 2, forbids the cumulation of offices of procurator and Promoter of Justice. Since the canon forbids the Promoter of Justice to act in cases in which he has heretofore appeared as procurator for one of the parties before the court, *a fortiori* the Promoter of Justice whose duty it is to defend justice in contentious cases cannot *ex officio* represent one of the parties and act as the Promoter in the same case. The Rota, in the decision cited, censures the Promoter who combined the two offices in a case involving the *mensa episcopalis*.

Since the Promoter of Justice who is being studied in these pages is principally the diocesan Promoter, he will be concerned only with the cases of those moral persons which the diocesan tribunals are competent to try. The common law reserves the contentious cases of certain moral persons to the tribunals of the Holy See, and in the adjudication of these the Promoter of Justice of these tribunals alone is competent to be present and defend the interests of the moral persons involved.[13] The common law, likewise, distinguishes between the rights of the bishop and the rights and goods of the episcopal curia and *mensa*. In the civil cases of the latter the diocesan courts are competent to adjudicate the issue provided the bishop consent to it.[14] The diocesan courts, of course, are competent to expedite all contentious proceedings involving moral persons of diocesan right, as long as the person of the defendant and the subject matter of the cause are under diocesan jurisdiction.

In the event of appeal, here, as in all other cases, the Promoter of Justice of the appellate tribunal will stand for the interests of the moral person which the diocesan Promoter defended before his own tribunals. No matter how much the case may pertain to the interests of the diocese he represents, the Promoter has no standing outside his own tribunal, and will leave the defense of the rights of

[12] *S. R. R. Decisiones seu Sentent.*, XV (1923), Dec. XXI, n. 13, 189.

[13] Canon 1557, § 2; 1558; Signatura Apostolica, Recursus—*A. A. S.*, XIII (1921), 271.

[14] Canon 1572, § 2.

the moral person involved to the Promoter of the court to which the appeal was taken.[15]

The Restitutio in Integrum

The most favorable protection offered by the ecclesiastical law to minors and to those who share their rights and privileges, the moral person, is the reinstatement into former condition by the authority of a judge as often as their rights and properties have been seriously or notably injured or transgressed. Whenever they have been gravely injured, minors and moral persons may, in addition to the ordinary means of redress provided in ecclesiastical law, apply to the court for the application of the extraordinary remedy of the *restitutio in integrum.*[16]

The purpose of the remedy is to repair the damage sustained by reason of a rescindible deed or act, even though the deed or act may in itself have been valid and therefore obligatory. This restitution to original state restores all the rights acquired in good faith before the restitution was asked. As was intimated, the principal beneficiaries of this legal remedy are minors and moral persons.[17]

Minors in Canon Law are those who have not yet completed their twenty-first year.[18] The privileges of minors are granted to moral persons.[19] The moral person may be collegiate bodies like the cathedral chapter, a religious community, etc., or it may be a non-corporate entity as a parish, a hospital, an orphanage, etc.

Minors have no authority to make contracts or other agreements but must do so through their parents or guardians. Since they are at the mercy of another and may suffer harm in their temporalities and rights through the carelessness and ill-will of parents and guardians, the law protects their interests by granting them a reinstatement into their previous condition, or, to put it more clearly, the court will set aside in their favor all offending agreements, con-

[15] Suprema Signatura, Recursus, 15 March, 1921—*A. A. S.*, XIII (1921), 271.

[16] Canon 1687, § 1.

[17] Canons 1687, § 1; 1688, § 2; Augustine, *A Commentary*, VII, 136.

[18] Canon 88, § 1.

[19] Canon 100, § 3.

tracts or other transactions made for them by their legal guardians just as though they had never happened. The same privilege is accorded to moral persons, collegiate or non-collegiate, because they also depend upon others to act for them, since the moral person is a fictitious being, a legal entity that cannot act for itself.[20] It should be noted that the reinstatement into previous condition refers not only to all types of valid contracts or transactions, *e. g.*, sales, renting, leasing, mortgaging, donations, etc., but also to court procedure, *e. g.*, sentences, *fatalia* through which the minor or the moral person may have suffered harm.[21]

The further favor of the law to minors and moral persons is manifested in the requirements which should be present for the legitimate invocation of this remedy. While it is an extraordinary remedy for others, it is for them an ordinary remedy. They may employ it in preference to other legal remedies at their disposal.[22] The only conditions that need be verified in their application for the remedy are that the offending act or deed be rescindible and valid, and that they have suffered a grave damage as a consequence of this deed or act.[23]

As to the question who may petition the court for the reinstatement, the minor, before he has reached the age of majority, may bring the matter to the attention of the local Ordinary who can appoint a guardian *ad litem*; the moral person who has suffered grave damage is to be defended by the local Ordinary and the Promoter of Justice under whose jurisdiction it has been placed.[24] Should the Promoter of Justice by report or observation perceive that an act, *e. g.*, a bargain or an alienation, is detrimental to the Church or the diocese, he may and should petition the ecclesiastical court

[20] Roberti, *De Processibus,* I, 389.

[21] Noval, *De Processibus,* I, 228; *S. R. R. Decisiones seu Sententiae,* XV (1923), Dec. XXI, n. 4, 183.

[22] "Habenti remedium ordinarium non est tribuendum extraordinarium, nisi hoc sit pinguis": Reiffenstuel, lib. I, tit. 41, § 2, n. 23; Lega, *De Jud. Eccl.,* I, n. 271; Noval, *De Processibus,* I, 228, 229.

[23] Canon 1687, § 2; *S. R. R. Decisiones seu Sentent.,* XV (1923), dec. XXI., n. 5, 183, 184; Noval, *De Processibus,* I, 227; Roberti, *De Processibus,* I, 386.

[24] Canons 1653, § 5; 1688, § 2.

for a *restitutio in integrum*,[25] since he is by office the vindicator and protector of the rights of moral persons, and the judge is empowered to grant the reinstatement *ex officio instante Promotore Justitiae*.[26]

The *restitutio in integrum* is not strictly a judicial action nor is it sought as a right deriving from strict law, but it is rather a petition directed to the court asking the judge to exercise in equity what the sources call his *nobile ministerium seu officium*.[27] Although it is not strictly a judicial procedure, the action or the petition follows the general rules of ordinary procedure outlined in the Code for determining competence.[28] The party against whom the petition is directed should be cited to defend himself against its concession.

The action of the petition for reinstatement is directed by the Promoter or the procurator for the minor or moral person to the court to which the defendant is subject; if several courts are competent the Promoter or the plaintiff has the right to choose the court most convenient to himself, and it will be the Promoter of Justice of the court chosen who will be present to defend the interests of the minor or the moral person.[29] To determine the competency of the court, both the defendant and the subject matter must be considered, as only the diocesan court which has both real and personal jurisdiction in the case, will be competent [30] to accept and examine the petition for reinstatement.

Time is a very important element in the prosecution of one's claims in any court. Canon 1688 defines the time in which the action for reinstatement may be brought. The law is very favorable to a minor, allowing him four years after he has attained

[25] Canon 1688, § 2; Muniz, *Procedimientos Eccl.*, III, 58; Augustine, *A Commentary*, VII, 136.

[26] Canon 1688, § 2; Suprema Signatura, Recursus—*A. A. S.*, XIII (1921), 272.

[27] Cc. 1 et 2, X, *de offic. judicis*, I, 32; *De Angelis*, lib. I, tit. 41, n. 5; A Coronata, *Institutiones J. C.*, III, 122.

[28] Roberti, *De Processibus*, I, 391 ss.

[29] Canon 1559, § 3; Suprema Signatura, Recursus, 15 March, 1921—*A. A. S.*, XIII (1921), 271.

[30] Canons 1556-1568 incl., 1906. This last canon will be considered later on.

majority to bring the action for reinstatement from obligations growing out of transactions made in his name while still in minority. Thus the law grants him ample time in which to discover any injury or harm done to his rights while a minor, and to discover the facts and grounds upon which to enter his petition for reinstatement. The minor need not wait until he has reached his majority but may bring the matter to the attention of the court, for the judge is authorized by the law, which adds that the Promoter of Justice is to assist the judge,[31] to investigate the wrong done to minors.

The juridical institute of the Promoter of Justice exists for the protection of the public good in contentious proceedings. The public good of any society demands that those who are unable to defend themselves against the deception, dishonesty, negligence or damaging counsel of others, should be defended by the law. The law in this instance entrusts the actual protection of minors to the Promoter of Justice, upon whom it will devolve, as often as the case is brought to his attention in any way, to seek the reparation of the harm done to the minor. As often as the case has already been brought to the attention of the court by the minor or his representative, the Promoter of Justice has the cumulative duty with the judge to verify all the conditions outlined in this article and compare them with the facts set forth in the petition. He will advise the judge, and should his examination of the facts in the case warrant the application of the remedy, he will motion that the judge grant the reinstatement, thereby using the prestige and influence of his public office to influence the judge in granting the petition of the plaintiff.[32]

The judge in the exercise of his *nobile officium* has the duty to protect these minors, but it is not an exclusive duty. The law reminds him that he must consult the Promoter of Justice in these matters before rendering the verdict. He need not follow the advice or motion of the Promoter but the obligation of consultation nevertheless remains. As seen above, the ordinary interpretation of Canon 105, n. 1, would demand this consultation for the validity

[31] Canon 1688, § 2.

[32] Canon 1688, § 2, " . . . audito vel instante promotore justitiae."

of the subsequent decree or sentence of the court granting the reinstatement.[33]

Moral persons, on the other hand, have the right to seek the reinstatement within four years. The time is useful time, and may run from the time of the injury done to them, or, in the case of inability to act, from the time of the cessation of the impediment preventing them from seeking the *restitutio*.[34] The words of the canon *dies laesionis factae* must certainly be understood not merely as the actual time when the damage was done, but when it was perceived and realized that damage had been done.[35] This interpretation seems evident from the apposition of the words *impedimenti cessati,* since one can not realize an obstacle unless he has perceived an injury to his rights and goods. This would be exemplified by the parish which has suffered injury or damage as a result of the transactions of a pastor who remained in office for some time after they were made, and the damage comes to light only with his death or removal. The time would run only from the latter moment as only then would the impediment cease.[36]

Moral persons enjoy the additional protection of the law, in as much as, in the case of minors, the judge can grant the reinstatement *ex officio* and place them in the status in which they were before the transaction occurred. If the administrator or the rector of the moral person has injured the rights of a church or institute and the judge or the Promoter have knowledge of the injury they may of their own initiative concede the reinstatement provided the defendant and the matter involved are subject to their jurisdiction.[37]

The same distinctions noted above in speaking of minors apply to cases of moral persons. If the judge desires to grant the *restitutio* of his own initiative, he must cite the Promoter and ask his opinion in the matter. If the moral person through its representative asks the reinstatement, the Promoter should, likewise, be cited in this

[33] Canons 105, n. 1; 1688, § 2; 1587, § 1.

[34] Canon 1688, § 1.

[35] Augustine, *A Commentary,* VII, 138; Engel, lib. I, tit. 41, n. 11.

[36] Canon 1688, § 1; Noval, *De Processibus,* I, 230; Wernz-Vidal, *Jus Canonicum,* VI, 279.

[37] Canon 1688, § 1; Augustine, *A Commentary,* VII, 136.

instance. If the moral person is already in court in the rôle of defendant or plaintiff and the judge perceives that the evidence submitted thus far justifies the concession of a *restitutio,* he will consult the Promoter who should be present at the proceedings involving the moral person; but if he is absent, the judge will cite him to examine the acts and give his opinion and do this under pain of invalidity of the decree of reinstatement.[88] The judge and the Promoter have a cumulative duty with regard to the reinstatement, and the judge may not proceed validly unless he has notified the Promoter and asked his advice.

Hence it may be concluded that while the presence of the Promoter is not essential to the ordinary cases involving moral persons, unless, as might easily happen, the Ordinary discerns that the case involves the public good and orders the Promoter to be present, he is essential in all actions granting a reinstatement to former condition. The judge must cite him and seek his advice if the decree of the court is to be valid. Moreover, he can and should seek the reinstatement of his own initiative as often as his extrajudicial investigation discloses that the knowledge which he has received of a grave injury to a moral person, is well founded. It is his duty to defend the moral persons before the courts from any injury at the hands of their administrators, rectors or third parties. The law itself establishes this as an integral part of his duty in the promotion of the welfare of the diocese for which he was appointed.

Relative to all the other actions in which the moral person may be involved, the prevailing canonical jurisprudence demands that he be present at the proceedings and actively insure that these persons will receive the adequate protection afforded them in the ecclesiastical law. He will vindicate to them all those rights and prerogatives which pertain to them as moral persons. He is not justified in leaving that protection to the judge or third persons; he has a cumulative duty with the judge to see that justice is administered to these moral persons and has that duty in virtue of the office he holds in the diocesan curia, the Promoter of the public good and welfare in the diocese which he serves.

[88] Canons 1688, § 2, 105, n. 1; 1587, § 1.

ARTICLE II. THE PROMOTER OF JUSTICE AND THE ACTIONS OF SEQUESTRATION AND INJUNCTION

The Code in a special section of the Fourth Book considers in detail various actions, or, rather, remedies of law and counterclaims which must be settled before the final and definitive sentence can be pronounced in a case, and which tend to secure a full adjustment as well as a security against damages and injuries while the litigation is pending. And since the Promoter of Justice is expressly mentioned in conjunction with the application of two of those remedies, it will be necessary to outline his rights and duties relative to these specific actions and remedies, in order to have a complete summary of his duties, as outlined in the Code. These two remedies are the actions of sequestration and injunction, and the possessory actions. Each will be treated in turn.

Under the prevailing law, sequestration consists in an order of the judge to set aside property or a person from the possession or control of the parties, pending the judicial decision on a controversy concerning it.[39] The injunction is an order of the court requiring some one to perform, or, more frequently, to refrain from performing some specified action.[40] When there is a question of personal or real goods between two litigants and one of them is in possession of the disputed property, the opposing party may have reason to fear that the property will be damaged or dissipated by the one in possession before the lawsuit can be definitely settled by the court. Now if the party can prove to the court that he has some right to the property and that there is danger that the possessor will do damage to it, the judge is obliged to issue a decree by which a third party is given custody of the disputed property until the court has established the rights of the respective parties to the disputed property. If there is a question of the exercise of rights before the court, and the plaintiff shows reason for contesting the rights claimed by another, and shows that this other party threatens to exercise the controverted rights pending litigation, and that such exercise is detrimental to him,

[39] Canon 1672, § 1.

[40] Canon 1672, § 2.

the judge must issue an injunction forbidding the party to exercise the right in question.[41] Any violations of these decrees will be considered attempts and may be made the object to further action by the injured party.

In criminal trials and other judicial proceedings involving the public good the judge may of his own initiative issue the decree of sequestration or injunction to protect the public good, a thing he is forbidden to do when only private interests are involved.[42] The Code adds that he will do this especially upon the motion of the Promoter of Justice to that effect, since the latter is bound by his office to protect the common weal, and, hence, must draw the attention of the court to matters that affect the common welfare of the diocese.[43]

As often as he deems the application of these remedies to be necessary or probably necessary to protect the public good, the Promoter of Justice should *ex officio* petition the court to apply them. The judge, as noted above, is also empowered to grant the decrees without consulting the Promoter of Justice. Unlike the concession of the *restitutio,* he is not bound to consult the Promoter; but the Code implicitly reminds the Promoter that the defense of the public good by the application of these remedies is peculiarly and primarily his duty, since the law says that the judge will grant the petition *ex officio* especially when the Promoter petitions for it.[44]

The Promoter should be extremely prudent in applying for the application to these two remedies, whether the case be one in which the parties before the court are privately engaged, or one in which he himself is the plaintiff. The reason for this is that injunction and sequestration always engender some suspicion of the one against whom they are directed and hurts that party's chances in the court.[45] Since the presence of the Promoter in these cases is normally a collateral one and is concerned only with interests of the public good, he must not favor either contending party, nor appear interested in

[41] Canon 1672, §§ 1, 2; *Regulae Servandae . . . S. R. R. Tribunal,* § 85—*A. A. S.,* II (1910), 811; Augustine, *A Commentary,* VII, 125.

[42] Canon 1672, § 3.

[43] Noval, *De Processibus,* I, 208.

[44] Canon 1672, § 3; Noval, *De Processibus,* I, 208.

[45] Wernz-Vidal, *Jus Canonicum,* VII, 253.

either one by suggesting methods of defense or attack. He must be absolutely neutral in the case, anxious only to apply the law with truth and justice according to the proofs which the parties have offered to establish their rights to things or to the exercise of rights which in themselves pertain by their nature to the public good.

An examination of the circumstances in the individual case will determine the Promoter whether or not it is to the interests of the public good to have the object of the trial sequestered, or to have either party enjoined from the exercise of controverted rights. Should his examination convince him that there is a necessity, he will follow the rules laid down for any other plaintiff and submit a petition to the judge setting forth the right or object which he wishes sequestered or enjoined, outlining at the same time, in summary fashion, the probability of damage or injury to the public good which seems to demand that the exercise of a right or the possession and use of an object be restricted by the court.[46] The judge is advised that he may grant the petition when it is asked by the Promoter, since the latter must have the same objective attitude towards the case as the judge himself.[47]

The Promoter may find the application of these remedies of assistance in his prosecution of the public good either in criminal or non-criminal cases.

The Promoter might have occasion to petition the relief of sequestration in a criminal process or prior to its inception, in order to safeguard and preserve a document or instrument which is valuable to the prosecution's presentation of its case against the accused. These documents may form the object of the delict or have an intimate connection with it and constitute what is known in criminal procedure as the *corpus delicti*. Not infrequently documents and instruments, *e. g.*, letters, contracts, records, etc., are invaluable to the prosecution in its attempt to establish the commission of a delict or the will and intention of the delinquent to commit the delict with which he is charged, and, therefore, establish him as the imputable cause of the delict. By petitioning the sequestration, the Promoter

[46] Wernz-Vidal, *Jus Canonicum*, VI, 253.

[47] Canon 1672, " . . . instante praesertim Promotore justitiae . . . "

insures himself against the possible loss, subtraction, alteration or malicious destruction of the evidence by having it placed in the custody of the chancellor or other persons appointed by the court.[48]

Not infrequently damages also grow out of a delict committed by the delinquent, and the Promoter may urge the sequestration of the goods which pertain to the public good and are held by the defendant, lest he dissipate them or use them in a manner prejudicial to justice, or, so as to render impossible the satisfaction of the verdict of the court, ordering him to make satisfaction for the damage his delinquency has occasioned to the moral person or institute which he represented.

The Code also mentions in connection with the criminal trial the sequestration of the person of the defendant. If there is danger that the defendant will be guilty of actions that will prejudice the Promoter's presentation of the prosecution's case and his attempts to obtain justice, the Promoter, after the first citation of the accused, may take the extraordinary remedy provided by the law, whereby the judge, after consultation with the Promoter, may order the defendant to leave the place in which he is stationed and remain in a particular place under the vigilance of the one to whom the prescribed place of residence is subject.[49]

The Promoter might also find it necessary to invoke the injunction in the course of a criminal trial, in order to restrain the exercise of rights which might prove prejudicial to the public good.[50] If the prosecution is intending to use the judicial accusses in order to establish the guilt of the defendant, the Promoter may petition the court for an injunction restraining the defendant from altering or changing the place involved in the judicial proceedings. Otherwise the defendant could make alterations which would destroy the chances of the prosecution to establish their case, and might even reduce to an absurdity their contentions that the accused committed the crime. The changed conditions of the place would tend to show that the allegations of the Promoter are absurd, since in view of the conditions

[48] Wernz-Vidal, *Jus Canonicum,* VI, 245.
[49] Canon 1957.
[50] Wernz-Vidal, *Jus Canonicum,* VI, 245.

existing in the place, it would be morally and physically impossible to verify the charges made by the prosecution.

The Code also speaks of an injunction forbidding the defendant to exercise the public functions of his office, as often as he is charged with a serious crime and the exercise of his office would be a source of scandal to the faithful.[51] It is the duty of the Promoter to call the attention of the Ordinary to all that is, or will become, a source of scandal to the faithful, and to seek its removal,[52] and, hence, in the present case, he will direct a petition to the Ordinary through the mediation of the court, seeking an injunction of the defendant's right to exercise publicly the functions attached to his office on the grounds that such exercise is scandalous to the faithful.[53] He may not invoke the application until after the citation of the accused and unless there is real danger of scandal, since such injunction is prejudicial to the reputation of the accused.[54]

Relative to the Promoter and his duty to seek the application of these remedies in contentious proceedings nothing very definite can be postulated. As the public good is usually involved in these proceedings by reason of circumstances, the conditions and circumstances arising in any given case will manifest whether or not the Promoter is justified in petitioning for the remedies. The ordinary cause for his invoking the remedies will be the protection of ecclesiastical property and the revenues, fruits or incomes accruing from ecclesiastical offices and benefices.[55] Since these persons cannot defend themselves against the malice and negligence of others or of those who represent them, or claim to do so, and, in as much as they pertain to the public good, the Promoter of Justice, if there is danger of injury being done to their rights and property through the misuse or dissipation of the property or incomes by the parties to contentious proceedings, will seek the sequestration of the same or

[51] Canon 1956.

[52] Noval, *De Processibus,* I, 569; Roberti, *Apollinaris,* III (1930), 250.

[53] A Coronata, *Institutiones J. C.*, III, 407; Muniz, *Procedimientos Eccl.*, III, 520, 521.

[54] Canon 1958; A Coronata, *Institutiones J. C.*,, III, 408.

[55] A Coronata, *Institutiones J. C.*, III, 109.

enjoin the party from the perception of the same, until such time as he establishes a clear title to them. An example may be had in the non-resident cleric or canon who obtains revenues from a juridical person of any kind. The Promoter may seek the sequestration of these revenues pending the litigation undertaken by the party to obtain them.[56] Moreover, as often as the asserted rights of the administrators or rectors of moral persons are in direct conflict with the moral persons before the court, the Promoter may petition the sequestration of the property and revenue of the moral person until the court has settled definitely the rights of the administrators or rectors, whenever there is danger that these things will suffer in the hands of their present possessor, if not be withdrawn entirely by him. Take, for example, the difficulties that arise from time to time when the personal funds and the funds of the moral person have become confused, or the funds of the moral person have been expended or withdrawn for purposes other than those for which the moral person was erected or approved, and now some one interested in the moral person steps forward to protest the use being made of the funds of that person and applies to the diocesan authorities for a ruling upon the matter. If the matter cannot be settled administratively but becomes the subject of judicial controversy, the Promoter, for the protection of the moral person, may petition the sequestration of its revenues and property.

The Promoter may also apply for an injunction against the exercise of rights whenever the exercise of those rights would prove detrimental to the public welfare. If a person were being forced into marriage, religious profession, or the priesthood, it would certainly devolve upon the Promoter who has reliable knowledge of such a situation to enjoin the persons from entering these states, and even seek their sequestration in a safe place, until such time as their free, voluntary acceptance of the state in question can be established.[57] So, too, if it was a question of a priest whose ordination is doubtful and who is exercising his ministry in a public capacity, the Promoter may seek the injunction of its exercise until the validity is substan-

[56] Ferreres, *Institutiones*, II, 272.

[57] Noval, *De Processibus*, I, 208; Wernz-Vidal, *Jus Canonicum*, VI, 246.

tiated or supplied.[58] Again, it may be a question of scandal given by two priests entrusted with the care of souls, who are engaged in a lawsuit, and who have given scandal to the whole vicinity by their actions. The Promoter can demand that they be enjoined from publicly exercising their offices, since their actions have rendered them ineffective, if not harmful, in their present capacities.[59]

The public good could likewise be involved in cases which have been appealed from the diocesan courts. The verdict in the first instance ordered the restoration of certain rights or objects pertaining to the public good to their apparently rightful possessor, but since the appeal suspends the execution of the sentence, there may be a well founded fear that the public good may be harmed by a dissipation of the property or an unrestrained exercise of the right in question. Here again, as long as it is a question of a public right or possession and the danger of injury to the public good is probable, the Promoter may demand the decree of sequestration or injunction for the protection of that public good.

In fine, as often as the public good is involved in a case, and it can be demonstrated to the court that unless the rights and property in question are sequestered or enjoined, there will be a resultant injury to the public good, the Promoter of Justice can and should petition the court to sequester the property or enjoin the exercise of the right, since the public good cannot be protected in any other way.[60] A straightforward evaluation of the circumstances in each case will show whether or not the remedy is necessary to forestall an injury to the public good, and thereby secure it against the harmful and scandalous actions of third parties. Should he feel that the danger is present, he is not justified in leaving the decision entirely up to the judge, but should take steps himself to point out to the judge that there is danger to the public good, and the law itself points out to him that this defense is primarily entrusted to him and to the judge only after he has failed to take cognizance of the danger and apply for the application of the remedies.

[58] Blat, *Commentarium,* IV, 187; Roberti, *De Processibus,* I, 196.

[59] Augustine, *A Commentary,* VII, 42.

[60] Noval, *De Processibus,* I, 208.

Article III. The Promoter of Justice and the Possessory Remedies

Canon 1693 states that a person who has a legitimate title to obtain possession of a certain thing or right, may petition the court that he be granted the possession of such a thing or the exercise of such a right.

Cardinal Lega defines possession as "the physical detention of a thing or some other relation to a thing, by which a person exercises actually or habitually some activity concerning the thing, claiming the right to do so to the exclusion of others and not momentarily, but for some time to which detention the law gives juridical effect and protection."[61] It is called possession when it is referred to corporeal things, quasi-possession when it is versed around a right or the exercise of a right. Thus, in quasi-possession or possession, one finds two elements. The first is the actual possession and the intention to possess as of right; the second completes the first and is the legal recognition and defense of the right.

If one has the legal right to the possession of a thing by contract, legitimate appointment, etc., and the one in possession refuses to surrender possession of the thing or right, the former may petition the court to force the one who opposes his right to relinquish the object to the petitioner. This is the first type of possessory action—one in which the plaintiff has not yet enjoyed the actual possession. The other two are remedies at the disposal of the plaintiff already in possession, the one to retain the possession, the other to recover what he already had, but has since lost. These latter two are technically known as the *actio retinendae possessionis* and the *actio spolii*. Since the Code expressly mentions the Promoter in relation to these two remedies, it will be necessary to consider their nature and his intervention in their application.

The Action for the Retention of Possession

The law grants to the possessor who has remained in full possession for one year or has held the detention of an immovable or mov-

[61] Lega, *De Judiciis Eccl. Civilibus*, I, n. 204; Noval, *De Processibus*, I, 246.

able object for the same length of time the right to sue anyone who molests him in that possession.[62] It makes no difference legally whether the possession, objectively considered, is just or unjust, as far as his right to sue the molester is concerned. The fact of possessions and the unmolested enjoyment of it are important factors in the good order of any society. Consequently, the law prescribes that the one who has been deprived of his possession should act promptly and vindicate it to himself and penalizes the one who is remiss in the vindication of his own rights by granting to the actual possessor for one year the right to enjoin any individual molesting him from any further interference with the right of possession. The fact that a person has waited a full year without upsetting the possession of the actual possessor sets up a presumption in the law that one who has been the actual possessor for one year is the rightful possessor and protects his apparent rights by granting him an injunction restraining interference with the enjoyment of his possession.[63] The injunction must be sought within a year from the date of the first act of molestation.[64]

In thus legislating the ecclesiastical society, much in the same way as the civil law, realizes the importance of the right of possession to good order of the society and forbids the disturbance of that right as detrimental to the public welfare. As a consequence of this necessary defense of the good order of the community, it recognizes that even persons who have obtained possession through theft, loan, deposit, finding, etc., have certain rights in relation to those objects which may not be indiscriminately violated; otherwise the way would be opened to acts of fraud and violence, since anyone would be free to invade another's rights and property on the ground that he had robbed or stolen what he possesses.

The suit may be brought against anyone's disturbers except the person from whom the possessor obtained the property or right by force or stealth or who gave him precarious possession.[65]

[62] Canon 1659.

[63] Canon 1695; Noval, *De Processibus*, I, 251.

[64] Canon 1695, § 2.

[65] Canon 1696, § 1.

While the law thus does not recognize the right of third parties to disturb the possession of goods or rights obtained unjustly, it contains an express exception in favor of the Promoter of Justice who may of his own initiative oppose the action for the retention of possession, as often as the object of the action is a thing or right which pertains to the public good and has been obtained unjustly by the possessor.[66] The canon thus accords a further recognition to the juridical institute of the Promoter of Justice and his right and duty to intervene in the interests of the public good.[67] Should the judge note the vitiated possession of an object or right pertaining to the public good, he may *ex officio* take action against the retention of possession through the intervention of the Promoter of Justice.[68]

The salvation of souls and the vindication of the common good may occasionally prompt the Promoter of Justice to oppose the action of the possessor who seeks retention of goods or rights which pertain to the public order and which he holds through stealth, force or precariously. Questions pertaining to the just possession of ecclesiastical offices and benefices and the ecclesiastical property and rights attached to them pertain not only to the private good of the faithful, but also to the common good.[69] Ecclesiastical offices and benefices imply the exercise of orders and jurisdiction in virtue of the appointment received from legitimate authority and the exercise of orders and jurisdiction is always of interest to the common good. The exercise of this jurisdiction over the properties and the rights, both spiritual and temporal, is connected with the office or benefice and the rightful institution of the incumbent in them. Hence, as often as an intruder asserts his rights to retain any of these things, the Promoter in virtue of his office will oppose the faulty possession and demand the dismissal of that intruder from the possession of the office or benefice or of any of the rights pertaining to either.[70]

[66] Canon 1697, § 2.

[67] Roberti, *De Processibus,* I, 403; Blat, *Commentarium,* IV, 217.

[68] A Coronata, *Institutiones J. C.,* III, 133.

[69] Wernz-Vidal, *Jus Canonicum,* VI, 299; Blat, *Commentarium,* IV, 217; Noval, *De Processibus,* I, 252.

[70] Ferreres, *Institutiones,* II, 283; Augustine, *A Commentary,* VII, 145.

The intervention of the Promoter in the case because of the public nature of the object in the controversy is conditioned by the canon itself. The possessor must have come into the possession of the controverted object or right by force, stealth or in a precarious manner; otherwise the presumption of the law is that the possession is just and the Promoter may not disturb the possessor in the enjoyment of his rights.[71] Hence, the Promoter in his objection of faulty possession must establish one of these defects recognized by the law as sufficient to evict the present incumbent from the possession he sought to protect by seeking an injunction from the ecclesiastical court, restraining some one from interfering with his own unjust possession.

Possession is had by force when the possession was acquired by violence or through the onset of a compulsion too great to be resisted by the legitimate incumbent of the possession.[72] This is also called "spoliation" by the law. This possession by violence is not necessarily effected by physical force, as there are occasions in which moral force may also be considered as being of sufficient influence that it could neither be resisted nor repelled, *e. g.*, the notoriously unjust sentence of the judge.[73]

Possession by stealth, as the name implies, is just the opposite. The possessor began his possession under cover lest the superior or owner discover his possession and upset him in it.

The precarious possession is the possession of a thing in the name, and at the pleasure, of the rightful possessor. If one gives to another possession and use of goods to be returned upon demand, so that the one who borrows the goods has no legal rights to the possession, that possession is called precarious.[74]

Whenever any of these defects can be demonstrated in the origin of the right of possession of ecclesiastical properties, offices or the spiritual and temporal rights connected with the same, the Promoter of Justice will intervene and oppose the retention by the

[71] Noval, *De Processibus*, I, 254.

[72] Canon 103, § 1.

[73] Noval, *De Processibus*, I, 253.

[74] Wernz-Vidal, *Jus Canonicum*, VI, 294; Noval, *De Processibus*, I, 253.

unjust possessor as often as the salvation of souls and the public good demand it.[75] Ordinarily this last condition will be found whenever it is a question of parishes or benefices having the care of souls. The Promoter will do well in certain instances to seek the advice of the Ordinary on the opportuneness of his action in these cases, as invariably there are factions involved who support each of the claimants to the rights of possession.

If the Promoter discerns that it is to the public good to oppose the faulty possession, he will simply direct his objection of faulty possession to the competent judge, indicating in summary fashion his proofs and witnesses. The presumption is in favor of the actual possessor and hence the burden of the proof is on the Promoter, who must substantiate his charges of faulty possession.[76] The hearing of the action will follow the rules of any other judicial action and the defendant will be afforded ample opportunity to vindicate his right of possession and the Promoter, if the grounds upon which he bases his objection to the possession are verified, will use the following remedy to recuperate the possession of the controverted right and vindicate it to legitimate authority.

The Action for the Regaining of Possession

A person who has been deprived of the possession of an object or right by force or stealth of any kind has the right to regain that possession through an action *de spolio* or, if the one who despoiled him takes action against him, he can enter the peremptory exception of spoliation against the spoliator. The action is not admitted after the lapse of a year from the time in which the person noticed the deprivation; the exception, however, is perpetual.[77]

Under the prevailing law the action is a highly privileged one and may be taken against anyone, whether a moral or physical person, who possesses rights or property removed from their actual possessor by stealth or force. This action may be directed against

[75] Augustine, *A Commentary*, VII, 145; Noval, *De Processibus*, I, 252.

[76] Canon 1676; Regula juris 56 in VI: *"Melior est conditio possidentis."*

[77] Canon 1698.

the one who detains the thing or right in good faith, though the latter, in turn, may sue for damages against the spoliator.[78] The reason for this extension against the possessor in good faith is the difficulty of establishing bad faith and in view of the fact that the possessor in good faith can remedy his loss by taking action against the spoliator.[79]

The Code sets forth two requisites for the licit use of the action. They are actual possession or detention and the privation of the same.

The possession of the movable or immovable object must have already been had.[80] This condition distinguishes the action from the preceding action since the action *de spolio* does not require possession for any special length of time nor does it presuppose any just reason for possessing. As a consequence, though one may use force to repel force in the protection of one's own property or in the defense of one's private right, once one has not repelled the invader in the act and the latter has obtained possession, he may not vindicate again that right or property by similar reprisal of his own authority. He must appeal to the authority of the courts and do so promptly, since his complaint will not be entertained by the court unless he files it within a year from the date in which he has knowledge of the spoliation; otherwise he must have recourse to the much more difficult petitory action. The property and the right must be vindicated according to the strict regulations of the law.[81]

The second condition follows from the very nature of the action, namely, that a true spoliation has taken place. The spoliation may have been perpetrated through force or theft. The law no longer requires that the spoliation be notorious but simply that it be capable of proof in the external forum.[82]

The Code mentions only the one who has suffered spoliation as enjoying the right to take the action *de spolio* [83] but all the authors

[78] Noval, *De Processibus*, I, 258, 259; Roberti, *De Processibus*, I, 408.

[79] Sebastianelli, *De Judiciis Eccl.*, 89.

[80] Canon 1698, § 1.

[81] Roberti, *De Processibus*, I, 408; Wernz-Vidal, *Jus Canonicum*, VI, 303.

[82] Roberti, *De Processibus*, I, 409.

[83] Canon 1698, § 1.

unanimously accord the Promoter of Justice the right to exercise the action whenever the public good is involved. They infer this right from the nature of his office as official defender of the public ecclesiastical weal.[84] The judge in the exercise of his *nobile officium* may promote the action, but he should do so through the Promoter of Justice.[85] Since *spolium* has its necessary forum it will be the Promoter of Justice of the forum where the spoliation took place that will enter the objection of vitiated possession in the name of the diocese against whom the spolium was committed.[86]

Hence as often as an act of spoliation has been committed whereby ecclesiastical public property or rights, such as ecclesiastical offices, parishes, benefices and the property and the rights connected with them, have been the object of spoliation, the Promoter of Justice, of his own initiative or at the instance of the judge, may enter the action *de spolio*. Very frequently pastors may find it distasteful to vindicate the rights and the properties which have been the object of spoliation by others and can obtain action in the matter by simply denouncing the spoliation to the Promoter of Justice. He will in all these cases appear as the plaintiff in the contentious proceedings and will vindicate the ecclesiastical rights and property against the usurpers of those things which pertain to the public good and have come into the possession of their present possessor through force or theft of any kind. Since the law makes no exception in the matter, he must show that the action has taken place within the year allotted by the law, *i. e.*, from the date in which the curia had knowledge of the unjust privation of the properties or rights.

This action may prove an effective weapon in the hands of the Promoter on occasional instances in vindicating the rights and properties of the Church since it permits him to vindicate to the common good all ecclesiastical rights and property which have been

[84] C. I. X, *De rest. spol.*, II, 13; Roberti, *De Processibus*, I, 407; Wernz-Vidal, *Jus Canonicum*, VI, 303; A Coronata, *Institutiones J. C.*, III, 133; Noval, *De Processibus.*, I, 261.

[85] A Coronata, *Institutiones J. C.*, III, 133.

[86] Canon 1560, n. 1.

unjustly impeded or withdrawn through fraud, stealth, threats, dishonesty in any form. What is more, he can vindicate these objects from the possessor in good faith as the prevailing law no longer requires that the present possessor be in bad faith. He can vindicate them from any one who detains them or has them in his possession.

He may, moreover, bring criminal action against the one guilty of the spoliation provided it constitutes a true delict.[87] The law enumerates some very severe penalties which may be imposed upon clerics who are guilty of notable or sacrilegious theft.[88] The Promoter would be justified in demanding the application of these penalties against a cleric who is guilty of the spoliation of ecclesiastical property or of sacrilegious theft or sale of the same, were he convinced that the cleric committed a delict inasmuch as the spoliation was voluntary on his part. At any rate, the Promoter can demand the recovery of damages occasioned to the property or suffered as a consequence of the loss of the property or of the rights by their legitimate possessor.[89]

The ordinary purpose of the action brought by the Promoter or by the ordinary plaintiff is the full restitution of the rights or the property which have been unjustly deprived. The quasi-possession of a right and the possession of the corporeal thing will be restored to the status in which they were before the spoliation took place.[90]

It was said that this is the ordinary purpose of any action *de spolio,* because the Code, with a view to full justice, restricts this effect in certain instances. These possessory actions respect only the fact of possession and not the right of possession and hence, while a party may vindicate the fact of possession, his right to that possession may be doubtful if not altogether faulty.[91] In view of this the full restitution of the possession of a thing or right might prove prejudicial to another who has the just right to the possession even though one party has satisfactorily established for the court the fact of his own possession.

87 Roberti, *De Processibus,* I, 407; A Coronata, *Institutiones J. C.,* III, 134.

88 Canon 2354, § 2.

89 Roberti, *De Processibus,* I, 407.

90 Roberti, *De Processibus,* I, 411; Wernz-Vidal, *Jus Canonicum,* VI, 305.

91 Roberti, *De Processibus,* I, 410, and n. 1.

The first reason for the suspension of restitution is the danger of damage or of the violation of another's right of possession. The fear of the damage or the injury to another's right is always sufficient for obtaining or granting an injunction or sequestration.[92] The text of the law itself gives an example of this, *e. g.*, the danger of cruelty to either spouse at the hands of the other, pending litigation of a cause of separation or nullity, is sufficient cause to grant an injunction restraining the rights to the resumption of marital relations of the party who brought the action *de spolio*. Moreover, if the dissipation, damaging or destruction of a thing is to be feared, that thing can also be placed in the custody of a sequester. The judge orders this at the instance of the party or of the Promoter of Justice if the action of spoliation has involved something pertaining to the public good.[93]

The Promoter of Justice is thereby empowered by the law to oppose the restitution and to seek the sequestration of the controverted thing or the injunction against the exercise of the right in question. Generally speaking, this will involve practically always questions of benefices, parishes and offices together with the rights annexed to them by law, *i. e.*, the administration of the sacraments and sacramentals, the impeding of parochial rights by determined persons either within or near the confines of the parish church, parochial rights over certain sections in the vicinity, the right of support, etc. It is never permissible to surrender a benefice into the hands of a lay person, since he is absolutely incapable of possessing it.[94] For the rest, in questions involving ecclesiastical benefices and institutes and the spiritual rights connected with them and exercised for the public good, it is the right of the faithful to require that they should not be possessed unjustly or dubiously and it is the duty of the Promoter of Justice to see to it that they are held and exercised only by their legitimate possessors. These difficulties arise chiefly in those places where *jus patronatus* still flourishes, although the Promoter may occasionally find use for the remedy in providing security

[92] Canon 1699, § 3.

[93] Canon 1699, § 3.

[94] C. 7, X, *de praescript.*, II, 26.

for ecclesiastical property or rights against the unjust possessor who has established the fact of possession and is bent upon retaining these things. The Promoter will oppose the restitution of the property or right to any possessor whose right and title to the same is faulty; the public good demands that the title to these things be certain.[95] The pastor who has the legitimate title to a right or thing need only notify the Promoter and he will seek the suspension of the restitution until such time as the question of the right is settled.

It need hardly be remarked that the Promoter may invoke the application of these remedies suspending restitution as often as one of the parties to the controversy is a moral person and the other party has brought an action *de spolio* against the moral person. These persons, as was seen in a preceding article, enjoy the protection of the law, and that protection is usually guaranteed by the presence of the Promoter who is to see to it that they do not suffer in any of their rights as moral persons and he will vindicate to them all that they have unjustly suffered as moral persons.

The second reason for the suspension of restitution to the one proving spoliation is the readily proved and evident right of possession vested in another. The law does not determine the limits of this reason and hence it must be derived from the nature of the cause before the court. Surely, no judge is justified in ordering a person to resume cohabitation with a person who is certainly guilty of adultery; or to concede the possession of a benefice to one whose title to it is evidently faulty; or to give a thing to the one despoiled which the one guilty of spoliation or a third party vindicates to himself as his own by the sentence of a court which has caused the matter to become a *res judicata,* etc. The Promoter may use these or similar reasons to forestall the restitution of objects or rights pertaining to the public good, until such time as the one, who has convinced the court that he has been the victim of spoliation, also proves to the court that he has a legitimate title to the possession of a thing of which he has been deprived.[96]

[95] Lega, *De Judiciis Eccl.,* I, 267; Noval, *De Processibus,* I, 298.

[96] Roberti, *De Processibus,* I, 411.

Since the exception of spoliation has the same effects of restitution to the one making it against the one who despoiled him of the possession of a right or an object,[97] the same conclusions relative to the suspension of restitution are to be postulated in the case. All that has been said of the suspension of restitution in the case of actions *de spolio* applies to the defendant in a case who makes the exception *de spolio* and for the same reasons as given above for the action.

In fine, the Promoter will intervene in all causes involving benefices, offices, parishes and other ecclesiastical moral persons, the property or spiritual rights of which have been unjustly impeded or withdrawn by a possessor whose title to them is faulty and vitiated. The spiritual welfare of the faithful and the freedom of ecclesiastical rights and property, which by reason of their public character pertain to the public good, will furnish a reasonable basis for his intervention in these cases. In the causes of private persons which involve matters touching upon the public good as the duty of cohabitation, the validity of marriage, of orders, of religious profession, of the rights of *jus patronatus,* he will oppose the restitution as often as it is evidently unjust and whenever it would be the occasion of scandal or spiritual harm to the faithful. As often as individuals have been deprived through fraudulent and threatening actions of their own legitimate rights to take an *actio de spolio,* the Promoter will relieve their sad condition in order to obtain for them a release from the occasions of sin and to remove the scandal that inevitably grows out of the deprivation of the strictly personal rights of individuals. In all these cases he may institute the actions *ex officio* or at the invitation of the judge who has a cumulative duty with the Promoter to protect the public good in all these cases. These duties flow from his office as the official plaintiff for the public good who is to defend the rights of that public good and prevent and remove all that is or will in the ordinary run of events become a scandal to the faithful.

[97] Canon 1699.

ARTICLE IV. THE PROMOTER OF JUSTICE AND THE TWO CAUSES DESCRIBED IN CANONS 1734 AND 1850

With the exception of those matrimonial causes in which the Promoter is bound to assume the rôle of plaintiff because of the incapacity of the parties to attack the validity of the marriage and of those occasional causes in which the rôle of plaintiff or defendant devolves upon him in virtue of a mandate of the Ordinary, the normal rôle of the Promoter in contentious cases which involve the public good is an objective one and, to use the language of the tribunals of the Holy See, a collateral one, that is, while he always appears as a party to the trial, it will be as a third party who appears solely in the interests of the public good. He will abstain from all private controversies at issue in the trial and will intervene only in so far as his intervention is necessary to protect such rights and things as belong primarily to the public good.

The general law, however, makes two express exceptions to this general disinterested attitude which the Promoter should adopt relative to private contentious cases in which the public good finds itself involved. In both instances the law prescribes that he become an actual party to the trial and in the rôle of plaintiff prosecute the object of the controversy in the interests of the public good which was involved in the trial. The first case contemplated in the Code is that in which the interruption or renunciation of proceedings concerning the right to a benefice or church has taken place.[98] The second is one in which the plaintiff in judicial proceedings has rendered himself in contempt of court, has been declared such and the instance which he forfeits by his contumacy pertains to the public good.[99]

The Promoter of Justice and the Causes Described in Canon 1734

The *litis instantia* or judicial proceedings begin with the issue in pleading and ends with the final definitive sentence.[100] This is the

[98] Canon 1734.
[99] Canon 1850.
[100] Canon 1732.

normal tenure of a judicial process. This tenure, however, may be interrupted, abated or renounced at any time after the issue in pleading.

The proceedings are interrupted as often as the juridical person who stands before the court or a representative of the same is wanting. This occurs whenever one of the parties dies, or changes his status, or goes out of the office in virtue of which he was the party to a cause, provided always that the pleadings have not been closed by order of the judge.[101]

The last phrase is important in relation to the interruption of judicial proceedings. If the proof has been submitted and the judge has declared the period for the introduction of proof closed, the judge has all the evidence necessary to pronounce a just sentence in the cause and many proceed to do so.[102] If, however, any of the three contingencies enumerated in the canon intervene while the probatory period is still in progress, the trial is necessarily interrupted since the basis for just judgment is of its nature incomplete and the judge must reserve his sentence in the matter until such time as the instance is resumed and the proofs are completed.[103]

Ordinarily, then, death or change of status interrupts the judicial proceedings relative to any right or thing. The Code, however, makes an express exception to this general rule when the object of a judicial controversy is the right to a benefice. Canon 1734 prescribes that, as often as one of the parties to a judicial trial involving the question of a right to a benefice dies or renounces his right, the instance is not necessarily interrupted. It empowers the Promoter of Justice to enter the judicial controversy and oppose the claims of the surviving litigant in order to establish the freedom of the benefice and vindicate its appointment to legitimate authority. Such action on the part of the Promoter presupposes that the Ordinary does not desire to confer the benefice upon the surviving litigant which he is free to do if the appointment is one of free collation.[104]

[101] Canon 1733.

[102] Canon 1733, n. 2; Noval, *De Processibus*, I, 297.

[103] Canons 1733, n. 1, 1860 ss.

[104] Canon 1734.

This last phrase is understood of all ecclesiastical benefices and offices not reserved to the Holy See.[105] If the office or benefice is of free collation, the Ordinary is free to confer it on the surviving litigant or rather to adjudge it to the surviving litigant and his decision will have the same effect as if the litigant had won the judicial cause; the *cessio* of the benefice or church thus made it equivalent to canonical appointment.[106] It is evident that such action taken by the Ordinary terminates the cause since the object for judicial controversy would no longer exist.

If the benefice is not one of free collation or the Ordinary has no desire to adjudge the benefice to the surviving litigant, the Promoter of Justice will enter the cause and oppose the claims of that litigant. The death of the other party or the renunciation made by him of the right, in so far as he enjoyed it, does not confer on the survivor an exclusive right to the benefice. Every ecclesiastical appointment presupposes canonical institution by legitimate authority and the fact that he alone remains of those who contested the right does not give him the canonical appointment or provision required by law for the legitimate possession of an office, benefice or parish.[107] The interruption of the judicial proceedings does not make his title to the benefice or parish certain and legitimate. The bishop, by his positive action in denying the appointment to the survivor, leaves his title doubtful and the Promoter of Justice is empowered by the Code to take up the controversy and to endeavor to disprove the doubtful title claimed by the survivor. The sole reason for the Promoter's intervention in these proceedings is to prevent the holding or retention of ecclesiastical benefices without the proper canonical appointment or provision.[108] Proper canonical provision pertains to the public good since it is to the interests of all the faithful that public offices in the Church should not be held and exercised unjustly.[109] Consequently, the Code entrusts the defense of these in-

[105] Canon 1435; Augustine, *A Commentary*, VII, 182.

[106] Wernz-Vidal, *Jus Canonicum*, VI, 355; Roberti, *De Processibus*, II, 6.

[107] Canons 147-151.

[108] Canons 147-151; A Coronata, *Institutiones J. C.*, III, 166.

[109] Canon 1734; Lega, *De Judiciis Eccl.*, I, n. 233, 267; Noval, *De Processibus*, I, 298.

terests to the public personality who functions for that purpose, the Promoter of Justice.[110]

This rule of the Code abrogates the old rule of the Apostolic Chancery which formerly granted the surviving litigant a month of grace before his right could be contested by anyone.[111] During this month no one could substitute himself for the deceased adversary, unless he could demonstrate against the surviving litigant that the deceased had been in unmolested possession of the benefice for at least three years or that the survivor was an intruder in the benefice. The Code more correctly has abolished this month of grace and has committed the immediate defense of the public interests to the Promoter of Justice[112] who becomes competent to enter the proceedings at the moment of their interruption.

The provision for his intervention is directly and clearly stated in the prevailing law. It is a question of two litigants who are contesting the right to a benefice, a right which in some way pertains to one of the contestants. The prescript of the Code is concerned with this question alone and does not extend to other action which may be had in connection with benefices as, for example, *jus patronatus*, the action of clerics taken against those who elect or confer a benefice, etc.[113] Moreover the canon presupposes the instance to have begun since it uses the term *lite pendente*. Hence the *litis contestatio* must have been reached, even though neither party had taken an active step after that point to prosecute their claims with proof. All that is necessary is that the issue in pleading had been formulated and that the issue involved the right to a benefice or church; for once the *litis contestatio* has been had the trial is pending and the judge should cite the Promoter to be present at the proceedings.[114]

It makes no difference whether the surviving litigant was the

[110] Canon 1734; Muniz, *Procedimientos Eccl.*, I, 202.

[111] Regula 2 Apostolicae Cancellariae—*A. A. S.*, II (1910), 287.

[112] Roberti, *De Processibus,* II. 6.

[113] Blat, *Commentarium,* IV, 236.

[114] Canon 1732; Roberti, *De Processibus,* II, 6; Blat, *Commentarium,* IV, 236.

plaintiff or the defendant as the Promoter upon entering the trial does not sustain the claims of the deceased party.[115] He appears solely to defend the liberty of the benefice against the claims of the remaining party and thereby leave the place open for appointment by the one who has the authority to make it. He will do this by proposing opportune arguments against the reputed right of the surviving litigant. These arguments will have for their purpose to show that the survivor has neither a certain nor a legitimate title to the benefice, according to the nature of the controversy.[116] The Code uses the terms benefice or church and Noval interprets it to mean all ecclesiastical offices.

The Promoter should proceed at his own intiative in these cases as often as he is aware of the Ordinary's intention not to confer the benefice or church upon the surviving litigant. The judge, since the Ordinary must notify him in the event that he adjudges the benefice or office to the survivor, will insure the Promoter's presence at the interrupted proceedings by citing him to appear and oppose the doubtful claims of the remaining party to the trial.[117]

The Promoter of Justice and the Contumacy of the Actor in Contentious Proceedings

Canon 1849 states that, if on the day and at the hour when the defendant appears in answer to the summons of the court, the plaintiff is absent and gives no excuse or an insufficient one for his failure to appear, the judge shall again summon the plaintiff at the request of the defendant. If the plaintiff does not obey the new summons or if, after answering the summons, he fails to begin the trial or after having begun it fails to prosecute it, the judge at the request of the defendant or the Promoter and the defender of the bond shall declare him guilty of contempt following the same rules as were laid down in Canons 1843-1845 for the declaration of the contempt of the defendant.

[115] Wernz-Vidal, *Jus Canonicum,* VI, 355.

[116] Noval, *De Processibus,* I, 298; Cocchi, *De Processibus,* 215.

[117] Roberti, *De Processibus,* II, 6.

Thus the Code apparently treats the plaintiff much more leniently than the defendant. A defendant who does not appear in court or fails to excuse himself can be declared in contempt of court for his first act of disobedience to the court; but the plaintiff cannot be declared in contempt of court for disregarding the first summons of the court to be present for the joinder of issue, but the defendant can walk out of court and wait until he is summoned again, or he can insist upon the plaintiff's being made to appear and try the case. Should the defendant desire the case to be tried, the judge will again issue a summons to the plaintiff and if he willfully disregards this second summons the case will be tried without the presence of the plaintiff. The defendant will then advance proofs against the claims of the plaintiff as they were set forth in the original bill of complaint presented to the court. If, however, the contumacy occurs in the midst of the proceedings there are those who maintain that the plaintiff need not be summoned again.[118] The majority of authors hold that whenever the plaintiff is disobedient to the first summons a second summons must be issued [119] before he can be declared in contempt.

The judge will not *ex officio* declare the plaintiff in contempt of court. Like the defendant, the plaintiff will not be declared in contempt except on the motion of his opponent, the Promoter or the defender of the bond if they are present at the proceedings. The Promoter of Justice will seek the declaration of contempt in all causes pertaining to the public good save those entrusted to the defender of the bond. Hence as often as the plaintiff is in contempt in causes involving moral persons, or in causes relative to ecclesiastical benefices, and the rights and property connected with them, etc., it will be the Promoter who will seek the declaration in the event the other party fails to do so.[120] If the Promoter does not happen to be present at the proceedings and it is not one of those causes entrusted to the defender of the bond and the judge perceives that it

[118] Woywod, *Homiletic and Pastoral Review,* XXXII (1932), 1057.

[119] Roberti, *De Processibus,* II, 136, 137; Wernz-Vidal, *Jus Canonicum,* VI, 509.

[120] Canon 1849.

is of interest to the public good that the cause be carried to its logical conclusion in the sentence, he may cite the Promoter to seek the declaration of contempt.[121]

Muniz notes the custom in his own country whereby the Promoter of Justice is present at all incidental causes on contumacy. His presence is an added guarantee that no one will be declared in contumacy and deprived of his rights because of it, unless there is undeniable proof of the contempt.[122] This intervention of the Promoter is *praeter legem* but it is an added assurance that, as often as the public good is involved, it will not be without representation in the tribunal and thereby insures the presence of the Promoter to promote the cause in accordance with the provisions of Canon 1850, § 2.

The Promoter should never seek the declaration of contempt against the plaintiff unless all the conditions laid down in the law have been observed. In justice to the plaintiff he must have in his possession proof which carries with it at least moral certitude that the plaintiff received both summons and yet wilfully let them go unheeded. In that event, since the public good is involved, he has no choice save to petition the court for the declaration of contumacy.

Contempt of court by a plaintiff is considered far more serious than the same offense committed by the defendant and justly so, because it was the plaintiff who involved the other party in the annoyance of court proceedings. Wherefore, if he is declared guilty of contempt of court, he forfeits the right to prosecute the cause and the Code makes no provision for recovering the right or restoring it to him after repentance.[123] In affairs which concern the public good, the Promoter or the defender of the bond may take the place of the plaintiff who has been declared guilty of contempt of court; otherwise the defendant is given various means to free himself from further molestation in the case started by the plaintiff.[124]

This last canon supplements the former canon mentioned. The

[121] Noval, *De Processibus*, I, 394.

[122] Muniz, *Procedimientos Eccl.*, III, n. 199, 151.

[123] Canon 1850, § 1.

[124] Canon 1850, §§ 2, 3.

Promoter will not only seek the declaration of contempt against an obstinate plaintiff in a case involving the public good but will also prosecute the action by substituting himself for the absent plaintiff since it is to the public welfare that these causes be definitively settled by a judicial sentence.

Hence in all judicial causes involving the public good, *e. g.*, in those causes relative to benefices, their possession, their retention, the exercise of rights connected with them, in cases concerning ecclesiastical offices or involving moral persons and their rights as moral persons, the Promoter will substitute for the absent plaintiff and prosecute the cause through to the sentence and in appeal, should he consider the sentence of the first court unjust. Relative to the last named causes, *i. e.*, those involving moral persons, the Suprema Signatura in a decision on an appeal taken to itself notes that while the Promoter generally exercises a collateral office in these cases, he may on occasion become the principal actor in their behalf. It quotes the present Canon 1850 in support of this opinion of the supreme tribunal.[125] The decision notes that, while the negligence and failure of the administrator or rector of these persons must be supplied by the Ordinary as often as this negligence and failure occurs outside the curia,[126] it is the Promoter who will supply it as often as it happens in the midst of trial proceedings. He is the natural defender of their rights in judicial proceedings and, as often as the conditions of Canon 1850 are verified in a case involving their rights, the Promoter will be present to prosecute their claims.

The reason for the intervention of the Promoter is always the same; the public good demands that the ecclesiastical offices, benefices, the rights connected with them or with other moral persons, erected by the Church because of the benefits accruing from them to the public good, should not be held unjustly or illicitly. The common welfare of the faithful insists that the possessors of all these rights and properties should hold and exericise them justly and the

[125] *Signatura Apostolica, "Tergestina," Recursus,* 15 March, 1921—*A. A. S.*, XIII (1921), 271.

[126] Canon 1653, § 5.

Promoter of Justice as the official plaintiff for the public good should see to it that this just possession is definitively determined by the sentence of the court to be in rightful hands.[127]

In matrimonial causes it will be the defender of the bond who will seek the declaration of contumacy against the absent plaintiff. Should the judge declare the plaintiff in the matrimonial cause to be in contempt of court, he should cite the Promoter to prosecute the cause of nullity as often as there exists probable grounds of invalidity in the cause before him. The defender of the bond may not prosecute the cause for invalidity since he is not free in his conclusions, but must always defend the bond; whereas the Promoter of Justice is perfectly free in his conclusions and seeks only justice and truth in any cause.[128] Wherefore, if there exists grounds for believing the marriage invalid, the Promoter will prosecute the cause in the willful absence of the plaintiff. The invalidity of marriage is always prejudicial to the public good and to the salvation of the defendant and when the proceedings have reached this far and there is no hope of a reconciliation in happy marriage, there is nothing to be done but to have the status of the parties defined by the ecclesiastical courts.[129] The present canon empowers the Promoter of Justice to step into the rôle of plaintiff and to thereby relieve the intolerable situation of the defendant and also to remove the scandal which invariably accompanies null or doubtfully valid unions. He will at least attempt within the bounds of truth and justice to have the court define this marital status which has already, or which will inevitably, become a source of scandal to the faithful.[130]

Moreover, the Promoter may accept any assistance which the plaintiff who has been declared in contempt may care to offer him in the way of additional proof or conclusions.[131]

In all these cases the Promoter may appeal from the sentence of

[127] Lega, *De Judiciis Eccl.*, I, 267; Noval, *De Processibus,* I, 298; Blat, *Commentarium,* IV, 357.

[128] Roberti, *De Processibus,* I, 196; Bernardini, *Apollinaris,* VII (1934), 439.

[129] Roberti, *Apollinaris,* III (1930), 250; Creusen, *Nouvelle Revue Theologique,* 56 (1929), 682, 685, and 57 (1930), 521; Blat, *Commentarium,* IV, 503.

[130] Noval, *De Processibus,* I, 569; Roberti, *De Processibus,* I, 196.

[131] Roberti, *De Processibus,* II, 137.

the diocesan courts and the Promoter of Justice of the appellate court will prosecute his appeal.[182]

This rôle of the Promoter is an important one since it obviates many diffculties which might otherwise confront the public good as a result of the obstinacy of plaintiffs. It expedites and facilitates the public administration of justice in causes in which the parties themselves become the obstacles to the dispensing of justice. Moreover, it gives a definite, positive assurance that these questions which pertain to the public good will be authoritatively settled and not left doubtful. It thus marks a further extension by the Code of the public personality of the Promoter as the legitimate defender of all rights and things pertaining to the public ecclesiastical weal.

Article V. Two Minor Applications of the Office of the Promoter of Justice in Contentious Cases

The Church is always solicitous that those who seek her services in judicial adjustments of their difficulties should obtain full justice and enjoy an adequate protection of their rights. This solicitude is aptly demonstrated in the two legal provisions which form the object of this article on the duties of the Promoter.

As often as a party is in danger of suffering an injustice, either in virtue of a denial of the services of her courts or because of their inability to provide skilled counsel for the proper protection of their rights, the ecclesiastical law makes express provision for the protection of the rights of those who seek justice through her and prescribes that the Promoter of Justice intervene in the proceedings and insure that the provisions placed by the law at the disposal of deserving parties are accorded to them. The presence of the Promoter is considered by the law to be an additional guarantee that the party petitioning the application of these legal remedies will certainly obtain them, if their claims are within the bounds of reason and justice. In both instances the presence of the Promoter of Justice is held to be legally necessary and the judge of the tribunal,

[182] Canon 1879; *Apostolica Signatura, Recursus—A. A. S.*, XIII (1921), 271.

otherwise competent, may not proceed to the exercise of its rights without first consulting the Promoter and hearing his official opinion in the matter.[133]

The first of these instances in which the Promoter must be heard is in the recourse against the decree of rejection of an introductory *libellus;* the second is in the granting of free legal services.

The Promoter of Justice and the Recourse Against the Decree of Rejection of the Libellus

Upon the examination of the introductory *libellus* petitioning the service of the court in the judicial adjustment of difficulties, the judge or the tribunal, according to the nature of the cause which forms the object of the judicial controversy, will either admit it or reject it.[134] In the event that the court decides upon the latter course, it will return the *libellus* to the petitioner stating the reasons for the rejection.

The rejection of the *libellus* may be of a twofold nature. It may be only a relative rejection, inasmuch as the bill contains minor errors which may be corrected and, if presented to the court again according to the suggested corrections, it will be acceptable to the court. On the other hand, the rejection of the *libellus* may be absolute because it labors under a defect which it is not within the power of the petitioner to correct. Such defects would be: the claim of the court that it is absolutely incompetent; the decision of the court that the plaintiff lacks the juridical capacity to stand in court; or the court feels that there are no grounds for action extant in the case, etc.[135]

As often as the judge or the tribunal absolutely rejects the *libellus,* the petitioner may take recourse against the decree of rejection if he feels himself aggrieved by it. The recourse is always proposed to the tribunal which is competent to receive the appeals from the court which rejected the *libellus.*[136]

133 Canons 1709, § 3; 1915, § 2; Roberti, *De Processibus,* I, 198.

134 Canon 1709, § 1.

135 Roberti, *De Processibus,* I, 431.

136 Canon 1709, § 3; Muniz, *Procedimientos Eccl.,* III, 91.

The nature of this recourse is absolutely singular in the Code.[137] It offers a striking analogy to appeal but differs from it as no sentence or process precedes it and, although no appeal is given from the decree of the second court, the affair does not become a *res judicata.* The legislator, however, practically endows this recourse with the character of an appeal and with the effects of one; for he prescribes that it is to be made to the superior tribunal and not to the superior himself and it is to be defined only after hearing the party and the Promoter of Justice or the defender of the bond.[138]

The recourse is interposed by a new petition in which the court of appeal is asked to set aside the decree of rejection and admit the petition of the plaintiff. This recourse must be interposed within ten days from the time of notification of the decree of rejection, but since the time is useful time it does not run unless it is unimpeded. A copy of the rejected petition and the decree of rejection should accompany the petition for the withdrawal of the decree of the lower court.[139]

If the petition concerns the rejection of a petition involving the bond of matrimony, the Promoter need not concern himself with it as the defender of the bond will be cited and his presence suffices in the expediting of the hearing. The Promoter will be cited to be present at the discussion on the rejection of the *libellus* as often as the rejected *libellus* pertains to any other matter, private or public.[140]

The reason for the intervention of the Promoter of Justice is that the rejection of the *libellus* always carries with it the danger lest the definitive rejection of the recourse be equivalent to denial of justice. Such refusal of the use of the ecclesiastical courts in the prosecution of one's rights or claims always pertains to the public good, since it is essential to the public good that every individual be given a reasonable opportunity to vindicate his own just rights. For this reason the law prescribes that the Promoter of Justice in-

[137] Roberti, *De Processibus,* I, 431.

[138] Canon 1709, § 3; Noval, *De Processibus,* I, 282.

[139] Roberti, *De Processibus,* I, 431.

[140] Canon 1709, § 3; Roberti, *De Processibus,* I, 432; Noval, *De Processibus,* I, 282; Blat, *Commentarium,* IV, 234.

tervene and that he be heard since it will become his official duty to vindicate to the individual the exercise of those rights, the unjust denial of which would prove injurious to the Church since it would serve to harm her good repute as the champion of the underprivileged and would weaken that full confidence and wholesome respect in her courts so essential to the full success of her mission on earth.[141] A further and practical reason is to be found in the fact that the court of appeal is ordinarily some distance away and the presence of the Promoter assures the one taking the recourse of a skilled legal official representative to protect his claims.

The Promoter will examine the reasons for rejection set forth by the lower court and will compare these with the proofs submitted by the petitioner and from these two sources he will form his own independent opinion in which he will set forth the reasons why he believes the decree of the lower court should be upheld or set aside. The tribunal must cite him and give him an opportunity to voice that opinion if its decree is to be valid.[142]

The Promoter of Justice and the Gratuitous Legal Service

It is evident that the legal costs of lawsuits initiated for the benefit of private individuals should be defrayed by the litigating parties. The government of the Church and the State has many expenses incidental upon the proper administration of justice. Many men must be employed and the supplies necessary to expedite judicial processes must be purchased and hence it is only just that these expenses should be defrayed by the parties who avail themselves of the services of the courts. The civil courts as well as the ecclesiastical courts compel the litigants to pay the costs of the trial.

While the justice of the law that requires the parties to pay the judicial expenses is not questioned by anyone, all admit at the same time that the poor who are not able to pay the costs of a judicial trial should enjoy free legal defense of their rights. In the laws of the various States of the Union one finds provisions made for a

[141] Noval, *De Processibus,* I, 252; Blat, *Commentarium,* IV, 234.

[142] Canons 1709, § 3, 105, n. 1; 1587, § 1; Muniz, *Procedimientos Eccl.,* III, 101, gives an exemplar of this votum of the Promoter.

public defender who will be appointed by the judge to defend the poor in criminal cases as often as they cannot provide defense for themselves. No such general provision is made for the defense of the poor in civil proceedings and it is impossible to ascertain satisfactorily whether or not the individual States make provisions for the gratuitous legal service in these cases also. The Canon Law, on the other hand, from ancient times provided for free legal protection of the poor both in civil and criminal trials. An early example of this solicitude is to be found in the Code of the African Church, codified in the year 419, and the provision which it embodies relative to the defense of the rights of the poor appeared in many earlier Councils of the African Church. The provision reads as follows: "Because of the affliction of the poor, whose molestations weary the Church unceasingly, defenders shall by provision of the bishops be appointed for them against the power of the rich."[143] At the time of Pope St. Gregory the Great, who died in the year 604, the Roman curia had an official defender of the poor and he was appointed with the formula: "Receive the office of the defenders of the Church so that you may without compensation and with energy execute whatever will be commanded you by us for the benefit of the poor.[144] During the troublesome time of the Middle Ages the Church provided free legal service where the State had refused it.[145] Still later one finds Paul IV enjoining the advocates of the poor to visit the jails of the city and to place their services at the disposal of those who could not afford legal counsel.[146] The office of advocate for the poor lapsed for a time but one sees Benedict XIII reestablishing it for the Province of Rome in the Council held at Rome in 1725.[147] It cannot be said that there were always of-

[143] Codex Canonum Eccl. Africanae, n. LXXV—Harduinus, *Acta Conciliorum,* I, 903.

[144] Galletti, *Del primicerio della S. Sede Apostolica i di altri ufficiali magiori del sagro palagio Lateranense* (Roma, 1776), 151.

[145] Cc. 10, 11, 15, X, *de foro comp.,* II, 1; C. 26, X, *de verb. signif.,* V, 40.

[146] *Bullarium Romanum,* VII, 219.

[147] *Coll. Lac.,* I, 358, 432.

fical defenders of the poor at the Roman curia through all the centuries, but free defense of the poor was always provided in the recourse of the poor to Rome and the Holy See.[148]

When, at the reorganization of the Roman curia, special rules were published for the Sacred Roman Rota and the *Signatura Apostolica,* the two established tribunals of the Holy See, these laws ruled expressly that the poor have a right to exemption from legal costs and to free legal services. The dean of the Rota or the Cardinal Prefect of the *Signatura* have the right to order an attorney from among those permitted to practice before the respective tribunals to take up the defense of the poor without payment for his services by his client.[149]

This law of the tribunals of the Universal Church has been made binding upon all ecclesiastical courts of the Catholic world in virtue of Canon 1914. The fact that the Code calls this a right of the poor precludes the possibility that any court may deny the favors which the Supreme Authority of the Church grants them. If then the litigant proves that he is not able to pay the costs of the trial and the services of an attorney and yet has a just reason to go to law, the court may not refuse to accept his lawsuit because of his inability to pay.

The Code nowhere states or defines what is meant by the term "paupers" nor can any general law state what it considers to be a poor person. The man who depends upon his wages for the sustenance of himself and his family and who, only by frugality, is able to save a small amount to invest in a home of his own or in some safe and profitable investment as a protection against old age and such misfortunes as come in life, is poor, although he does not lack the necessities of life and perhaps enjoys a few of its comforts.[150] Most American Catholics are in this class who have little more than the necessities of life and are for the most part more than willing to do their share in the external works of the Church as the history

[148] Pertile, *Storia del Diritto Italiano,* § 222; Wernz-Vidal, *Jus Canonicum,* VI, 598.

[149] Lex Propria S. R. Rotae et Sig. Ap., Cap. IV—*A. A. S.,* I (1909), 34.

[150] Noval, *De Processibus,* I, 454.

of the Church in this country readily attests.[151] If the Catholic has been faithful in his attendance at Church, he is most certainly deserving of deepest consideration from the ecclesiastical judge, should he petition the diminution or exemption from legal expenses and fees. These people have made the many external works of the Church possible by their sacrifices and donations and when they petition the services of her tribunals the judge should grant them the consideration they justly merit.

The law commands that the judge be conscientious in his investigation into the financial status of the petitioner, so much so that it authorizes him to make private investigation into their resources.

The other point which the poor person must establish is common to all trials before the Church and not peculiar to him. The Church abhors lawsuits and, after the example of her Founder, favors the amicable and private settlement of difficulties if that is at all possible. Every civilized court demands that a person have a reason before he will be admitted to use its services.

Before the judge proceeds to grant free legal services and to appoint an attorney, he must confer with the Promoter of Justice, whose business it is to see that justice is accorded to all who appear before the ecclesiastical courts and hence that the genuinely poor receive a full defense of their rights.[152]

The Promoter of Justice has a cumulative duty with the judge to see that no one is denied a full defense of his rights because he lacks the temporal means to provide it himself. He will conscientiously examine the petition and the proofs alleged to support the two points, described above, which must be verified in every petition for gratuitous legal services. Should he deem that the petitioner warrants the consideration of the court, he will use the influence of his public office to obtain the decree of free legal services or of lower costs in favor of the petitioner. If, on the other hand, he feels that the petition as submitted is unwarranted, he will oppose the granting of the concession unless further additional proof is forthcom-

[151] Woywod, *Homiletic and Pastoral Review*, XXXIII (1932, 1933), 492, 493.

[152] Canon 1915, § 2; Noval, *De Processibus*, I, 456; Roberti, *De Processibus*, II, 181.

ing which undoubtedly establishes the petitioner as poor. He has not only the duty to vindicate full defense to the poor, but also has the duty to protect the diocesan fisc and its just right to the expenses for private judicial causes against the fraudulent and undeserving petitioner who would defraud that fisc of what is its just due.[153]

The new norms of the Rota place an additional obligation upon its Promoter to see to it that the advocates assigned to the cases of the poor diligently perform their duties and to report any laxity in the performance of the same.[154] This seems but natural since his duty to see that the poor obtain a full defense of their rights does not cease with the appointment of an advocate.

The Code is silent on what recourse may be taken should the judge deny the petition of the party. The Rota permits the party or the Promoter to have recourse against the decree of the judge to the *turnus* or to the whole body of the tribunal.[155]

The petitioner who feels himself aggrieved by the decree of the diocesan court may appeal to the Ordinary.[156] The Promoter of Justice who advised the granting of gratuitous *patrocinium* to the petitioner may also call the attention of the Ordinary to the adverse decree of the court if he feels the party aggrieved by it. The law commands that he be cited and heard in its granting and if the petition is just and is denied his defense of the rights of the poor certainly does not stop there or it is a nude defense. His office certainly implies that he will oppose any adverse decree in this matter which is obviously unjust.

[153] Regulae Servandae . . . S. R. R. Tribunal § 217—*A. A. S.*, II (1910), 845; Roberti, *De Processibus*, II, 281.

[154] Normae S. R. R. Tribunalis, art. 21—*A. A. S.*, XXVI (1934), 458.

[155] Normae S. R. R. Tribunalis, art. 181—*A. A. S.*, XXVI (1934), 491.

[156] Roberti, *De Processibus*, II, 282; D'Angelo, *Apollinaris*, II (1929), 515.

CHAPTER VIII

THE RIGHTS AND DUTIES OF THE PROMOTER OF JUSTICE IN THE PROSECUTION OF CRIMINAL CAUSES AND OF THOSE CAUSES WHICH PERTAIN TO THE PUBLIC GOOD

THE rights and duties of the Promoter to introduce causes and to intervene in criminal causes and certain contentious cases, as expressly provided by the law, has been considered in the previous articles. There the general duties of the Promoter as outlined in Canons 1586, 1934, 1955 and 1971 were considered. There still remains the consideration and study of his rights and duties in prosecuting these causes before the courts until a final settlement has been reached which is satisfactory to the public good he represents. The Code does not content itself with this general statement of his duties. It mentions him in connection with a large number of canons to be found scattered throughout the whole Fourth Book of the Code in which his rights and duties in the prosecution of causes are noted and stressed.

In order to simplify the study of his duties in the subsequent stages of the trial, the general outline of a trial as given in the Code will be followed, treating first the general duties of the Promoter relative to the trial proper and then considering him in relation to the individual steps which go to make up the trial and its subsequent contingencies.

ARTICLE I. THE PROMOTER OF JUSTICE AND THE JUDICIAL CONFESSION

Canonists in treating of specific proofs generally begin their treatises with a discussion on confession and rightly so. The judicial confession has always been considered the queen of proofs. Especially in the early inquisitorial procedures every conceivable effort was made to obtain a confession.[1] But under the prevailing

[1] Wernz, *Jus Decretalium,* V, 442, 443.

legislation no coercive means of any nature may be employed to procure a confession from the accused.[2] The Promoter and the judge must bear in mind that the shrewd and browbeating methods sometimes found in the civil courts have no place in the ecclesiastical procedure.

This may be concluded from the fact that the rules of the common law forbid the requirement of an oath to tell the truth from the defendant in criminal causes and from the stringent rulings on the examination of parties which forbid the judge and the Promoter to put questions in such a way that the defendant will be unavoidably led to commit himself on the delict perpetrated by himself.[3]

Confession may be defined as a statement, oral or written, made before the ecclesiastical judge by one party against himself and in favor of the other party, spontaneously, or upon the demand of the judge.[4] The text permits not only spontaneous confession but also elicited confession. That one may confess of his own accord is evident. On the other hand, the judge also may solicit a confession; but, as previously remarked, he may not resort to questionable tactics in order to obtain it and the blistering, ensnaring cross-examination of the civil courts is not tolerated in ecclesiastical courts.

Besides this express confession authors before the Code speak of the tacit confession.[5] The Code still retains this idea of implicit confession in several canons, *e. g.*, Canon 1800, § 4, permits the refusal to submit specimens of handwriting to be interpreted as a confession of the authenticity of a document. Some authors would evaluate the contempt of court as an implicit confession of guilt.[6] Other canons leave it to the discretion of the judge as to whether certain actions or failures to act are to be considered as confessions.[7]

[2] Canons 1750-1753.

[3] Canons 1743, § 1; 1744.

[4] Canon 1750; Augustine, *A Commentary*, VII, 197.

[5] Lega, *De Judiciis Eccl.*, I, 472; Reiffenstuel, lib. II, tit. XVIII, n. 5.

[6] Muniz, *Procedimientos Eccl.*, III, 230, n. 1.

[7] Canons 1743, § 2; 1831, § 2; 1836, § 4; Roberti, *De Processibus*, II, 34.

A confession may also be extrajudicial. A confession is a judicial confession when it is made in court before the competent judge acting in his official capacity as judge. Both conditions are necessary for a valid judicial confession.[8] Hence a confession made to the judge, but not in court, is extrajudicial or if it was made in another trial, ecclesiastical or civil, but not made in the present proceedings, it would likewise be extrajudicial. The same must be said of the confession made to private individuals or to the Promoter of Justice even though it be made under oath and signed by the defendant.[9] In this the Canon Law is stricter than the common law.[10]

A confession to constitute full proof in court must have certain qualities. These qualities are set forth in the Code and have been derived from the Decretals.[11] The confession to have the value of proof must be judicial in the sense explained above. It should be clear and definite and allege something against oneself and in favor of the other party.[12] It should be spontaneous and made with full knowledge, that is, free from the stress of passion, provocation, error of fact, etc.[13]

When all the conditions required by the law are verified one has a confession in the full sense. What will be the effect of such confession upon the action of the Promoter? An extrajudicial confession and a tacit confession, whether considered such by the law or by the judge, does not constitute full proof in causes involving the public good. They at most form presumptive evidence and must be joined to other strong evidence if the Promoter hopes to win his

[8] Canon 1750; Wernz, *Jus Decretalium,* V, 441, n. 8; Augustine, *A Commentary,* VII, 197.

[9] Reiffenstuel, lib. II, tit. 18, n. 9; A Coronata, *Institutiones J. C.,* III, 185.

[10] Droste-Messmer, *Canonical Procedure in Disciplinary and Criminal Cases of Clerics,* p. 98.

[11] Canons 1750, 1751; c. 2, X, *de confessis,* II, 18; c. 4, X, *de judiciis,* II, 1.

[12] Relative to the qualified confession and its probatory value, *cf.* Reiffenstuel, lib. II, tit. 18, par. 1, n. 23; Noval, *De Processibus,* I, 318-320.

[13] Muniz, *Procedimientos Eccl.,* III, 231; for a full explanation of the qualities of a judicial confession, *cf.* Noval, *De Processibus,* I, 320, 321; Wernz-Vidal, *Jus Canonicum,* VI, 388; Roberti, *De Processibus,* II, 34, 35.

case. The qualified confession is admissable in criminal trials but its value as proof is left to the estimation of the judge.

The effect of an unqualified confession made freely and deliberately is very moderately stated by the law in Canon 1751: "It frees the other party from the burden of proof." Hence if the defendant confesses his obligation or guilt, the plaintiff has won the case and in private contentious cases the judge may proceed to pass sentence. In causes affecting the public good, and such would be all causes in which the Promoter was present, the confession of the party does not produce full proof.

The other effect of the judicial confession stated in Canon 1752 is that the confession once made cannot be retracted. This rule admits of two exceptions and the party can revoke his confession, provided he does so immediately before he leaves the court and can prove that the confession was not made legitimately or that it was made in virtue of an error of fact.[14]

These are the only two effects retained by the Code from the prior legislation on the effects of confession. Thus the prevailing law passes over all the other effects attributed to a judicial confession by the authors who interpreted the legislation before the Code.[15]

Under the pre-Code legislation, once a valid confession had been obtained, there was no need to proceed further even in criminal proceedings. The *Promotor Fiscalis* was relieved of the burden of further proof and the judge merely determined the presence of the necessary conditions and pronounced sentence without further prosecution by the Promoter.[16]

It is evident from the present law, as stated in Canon 1751, that this is no longer true. The valid judicial confession indeed simplifies the task of the Promoter; but it does not exempt him from the obligation of producing further proof, since the judicial confession does not constitute full proof in causes involving the

[14] Canon 1750.

[15] Schmalzgrueber, lib. II, tit. XVIII, nn. 22 ss.; Wernz, *Jus Decretalium*, V, 445.

[16] Heiner, *De Processu Criminali Eccl.*, 53, 54; S. B. Smith, *Elements of Ecclesiastical Law*, II, 81; Wernz, *Jus Decretalium*, V, 445.

public good. Now all the causes in which the Promoter will be involved pertain to the public good in which, therefore, the defendant's confession does not carry with it the canonical notoriety of law exempting the Promoter from establishing his claims or charges with proof independently of the confession.[17]

The judicial confession is, nevertheless, an exceptionally fine proof in aiding the judge to obtain moral certitude and in passing sentence. If it occurs in a criminal cause and the crime admits of judicial correction, it should be administered and the action of the Promoter is suspended until such time as the defendant lapses from his good behavior.[18] If the judicial correction cannot be used or the Ordinary adjudges it to be useless, the public good will demand that the Promoter establish the truth concerning the delict and its author by judicial proofs other than the confession of the defendant and that the defendant be punished by judicial sentence.[19] The public good will demand that the court determine the exact delict committed, the degree of imputability to its author and the penalties to be imposed upon him. The Promoter, consequently, will proceed to establish these three things, a comparatively easy task in view of the confession of the defendant already in the possession of the court. In the remaining cases in which he appears, the Promoter will vindicate the object of the controversy by additional proofs and will seek any damages that may be connected with the action.

Before leaving the question of the Promoter and judicial confessions, it should be remarked that the Promoter is never permitted to make one. The Code, indeed, allows it to both parties[20] and, although the Promoter does occasionally come under the name of a party, he may not make a confession in those cases in which he appears as plaintiff. The reason is self-evident; for the Promoter in exercising his office is the representative of the public good and he may not do anything that would be prejudicial to that public

[17] A Coronata, *Institutiones J. C.*, III, 186; Noval, *De Processibus*, I, 321; Roberti, *De Processibus*, II, 36; Augustine, *A Commentary*, VII, 199.

[18] Canon 1950.

[19] Noval, *De Processibus*, I, 535.

[20] Canon 1751.

good.[21] In criminal trials and in those contentious cases which involve the public good the necessity of conducting the proceedings has been carefully weighed by the bishop and the Promoter in their previous extrajudicial investigation into the matter. These investigations have resulted in the decision that the best interests of the diocese demand a judicial prosecution which, in turn, was entrusted to the Promoter of Justice. In the event that he notices his case is not too strong, he may make the bishop aware of it and let him take any action he sees fit as to the withdrawal of the case or he may continue to present his case for the public good as clearly and as justly as he can, leaving to the judge the decision as to what is justice in the case and not taking upon himself the exculpation of the accused or the defendant by his own judicial confession.

Article II. The Promoter of Justice in the Probatory Period

A. *His Right to Call Witnesses*

Among the evidence strictly so called, the testimony of witnesses holds the first rank in all trials. It is the best weapon in the hands of a plaintiff in establishing the claims or charges which he has caused to be brought against the defendant. Hence the calling and the examining of witnesses form an all important part of the trial in which the public good has caused the Promoter of Justice in his rôle of official plaintiff to bring certain charges or to promote certain interests pertaining to the common weal of the Church in the diocese.

The duty of the Promoter of Justice in that part of the trial in which the proof and evidence of the trial are set forth by the parties and the witnesses is not satisfied by a mere presence on the part of the Promoter. On the contrary, from the very nature of the proceedings in which he appears, the whole brunt of the case for the public good falls upon his shoulders. In the criminal trial he has brought charges against the accused and since it is his duty to see

[21] Noval, *De Processibus,* I, 321; A Coronata, *Institutiones J. C.,* III, 184; Muniz, *Procedimientos Eccl.,* III, 228, n. 2.

to it that the defendant is justly punished because of his offense against the ecclesiastical society, it will likewise be his duty to be present actively to sustain by means of substantiating evidence the charges he has brought. So also in those cases which the public good has caused him to introduce or to intervene, the defense of that public good will entail an active participation in this part of the trial or it will constitute no defense whatsoever. In these cases, criminal and contentious, he appears as the official plaintiff for the public good and just as every plaintiff is expected to support actively his claims, so also is the Promoter of Justice, and especially since he has been designated by law as the sole official plaintiff in the prosecution of the public interests.[22]

Little wonder then that the Code expressly grants the Promoter the right to call witnesses. He enjoys this right for a twofold reason. He enjoys the right in common with all parties to a trial as often as he appears as the plaintiff in a cause in order to substantiate the charges or the claims he has set forth in his *libellus* and to defend them against the challenges and counterclaims of the defendant.[23] He also enjoys the right to call witnesses in those cases in which he does not appear as plaintiff but acts in a collateral capacity inasmuch as the cause pertains to the public good and in which he appears only to defend the public good in the issues of the trial which touch upon it. Consequently, in virtue of his office, he can call witnesses even in private cases as often as these cases involve the public welfare.[24]

The production of witnesses in criminal and contentious cases is ruled by the same general regulations set forth in the Code to govern this step in any trial.[25] In general, the production of witnesses observes the following legal form. The Promoter who is

[22] Canons 1586, 1934, 1955; Noval, *De Processibus,* I, 333; Roberti, *De Processibus,* II, 51, 62, 63, n. 1, 63; Heiner, *De Processu Criminali Ecclesiastico,* 67.

[23] Canon 1759, § 1.

[24] Canon 1759, § 2; Noval, *De Processibus,* I, 333; certain authors also quote Canons 1968, 1969 to vindicate this right to the Promoter but the Code gives him all the authority he needs in the canon cited above.

[25] Canon 1959.

calling the witness directs a written petition to the judge clearly stating the full name of his witnesses together with their place of residence. He also includes in the petition *positiones* or articles which he requests the judge to use as the basis for the questioning of his own witnesses and of those called by the opposing parties. This petition is ordinarily addressed to the chancery office.[26]

In the pre-Code legislation these *positiones* had a very definite form.[27] They were akin to the contestation of the cause and had the same purpose as the *litis contestatio,* namely, to fix the issue or the charges to be proved. These *positiones* were nothing more than certain, brief, concise, categorical questions, assertions, specifications or counts pertaining to the cause which one of the litigants (usually the plaintiff) submitted to the judge with the request that the other litigant (usually the defendant) be compelled to answer categorically "yes" or "no," or whether he admitted or denied them, and that for the purpose of being relieved from the burden of proving these points or specifications which were admitted by the opposing party to the trial.[28] Their name was derived from their affirmative character and their value is readily seen; for if the *Promotor Fiscalis,* for example, proposed such specifications and *positiones* and the defendant admitted five and contended that only five were false, it would be necessary to prove only five as the other five are already established by the defendant's confession which, as was seen, constituted full proof under the old law.

These forms are no longer used and the question lists are now submitted for the questioning of both the parties and the witnesses alike. In fact, the *positiones* which formerly had for their objective the soliciting of the confession of the accused generally are not used in modern criminal trials; the prevailing curial practice finds the question lists much more preferable since they have as their object to discover the objective truth in any given case. This had become

[26] Canon 1761, §§ 1, 2; Roberti, *De Processibus,* II, 51.

[27] C. 2, *De verb. signif.,* V, 11, in Clem.

[28] Glossa in c. 1, *De confessis,* II, 9 in VI; Bouix, *De Judiciis Eccl.,* II, 207; Reiffenstuel, lib. II, tit. XVIII, nn. 89 ss.; A Coronata, *Institutiones J. C.,* III, 172.

the curial practice in criminal trials at the close of the last century.[29]

These question lists are intended to show the indentity of the witness, the knowledge he is thought to possess concerning the issue on trial, and especially the source of that knowledge in his possession. The questions themselves follow the general rules on questioning and hence leading and suggestive questions are not permitted. A leading question is that which puts into the mouth of the witness the words to be echoed back or the answer which the party expects to get from him.[30] The best procedure for the Promoter in framing his questionnaire is to proceed gradually from the general to the particular. Then, too, the questions should not be captious or obscure, misleading the witnesses and attempting to wring from him an admission he does not intend.[31]

Moreover, the general rules on procedure prescribe that ordinarily the names of the witnesses should be interchanged between the parties even before the examination of witnesses has taken place.[32] This interchange is effected through the judge to whom the names of the witnesses had been submitted along with the petition that they be cited and examined in the case. However, if such action would considerably embarrass the witness or there is danger of reprisal or bribery, the judge may exercise the discretionary power granted him by the law and withhold the exchange of names until after the publication of process.[33]

The reason for this interchange of names is to give the parties an opportunity to exercise their right to exclude objectionable and prejudicial witnesses, thereby affording them a legitimate form of defense guaranteed them in the ecclesiastical law. They have the right to seek the exclusion of the witness in the three days following the disclosure of the names of the witnesses. They may not exercise this right after the peremptory period of the three days

[29] A Coronata, *Institutiones J. C.*, III, 198; Craisson, *Manuale Juris Canonici*, IV, n. 5938, 169; Bouix, *De Judiciis Eccl.*, II, 210.

[30] Bouvier, *Law Dictionary*, "The Leading Question."

[31] Canon 1775; Wernz-Vidal, *Jus Canonicum*, VI, 370.

[32] Canon 1763.

[33] Canon 1763; Roberti, *De Processibus*, II, 51.

has expired, unless they can prove or affirm under oath that the objection to the witness was not previously known to them.[34]

The Promoter has the express right to call witnesses and may exercise all the rights which all the other parties to the trial enjoy relative to that form of proof.[35] Since the parties have the right to seek the disqualification of a witness, he, as the official plaintiff or protector of the public good in criminal causes or contentious cases in which he acts in virtue of his office, may also exercise a similar right; otherwise his defense of the charges which he has brought or the claims which he has set forth would be hopelessly weakened. Canonists recognize this right as coextensive with his duties in criminal proceedings [36] and the same reasons would be applicable to his duties in the contentious cases in which he appears in the pursuance of the duties of his office.

The question naturally arises: Is the Promoter bound to give the names of the witnesses to the defendant in criminal proceedings? The question was partially discussed in connection with the presentation of the *libellus* in criminal trials. It was noted then that the authors and the practice of courts permitted the suppression of names for grave reasons, provided these reasons were admitted by the judge. The present canon implies that the interchange of names between the parties is the ordinary procedure. It makes no distinction between the criminal and contentious proceedings and hence the Promoter is not exempted from the obligation of this canon. The reason for this is that the disqualification of witnesses is considered by the law as a very effective part of a legitimate defense. It is very important for the accused to reveal the character of the witness in the criminal trial and thereby upset his credibility.

The canon, however, admits of an exception which may be more easily verified in criminal causes, whereby the judge is permitted to suppress the publication of names until the moment of the publication of process as often as there is a grave reason for doing so. Canonists go even further and say that the names of the wit-

[34] Canon 1764, § 4; A Coronata, *Institutiones J. C.*, III, 201, 202.

[35] Canon 1764, § 4; Noval, *De Processibus*, I, 333.

[36] A Coronata, *Institutiones J. C.*, III, 204; Muniz, *Procedimientos Eccl.*, III, 241.

nesses need never be published should the grave reason persist and care be taken to examine the witnesses properly and justly and provided their testimony has been delivered to the defendant.[37] They base their contentions not upon any positive prescript of law, but upon justice and fairness to the witness who might suffer any injustices as a result of his services to the public good as a witness.

It is the judge and not the Promoter who is to evaluate the presence of grave reasons permitting the suppression of the names of the witnesses. Nor should the Promoter seek the suppression unless the grave reason is actually verified in the case. The presence of the grave reason required for the suppression of the names of the witnesses is not to be easily imagined in this country according to the opinion of our own American canonist S. B. Smith.[38] He is most insistent upon the right of the defendant to know the names of the witnesses and excuses the Promoter from the obligation only in cases of heresy and admits of this exception only because the prevailing law made it.

In the event that the judge decides that the reasons for not publishing the name of a witness are satisfactory, it becomes the absolute duty of the Promoter to examine carefully the competence and credibility of the witness, whether he be for the defense or the prosecution. He must sincerely endeavor to determine whether there be any solid ground for the challenge of such a witness and he should anticipate the exceptions of the court, which will be more exacting in its examination of this witness and will demand proof of his reliability as a witness and his freedom from such challenge as might be made were the defendant fully cognizant of his identity. Then, and only then, will the court admit the petition of the Promoter requesting that his witness be heard but that his identity be kept a secret.[39]

[37] *Regulae Servandae . . . S. R. R. Tribunal*, par. 116—*A. A. S.*, II (1910), 821; Wernz-Vidal, *Jus Canonicum*, VI, 420; Heiner, *De Processu Crim. Eccl.*, p. 147 ss. and p. 151 ss.; Pierantonelli, *Praxis Fori Eccl.*, n. 22, p. 144.

[38] S. B. Smith, *New Procedure in Criminal and Disciplinary Causes of Ecclesiastics in United States*, 145, 146.

[39] *Regulae Servandae . . . S. R. R. Tribunal*, par. 116, n. 3—*A. A. S.*,

This would seem to give the Promoter an unfair advantage over the defendant because the former is permitted to be present at the examination of the witnesses of the accused and in the case under consideration the names of the witnesses are not even disclosed to the defendant. Does this not militate against the principle that the accused is the privileged party to any trial? At first sight it would seem so; but the objection loses force when one considers the reasons in behalf of which the Promoter exercises his office. The Promoter is bound by his oath of office to respect the just rights of the accused and to do all in his power to accord him a fair trial. In the case under consideration the Promoter will be bound in conscience to investigate thoroughly the character of his witness and to examine his past life, his relationship with the accused and the reputation he enjoys in his own community. Besides, the court in its examination will be stricter with this type of witness and will employ every reasonable safeguard to protect the constitutional rights of the accused. It is to be expected that the Promoter will do all these things since the Code demands of him the same qualifications as are demanded of the judge himself; for the law demands that the Promoter of Justice be straightforward and zealous for justice.[40]

When the names have been disclosed, and this will be the ordinary course, the party has three days in which to challenge the witness. These three days run from whatever moment in the trial the names are made known to the party; otherwise he loses the right to challenge the admission of the witness unless he can establish the exception admitted in paragraph 4 of Canon 1764. The Promoter is bound by the same rules of procedure and must exercise his right of challenge within the periods prescribed by the law since the law mentions no exceptions.

Nor may the Promoter drop or reject the testimony of a witness introduced by himself; for in producing him he has expressly approved his qualifications as a witness. Only if a reason to object to

II (1910), 822; Wernz-Vidal, *Jus Canonicum,* VI, 420; Pierantonelli, *Praxis Fori Eccl.,* 144.

[40] Canons 1589, 1573, § 4; 1613, §§ 1, 2.

the witness developed after he was summoned would the Promoter be permitted to place an exception against him.[41] This could easily happen in the causes for which the Promoter functions. Suppose a witness were to perjure himself, become infamous or, from a false sense of pity, contradict the original statements he made to the Promoter and which the latter knows to be true. Even though no new reason arose for the repudiation of his witness, the Promoter always has the right to contradict anything the witness says against his prosecution of a cause, because, although he may know the witness, he cannot know what he intends to say or what his intentions are until he has appeared in the court.

Relative to the number of witnesses which the Promoter may introduce, the present law is indefinite. It leaves it entirely to the discretion of the judge to regulate this matter by determining and restricting the number of witnesses so that the trial may not be unnecessarily prolonged.[42] The Promoter, however, should bear in mind that an unnecessary array of witnesses serves only to delay the decision, confuse the issue and annoy and disquiet all those connected with the trial. He will be prudent and invite only as many witnesses as are necessary to establish the truth of his charges or claims.[43]

Finally, can the Promoter demand the penalties mentioned in Canon 1755, § 3, to compel witnesses to testify in the causes in which he functions? It would seem so from the context of the canon. The Promoter *per se* has the right to seek the application of penalties and this canon gives the right to the judge to inflict the penalties on both lay persons and clerics who refuse to testify. The witness, however, should be first admonished to appear and testify or, if he has already appeared, he should be admonished to testify. If he declines to do so, he must make known his reason for his refusal.[44] In the event that further suasion by the judge and the Promoter fails to move him to testify, the usual canonical warnings

[41] Canon 1764, § 3.

[42] Canon 1762; c. 37, X, *De testibus,* II, 20.

[43] *A. S. S.,* II (1867), 406.

[44] Canon 1766.

having been made, the ecclesiastical law permits the application of penalties.[45] The reason for this is that the office of witness is one of public interest and affects the public welfare. All the more is this verified in the cases in which the Promoter acts since they, more than any other type of case, affect the common welfare. The common good will demand that persons exercise the office and that they may be compelled to do so.[46] All law recognizes the validity of compelling such service.

It was said that *per se* the Promoter had the right to seek the application of these penalties; but whether or not this would be a practicable procedure is another question. A distinction would seem to be advisable. If the witness is a lay person it would seem that the conclusion of S. B. Smith that compulsion by penalties should not be used on them in this country is correct.[47] Should the suasion of the Promoter or the judge fail to arouse their sense of duty to the ecclesiastical society, no further measures should be taken. With clerical witnesses, however, it does seem advisable to compel them to testify in the interests of the common ecclesiastical good since, by seeking ordination, they profess a special interest in the common welfare and therefore should be compelled to accept the public office in the interests of that welfare. All this presupposes, however, that the witness is not one of those persons expressly exempted by the law [48] since it was stated that he had no reasons for his refusal to testify.

B. *The Order in Which the Witnesses Are to Be Heard*

The order in which the witnesses are to be heard may be regulated by the judge. The plaintiff should present his witnesses first unless some reasonable cause dictates a change of order. After the witnesses of the plaintiff the witnesses of the defendant are heard and finally those called by the *Defensor Vinculi.* Witnesses

[45] Cc. 1-5, X, *De testibus cogendis vel non,* II, 21.

[46] Augustine, *A Commentary,* VII, 202, 203; S. B. Smith, *Elements of Ecclesiastical Law,* II, 104, 105; Droste-Messmer, *Canonical Procedure,* 111, 112.

[47] S. B. Smith, *Elements of Ecclesiastical Law,* II, 104.

[48] Canons 1755, § 2, nn. 1, 2; 1757, § 3.

called by the Promoter of Justice in cases in which he is not the plaintiff are heard after those called by the parties and, in the event that he is involved in a matrimonial trial, his witnesses will be heard after those of the parties and before those of the *Defensor Vinculi.*[49]

The preceding order is the ordinary order prescribed for contentious proceedings. It was noted previously, however, that in criminal trials the probatory period, unlike the order usually followed in contentious cases, was not common to both parties; but was preferably divided into two distinct periods, the first to be assigned to the Promoter, the second to the defendant. This division is based upon the practice of the ordinary ecclesastical tribunals and corresponds more closely to the nature of the criminal cause in which the defendant is the privileged party enjoying the right to be heard last.[50] The defendant is always given the full benefit of the law in his presentation of his defense and hence he need not present that defense until the prosecution has established its case against him. In the event that the prosecution fails to establish his guilt, he need not present a single witness to refute the demands of the Promoter; but will simply request the judge to dismiss the charges against him as unfounded and unproved.[51]

Hence, the Promoter will ordinarily present his witnesses in the term assigned by the judge at the moment of the formulation of the issue and in criminal trials the term will precede that for the production of the witnesses for the defense.

Any reasonable cause will justify the judge in departing from the order described for either criminal or contentious cases. The main purpose for the order is to keep the witnesses apart, so that they may be examined separately and to obviate all communication between the parties and the witnesses, thereby precluding the dangers which such meetings might occasion. Not infrequently these

[49] Muniz, *Procedimientos Eccl.,* III, 235, 236; S. B. Smith, *Elements of Ecclesiastical Law,* II, 398; Dolan, *Defensor Vinculi,* p. 60.

[50] Pellegrini, *Praxis Vicariorum,* Pars II, Sect. 2, Subsect. 3, n. 1; Bouix, *De Judiciis Eccl.,* II, 214; Noval, *De Processibus,* I, 296; *Regulae Servandae . . . S. R. R. Tribunal,* par. 41.

[51] Canons 1748, § 2, 1827.

cases involving the public good engender deep feelings on both sides and, were the parties and the witnesses confronted, it might work to the detriment of the interests of justice and lead to embarrassing situations which could otherwise be easily avoided by preventing the witnesses for both sides from appearing at the same time. The greater convenience to the witnesses and in some cases a real necessity on their part will demand a departure from the order described at least in individual instances. The witness should not be forced to lose work, suffer unwarranted expenses or inconvenience, if that can be avoided by hearing him at a later or earlier time than that assigned for the other witnesses of the party for whom he is to testify. Such reasons will justify the judge in arranging the time so that the witness may be heard outside the period assigned to him.

Witnesses may be called at any moment between the *litis contestatio* and the *publicatio processus,* when the judge by decree gives both sides the right to see the testimony that has been taken thus far in the process. These two stages mark the normal periods for the production of witnesses and the presentation of evidence.[52] The issue in pleading marks the opening of the probatory period [53] and the publication of process marks the close of the same period, since the parties have signified to the judge that they have exhausted their proofs and have nothing further to bring before the court.[54] Both of these terms admit exceptions of which the Promoter may avail himself in any cause in which he acts.

It was already noted when speaking of the *litis contestatio* and its effects on the action of the Promoter in criminal causes that prior to it and the fixation of the controverted points, the judge might not lawfully proceed to hear witnesses, to receive depositions or examine experts. It was noted that the law admitted of exceptions.[55]

The first exception is in cases of contumacy. In such cases when

[52] Canons 1730, 1860, §§ 2, 3.

[53] Canon 1731, § 2; Wernz-Vidal, *Jus Canonicum,* VI, 348.

[54] Canon 1860, §§ 2, 3; Roberti, *De Processibus,* II, 67.

[55] Canon 1730.

the defendant is in contempt from the first moment of his citation, the Promoter of a certainty may introduce witnesses to prove the contempt of the accused in order that the judge may declare it and proceed to define the issue in pleading, thereby leaving the former free to establish by witnesses and other proof the guilt of the accused and to demand the application of the correlative penalties and in other cases involving the public good to settle the issue by a definitive sentence.[56]

The canon itself cites a few instances in which the judge may proceed to hear witnesses before the *litis contestatio* because the condition of the witness makes it imperative that he be heard as soon as possible. A witness may be advanced in age so that his memory is weak; or he may be in danger of death; or he may be on the point of leaving for some distant place. These reasons for anticipating the hearing of witnesses are enumerated demonstratively for the canon adds that any other good reason of a similar nature which would render it impossible or highly difficult for the witness to testify during the trial would justify his examination before the *litis contestatio.*[57] Augustine gives another reason which might be easily verified in cases involving the public good, namely, it might be doubtful that the witness will be as willing to testify later as he is at present.[58] Whenever these or any other good reason are present, the Promoter would be justified in availing himself of the exception and should do so in the interests of the public good. It goes without saying that as often as the criminal procedure is by way of inquisition, the Promoter may suggest that certain witnesses be heard, even though there has been no *litis contestatio.* Should the Promoter know of available witnesses, either for the defense or the prosecution, his office would demand that he make these witnesses known to the bishop or the inquisitor.[59]

Relative to the concluding term of the probatory period and the prohibition against the introduction of further witnesses after the

[56] Wernz-Vidal, *Jus Canonicum,* VI, 349.

[57] A Coronata, *Institutiones J. C.,* III, 161; Noval, *De Processibus,* I, 295.

[58] Cc. 2, 3, X, *De testibus,* II, 20; Augustine, *A Commentary,* VII, 178.

[59] Canon 1586.

publication of the testimony, it should be borne in mind that the Promoter does not enjoy any special privileges in the matter.[60] He enjoys the same rights as any other party and no more. It was stated that the Promoter had the same duties as those mentioned in Canons 1968 and 1969 for the defender of the bond and that canonists recognized these duties as a part of his office, but that does not mean that he enjoys the privileges which those canons expressly confer upon the defender of the bond. There it is expressly stated that the *Defensor Vinculi* has the right to call witnesses at any time in the trial, even after the *publicatio processus* and needs no grave cause for this but may do so as long as he deems it useful in the case.[61] The Promoter enjoys no such privilege in the presenation of witnesses. He may present them after the publication of process only when the conditions laid down in Canon 1786 are verified. As often as these conditions are present, he, like any other party to a trial, may petition the judge to call witnesses, but not otherwise.[62]

What constitutes the very serious reason permitting the exception, the Code does not specify; but rather leaves it to the discretion of the judge.[63] Authors before the Code discussing grave reasons which would justify the examination of a witness after the testimony has been made accessible to the parties propose the following; if some doubt arises as to the veracity of some of the testimony already taken or if one of the witnesses should be convicted of perjury; if new proofs could be furnished which were not heretofore available; if the acts containing the testimony were destroyed or lost and the witnesses who testified are no longer available, but new ones equally reliable may be had to substantiate the facts in the cause; if the judge believes it necessary in order to safeguard a legitimate defense to the accused; if, from the publication of testimony, a fact would result which could not be foreseen by the opposing party.[64]

[60] Canon 1786.

[61] Canon 1968, n. 3; Dolan, *Defensor Vinculi*, p. 61.

[62] Muniz, *Procedimientos Eccl.*, III, 237.

[63] Canon 1786.

[64] Reiffenstuel, lib. II, tit. 19, nn. 154, 158; Lega, *De Judiciis Eccl.*, I, 437.

While these reasons are listed by the authors of the old law as grave causes which admit the introduction of new witnesses after the close of the probatory period, modern authors profess that any of these causes is sufficient to permit the judge to allow the introduction of new witnesses by either party when the cause never becomes a *res judicata*. They all insist, however, that the judge be much stricter in the verification of the presence of these reasons in a cause that becomes a *res judicata* than in those which never become such and this because of the greater danger of fraud and bribery [65] in the former cases.

The reason for this wise legislation on the part of the Church is to preclude the danger of bribery, perjury, unjust influence on witnesses and similar other evils which subvert justice. There is a special danger in those causes which become a *res judicata* that parties, realizing from the publication of testimony that their cause is lost, will resort to bribery or other corruption of witnesses so that they may bring before the court previously instructed witnesses.[66]

In the event that the party is desirous of interjecting new witnesses into the procedure after the final publication of testimony he must petition the judge to permit it. The judge must satisfy himself that there is just cause and that all danger of fraud and subornation has been removed. In addition, before he has done this, he must give the other party and the Promoter of Justice, when he is a party in the trial, an opportunity to interpose any objection they may have to the admission of the witness at this stage of the trial. The judge then admits the witness by a decree in which it is stated that all the above requirements have been satisfied.[67]

Wherefore, the Promoter, either in his rôle of plaintiff or of a participant in a trial involving the public good, can request that a new witness be introduced as often as there is a serious and just reason for doing so. He may not do so unless the reason is very

[65] Muniz, *Procedimientos Eccl.*, III, 237, n. 2; Roberti, *De Processibus*, II, 68; Wernz-Vidal, *Jus Canonicum*, VI, 417, n. 65.

[66] C. 2, *De test. et attest.*, II, 8 in Clem.; Reiffenstuel, lib. II, tit. 20, nn. 461 ss.

[67] Canon 1786.

grave and the judge is satisfied that it is very grave. He would be bound, however, as a minister of justice to make certain that all danger of fraud or prejudice is absent, as often as he calls a witness after the publication of process. This obligation does not derive from any particular canon, but from the whole purpose of his office, which demands a full respect of the rights of the defendant and a safeguarding of truth and justice in the trial.

Should the defense request the hearing of a new witness, the judge should consult the Promoter and permit him to make any objections he may see fit to make to the hearing of the witness at that period of the trial. The opinion required of the Promoter is not a deliberative one but only consultative.[68] This provision that the judge consult the Promoter in those trials which pertain to the public good is a further protection added to the prohibition of Canon 1786 against fraud or the corruption of witnesses in these causes which vitally affect the public good.

In fine, the Promoter has the same right as any other party to call witnesses, although he does not enjoy the wide prerogatives enjoyed by the *Defensor Vinculi* in the same matter. The judge, however, need not be as severe and as exacting as he would have to be with other plaintiffs in these matters. The law itself frankly states the reason for the limitation in the calling of witnesses. It is for no other reason than to avoid fraud and collusion. The Promoter labors under no such suspicions, as he has been chosen by the bishop according to the requirements of the law with the same care with which the judge has been chosen. His office and his oath of office bind him to a straightforward, disinterested prosecution of the interests of the public good in all causes in which he has a part. He, however, has no right to delay the proceedings unnecessarily or to complicate them further after the *publicatio processus,* by the introduction of new witnesses who might have been heard just as easily had they been called at the customary time. Nor is a unanimous vote required as in the case of the defender of the bond to reject his petition for the examination of a new witness.[69] A majority suffices

[68] A Coronata, *Institutiones J. C.*, III, 221.

[69] Canon 1969, n. 4.

for the rejection of the petition as it does for any other plaintiff or party to a trial.[70]

C. *The Promoter and the Examination of the Parties and the Witnesses*

The parties in the trial have the right to present to the judge either the *positiones* or the questions with which they wish the parties or the witnesses to be questioned.[71] These *positiones* or positive categorical assertions of fact, as was already observed, are little used now and the word is used indiscriminately to designate a prepared list of questions. The ordinary practice of modern tribunals is to submit a prepared list of questions.[72]

Since it is an auditor who generally conducts the examination of witnesses and the parties, the right and duty to put the questions to them falls to him. He exercises this duty, however, under the general direction of the Promoter of Justice who has been assigned to the case.[73] Regularly these question lists will be prepared by the Promoter of Justice, although, if he so desire it, he may present *positiones* also to be used in the examination of the witnesses and the parties.[74]

The judge or auditor in the examination of witnesses or parties should use the questions of the Promoter of Justice. The prosecution of the charges or of the claims of the public good and their substantiation rests with the Promoter and unless he is given an opportunity to draw out his own witnesses before the court, his presentation of the case will be to no avail. He is better qualified than the judge to prepare the questions since he has made a thorough study of the information and has conscientiously striven to draw the proper conclusions from it. His questions to the witnesses will serve to demonstrate that his conclusions are warranted and

[70] Muniz, *Procedimientos Eccl.*, III, 236.

[71] Canon 1745, § 1.

[72] A Coronata, *Institutiones J. C.*, III, 172; Roberti, *De Processibus*, II, 20, 21.

[73] Wernz-Vidal, *Jus Canonicum*, VI, 364, 365.

[74] Canon 1745, § 1; *Normae S. R. R. Tribunalis*, art. 93—*A. A. S.*, XXVI (1934), 473, 474.

that the penalties demanded by him in a criminal trial or the conclusions set forth by him in the contentious case are deserving. Other plaintiffs are accorded this right and, while in cases that involve the public good the judge has a cumulative right with the Promoter to protect that public good, it is by no means an exclusive one.[75]

The Promoter in framing his questions should faithfully observe the rules laid down in the Code for the questioning of the parties and witnesses under pain of the possible rejection of his petition and lists by the judge. He should be most careful in criminal trials because of the privileged position enjoyed by the defendant in such proceedings. He will prepare the interrogatories for each witness. They will manifest such general things as the name, residence, condition, age, etc., of the witness. Besides these general questions he will prepare special questions which must refer to the crime in criminal matters and to the object of the trial in contentious cases; they ought all to be relevant to the fact at issue and to the particular fact in proof of which he calls them. The questions will bring out the circumstances of place, time, persons, etc., so as to show to advantage the type of knowledge possessed by the witness, *i. e.,* whether he is an eyewitness, etc. The questions will always be as clear as possible and capable of a direct, definite answer. The wily examination occasionally permitted in the civil courts has no part in ecclesiastical procedure.[76] Discretion, tact, charity and the information already in the possession of the Promoter will serve to guide him in this delicate task. An excellent specimen of the questioning by the Promoter in criminal trials, always a delicate question for the authors, is to be found in Bouix's very practical commentary on criminal trials in the courts of the Church.[77]

[75] Wernz-Vidal, *Jus Canonicum,* VI, 365; *Regulae Servandae . . . S. R. R. Tribunal,* par. 137, n. 2, expressly accords the right to the Promoter.

[76] Canon 1775; Roberti, *De Processibus,* II, 62; Sebastianelli, *De Judiciis Eccl.,* 165; S. B. Smith, *Elements of Ecclesiastical Law,* II, 96.

[77] Bouix, *De Judiciis Eccl.,* II, 565-568, 539-541. This is reproduced in other authors as a model for the examination of the parties and the witnesses in criminal trials.

The Promoter of Justice has the right also to be present at the examination. While in a broad sense he is a party in many trials, he is not included in the general prohibition against the presence of the parties at the examination of the witnesses.[78] Coexistent with this right to be present at all the sessions of the trial which deal with the examination of witnesses and parties is his right to present new and additional questions as often as the answers of the witnesses or the parties suggest the new questioning and he deems it useful or necessary to establish or clarify a point in the trial.[79]

The interrogatories or questions are to be put to the witness by the judge or auditor. If the Promoter of Justice should wish to ask other questions, these questions may be proposed to the witnesses not directly, but by means of the judge.[80]

Thus, though cross examination properly so called has no place in Canon Law, as neither the Promoter nor the attorney for the defendant examines the witness, but only the judge, there is what might be termed the quintessence of cross examination, inasmuch as the accused himself or his counsel and the Promoter of Justice may request the judge to reexamine the witness before the publication of the testimony on certain points of the issue or relative to the witness's competency and in certain circumstances may request the same reexamination even after the publication has taken place. This quintessence of cross examination is also noticeable in the closing stages of the trial.

D. *The Promoter of Justice and the Experts in the Trial*

Closely related to the testimony of witnesses is the opinion of experts. If they merely testify to the facts that are observed by them they are simply witnesses, though their testimony may be es-

[78] Canon 1771; Roberti, *De Processibus*, II, 60; Augustine, *A Commentary*, VII, 225.

[79] *Regulae Servandae . . . S. R. R. Tribunal*, par. 108; Roberti, *De Processibus*, II, 63.

[80] Canon 1773, §§ 1, 2; *Regulae Servandae . . . S. R. R. Tribunal*, par. 114, n. 5; Roberti, *De Processibus*, II, 63.

pecially valuable since their observations are made with an expert knowledge on the matter. They may, however, be especially appointed by the judge to examine certain matters and to give their expert opinion on them; it is in this latter sense that the law evolved by the Rota calls them experts.[81]

Experts, then, are called into a trial as often as the law or the judge demands them in order to prove a fact or to establish the true notion of a thing, as the reading of a difficult document. Their office and duty consists in applying their skill and science to the subject in dispute according to the rules of truth and justice.[82]

The judge can, and occasionally should, call upon experts in these trials pertaining to the public good. They might be called to examine a document, to verify a signature, to determine whether or not a certain injury constitutes a delict, to estimate the damages to or the value of objects, to give medical testimony which might be needed in a case to verify certain assumptions of parties to the trial,[83] etc.

These experts are to be selected by the judge in all cases pertaining to the public good, whether they be criminal or contentious; but in making the selections he must give the Promoter the opportunity to take such exceptions to the expert as he may see fit. The causes justifying the exceptions are the same as those for witnesses.[84]

There is no need to consider when these experts shall be considered necessary in a trial as the judge is the sole judge of their necessity in the cases in which the Promoter appears. Unlike matrimonial procedure in which the judge is required to use experts in certain cases,[85] the judge in all other cases pertaining to the public good is free to use them whenever the Promoter or the defendant

[81] *Regulae Servandae . . . S. R. R. Tribunal*, pars. 120-136—*A. A. S.*, II (1910), 822-826.

[82] Canons 1792, 1793; Augustine, *A Commentary*, VII, 242.

[83] Roberti, *De Processibus*, II, 81; Heiner, *De Processu Criminali Ecclesiastico*, p. 74.

[84] Canons 1796, § 1, 1880; Roberti, *De Processibus*, II, 82.

[85] Canons 1976, 1982.

requests them and he adjudges that they are useful or necessary in the case.[86]

One class of experts, however, may prove very helpful in the cases involving the public good and the Code accords special notice to their work.[87] These are the handwriting experts. Not infrequently the cases in which the Promoter appears will revolve around accounts, records, documents, instruments, the authenticity of which the parties will deny.[88] In these cases the judge selects other writings of the defendant which are unquestionably his and orders a comparison made with the written evidence submitted by the Promoter. If the written material selected by the judge is insufficient to make a valid test, the judge may order the party in question to appear and in the presence of the court give a specimen of his handwriting. The refusal of the defendant to write the specimen will legally constitute a tacit confession or admission to the authenticity of the controverted writings, a presumption which the Promoter may use as admunicular proof in his efforts to establish his case with moral certitude in the mind of the court.[89] The legal proof of Canon 1800, § 4, can be attacked on the same grounds as the express confession which was previously described.

The judge and the Promoter should be very cautious and circumspect in their employment of handwriting experts. In this matter Droste advises that not only specimens of the handwriting of the defendant but also of other authors should be mingled together and the expert should detect from among the writings which corresponds to the evidence submitted by the Promoter of Justice.[90]

The Promoter has the duty cumulatively with the judge to see to it that the experts meet all the requirements of the law, namely, that they are personally qualified to give testimony and that their reputation in their science is merited and that in the exercise of

[86] Canon 1793.

[87] Canon 1800.

[88] *Regulae Servandae . . . S. R. R. Tribunal,* par. 132; A Coronata, *Institutiones J. C.,* III, 235; Heiner, *De Processu Criminali Ecclesiastico,* pp. 75, 76.

[89] Canon 1800; Roberti, *De Processibus,* II, 90; Heiner, *De Processu Criminali Ecclesiastico,* pp. 75, 76.

[90] Droste, *Kirchl. Disciplinar-und-Kriminalverfahren* (1882), p. 116.

the office they have faithfully executed the mandate of the court made to them at the time of their appointment.[91]

The Promoter also has the general duty in common with the judge to see that all the regulations as laid down in the Code in Article II, of the First Part of the Fourth Book are carried out faithfully. This examination of experts whether they testify for the defense or the prosecution may well prove the turning point in his presentation of the case for the public good and hence it is all important for him to see to it that the requirements of truth and justice are satisfied by the experts; otherwise expert opinion may defeat the very purpose for which it was introduced into the trial.[92]

Each expert must submit an individual report to the judge in writing after each of them has individually examined the matter in question.[93] These reports are available to the Promoter and he may request that the experts be asked additional questions which the reports suggest to him. After studying the reports, he will submit to the judge the desired questions upon which he wishes the experts to be examined. It makes no difference whether the experts were introduced by the prosecution or the defense; the public good gives him the right to be present at their examinations and to advise and counsel the judge in the further examination of the experts based upon their reports.[94]

E. *The Promoter of Justice and the Ocular Inspection (Accessus Judicialis)*

To clarify a point or a proof which has arisen in the course of the trial, judicial visit and investigation is often of advantage. This judicial investigation in certain circumstances may afford prime and incontrovertible proof as to the notoriety of criminal fact, ren-

[91] Canons 1794, 1795; A Coronata, *Institutiones J. C.*, III, 234; Augustine, *A Commentary,* VII, 242, 243.

[92] Canon 1793, § 2; *Regulae Servandae . . . S. R. R. Tribunal,* par. 108.

[93] Canon 1802.

[94] *Regulae Servandae . . . S. R. R. Tribunal,* par. 108, n. 1; Wernz-Vidal, *Jus Canonicum,* VI, 364, 365.

dering all other proof superfluous [95] or as to the facts alleged by the Promoter in contentious proceedings involving the public good. Such investigation of a place, a locality, a house or a recognition in cases involving portable objects will often give the judge a better insight into the case and enable him to better evaluate the arguments adduced by the Promoter or the other parties to these trials involving questions of public interest.[96]

While this type of proof is seldom employed, yet it may occur at any time. Perhaps the entire value of an all important witness may depend upon whether it was humanly possible to see and hear in one place what occurred in a place nearby. Suppose at the same time there are noteworthy discrepancies in the testimony of witnesses relative to circumstances closely connected with *corpus delicti* in criminal trials and with the object at issue in the contentious case. This would indeed be an instance in which the judge could opportunely resort to an ocular inspection, go himself and examine the site or locality involved in the trial and in the light of this first hand information evaluate the testimony he has received in the trial.

Not infrequently in criminal cases this judicial visitation or recognition of an object will have been made during the inquisition which proceeds the actual criminal trial.[97] In the event that this has been the case, the intervention of the Promoter will depend entirely upon the invitation of the inquisitor to be present. If invited by the latter, his activity will be entirely within the limits fixed by the judge at the moment of invitation. Should the inquisitor invite him and ask his assistance in the examination of experts, witnesses and parties, he will assume an active rôle; otherwise he has neither the right nor the duty to intervene in any way.[98]

In cases involving the public good, the judge may decree the

[95] Roberti, *De Processibus,* II, 91, 92; Bouix, *De Judiciis Eccl.,* II, 151; Heiner, *De Processu Criminali Ecclesiastico,* 60.

[96] Sebastianelli, *De Judiciis Eccl.,* II, 149.

[97] Wernz-Vidal, *Jus Canonicum,* VI, 445, n. 2.

[98] Canon 1945; Muniz, *Procedimientos Eccl.,* III, n. 566, 482.

judicial visitation or recognition of his own initiative or at the instance of the Promoter who has the right to demand the use of this procedure, should he deem it necessary to establish his own contentions or to disprove the defenses evolved by the other parties to the trial.[99] In like manner, he may also oppose the request of the defendant, if, for example, he had reason to believe that conditions had been notably altered so as to discredit his case and deceive the judge. He may do this in virtue of the general duties imposed upon him by his prosecution of the interests of the common good in any case in which he functions in his official capacity.[100]

Should the judge decree the visit to the place, site, etc., during the proceedings, the Promoter would enjoy the right to accompany the judge and the notary; for this is a judicial act and consequently he is entitled to be present and should be present unless otherwise impeded.[101]

The Code leaves no doubt that this is a judicial act since it empowers the judge to examine experts, witnesses or the parties at the place where the judicial inspection is to take place and to do this so far as their examination is necessary to accomplish the end for which the judicial visit was made. The notary records all the testimony that is given in response to the questioning of the judge.[102] The law gives the parties the right to be present and to suggest questions provided that there is no danger of disturbances or disorders.[103] This reason for interdicting the presence of the parties would have no value in relation to the Promoter of Justice. Besides, as already insisted upon, he has the general right and duty to be present at all examinations of the trial and the fact that this examination is held outside the court is no reason to exclude him. It is a judicial act and hence he must be cited to insure its validity as well as to permit him a fair opportunity to enjoy a

[99] Roberti, *De Processibus,* II, 92.

[100] Noval, *De Processibus,* n. 765, 502; Vermeersch-Creusen, *Epitome,* III, 116.

[101] Canon 1587, § 2.

[102] Canon 1810; Roberti, *De Processibus,* II, 93.

[103] Canon 1809.

legitimate means of providing proof or defense according to the nature of the visit.[104]

F. *The Duty of the Promoter Relative to the Documents Submitted in the Trial*

Evidence in criminal or contentious cases is frequently supplied by means of documents. The word "document" is understood here in the wide sense of any record expressed in writing or symbols, no matter what may be the nature of the material on which the writing may be recorded.[105]

In order that a document may serve as evidence it must be genuine and authentic. Genuine means that it is the same as that written by the author and is not spurious, interpolated, forged or corrupted in any way. The authenticity, on the other hand, merely means that the document is authoritative, *i. e.*, that the contents of the writing are reliable and trustworthy because they are attested by a certain form, seal or signature. A document therefore may be genuine without being authentic.[106]

Relative to the probatory value of the various classes of documents the Code is very explicit. In Canon 1813, §§ 1, 2, it enumerates the various documents, ecclesiastical and civil, which are recognized as public and authentic, provided, of course, that all the formalities required in the law for their proper execution have been fulfilled. These public documents are presumed genuine until the contrary is proved. They prove all that is directly and principally affirmed in them. In other words, such documents afford *prima facie* evidence of the direct action which is proved by the document, *e. g.*, a civil marriage certificate issued by the recorder proves that the parties have gone through a civil ceremony of marriage as required by law. The burden of the proof is upon the one who attacks such a document.[107]

[104] Canon 1587, § 2; *Regulae Servandae . . . S. R. R. Tribunal*, pars. 108 and 170.

[105] Reiffenstuel, lib. II, tit. XIX, nn. 221 ss.

[106] A Coronata, *Institutiones J. C.*, III, 249; Augustine, *A Commentary*, VII, 254, 255.

[107] A Coronata, *Institutiones J. C.*, III, 251; Noval, *De Processibus*, I, 370.

The third paragraph of the same canon states that all letters, contracts, or last wills which are drawn up by private persons as such must be regarded as private documents. To this last class belong private letters written by persons in public office.

This last class of documents often becomes important in trials in which the Promoter is acting as plaintiff or in a collateral capacity.[108] Whenever they are introduced into the trial the main object of the Promoter will be to prove or disprove the genuineness, authenticity, existence, loss of documents, etc. It will suffice to say that all these points will be established by witnesses, either because they are signatories or parties to the content of the writings, or because they have seen or read it, or know its handwriting or have heard the content, etc. If necessary, the opinion of experts may be injected into the trial. But to establish the authenticity of documents the Promoter and the judge should act with the greatest caution. They must first ascertain whether the witnesses or the experts are acquainted with the person whose instrument the writing is alleged to be; whether they have been in correspondence with him or accidentally know his writing; whether they know it well and can now recognize it. The documents must then be placed among other documents of different authors covering the signatures and the witness or expert who professes to know the handwriting in question should be asked to pick it out.[109]

The Promoter of Justice has the right as the official plaintiff or as a party to the trial to submit to the court any written evidence pertaining to the cause that he may have in his possession.[110] Whenever these writings are private and their authenticity is denied by the party to whom he attributes them, he must further establish their authenticity and genuineness by parol evidence at his disposal and may, if the occassion warrants it, request the judge to call in experts. He should submit questions for and as-

[108] Muniz, *Procedimientos Eccl.*, III, 307, lists various private documents which frequently appear in trials involving public good.

[109] Droste-Messmer, *Canonical Procedure in Disciplinary and Criminal Cases of Clerics*, p. 133; A Coronata, *Institutiones J. C.*, III, 250.

[110] Canon 1812; *Regulae Servandae . . . S. R. R. Tribunal*, par. 108.

sist at the examination of all the witnesses and experts whom he has introduced into the trial to establish the authenticity and genuineness of the written evidence submitted by him.[111]

The Promoter has the right to examine all documents submitted by the defense as proofs in the trial.[112] This implies that he ascertain whether the writing is truly genuine. From the general mandate of his office he has the duty to attack the documents if forgeries, to demonstrate the falsification of records and in general to forestall any attempt of the defendant or any party to a trial in which he is acting from perpetrating a fraud on the court.[113] To this end the Promoter may request the citation of new witnesses and their examination by the court in order to substantiate his attacks on the documentary evidence of the other parties.

It frequently happens that documents which are necessary to the trial are in the possession of the other party. In this case the party desiring to introduce the document petitions the judge giving a description of the document, and the reason for the petition, indicating also the possessor. If the other party denies that he has the document, or refuses to present it to the court, the judge after hearing the Promoter of Justice, may by interlocutory sentence order the holder to bring it into court.[114]

It will be noted that as often as the Promoter is in the case in any capacity, he must be heard before the judge issues this decree or interlocutory sentence. It might also be added that the Promoter has the right also to petition the exhibition of a document which is in the possession of the parties opposing him.[115] Relative to the defendant in a criminal trial a distinction is in order. If he has a document in his possession and the Promoter desires to introduce it into the trial, despite the order of the judge he would not be bound to pro-

[111] Heiner, *De Processu Criminali Ecclesiastico,* p. 79; Boriero, *De Processu Canonico,* p. 92, gives an exemplar of the question list to be used in the establishing of the authenticity of a document or to deny the same.

[112] Canon 1820; *Regulae Servandae . . . S. R. R. Tribunal,* par. 108.

[113] Heiner, *De Processu Criminali Ecclesiastico,* p. 79; Noval, *De Processibus,* I, 502.

[114] Canon 1824, § 1.

[115] Canon 1824, § 1; Roberti, *De Processibus,* II, 105.

duce it into the court. His duty to produce documents extends no further than his duty to testify in the case. The only possible exception to this rule would be that the production is demanded for the common good of religion, a reason which can hardly be said to be present in most disciplinary cases.[116]

G. *The Promoter of Justice and the Interpreters in the Trial*

The language of the ecclesiastical courts is to be in the vernacular; but the witnesses and the parties are to be examined in the language in which they are fluent. In the event that the witnesses and the parties do not speak the vernacular of the court sufficiently to answer intelligibly the questions of the court or the documents submitted in the trial are not in the vernacular, there arises the natural necessity of an interpreter who will act as the intermediary of the court. This interpreter obtains his appointment from the judge and may not exercise his rôle until he has been sworn in.[117] The interpreter must be acceptable to the parties and to the Promoter of Justice. He must be proficient in the required language and must be free from all exception of suspicion either on the part of the Promoter or the parties to the trial.[118]

The Promoter, therefore, has the right to take exception to the interpreter, if he feels it necessary to protect the ends of justice. The grounds for exceptions are the same as those against witnesses, although exceptions may also be taken against their knowledge of the language. The Promoter, since he may be present for the appointment of the interpreter, should lodge at that time any objections he may have against the naming of a certain interpreter, whose appointment he may feel to be prejudicial to the interests the Promoter represents in the case.[119]

Hence the Promoter is bound to see to it that the interpreter is capable and that he fulfills the oath of his office.

[116] Canon 1823, § 1; Noval, *De Processibus,* I, 374.

[117] Canon 1641.

[118] Canon 1614; Roberti, *De Processibus,* I, 201.

[119] Roberti, *De Processibus,* I, 201.

H. *The Promoter of Justice and Rogatory Commissions*

Neither the pre-Code law nor the present law of the Code refer expressly to any duties of the Promoter in these matters. His duties relative to rogatory commissions must be deduced from his general duties and from parallel passages in the Code.

The prevailing law ordinarily demands that the witnesses be heard in court; but where there is a just reason for the non-appearance of the witness in the court, two remedies may be employed so that the evidence may not be entirely lost to the trial. If the witness lives in another diocese, the tribunal which is trying the case may call upon the tribunal of another diocese to cite the witnesses and examine them or any documents they may have in their possession.[120] The second remedy may be used where the witness lives at a great distance from the cathedral city and cannot appear himself or cannot be reached by the judge without grave inconveniences or expenses. In this instance a priest may be delegated to ask the questions and he will associate with himself another priest who will act as notary at the examination.[121] In this second class may be included such witnesses as are willing to testify but will not appear in court under any circumstances.[122]

In the first instance the court hearing the case will forward to the second diocese *litterae remissoriales* giving the necessary information as to the witnesses and documents desired and enclosing question lists to be used in the examination of the witnesses or the documents. In the latter cases the procedure will be the same but the letters sent to the delegated priest are technically known as *litterae delegationis*.[123]

Since the Promoter has the right to call such witnesses as are necessary or useful to his cause, he should not be denied the exercise of that right simply because the witnesses are too far removed from

[120] Canons 1570, § 2; 1770, § 2, n. 3.

[121] Canon 1770, § 2, n. 4.

[122] Droste-Messmer, *Canonical Procedure in Disciplinary and Criminal Cases of Clerics*, p. 114.

[123] A Coronata, *Institutiones J. C.*, III, 212.

the tribunal to be present. Not infrequently the criminal will have been remanded to his own diocese for punishment, or the witnesses who are important to the Promoter's case will have moved to other parts, or will have been transferred to some place outside the diocese. He has the right to petition the judge that the provisions of Canons 1570, § 2, and 1770, §§ 2, 3, be employed to reach the important witness. The judge, however, is the one to decide whether the evidence is useful or important enough to warrant the use of these extraordinary means.[124]

Should the judge grant the request of the Promoter, the latter certainly has the right and the duty to present the question lists which will be included in the remissorial letters or letters of delegation as the case may be. This is sufficiently evident from what has already been said concerning the right of the Promoter to be present at and contribute to all examinations of witnesses in all cases in which he acts. He has the same right, should the defendant or other parties to a trial in which he acts invoke the use of this remedy in order to bolster up their alibi or the claims which they oppose to the Promoter. Should the judge accede to the request of the other parties, the Promoter has the right to see the interrogatories which are addressed to the other tribunal or to the delegated priest and to suggest any others he may see fit in order to discover the truth.[125]

Thus far there is no difficulty but the practical application of the law of the Code, as set forth in Canon 1570, § 2, might give rise to some speculative difficulty. In the canon it is expressly stated that each tribunal: *Jus habet in auxilium vocendi aliud tribunal, quod normas pro singulis actibus jure prescriptas servare debet.* Does this mean that the Promoter of Justice of the second tribunal should be present at the examination of witnesses and documents by his tribunal?

Considering the law as it stands it would seem so. The canon

[124] Canon 1749; Bouix, *De Judiciis Eccl.*, II, 402, 403.

[125] *Regulae Servandae S. R. R. Tribunal*, par. 108, n. 1; *Normae S. R. R. Tribunalis*, art. 94—*A. A. S.*, XXVII (1934), 474; Noval, *De Processibus*, I, 502.

commands that all the prescripts of the law be observed in the examinations of witnesses and one of the regulations is certainly that the Promoter of Justice be present at the examination of witnesses and documents to suggest any questions which the public good might demand. Moreover, Canon 1587, § 1, demands under pain of nullity the citation of the Promoter of Justice to all acts of the trial at which he should be present.

Other than this general rule of Canon 1570, § 2, there are no positive regulations or instructions on the execution of the *litterae remissoriales* relative to the action of the Promoter. This is quite understandable because for the most part criminal and disciplinary legislation was pretty much neglected until 1880, being left for the most part to local particular legislation and to custom. The Instruction of 1880, introducing as it did a new procedure, gave rise to many important difficulties which more than occupied the attention of leading canonists at the turn of the century.[126] The activity of the Promoter in contentious cases became extensive and universal only with the Code. The Code clarified many of the difficulties which had arisen in the criminal procedure but naturally could not advert to all the manifold ramifications of procedural difficulties and technicalities and, as it was noted, is silent upon the presence of the Promoter in the assisting tribunal.

The defender of the bond, on the other hand, and his duties in this matter were the object of special attention in several instructions of the Holy See.[127] These required that the *Defensor Vinculi* of the assisting tribunal be present at the examination of witnesses for another tribunal to safeguard the sanctity of the marriage bond. It would seem that there are at least equal reasons why the Promoter should perform a similar function in those cases which affect the public good, since he has the cognate duty to defend the public good and morality in all other contentious cases and in criminal cases. To this end the practice of courts and the unanimous opinion of canonists both before and after the Code demanded the citation

[126] Noval, *De Processibus,* I, 490, 491.

[127] Dolan, *Defensor Vinculi,* pp. 74, 75.

and presence of the Promoter of Justice at the examination of witnesses and documents.[128]

The new norms of the Roman Rota, published in 1934, afford some interesting and pertinent observations relative to the present question. They prescribe that as often as the rogatory commissions are concerned with criminal trials or trials involving the public good, the Promoter of Justice of the diocesan tribunal is to be present at the examination of the witnesses and the parties notwithstanding the fact that as a rule the questionnaires, prepared by the Promoter of the Rota and the Ponens of the same tribunal, had been included in the remissorial letters.[129]

It goes without saying that, when the Rota entrusts the composition of the questionnaires to the discretion of the assisting tribunal, the Promoter of Justice of the diocesan tribunal will draw them up from the knowledge of the cases afforded in the rogatory commissions themselves. The Promoter will also be present at the examination of the witnesses and the parties; all this is clear from the description given in the Rota rules of the second method of effecting a rogatory commission.[130] Yet even when the Ponens and the Promoter have already framed the questionnaires to be used and have forwarded them to the assisting tribunal, the Rota expressly prescribes that the Promoter be present at the examinations requested in the commission and add his own pertinent questions as often as this last faculty is included in the commission.[131]

In view of these facts there would seem to be an obligation on the part of the Promoter of the assisting tribunal to be present at the examination of witnesses in cases involving the public good. This obligation would not arise from any particular statute but

128 Pellegrini, *Praxis Vicariorum,* Pars IV, sec. 1, n. 18;*Acta et Decreta Concilii Plen. Balto. III,* n. 325; Heiner, *De Processus Criminali Eccle.,* p. 67; Roberti, *De Processibus,* II, 60-63; Wernz-Vidal, *Jus Canonicum,* VI, 364, 365.

129 Articles 93, par. 1; 94—*A. A. S.,* XXVI (1934), 473, 474.

130 *Normae S. R. R. Tribunalis,* art. 93, par. 2—*A. A. S.,* XXVI (1934), 473.

131 Articles 93, par. 2, n. 2; 94—*A. A. S.,* XXVI (1934), 473, 474.

from the general duties of the Promoter in his prosecution of the public good in cases affecting that good. The exclusive right given to him by the ecclesiastical society to prosecute its interests in the ecclesiastical tribunals carries with it the cumulative duty to seek the full execution of justice to and protection for the public moral order. The constant practice of tribunals and the teaching of the authors indicate the right and the duty of the Promoter in cases involving the public good to be present at all examinations of witnesses in cases prejudicial to the public good. The assisting tribunal would do well to cite its Promoter in the execution of rogatory commissions in order to insure justice to both the ecclesiastical society and to the parties in the trial.

However, since the Code does not expressly or specifically demand the presence of the Promoter and since the questions of the remitting tribunal are to be used, the exception of nullity may not be urged against these acts and this for a twofold reason. First, Canon 15 declares that laws which void acts have that effect only when the law sets forth the requirements and conditions for validity in a decisive manner. Now the present requirement is at most a doubtful obligation.[132] Then, too, the Promoter on the return of the *acta* from the second tribunal will study and examine the acts and thus the *acta* would be validated, if by any chance their validity were to be frustrated by a violation of Canon 1587, § 1.[133]

Nevertheless, it seems quite proper for the assisting tribunal to call upon its Promoter of Justice to be present in the execution of rogatory commissions. The fact that witnesses are examined outside the diocese does not justify the dispensing of the ordinary safeguards provided by the law. This fact would warrant all the more the citing by the second tribunal of the official who is entrusted with the duty of seeing to it that crime and all other actions which are prejudicial to the public good are bridled by the application of the proper safeguards against the actions of interested parties to cases involving that good.

[132] Canon 15: "Leges, etiam irritantes et inhabilitantes in dubio juris non urgent."

[133] Canon 1587, § 2.

I. *The Promoter of Justice and the Oaths of the Parties*

As was already noted, the Promoter of Justice may not demand that the defendant in the criminal trial take the oath, which is given to the witnesses, to tell the truth. This practice, formerly much used and abused, was abolished by Benedict XIII at the Council held in Rome in the year 1725.[184] The prevailing law retains the same prohibition, confining the judge to admonishing the accused to tell the truth.[185] In all other cases pertaining to the public good, the oath is administered to the parties.

Another oath which plays a great part in civil cases and proceedings is the suppletory oath. Parties who have proof, but insufficient, may in certain cases by means of the suppletory oath complete the proof and have the trial proceed to its normal conclusion—the sentence.

Previous to the Code, there was a species of suppletory oath employed in criminal procedure. It was technically known as the *purgatio canonica.* The Promoter in those cases in which he was unsuccessful in marshalling sufficient proof to warrant a sentence against the accused could demand that the accused purge himself of the suspicion still attached to him by taking an oath in the presence of the judge.[186] This canonical purgation did not serve to complete the proof, but only to give the judge greater security when he passed sentence in virtue of the canonical maxim: *actore non probante, reus absolvitur.* Hence it may be called suppletory only in a wide sense of the term.[187]

At any rate canonical purgation had fallen into desuetude at the end of the last century. The present law is silent on that form of proof and so in virtue of Canon 6, n. 6, it has no place in the prevailing law.[188] Although canonical purgation was a suppletory oath only in a wide sense, Vermeersch-Creusen are probably correct in

[184] *Coll. Lac.*, I, 364.

[185] Canon 1744.

[186] Cc. 5, 6, X, *de purgatione canonica,* V, 34; Lega, *De Judiciis Eccl.*, IV, 363 ss.

[187] Wernz-Vidal, *Jus Canonicum,* VI, 499.

[188] Noval, *De Processibus,* I, 316.

their contention that Canon 1830, § 2, which forbids the use of suppletory oaths in criminal proceedings, is a further abrogation of the old juridical institute of canonical purgation.[139]

Consequently the various oaths so important in contentious proceedings may never be given to the defendant in criminal trials either *ex officio* or upon the motion of the Promoter.[140]

Nor may the Promoter request that the parties to most of the contentious cases in which he will be involved be given the suppletory oath. The law expressly interdicts its use in all proceedings which deal with matters of great moment or where the object involved is of great price. The reason is self-evident, since it is asking too much of human nature when so much hangs in the balance. Since most of the cases in which the Promoter will be involved include these cases of great moment, *e. g.,* cases involving the status of persons, the possession of benefices, certain rights of major importance, etc., he may not permit the suppletory oath to supply the insufficiency of proof. He may, however, request that it be used in matters of minor value or importance as sometimes occur in cases of moral persons at which he happens to be present.[141]

J. *The Promoter of Justice and the Incidental Trial*

An incidental trial (*causa incidens*) is one which, though not expressly contained in the original *libellus* or introductory bill of the trial, is so intimately connected with the point at issue that it must be settled before the principle cause is defined, *e. g.*, the competency of the judge, the reprobation of witnesses, etc.[142] Every such secondary question must be proposed after the trial has actually begun, that is, after the summons has been duly made and it may be entered by the Promoter of Justice, the other parties in the trial and by third parties interested in the issue of the trial.[143]

[139] Vermeersch-Creusen, *Epitome,* III, 82.

[140] Noval, *De Processibus,* I, 380; A Coronata, *Institutiones J. C.,* III, 266.

[141] Canon 1830, § 2; Roberti, *De Processibus,* II, 109; Wernz-Vidal, *Jus Canonicum,* VI, 476-478.

[142] Canon 1837; Augustine, *A Commentary,* VII, 283.

[143] Roberti, *De Processibus,* II, 121.

The incidental cause is a true trial, though a secondary one, and, therefore, must be introduced by a petition, either oral or written, according as the judge decides.[144]

When the Promoter proposes the incidental question it devolves upon him to prepare the *libellus* according to the regulations laid down in Canons 1706-1710 for the preparation of any *libellus* in the trial. He will briefly and concisely set forth the purpose of the incidental cause and will allege its connection with the issue involved in the principal trial to be such that it requires a preliminary settlement.[145] Since the defendant or the parties in the case must be heard, the Promoter must defend the introduction of this issue against any opposition which the defendant or any other party to the trial may raise against its introduction and admission into the proceedings.[146] It will be his duty to demonstrate to the tribunal by solid arguments the necessity of admitting the secondary cause and its connection with the main issue of the trial.

In the event that the defendant or third parties seek to interject an incidental cause into any trial in which the Promoter is functioning, the judge must notify the Promoter of the petition and grant him an opportunity to oppose its acceptance by the tribunal, should he feel it unwarranted.[147] He is not obliged by his office to oppose the petition simply on the grounds that it was petitioned by the defendant in the criminal trial or by the parties opposed to him in contentious cases; for he is bound by his office to respect the just rights of all parties in the trial. He will oppose the petition for an incidental cause only when he believes that it lacks a solid foundation, or has no connection with the main trial, and has been introduced simply to retard the trial and obscure the main issue represented by the Promoter. To act otherwise would be to obstruct the trial and the judge would be within his rights in reprimanding him.

It is the judge, however, who in the last analysis will decide

144 Canon 1839; Roberti, *De Processibus,* II, 122.

145 Canon 1838; Augustine, *A Commentary,* VII, 384.

146 Canon 1839.

147 Canon 1839; *Regulae Servandae . . . S. R. R. Tribunal,* par. 97, n. 2; *Normae S. R. R. Tribunalis,* art. 107—*A. A. S.,* XXVI (1934), 476.

whether or not the incidental cause is to be admitted or rejected; but since it is a judicial act he may not take any action without citing the Promoter to be present.[148] The decision of the judge as to whether the proceedings of the incidental trial are to be oral or written will guide the Promoter in his subsequent preparations for this session of the trial.[149]

In general, the Promoter will have the same rights and duties which he exercises in the main trial. He is bound to be present at the sessions of the incidental trial in virtue of the same general mandate of his office which imposes the duty of presence at all judicial sessions of the trial; for though the incidental cause is a secondary trial it is an integral part of the principal trial.

Against the decree of the judge rejecting the petition for the incidental cause, it would seem that the Promoter and the parties have the same remedies that they enjoy against the rejection of the original *libellus.* Canon 1838 applies *servatis servandis* all the regulations of Canons 1706 to 1725 to the incidental trial. Canon 1709 gives the right of recourse to the higher tribunal against the rejection of the *libellus.* This right must be exercised within ten days useful time and its exercise should be indicated to the court. The higher court in passing upon the recourse will cite its own Promoter of Justice.[150]

Nor may the enumeration of Canon 1880 be objected to this opinion. In the first place this is recourse and not appeal. Paragraph 6 of the canon cited does forbid appeal or recourse from the sentence or decree defining an incidental cause but that is all. The present question of recourse against the rejection of a *libellus* does not come under that classification.

Some argue that appeal or recourse may not be taken against a decree or sentence unless it has definitive force and that the same principles apply to the refusal to admit the recourse against the *libellus.* This may apply in virtue of Canon 20; but since the

[148] Canons 1587, 1839; *cf.* Roberti, *De Processibus,* II, 122, 123, for the rules of procedure in the incidental trial.

[149] Canon 1838.

[150] Canon 1709, § 3.

question is not discussed by the authors, no final settlement of the question can be given.

Should the judge persist in his refusal to admit the incidental cause to such an extent that he denies the Promoter the right to interpose recourse against his decree of rejection, the Promoter could attack the obstinate decree in his appeal from the final sentence provided the latter is also unjust and unwarranted.

If the action of the judge in refusing the admission of the incidental trial was manifestly unjust or prejudicial, the Promoter would be perfectly justified in appealing to the Ordinary.[151]

Against a decree or sentence defining an incidental cause, there is no appeal or recourse unless the sentence or decree has definitive force.[152]

The interlocutory decree or sentence is definitive in character and has the nature of a definitive sentence in the following cases: when it relieves the judge of further participation in the cause; when it admits or rejects a peremptory exception; when it imposes an obligation upon one of the parties which cannot be remedied or corrected by the definitive sentence; and finally, when it is of such a nature that it so defines a point or question raised in the trial that the entire proceedings are thereby terminated, thus rendering a definitive sentence in the principal trial unnecessary.[153]

In these cases only may appeal or recourse be taken against an interlocutory decree or sentence and that appeal or recourse must be interposed within ten days useful time. If the Promoter feels himself and his prosecution of the case aggrieved by the interlocutory sentence, he must pursue the appeal in the regular way; otherwise, the decree or the sentence relieves the defendant or parties of further proof or obligation relative to the trial as such a sentence or decree decides a substantial incidental question from which the solution of the principal question necessarily follows, thereby forcing the sentence of the judge.[154]

[151] Canon 1625, §§ 1, 3.

[152] Canon 1880, § 6.

[153] Reiffenstuel, lib. II, tit. XXVI, nn. 18 ss.; Wernz-Vidal, *Jus Canonicum*, VI, 559, n. 61.

[154] Roberti, *De Processibus*, II, 171, 172; Connolly, *Appeals*, p. 81.

The Promoter of Justice, therefore, is certainly to be admitted to the incidental trial and is to actively participate in it. The Code in legislating for the incidental trial expressly provides for his presence at these proceedings by enacting express regulations pertinent to his rôle in them.[155]

Since the intervention of the Promoter in criminal trials is essential, it necessarily follows that the absence of the Promoter of Justice from the incidental proceedings will nullify the results of these proceedings unless the rules laid down in Canon 1587 are observed. The same is true as often as his presence in the contentious case is essential to the validity of the principal cause.

In the event that he was cited for the incidental trial and did not appear, he should be granted an opportunity to see the *acta*, even though they are already valid.[156] Were he not cited and at the same time was not present, the *acta* of the incidental trial must be submitted to him if they are to be recognized as valid.[157] He might later on in the trial accept the findings of the tribunal in the incidental trial and thus eliminate the possibility of the charge of invalidity being placed against the *acta* because of his absence. Without this acceptance by the Promoter these *acta* may not be validly integrated into the *acta* of the principal trial which are to serve as the basis of the definite sentence of the judge.

The judge may countenance an action to revoke or set aside the findings of an incidental cause at any time prior to the final sentence. In like manner a change or correction of the sentence or the decree may be requested. The action may be taken by the judge of his own initiative or upon the motion of the Promoter or of any of the parties to the trial. If the judge desires to revoke or correct the sentence of his own initiative he must have a just reason and he must consult the Promoter of Justice and the other parties to the trial. If the Promoter or one of the interested parties to the trial request the revocation or revision, the judge shall hear the other parties in order to learn whether they feel themselves aggrieved or curtailed

[155] Canons 1837, 1839, 1841.
[156] Canon 1587, § 2.
[157] Canon 1587, § 2.

in their rights by the interlocutory sentence or decree. If one party petitions a change or correction the other party must be heard. Hence as often as the judge seeks to change, correct or revoke an interlocutory decree or sentence of his own initiative or upon the motion of one of the parties, he must consult the Promoter of Justice who is acting in the case and hear his opinion before taking any action in the matter.[158]

Article III. The Promoter of Justice in the Remaining Stages of the Judicial Trial

A. *The Promoter and the Conclusio Causae and the Publicatio Processus*

The first part of any trial is devoted to the hearing of witnesses and experts, and to examination of the documentary evidence, in a word, to the gathering of evidence. It is concerned solely with the facts in the case. When all the facts pertinent to a case have been exhausted, the trial enters the second major phase, wherein the opposing advocates take the facts and explain them in the light of the law."[159]

The presentation or instruction of the cause is divided from the legal discussion of the cause by a procedural act technically known as the *conclusio in cause.*[160] This is effected by a decree of the judge. Once this decree has been issued, the entire nature of the process changes. The sole concern in this period of the trial is the application of the law to the facts presented to the court in the earlier sessions of the trial.[161]

The judge may issue this decree concluding the instance after he has consulted the parties and they signify that they have nothing more to add to the facts already presented. The judge may also decree the *conclusio in causa* if it is evident that the parties are abusing their privilege to call witnesses in order to delay the trial

[158] Canon 1841; Roberti, *De Processibus,* II, 123, 124.
[159] Roberti, *De Processibus,* II, 156.
[160] Canon 1860, § 1.
[161] Roberti, *De Processibus,* II, 156.

and confuse the issue, or if the tribunal feels that the issue has been sufficiently instructed.[162]

Since the next step in the trial is the discussion of the cause in which both parties are permitted to apply the law to the facts in the case and since all the testimony taken in the case has been kept secret by the court, at least as far as the defendant in the criminal trial and the parties in the contentious cases are concerned, the judge must issue another decree, that of the publication of the process. The Promoter and all the parties to the trial are given an opportunity to examine all the procedural acts thus far enacted in the case together with all the evidence thus far presented in the proceedings as well as all the inferences, conclusions and the motions based upon this evidence by the parties. In a word, they are given an opportunity to examine and make a copy of the entire proceedings which have transpired up to that moment.[163]

Under the pre-Code legislation, there was a twofold publication of process in the mixed criminal procedure as enacted in the Instruction of 1880. The prevailing law makes no distinction between the mixed and the purely accusatorial procedures and provides for but one publication of process, that described in the present canons.[164] In both criminal procedures it takes place in virtue of the decree declaring the instance closed as the criminal case is sufficiently instructed.

It is impossible to consider the effects of the *publicatio processus* without considering the effects of the *conclusio in causa*. The two decrees are necessarily interwoven in the one procedural act. It is possible to theorize on the order in which the decrees should follow, but the question is of no practical importance. The two decrees divide the trial into equal parts and belong to neither section themselves. They have, however, important effects upon the action of the Promoter of Justice and his direction of the prosecution in any given case and these should be noted before proceeding to the discussion in the trial.

[162] Canons 1858, 1859; Roberti, *De Processibus,* II, 159.

[163] Canons 1858, 1859; Roberti, *De Processibus,* II, 157.

[164] Canons 1858, 1859; Noval, *De Processibus,* I, 540.

Before proceeding to the declaration by decree that the process is closed, the judge must have first obtained the admission of the Promoter that he has rested his case. The Promoter must inform the tribunal that he had nothing further to add or the judge may presume that, inasmuch as the Promoter has not exhausted the complete terms assigned him by the court for the introduction of witnesses and evidence.[165] The judge, however, may issue the decree even over the protest of the Promoter, if he believes that the latter is unnecessarily prolonging the trial by the presentation of irrelevant and useless evidence provided that he considers the case of the Promoter for the public good is sufficiently instructed. It is the duty of the judge to curb and check any practices which serve only to complicate and retard the trial of the issue, even though the Promoter is the offender in that regard.[166]

After the issuance of this judicial decree as a general rule no new evidence is to be introduced,[167] since both the Promoter and the parties have rested their cases and have indicated to the judge that they have presented to the court all those things which they deemed necessary to the case.[168] The new evidence may not be accepted by the judge except under the conditions fixed by law.[169]

While the *publicatio processus* is chiefly of advantage to the other parties in the trial, since it makes known to them all that heretofore had been kept secret in the trial, it is also of decided advantage to the Promoter.[170] True, the Promoter had ample opportunity during the trial to impugn the documents introduced by the parties and to discredit and disprove the witnesses called by them, as well as to propose his views relative to the other types of proof in the trial, as judicial visit, experts, etc. Still this challenge of individual proofs is insufficient to the Promoter's presentation of his case. A full and entire presentation of any case requires that not only the individual proofs be challenged but that the entire evi-

[165] Canon 1860, § 2.

[166] Canon 1860; Roberti, *De Processibus,* I, 402.

[167] Canon 1861, § 1; Roberti, *De Processibus,* II, 160, 161.

[168] Canon 1860, § 2.

[169] Canon 1786; *cf.* Previous article on witnesses.

[170] Canon 1858.

dence as presented by all the parties to the trial be weighed and prudently compared. It will then become the duty of the Promoter to study minutely the individual proofs offered by the parties and to compare them with the single links of his own case. He will note especially the observations made by the judge, the parties and their counsel in the course of the trial. This prudent comparative study of the facts made available in their entirety by the publication of the process will serve as the groundwork for his preparation of the summary of the case which will mark a vital step in his prosecution of any cause.

The period within which the defenses should be presented will be defined by the judge either in the decree in which he closes the process or by a special decree. The length of these periods will be determined by the circumstances in any given trial since the amount and type of evidence submitted will necessitate a longer or shorter period according as it is lengthy and involved or short and clear. The Promoter or the parties can petition the judge to prorogue the terms as often as they feel the extension necessary to prepare their respective defenses; but the judge may not shorten or prorogue the period previously granted by the court without the permission of the parties and the Promoter of Justice.[171]

B. *The Promoter of Justice and the Summing Up (Discussio Causae)*

Once the case has been closed by the aforementioned decree of the judge, the second and forensic stage of the trial begins. In the first part of the process all the circumstances of fact have been gathered together and the Promoter was solely concerned with proving to the judge the facts in the case upon which he based his accusation or his claims according to the nature of the process. In this second period he must apply the law in the case; for although the law in the case is clear in itself and is known to the judge, the Promoter

[171] Canon 1862; Roberti, *De Processibus,* II, 164; *Normae S. R. R. Tribunalis,* art. 126—*A. A. S.,* XXVI (1934), 479, assign thirty days as the limit for the preparation of defenses by the Promoter or the parties.

must demonstrate to the court the connection and application of the law to the facts he has presently alleged and proved.[172] While the Promoter has opposed the individual proofs of the defendant or the parties at the time of their presentation, the certitude and existence of a true delict or of a reasonable contention may be more perfectly demonstrated by a complete and orderly summation of all the proofs presented in the trial, drawn both from the assertions of the Promoter and from the attempts of the parties or their counsel to impugn the conclusions of the Promoter together with the specific conclusions of law based upon this evidence by the Promoter.[173]

The defense, of course, has the same right as anyone who is a party to the trial. This is an excellent weapon in the hands of the defense, as their name implies, since they are technically known as defenses. These defenses are intercommunicated among the parties to the trial. This interchange of briefs of defense between the Promoter and the parties may be called the *discussio causae* although the law reserves the title for the oral discussions which are rarely if ever admitted.[174]

Although this defense may be waived in contentious proceedings where the weight of evidence leaves the judge only one possible conclusion, it is never permissible to dispense with it in criminal causes. The positive law of the Church demands that these defenses be written and interchanged between the Promoter and the defendant in every criminal trial.[175] Should the defendant fail to prepare a defense in the useful time allotted him by the court, the attorney assigned to the defendant by the court must always prepare the defense.[176] He will always prepare this defense as a duty of his office irrespective of the wishes of the defendant.

Consequently, the Promoter will be very active in this session of the trial. He will draw up his defenses within the period fixed by

[172] Roberti, *De Processibus,* II, 156.

[173] Wernz-Vidal, *Jus Canonicum,* VI, 529.

[174] Wernz-Vidal, *Jus Canonicum,* VI, 529.

[175] Canon 1867.

[176] Canon 1655, § 1; A Coronata, *Institutiones J. C.,* III, 298; Roberti, *De Processibus,* II, 162; Heiner, *De Processu Criminali Ecclesiastico,* p. 109.

the judge and must not obstruct the trial by non-compliance with the decree of the judge assigning the terms.[177]

Under the old law this defense was effected in criminal trials chiefly by parol pleading. The Promoter and the advocate for the defense and the defendant himself, if he so desired, appeared before the tribunal and pleaded their defenses orally after the written defenses had already been submitted to the tribunal.[178] Under the prevailing law the defenses are to be in writing although as will be seen, the judge may permit oral discussion in order to clarify a point or to make specific applications of law, but may not do so for the entire defense.[179]

The object of the defense of the Promoter, as noted, is a summation of his case, with particular stress being placed on the application of the law to the facts proved in the previous court sessions. It will endeavor to show that the opposing parties have not weakened his contentions by repeating the individual facts with their correlative proof, by substantiating and explaining the identical motions, allegations and conclusions he made during the course of the trial. The Promoter will confine himself entirely to the charges or specifications fixed in the *litis contestatio* and in the event that new crimes committed by the defendant have been disclosed during the proceedings, he will not advert to them in his present summation, although he may later take separate criminal action against the accused on the basis of the newly-discovered evidence provided that the delict is not simply occult but public.[180] The Code in its legislation on the sentence clearly indicates that it is to be conformable to the *litis contestatio* and hence unless the judge ordered it to be amended in view of the new facts or delicts uncovered in the process, it would be useless for the Promoter to substantiate them in his summation, since the judge may only advert to those contentions and

[177] A Coronata, *Institutiones J. C.*, III, 299.

[178] Heiner, *De Processu Criminali Ecclesiastico*, pp. 112, 113; Droste-Messmer, *Canonical Procedure in Disciplinary and Criminal Cases of Clerics*, 173.

[179] Canon 1866, §§ 1, 2.

[180] Canon 1726; Noval, *De Processibus*, I, 413; *Apollinaris*, II (1927), 76, 77; Boriero, *De Processu Canonico*, p. 302; Roberti, *De Processibus*, II, 183.

accusations made in his *libellus* and included in the formula of doubts at the outset of the judicial trial or as it was amended by judicial order in the course of the trial.[181]

The common law says nothing or very little about the form of these defenses. It leaves it to the prudent judgment of the judge to moderate the defense, advising him, however, that it should not be too long.[182] It, likewise, states that the Promoter should follow the particular law of the tribunal in this matter. Hence if the particular law of the tribunal demands that the copy of the summation be typewritten and that it should not exceed a certain number of pages or lines, the Promoter should conform to these rules [183] unless the unusual amount of evidence submitted requires that a longer defense be submitted in order to protect effectively the interests of the public good against the attacks of the other parties in the trial. In this event the judge may upon petition of the Promoter waive the rule. The new norms of the Rota interpret Canon 1864 as permitting twenty printed pages for the defenses which may be increased by permission of the judge, but never to exceed forty pages.[184]

The Promoter should be as dispassionate as possible in his summation or charge to the tribunal. The impassioned charges to the jury or the judge too frequently heard in our secular courts have no place in Canon Law. The defense of the Promoter should be a simple, inornate, inoffensive presentation of the fact and the law in the case according as it supports his contentions in the case. The Promoter while endeavoring to maintain the effectiveness of his arguments will do so as concisely and as forcibly as possible.[185]

Ordinarily the parties will present to the court a sufficient number of copies of the defenses so that a copy may be given to each of the judges, the parties and the Promoter and the defender of the bond if they are to be present, so that each person may make a private study of it. The number of copies to be presented by the

[181] Canon 1873, § 1, nn. 1, 2; Heiner, *De Processu Criminali Ecclesiastico*, p. 113.

[182] Canon 1864.

[183] Canon 1864.

[184] *Normae S. R. R. Tribunalis*, art. 124—*A. A. S.*, XXVI (1934), 479.

[185] Roberti, *De Processibus*, II, 163.

Promoter will depend upon the rôle he is exercising in the process. If he is acting as plaintiff in either criminal or contentious cases, he will follow the rules laid down for all parties and present copies for all those enumerated above. If, however, he appears in a collateral rôle simply out of vigilance for the rights and things pertaining to the public good and not in the rôle of an actual party to the trial, he will only prepare copies for the judges. This copy will set forth the allegations of the Promoter in favor of the public good and is for the instruction of the judge and not to be attacked by the parties.[186]

In non-criminal cases, the Promoter enjoys the right to give his defense observations last, unless the defender of the bond is also present in the case. In this latter event only the defender of the bond will follow him and all the parties must present their defenses to him before he presents his own. In all contentious cases he presents his defenses only after he has viewed the defenses of the other parties to the trial; but in criminal cases he enjoys no such privilege. The accused and not the Promoter is the privileged party to this latter type of proceedings and since he is the accuser in the trial he must submit his briefs of defense at the same moment that the judge assigns for the filing of the defense brief for the accused. He will receive the brief of the defense attorney only after he has filed his own brief with the notary of the court.[187]

After ordering the notary to give copies of the defenses to the Promoter and to the parties in the trial, the judge assigns a term within which they must reply to each other's briefs in writing. If the tribunal has its own rules concerning the filing and distribution of briefs, the Promoter will abide by these regulations.[188] The parties and the Promoter have the right to answer only once, unless the judge extends this right by decree. Should the judge find it necessary to permit the repetition of answers in order to clear up a doubt or to discover the truth in the cases, he must allow all parties to the trial equal opportunity to respond and this under pain of nullity

[186] Wernz-Vidal, *Jus Canonicum,* VI, 531.

[187] *Normae S. R. R. Tribunalis,* arts. 126, par. 2, 131—*A. A. S.,* XXVI (1934), 479; Bernardini, *Apollinaris,* VII (1934), 464, 465.

[188] Canon 1865, § 1.

to the process, since the full defense of one's position is guaranteed by both the law of nature and the positive law of the Church.[189]

These responses follow the general rules laid down in the Code for the preparation of defenses.[190] They also must be in writing and should be direct answers to the briefs submitted by the opposition. They should be brief, concise and to the point. In fact the Rota permits only ten printed pages. The length of the responses in the cases before the diocesan curia will depend upon the particular regulation of the curia and in the absence of specific regulations in the matter the prudence of the judge will regulate it.[191] The Promoter should prepare the same number of copies of the responses as he did briefs for the defenses; for these responses together with the briefs will form the principal object of private study by the judges before the pronouncement of the sentence. All that has been said of simplicity of style and freedom from impassioned and offensive observations should, likewise, mark the response of the Promoter to the brief of the parties.

The judge may also permit an oral discussion of the case at the instance of the Promoter of Justice or of one of the parties.[192]

When this procedure is permitted, the parties may submit statements of facts which the discussion is to cover. Generally, however, this discussion will take the form of questions and answers, for ecclesiastical procedure abhors forensic oratory.[193]

If the Promoter has petitioned its use it will naturally devolve upon him to propose the questions relative to the fact or to application of law and the judge will propose them to the parties concerned. In the event that the satisfactory settlement of the doubt or difficulty requires the assistance of experts, the judge may appoint them and invite them to be present. In the event that the lawyer for the defendant is granted the request, the judge will propose the questions prepared by him to the Promoter of Justice.

[189] *Regula Juris 32* in VI°; Blat, *Commentarium,* IV, 371.

[190] Canon 1865, § 1.

[191] Canon 1865, § 1.

[192] Canon 1866, §§ 1, 2.

[193] *Regulae Servandae . . . S. R. R. Tribunal,* par. 67, n. 1; Roberti, *De Processibus,* II, 166.

Since the Promoter is a party to the trial and in cases in which he acts as the plaintiff a party to the discussion itself, he must be cited to be present at it. In the latter cases it would be hardly possible to conduct the oral discussion unless he were there to answer the questions of the defense or of the party.[194]

The Promoter has no right to interject additional questions into the proceedings at this special discussion permitted by the judge for single doubts or difficulties. The Promoter must confine himself to the questions admitted by the judge and in the event that the question lists of the defense or of the party appear prejudicial to his case, he may petition the judge to admit his own question lists in order to counteract this prejudicial effect. The judge is the sole moderator of the whole procedure and he may admit it as often as doubt still persist concerning the issue involving the public good, even to this late period of the trial.[195]

The time for this oral discussion must be after the defenses and the responses have been submitted to the court, since at that moment all that is necessary for the definition of the cause has been presented.[196] Consequently, once the oral discussion is completed, no matter what the results may be, neither the Promoter nor the parties to the trial may resort to further written defenses or responses to oppose any point they may fear to have been gained by the opposition. The value of the oral discussion rests entirely with the tribunal for upon its completion the judges proceed immediately to the pronouncement of the sentence.[197]

C. *The Promoter of Justice and the Sentence*

After the final pleading of the Promoter and the parties, the presiding judge will assign a day and hour for the meeting of the judges to deliberate on the sentence. The complicated nature of the testimony and the gravity or difficulty of the question to be solved by

[194] Canon 1586, §§ 1, 2; Wernz-Vidal, *Jus Canonicum,* VI, 531; *Regulae Servandae . . . S. R. R. Tribunal,* par. 73, n. 1.

[195] Canon 1866, § 2.

[196] Roberti, *De Processibus,* II, 167.

[197] *Regulae Servandae . . . S. R. R. Tribunal,* par. 71, n. 4.

sentence will be the determining elements in the length of time to be given to the individual judges for their private study of the case. Unwarranted and unreasonable delays should be avoided since the pronouncement of the sentence should take place as soon as possible after the completion of the discussion of the cause or the summing up by the parties.[198]

The sentence is the legal pronouncement by which the court defines the question proposed to the tribunal by the parties and examined by the court.[199] In criminal proceedings this sentence may be declaratory or condemnatory according to the nature of the charges brought by the Promoter and the nature of the delict proved by him.[200]

After the *conclusio in causa* has been reached the Ordinary may no longer employ judicial correction and the trial proceeds to the sentence despite the valid judicial confession made after that moment.[201]

As often as the case has been tried by a collegiate tribunal, the judges follow the regulations laid down in the law for the meeting of the judges and for the evolution of the sentence which this meeting occasions.[202]

Has the Promoter of Justice the right to be present at this meeting of the judges and to participate in the informal discussions? The common teaching is that the Promoter has neither the right nor the duty to be present at these informal meetings of the judges held for the purpose of arriving at a definitive sentence in the case.[203]

The right and duty of the Promoter to presence extends only to the judicial sessions of the trial. The discussion of the judges for the formation of the sentence is not a part of the judicial trial. This

[198] Canon 1870; Wernz-Vidal, *Jus Canonicum*, VI, 544.

[199] Canon 1868, § 1.

[200] Roberti, *De Processibus*, II, 173; Heiner, *De Processu Criminali Ecclesiastico*, pp. 118, 119.

[201] Canon 1950.

[202] Canons 1871, §§ 1-5 incl.; Muniz, *Procedimientos Eccl.*, III, 368.

[203] Roberti, *De Processibus*, II, 181; Muniz, *Procedimientos Eccl.*, III, 368; *Regulae Servandae . . . S. R. R. Tribunal*, par. 177, n. 1.

is proved by the absence of the notary.[204] The meeting is merely a private informal discussion of the judges from which all others are to be excluded. The reason for this exclusion of the other officials of the tribunal is that the judges may have complete freedom in expressing their opinions and in discussing the case, the solution of which is exclusively their concern.

The absence of the notary is a strong proof of the non-judicial character of the meeting since his place is filled by the relator. Additional proof of the Promoter's exclusion is the absolute secrecy with which the law cloaks this meeting of the judges and the opinions and votes of the dissenting judges in a collegiate sentence.[205] While the conclusions are to be integrated into the *acta*, they do not become a part of the *acta* properly so-called but are preserved in a separate sealed folio attached to the acts for safekeeping in the diocesan archives.

The relator draws up the sentence. This sentence must contain the name of the Promoter who acted in the trial.[206]

The publication of the sentence in the prevailing law is made *ex officio*. In all trials this publication extends to the interested parties and therefore to the Promoter and to all those who participated as parties in the trial. The Code permits three methods of publication.[207]

It makes little difference which method the tribunal chooses for the publication of the sentence. The fact remains that the Promoter of Justice who had acted in an official capacity at the trial should receive notice of the sentence or be actually notified where he may hear or obtain the sentence.[208] Whenever the first method is used, whereby the judge sitting in court pronounces the sentence, it seems that the citation of the Promoter would be required for validity unless he is already present.

[204] Canon 1871.

[205] Canons 1623, § 2; 1871, § 2; Roberti, *De Processibus*, II, 182.

[206] Canon 1874, § 2; Wernz-Vidal, *Jus Canonicum*, VI, 544.

[207] Canon 1877.

[208] Canon 1877.

Article IV. The Promoter of Justice and the Remedies Against the Sentence

While a definitive sentence ordinarily settles in a decisive and final manner all cases in which the Promoter of Justice appears with the exception of those cases which pertain to the status of persons and require two conformable sentences and, as such, is presumed to be right and just and to have been pronounced in accordance with the provisions of the law and in compliance with the requirements of strict justice, yet it can happen that the sentence in question may be unjust, considered in itself or with respect to the merits of the cause as presented to the court. To guard against any of the unfortunate results which naturally flow from such possible miscarriage of justice, the judiciary system of all perfect societies and the Church is no exception, provides certain legal remedies the application of which will protect the rights of the parties engaged in a legal action who may feel that their rights have been violated or unduly abridged by an unjust sentence of the court. The plaintiff as well as the defendant has the right to call upon the higher courts for redress against any injustice which the offending sentence may occasion. This redress in Canon Law may take any one of three possible forms, *e. g.*, appeal, the complaint of nullity and the ***restitutio in integrum***. The first two are called ordinary remedies against the sentence, the third an extraordinary remedy.[209]

A. *The Promoter of Justice and the Appeal*

Appeal is taken here in the strict sense. It is to invoke the aid of a superior judge for the purpose of seeking redress against an injury or grievance, either already inflicted or about to be inflicted by an inferior judge.[210] It is a legal application made to the higher court for assistance in the protection of one's legal rights which have already been violated or unduly curtailed by the sentence rendered in the court of first instance. Appeal, then, affects an unjust sentence

[209] Vermeersch-Creusen, *Epitome*, III, 98; Noval, *De Processibus*, I, 417; Roberti, *De Processibus*, II, 191, 192.

[210] Canon 1879; Schmalzgrueber, lib. II, tit. XXVIII, n. 1.

and not an invalid one. It was instituted to remove a grievance or injury inflicted; or to correct the inexperience, lack of knowledge or other defect in the judge who passed the sentence in first instance; or finally, to give the litigant who through ignorance or negligence has failed to establish his case properly in the first instance an opportunity to remedy this defect in the court of appeal.[211] The primary object of appeal is the revision of the impugned sentence for the benefit of the aggrieved party and in the interests of justice.[212]

The Promoter of Justice may also entertain a just complaint against the sentence not indeed personally but officially, inasmuch as he believes the public order or good has been injured by the sentence. Consequently, he too may appeal from the sentence of the court of first instance and his right to do so is expressly recognized by the law itself.[213] As a rule appeal is permissible to him in all cases of grievance except those expressly exempted by the law.[214]

The fact that the Promoter might entertain a just complaint against the sentence was recognized in the pre-Code legislation.[215] The authors for the most part discuss the appeal of the defendant since this is the ordinary case; but in passing they note that the Promoter of Justice may and should interpose an appeal as often as the interests of justice would seem to demand it. They realized that even after the criminal trial had wound its way through all the ordinary stages of criminal procedure, the judgment may yet be false, since judges err in these cases in which all too easily personal sympathy, passion or prejudice may enter and betray or mislead the better judgment.[216]

While the Code recognizes the right of the Promoter to interpose an appeal in all cases of grievance which are not prohibited by law, this right does not impose upon him the same obligation of exercise

[211] Bouix, *De Judiciis Eccl.*, II, 246; Wernz, *Jus Decretalium,* V. 527.

[212] Roberti, *De Processibus,* II, 197; Connolly, *Appeals,* p. 4.

[213] Canon 1879; Augustine, *A Commentary,* VII, 318; Roberti, *De Processibus,* II, 198.

[214] Canon 1880; Vermeersch-Creusen, *Epitome,* III, 116.

[215] S. C. EE. et RR., 1 Aug. 1851; *A. S. S.,* XV (1882), 547 ss.; Heiner, *De Processu Criminali Ecclesiastico,* p. 125; Boriero, *De Processu Canonico,* p. 310.

[216] Bouix, *De Judiciis Eccl.,* II, 246.

as it does on the cognate office of the defender of the bond. With the latter the positive law requires that he automatically appeal against a sentence of nullity whether the sentence seems unjust to him or not; for the positive law requires two conformable sentences before the marriage cause attains the status of a *quasi-res judicata.*[217] There is no such requirement in the causes in which the Promoter appears (save marriage cases in which he appears as plaintiff), the single sentence being sufficient to make the case a *res judicata,* unless the defendant or one of the parties, if it is a contentious case, appeals.[281] Consequently, the Promoter will appeal from the sentence only when he in his official capacity feels that the sentence is unjust and he is convinced that the sentence of the lower court does not adequately protect the public welfare.[219]

In view of this, authors who advert to the subject both before and after the Code have taken the view that the Promoter should not interpose an appeal in a criminal trial unless the sentence of the first court is manifestly and certainly unjust.[220] These authors contend that when the accused person has once been regularly tried and justly acquitted in the diocesan curia, the Promoter cannot appeal to a higher tribunal and have the accused tried again on the same charges. This opinion is more conformable to the general norms at the end of the Fourth Book of the Code regulating the criminal trial; one cannot help in examining them but be impressed by the mildness and tempered justice of the law. Every effort is made to seek the emendation of the accused and to avoid the severity of punishment attendant upon the trial. In the present question the Promoter in his official capacity has done all that was possible to see that justice was satisfied and yet the court has felt that the accused should not be punished for the charges brought against him. It would seem that the Promoter should be satisfied with this execution of his duty and permit the accused to take advantage of the decision of the

[217] Canons 1986, 1987.

[218] Canon 1903; Noval, *De Processibus,* I, 444, 445.

[219] Roberti, *De Processibus,* II, 198; Blat, *Commentarium,* IV, 137.

[220] Noval, *De Processibus,* I, 502; Boriero, *De Processu Canonico,* p. 310, n. 3; Baart, *Legal Formulary,* p. 75; Monacelli, *Formularium leg. pract.,* I, tit. I, formula 8.

court to reestablish himself in the ranks of the clergy and to vindicate by his subsequent conduct the absolution granted him by the court, unless of course the sentence is manifestly unjust or has been given in consequence of the chicanery and deception practiced by the defendant.

This teaching of canonists has been the object of a centenary custom prevailing here in the United States. Dating from the establishment of the hierachy in this country the custom of the prosecutor not appealing from the just absolving sentence of a diocesan court has run the prescribed one hundred years.[221] Prior to the Code this unviolated prescription had the force of law and hence any attempt on the part of the prosecutor to appeal from a just absolving sentence would not only render him odious but would be illegal.[222] The Code in its prescriptions on appeal has not abrogated this centenary custom and so, in virtue of Canon 5, it would still be in force. The writer knows of no bishop who has suppressed the custom; it still enjoys the force of law here in the United States.

In the event that any trial in which he has participated in the interests of the public good has not been regular or the sentence has been unjust, the Promoter has not only the right but the duty of appealing the sentence. His official duties demand that the ecclesiastical law be protected, that scandal be removed and that the public good which has been violated be repaired. As often as the court circumvents his efforts to obtain these ends by the pronouncement of an apparently unfair sentence, the mandate of his office requires him to appeal the sentence and to seek the removal of the grievance against the public good by a revision of the sentence in the higher court. The Promoter is to determine whether the court has closed its eyes to or erred in the facts in the case and pronounced a sentence that is unwarranted in the light of his own conclusions and the evidence with which he substantiated these conclusions.[223]

Should the Promoter desire to appeal from the sentence he must

[221] Baart, *Legal Formulary*, p. 75.

[222] Baart, *Legal Formulary*, p. 75.

[223] Canon 1879; Boriero, *De Processu Canonico*, p. 310; Heiner, *De Processu Criminali Ecclesiastico*, p. 125.

do so within the period of time set by the law for such action. The related public officer, the *Defensor Vinculi,* is not so strictly affected by these terms since the law requires an automatic appeal from the sentence of first instance when it is one of nullity.[224] The Promoter, on the other hand, is not bound by law to appeal from a sentence adverse to himself. His obligation to appeal arises not from any particular prescript of law but from the general nature of his office. He is bound to appeal only when he considers the sentence to be unjust and insufficient to provide for the public good. He enjoys no special privileges in exercising his right of appeal: the Code simply grants him the same rights in the matter which it grants to any other plaintiff who feels himself aggrieved by the sentence.[225]

Consequently, the Promoter of Justice must file his appeal within the ten-day period established by the law [226] and must prosecute his appeal within the thirty-day period set by the law.[227] Both these legal terms *(fatalia)* are of useful time and therefore time during which the right to appeal and to prosecute the appeal have not been impeded.[228] Canons 1733 and 1884 state the reasons capable of interrupting or abating the period.

Both these legal terms are peremptory in the ordinary trial, that is, they have been conceded by the law for the definite purpose, the right to appeal and to prosecute the appeal and the non-fulfillment of these ends within the respective legal periods ends in the annulment of the right to appeal.[229] Both these terms come under the *fatalia legis,* so that if no effort is made to interpose an appeal or no effort is made to prosecute the appeal which was interposed, the right to do so is thereby extinguished and it is not within the power of the judge to restore it.[230]

Wherefore, if the appellant permits these terms to pass without

[224] Canons 1986, 1987; Dolan, *Defensor Vinculi,* p. 105.

[225] Canon 1879.

[226] Canon 1881.

[227] Canon 1883.

[228] Canons 1885, 35; A Coronata, *Institutiones J. C.,* I, n. 55; Connolly, *Appeals,* pp. 103-107.

[229] Wernz-Vidal, *Jus Canonicum,* VI, 562; Roberti, *De Processibus,* I, 285.

[230] Canon 1634, § 1; Noval, *De Processibus,* I, 141.

interposing an appeal or without prosecuting the appeal he has interposed, the right of doing so is thereby forfeited.[231] The process is extinguished by the negligence or inertia of the appellant and this failure on his part is justly regarded by the law as a tacit renunciation or desertion of appeal.[232] When the appeal thus goes by default the sentence, if it does not pertain to the status of persons, becomes a *res judicata* and the execution thereof follows as a matter of law and right.[233]

The Promoter of Justice is similarly obliged by the tenor of Canon 1883 to prosecute his appeal within the legal term. If he desires to introduce the cause in the appellate court where the Promoter of the latter tribunal will take over the actual prosecution of his cause, he must not only interpose a complaint against the obnoxious sentence within ten days, but he must also prosecute that appeal within thirty days from the notification of the acceptance of the appeal by the judge of the lower court. The reason for this is that despite his official capacity in a trial he has only the rights granted to other aggrieved plaintiffs and nothing more. His failure to observe the *fatalia legis* relative to the prosecution of the appeal will result in the offending sentence becoming a *res judicata* and will therefore defeat the Promoter's attempts to protect the common good and to obtain justice in the case. Hence as often as the Promoter considers the sentence of the first instance detrimental to the public good, he shall take care to observe all the *fatalia legis* relative to appeal so that his efforts to protect the common welfare may not prove abortive.

Naturally, it is the Promoter of Justice of the curia issuing the sentence who will interpose the appeal. This means that the Promoter will declare his intention to appeal before the judge of the court or will present a written petition to that effect. According to the Code this oral declaration of appeal may be used only when the sentence is solemnly pronounced by the judge presiding in court,[234]

[231] Canon 1886; *cf.* Connolly, *Appeals,* pp. 103-107, on the *fatalia* in appeals.

[232] Canon 1738.

[233] Canons 1902, n. 2; 1917.

[234] Canons 1882, §§ 1, 2; 1877.

a procedure seldom employed in modern ecclesiastical trials. The Promoter will generally be obliged to submit a written petition of appeal.

This judicial petition is directed to the judge who pronounced the sentence [235] and if it was made orally it will be immediately committed to writing by the notary of the court. There is no required form for the petition of appeal, although Roberti declares that the rules governing the introductory *libellus* are to be applied to all petitions which invoke any legal favor of law against an unjust sentence with due regard, however, to the observance of appropriate changes necessitated by the circumstances of a particular case.[236]

Relative to the prosecution of the appeal, Canon 1884 declares that it suffices to invoke the help of the higher court to change or remedy the sentence, presenting at the same time an authentic copy of the sentence of the lower court against which the appeal is taken. The judicial petition must contain the name of the party against whom the appeal is directed; it should clearly determine the sentence or particular part of the sentence appealed; the reasons upon which the appeal is based should also be included in the petition. These reasons do not have to be developed to any great length; it is sufficient that they be sound, clearly and concisely stated so that the appellate judge may recognize immediately the justice of the claim. They may not be omitted entirely, but it will suffice if such reasons are expressed as will convince the judge that the appeal was not taken merely to delay the execution of the sentence.[237] To this petition are added authentic copies of the petition of appeal and of the impugned sentence of the lower court. The interposition of these three documents by the Promoter confirms the interposition of his appeal and fulfills the legal requirements for the valid prosecution of appeal.

The Promoter would do well to take particular care in his preparation of the reasons for the appeal from the impugned sentence; inasmuch as this information will prove invaluable to the Promoter

[235] Canon 1882, § 1.

[236] Wernz-Vidal, *Jus Canonicum,* VI, 563; Roberti, *De Processibus,* II, 211.

[237] Connolly, *Appeals,* p. 153.

of the appellate tribunal who must prosecute the appeal before that court in the name of the Promoter of the first instance.

Upon the reception of the *acta* from the lower court the Promoter of Justice of the appellate court will prosecute the appeal. The transmission of the acts will be effected by the lower court according to its own methods for effecting this action and the Promoter need not concern himself about it.

Wherefore, the duties of the Promoter of the first instance are confined solely to the interposition of the appeal and the preliminary prosecution of the appeal before the appellate court. His only functions in appeal will be the observance of the *fatalia* and the preparation of the twofold judicial petition, one for the interposition, the other for the prosecution of the appeal. The Promoter of the first instance never appears before the superior tribunal in that capacity in order to prosecute his appeal. His office is a public one and it will be exercised in the higher courts by the officer of that tribunal who exercises a rôle identical to his own before that instance. The Promoter of Justice has no official standing outside the tribunal for which he was appointed.[238]

When the defendant appeals and this will be the normal procedure, the Promoter of Justice in the second instance will be cited to defend the victory won in the first instance by the related officer. Once the appeal is taken, it is the concern of the Promoter of the second instance since the case is removed entirely from the duties of the Promoter of the first instance. If the defendant or the party has filed his appeal with due regard to all the requirements of the law, the judge must permit him to file it.[239] If he is doubtful concerning the justice of the appeal, he must, likewise, receive it and leave the approval or rejection of it to the decision of the appellate court.[240] The judge will indeed notify the Promoter of Justice, as the appellee in the case, of the interposition of an appeal by the de-

[238] *Suprema Signatura, Recursus,* 15 March, 1921—*A. A. S.*, XIII (1921), 271; Roberti, *De Processibus,* I, 198; Muniz, *Procedimientos Eccl.*, III, 396, n. 1; Lega, *De Judiciis Eccl.*, I, 147.

[239] Roberti, *De Processibus,* II, 212.

[240] Wernz-Vidal, *Jus Canonicum,* VI, 563, 564.

fendant but there is nothing that he can do to prevent it, no matter how unfounded or unjust it may seem to him, since the lower court can only accept the appeal. It will be the duty of the Promoter of the second instance to attack the justice of the appeal and to sustain the arguments presented in the lower court by the Promoter of that instance. The Promoter of Justice of the lower court might be obliged to intervene, were he aware of the fact that fraudulent and dishonest methods were being employed by the party to undermine and discredit the proofs, submitted by him in the first trial. In this latter event he would be obliged to transmit his information to the Promoter of the superior court. This duty would not derive from any statute or canon but from the obligations of his office to protect the public good by the just prosecution of all those who offend against the public welfare. The actual presentation of the entire defense, however, is in the hands of the Promoter of the appellate court.

The new norms of the Rota have introduced a further change in the rights of its Promoter. No longer need he seek the aid of the Promoter of the lower tribunal through the medium of the Ponens. He has the right to seek this assistance directly from the Promoter of the court from which the appeal was taken to the Rota as often as he feels that the latter may be of assistance. The Promoter of the lower court in virtue of his office is bound to cooperate with the Promoter of the Rota in all questions pertaining to the public welfare.[241]

B. *The Promoter of Justice and the Complaint of Nullity*

The Promoter of Justice may also have recourse to the second ordinary remedy against an unfavorable and invalid sentence. This remedy is technically known as the complaint of nullity *(querela nullitatis)*.[242]

It is a judicial action by which the party or the Promoter contends that the verdict of the court is null and invalid, because it labors under some substantial defect.[243]

[241] *Normae S. R. R. Tribunalis,* art. 26, *A. A. S.*—XXVI (1934), 457.
[242] Canon 1897; Heiner, *De Processu Criminali Ecclesiastico,* 136.
[243] Reiffenstuel, lib. II, tit. 28, n. 23; Noval, *De Processibus,* I, 435.

The law distinguishes two types of nullity which can upset a sentence or at least retard its execution: the one is remediable, the other an irremediable defect.

The sentence is irremediably null if it has been rendered by an absolutely incompetent judge or if the tribunal which pronounced it was composed of a number less than that prescribed by the law;[244] or if the sentence was pronounced in a case in which at least one of the parties is not entitled to bring suit in the ecclesiastical courts, or in which some one has acted in the name of another without the necessary mandate.[245] In all these cases a sentence can never be rendered valid by any subsequent act of the tribunal. Against the execution of such a sentence the party condemned or ordered to do something by it has an exception which amounts to a peremptory exception and which may be employed against the judge attempting to execute it. The complaint of nullity may also be exercised as an action for a period of thirty years from the date on which it was passed. As an action it is a petition asking the judge to declare his own sentence null and void.[246]

The Promoter of Justice may institute the action as often as he is convinced that the sentence labors under one of these irremediable defects.[247] It makes no difference whether the sentence was favorable or unfavorable to him and in criminal trials whether it was condemnatory or absolving in character, for it pertains to the public good that sentences in trials involving that good which are certainly null should be set aside and the error repaired by a repetition of process; otherwise the sentence obtained by the Promoter in favor of the public good cannot be carried out and executed in the matter which formed the object of the trial.[248] If he is successful in his interposition of the complaint, his only redress will be to have the

[244] Canon 1576.

[245] Canon 1892.

[246] Canon 1893.

[247] Canon 1897, § 1.

[248] Heiner, *De Processu Criminali Ecclesiastico,* 135 ss.; Muniz, *Procedimientos Eccl.,* III, 427 and n. 1; Noval, *De Processibus,* I, 502.

tribunal that passed the sentence declare it null and reopen the process with a new introductory *libellus* or with a new bill of accusation according to the nature of the proceedings he is undertaking.[249] He may take this action at any moment within thirty years from the date of the sentence. However, it may happen that the null sentence was an absolving sentence and the examination of the grounds of nullity show that there are no grounds or insufficient ones for a new trial. In this event things should be left the way they were before the first proceedings since justice demands that an innocent person should not be retried simply because a sentence has been rendered invalid by some error of the tribunal. The same would be true in the contentious cases in which the Promoter had acted. Should the investigation into the complaint of nullity show insufficient grounds upon which the Promoter has to found his *libellus,* things will be left the way they were before the first proceedings were undertaken. To all practical purposes it might in a sense be called a reinstatement into former condition.

The second type of sentence against which a complaint of nullity may be levelled is a sentence that is null, but which may be corrected and thus rendered valid. This remediable defect of nullity is had as often as the legitimate summons was not made, or the sentence does not contain the reasons or motives that prompted the judge to pronounce it, or if the necessary signatures or the date and place are missing from the sentence.[250]

The effect of this remediable defect or cause of nullity will differ according to the nature of the cause of the nullity. In the first case, in which the nullity results from the omission of legitimate citation, unless the parties of their own will appeared and thereby healed the defect of citation, all subsequent citations and procedural acts are invalid. If the legitimate citation was not made at the beginning of the trial and the presence of the parties did not supply the defect, the whole process must be repeated.[251] It must be repeated from whatever point the citation was omitted and the parties did not sup-

[249] Roberti, *De Processibus,* II, 228.

[250] Canon 1894.

[251] Roberti, *De Processibus,* II, 225.

ply the omission. If, however, the defect affects only the written transcription of the sentence, the cause of nullity can be removed by the judge *ex officio* in cases involving the public good or at the instance of the parties to the trial and he can publish the sentence anew. The sentence once corrected and republished, the process and the sentence are sustained as valid. Moreover, if the parties should fail in the period allotted by the law to interpose an action against the sentence, all these material defects in the sentence are considered to be healed and the sentence stands as it was legitimately published despite the remediable defect present in it.[252]

The Promoter of Justice enjoys the right to enter the complaint of nullity against a sentence vitiated by a defect of this type.[253]

The Promoter will enter a complaint of nullity as often as the sentence is certainly null. If the process must be repeated, he will take steps to have this done only when the public good demands this procedure and it is evident from the trial which has already transpired that the case pertains to the public good and can result in a decision favorable to the common welfare of the diocese.

In the event that the Promoter files the complaint of nullity against an unfavorable sentence, he may enter it together with his appeal to the superior court or as a separate action. In the first case, he should do so within the ten-day period fixed by the law, whereas in the latter instance he has the three-month period allowed by the law for such action.[254]

Since in either case the discussion on the merits of the cause of nullity will take place in the diocesan court of first instance, the Promoter of Justice will be present to urge the nullity of the sentence and its correction according to the nature of the nullifying cause.[255] In the event that the judge who gave the first invalid sentence is assigned to hear the complaint of nullity, the Promoter of Justice may object to him as prejudiced in view of the former sen-

[252] Roberti, *De Processibus,* II, 225; Muniz, *Procedimientos Eccl.,* III, 430.

[253] Canon 1871, § 1; Wernz-Vidal, *Jus Canonicum,* VI, 568; A Coronata, *Institutiones J. C.,* III, 338.

[254] Canon 1895.

[255] Roberti, *De Processibus,* II, 231; Wernz-Vidal, *Jus Canonicum,* VI, 569.

tence and demand that another judge hear the complaint; nor need he allege any other cause.[256]

Should the defendant enter the complaint of nullity the Promoter will be present to assist the judge in the settlement of the complaint. The authors unanimously require his presence in all cases which involve the nullity of a judicial sentence on the grounds that the nullity of the sentence always affects the public good.[257] If he is to be present in these cases which involve the nullity of any sentence, *a fortiori* he will be cited to be present at the hearing on the nullity of sentences in which he actually was a party to the trial defined by them.[258] In all these hearings the Promoter of Justice will endeavor to protect all that has accrued to the public good in virtue of the sentence which is now attacked on technical grounds and in the event that it is decided that the sentence is null, he will take the proper steps to retrieve for the public good whatever has been lost to it by the declaration that the sentence of the first instance was null. It goes without saying that he will do all this within the bounds of truth and justice, never using his office to harass an innocent person by causing him all the inconveniences of another judicial trial when such action in no way contributes to the public good.

C. *The Promoter of Justice and the Restitutio in Integrum*

The object of all judicial procedure is to serve truth and justice. In the search for truth man frequently errs, especially where human feelings may enter the search. To restrain these as much as possible and to do all that man can to come at least near the truth, there are legal rules and norms of judicial procedure, the prosecution and the defense, the examination of witnesses, offensive and defensive pleadings, and lastly appeal. Yet, after the canonical trial has wound its way through all these steps and even passed the court of appeal,

[256] Canons 1896, 1615; Noval, *De Processibus,* I, 438.

[257] Muniz, *Procedimientos Eccl.,* III, 427, n. 1; Roberti, *De Processibus,* II, 234; A Coronata, *Institutiones J. C.,* III, 338; Wernz-Vidal, *Jus Canonicum,* VI, 570, n. 9.

[258] Noval, *De Processibus,* I, 502.

some one error may still be undiscovered, judgment may still be false and the sentence rendered unjust. For this reason it has often been said that no sentence and especially a sentence in a criminal trial ever becomes irrevocably a *res judicata.* For no punishment can ever be imposed for crime erroneously presumed or which is not fully deserved; nor in contentious cases may the rights of a party ever be proscribed when there is evidence of injustice in the sentences rendered in the case. Hence when one speaks of the validity of a sentence he simply means that it may no longer be set aside by the ordinary means of law and that as a consequence it is to be executed. But if that sentence is later proved to be manifestly unjust, the Church places at the disposal of the aggrieved party the extraordinary remedy of the reinstatement into former condition *(restitutio in integrum).*[259]

The *restitutio in integrum,* as a remedy, is a judicial petition asking the court to set aside the status of *res judicata,* which arises in cases which do not deal with the status of persons from two conformable sentences or from a single definitive sentence joined with the failure to interpose or prosecute a valid appeal. Those cases which pertain to the status of persons obtain a status of *quasi-res judicata,* but never become a *res judicata* in the strict sense of the term.[260] The reinstatement is a petition requesting that the execution of a sentence which has the absolute force of law be stayed and withdrawn and that the petitioner be reinstated in the condition or status he enjoyed prior to the time the first trial was undertaken.

The common law, having the interests of the public good in mind, demands that certain sentences have a degree of stability even though they be objectively false and unjust as regards the party aggrieved by the sentence.[261] The reason for this is that it is more expedient to the public good that the sentences pronounced by the court after all the procedural requirements and norms have been observed should

[259] Noval, *De Processibus,* I, 443.

[260] Canons 1902, 1903; A Coronata, *Institutiones J. C.,* III, 342-344; Roberti, *De Processibus,* II, 245-247; Heiner, *De Processu Criminali Ecclesiastico,* p. 137.

[261] *S. R. Rotae Decisiones seu Sententiae,* dec. XIX, n. 3, XIV (1922), 192; Roberti, *De Processibus,* II, 243.

be held firm and irrevocable than that they be just; otherwise controversies would never be securely and definitely settled.[262] The basis of the *res judicata* is to be found in the requirements of the public good which demands that after a controversy has been sufficiently adjudicated, some limit be fixed to end the controversy and define the respective rights of the parties to it. When this point has been reached the Church presupposes that the ecclesiastical judge has done all in his power to conduct the trial along the lines of truth and justice, until the contrary has been proved.[263] The Code substantially approves this opinion by constituting the *res judicata* as an irrebuttable presumption *(juris et de jure)*. The law does permit this presumption to be directly attacked.[264] The law, itself, admits that the status of stability which is accorded to two conformable sentences or to one sentence from which an appeal is not taken may be based upon an unjust sentence and nevertheless it does not permit the unjust sentence to be attacked directly. It may be attacked only by the *restitutio in integrum* which itself attacks the basis upon which the sentence is based.[265]

Canon 1905 lists the causes which will permit a petitioner to seek the *restitutio in integrum*. Roberti holds that the list of causes is taxatively given and that the clause which refers to the violation of a prescript of law refers to substantive law.[266] Muniz and Vidal, on the other hand, hold that the enumeration of Canons 1892 and 1894 on the basis for the complaint of nullity is taxative and that the enumeration of Canon 1905 includes not only violations of substantive law but also violations of merely procedural regulations.[267] Both opinions are probable but the latter seems to be preferable.[268]

262 Canon 1868, § 1; Pichler, lib. II, tit. 27, n. 20; Roberti, *De Processibus*, II, 243.

263 C. 16, X, *De sent. et de re jud.*, II, 27; C. 15, X, *De sent. et de re jud.*, II, 27; Lega, *De Judiciis Eccl.*, I, 570.

264 Canon 1904, § 1.

265 Roberti, *De Processibus*, II, 244.

266 Roberti, *De Processibus*, II, 228, 229; *Apollinaris*, III (1930), 476 ss.

267 Muniz, *Procedimientos Eccl.*, III, 430; Wernz-Vidal, *Jus Canonicum*, VI, 573; *cf.* Vermeersch, *Periodica*, XVIII (1929), 37*-62*.

268 A Coronata, *Institutiones J. C.*, III, 347.

Relative to the tribunal competent to grant the *restitutio* the matter is tersely stated in Canon 1906. The canon contents itself with saying that the judge who rendered the sentence which caused the matter at issue to become a *res judicata* is the competent judge to grant the reinstatement unless he himself had been guilty of some violation of the prescripts of law. In this latter case it will be the judge of the appeal court who will hear the petition for reinstatement. Whenever the matter has become *res judicata* through the sentence of an appellate court, there is a division of authority as to the court competent to grant the reinstatement. Roberti maintains it is the judge of the appellate tribunal, whereas Muniz and Vidal maintain that it is the judge of the court of first instance who is designated by the words *qui sententiam tulit* of Canon 1906.[269]

As often as the petition for the reinstatement to former condition is accepted and adjudicated in the tribunal of first instance, the Promoter of Justice of that instance should be cited to be present and to defend the status of *res judicata*.[270] The status of *res judicata,* as was noted above, is indispensable to the public good and must be defended against those who seek to set it aside by attacking the basis upon which the irrebuttable presumption rests. It will fall to the lot of the Promoter as the official defender of the public good to protect the honor of the courts and the firmness and stability of their sentences. The jurisprudence of the Roman tribunals approves this practice of citing the Promoter to be present as often as the cause before them is one involving a question of *res judicata*.[271] Moreover, if he has been a party to the trial and the sentence which defined that trial is the object of the petition for reinstatement, he has an additional right to be cited.[272] Again, if the persons aggrieved by the unjust sentence are minors or moral persons he may *ex officio* intro-

[269] Roberti, *De Processibus,* II, 265; Wernz-Vidal, *Jus Canonicum,* VI, 588; Muniz, *Procedimientos, Eccl.,* III, 444.

[270] Roberti, *De Processibus,* I, 197; Muniz, *Procedimientos Eccl.,* III, 445.

[271] *S. R. R. Decisiones seu Sententiae,* dec. XIX, XIV (1922), 191, 198 and in the same volume dec. V, 43, dec. VII, 65; Bouscaren, *Canon Law Digest,* p. 760.

[272] Canon 1904, § 2: "Facit just inter partes et dat exceptionem ad impediendam novam ejusdem causae introductionem."

duce the petition for reinstatement or, if another has introduced it, the judge must cite him and consult him before proceeding to concede the reinstatement.[273] It will be his duty, cumulatively with the judge, to see to it that the evidence submitted by the party is valid, trustworthy and conclusive. In the event that it is, he will withdraw all objections to the reinstatement, but if the contrary is true and the evidence is of a questionable or dishonest character, he will oppose the efforts of the party to set aside what the law presumes to be correct and just in the case.

Should the party seek the *restitutio* in the court of appeal it will be the Promoter of the second instance who will defend the *res judicata* before that tribunal. If the second instance is the Rota, the Promoter of that tribunal may call upon the Promoter of the first instance for any assistance he may deem necessary to defend the *res judicata* affecting the diocese of the second officer.

[273] Canon 1688, § 2; Noval, *De Processibus*, I, 228, 231.

BIBLIOGRAPHY

Sources

Acta Apostolicae Sedis (A. A. S.), Romae, 1909.

Acta Sanctae Sedis (A. A. S.), 41 vols., Romae, 1909.

Codex Juris Canonici Pii X Pontificis Maximi jussu digestus Benedicti Papae XV auctoritate promulgatus, Romae, 1917.

Codici Juris Canonici Fontes, cura Emi. Petri Gasparri editi, 6 vols., Romae, Typis Polyglotis Vaticanis, 1923-1929.

Collectanea Sacrae Congregationis de Propaganda Fide, 2 vols., Romae, 1907.

Collectanea Sacrae Congregationis Episcoporum et Regularium, Bizzari, A., Romae, 1885.

Collectio Lacensis, Acta et Decreta Conciliorum Recentiorum, 7 vols., Freiburg in Breisgau, 1870-1879.

Concilii Plenarii Baltimorensis, III, Acta et Decreta, Baltimore, 1886.

Corpus Juris Canonici, A. L. Richter, 2 vols., Leipsig, 1839.

Corpus Juris Civili, P. Krueger, 3 vols., Berlin, 1928.

Causae Selectae in S. Congregatione Cardinalium Concilii Tridentini Interpretum ab 1823-1869, C. Lingen et P. Reuss, Parisiis, 1871.

Hardouin, *Conciliorum Collectio Regia Maxima*, 12 vols., Parisiis, 1715.

Mansi, *Sacrorum Conciliorum Nova et Amplissima Collectio*, 59 vols., Paris, Arnhem-Leipzig, 1901, 1927.

Migne, *Patrologia Latina*, 221 vols., Parisiis, 1847-1870.

Normae S. Romanae Rotae Tribunalis, Romae, 1934.

Regulae Servandae in judiciis apud S. Romanae Rotae Tribunal, Romae, 1910.

Regulae Servandae in judiciis apud Supremum Signaturae Apostolicae Tribunal, Romae, 1912.

Sanctae Romanae Rotae Decisiones seu Sententiae, 14 vols., Romae, 1912-1930.

Thesaurus Resolutionum Sacrae Congregationis Concilii, 167 vols., Romae, 1718-1908.

Pallotini, Salvator, *Collectio Omnium Conclusionum et Resolutionum apud Sacram Congregationem Cardinalium Sacri Concilii Tridenti*, 17 vols., Romae, 1886.

Reference Works

Ayrinhac, Henry A., *General Legislation in the New Code of Canon Law*, New York, 1920.

Ayrinhac-Lydon, *The Marriage Legislation in the New Code of Canon Law*, New York, 1932.

Baart, Peter A., *Legal Formulary*, 2 ed., New York, 1898.

(Bachofen), Charles Augustine, *A Commentary on the New Code of Canon Law*, 8 vols., St. Louis, 1918-1922.

Bassibey, *Procedure Matrimoniale generale*, Paris, 1889.

Benedictus XIV, *Bullarium*, 18 vols., Mechlin, 1826.

——— *De Synodo Dioecesana*, 8 vols., Romae, 1806.

——— *De Servorum Dei Beatificatione et Canonizatione Beatorum*, 2 vols., Prati, 1834.

——— *Quaestiones Canonicae et Morales*, Prati, 1844.

Blat, Albert, *Commentarium Textus Codicis Juris Canonici*, 5 vols., Romae, 1921-1927.

Bonfante, *Istituzioni di Diritto Romano*, Turin, 1910.

Boriero, F., *De Processu Canonico*, Padua, 1909.

Bouix, D., *Tractatus de Judiciis Ecclesiasticis*, 3 ed., 2 vols., Paris, 1884.

Bouuaert-Simenon, *Manuale Juris Canonici*, 2 ed., Bandae et Leodii, 1926.

Bouvier, *Law Dictionary*, Philadelphia, 1878.

Calisse, Carlo, *A History of Italian Law*, Boston, 1928.

Cappello, Felix, *Tractatus Canonico-Moralis de Sacramentis*, 2 ed., 3 vols., Vol. III, *De Matrimonio*, Romae, Marietti, 1933.

Catholic Encyclopedia, 15 vols., New York, 1917.

Cencio, Ludovicus, *Tractatus de Procuratoribus*, Florence, 1857.

Chelodi, Joannes, *Jus Matrimoniale*, 3 ed., Trent. Libr. Edit. Trident., 1921.

——— *Jus de Personis*, 2 ed., Trent. Libr. Edit. Trident., 1921.

——— *Jus Poenale et Ordo Procedendi in Judiciis Criminalibus juxta Codicem Juris Canonici*, Trent. Libr. Edit. Trident., 1925.

Cocchi, Guidus, *Commentarium in Codicem Juris Canonici*, 7 vols., Turin, 1925-1927.

Connolly, Thomas, *Appeals*, Washington, D. C., 1932.

Coronata, Matthaeus a, *Institutiones Juris Canonici*, 3 vols., Romae, 1933.

Craisson, D., *Manuale totius juris canonici*, 4 ed., 4 vols., Pictavii, 1895.

De Angelis, *Praelectiones Juris Canonici*, lib. I, Romae, 1877, lib. II, 1884-1887.

De Becker, Julius, *Praelectiones Canonicae de Matrimonio*, ed. nova, Lovanii, 1931.

De Luca, Cardinalis, *Sanctae Romanae Rotae Decisiones*, 4 vols., Venice, 1734.

De Meester, A., *Juris Canonici et Juris Canonico-Civilis Compendium*, 3 vols., Bruges, 1921-1928.

De Justis, Vincentius, *De Dispensationibus Matrimonialibus*, Lucae, 1726.

De Smet, *Betrothment and Marriage*, 2 vols., St. Louis, 1923-1925.

De Smet, A., *Tactatus Theologico-Canonicus de Sponsalibus et de Matrimonio*, 4 ed., Bruges, 1927.

Dolan, J., *Defensor Vinculi*, Washington, D. C., 1934.

Drage, Geoffery, *The Criminal Code of the German Empire*, London, 1885.

Droste-Messmer, *Canonical Procedure in Disciplinary and Criminal Cases of Clerics*, New York, 1887.

Durandus, Gulielmus, *Speculum Juris*, 5 vols., Venice, 1575.

Eichmann, Edward, 2 ed., 2 vols., *Das Prozessrecht des Codex Juris Canonici*, Paderborn, 1921.

Esmein, A., *History of Continental Criminal Procedure,* translated by John Simpson, Boston, 1913.

Fagnanus, Prosper, *Commentarium in V Libris Decretalium,* 4 vols., Venice, 1696.

Farrugia, P., *De Matrimonio et Causis Matrimonialibus,* Romae, 1924.

Feije, Henricus, *De Impedimentis et Dispensationibus Matrimonialibus,* 3 ed., Lovanii, 1885.

Ferreres, Joannes, *Institutiones Canonicae,* 2 vols., Barcinonae, 1920.

Fournier, Paul, *Les Officialités au Moyen Age,* Paris, 1880.

Gasparri, Petrus, *Tractatus Canonicus de Matrimonio,* 3 ed., 2 vols., Parisiis, Beauchesne, 1904.

———, *Tractatus Canonicus de Matrimonio,* ed. nova ad mentem Codicis Juris Canonici, Typis Polyglottis Vaticanis, 1932.

Haring, Johann B., *Grundzüge des Katholischen Kirchenrechts,* 2 vols., Graz, 1924.

Hefele-Leclerc, *Histoire des Conciles,* 8 vols., Paris, 1908-1921.

Heiner, F.-Wynen, A., *De Processu Criminali Ecclesiatico,* Romae, 1912.

Hericourt, Louis De, *Les Lois Ecclesiastiques,* Paris, 1771.

Holdsworth, A., *History of English Law,* 9 vols., Boston, 1925-1931.

Hostiensis, *Commentaria in V Libris Decretalium,* 3 vols., Venetiis, 1581.

League, R. W., *Roman Private Law,* 3 ed., London (MacMillan and Co.), 1920.

Lega, M., *Praelectiones in textum juris canonici de judiciis ecclesiasticis,* 4 vols., Romae, 1896-1901.

——— *De Judiciis Ecclesiasticis Civilibus,* vol. I, 3 ed., Romae, 1905.

——— *Praelectiones in textum juris canonici, De delictis et poenis,* 2 ed., Romae, 1910.

Leurenius, Petrus, *Jus Canonicum Universum,* 5 vols., Venice, 1729.

Maroto, Philippus, *Institutiones Juris Canonici,* 3 ed., 2 vols., Romae, 1921.

Matthaeuci, Augustinus, *Officialis Curiae Ecclesiasticae,* Venice, 1734.

Michiels, Gommarus, *Normae Generales Juris Canonici,* 2 vols., Lublin, 1929.

Molitor, Wilhelm, *Über Kanonisches Gerichtsverfahren gegen Kleriker,* Mainz, 1856.

Mommsen, *Le Droit Penal Romain,* 3 vols., Paris, 1907.

Muniz, T., *Procedimientos Ecclesiasticos,* 3 vols., Seville, 1926.

Noldin, Henricus, *Summa Theologiae Moralis,* 20 ed., revised by A. Schmitt, 3 vols., Oeniponte, 1930.

Noval, Joseph, *Commentarium Codicis Juris Canonici,* lib. IV, *De Processibus,* 2 vols., Romae, 1920.

Ojetti, B., *Commentarium in Codicem Juris Canonici,* 3 vols., Romae, 1928.

Panormitanus, Abbas, *Omnia quae extant Commentaria,* Jacobi Napolitani et Antonii Corsetti, 8 vols., Venice, 1588.

Payen, G., *De Matrimonio in Missionibus,* 3 vols., Zi-Ka-Wei, 1928-1929.

Pellegrini, C., *Praxis Vicariorum,* Venice, 1706.

Peregrinus, Antonius, *De Privilegiis et Juribus Fisci,* Venice, 1611.

Pierantonelli, Pacificus, *Praxis Fori Ecclesiastici ad Praesentem Ecclesiae Conditionem Accomodata,* Romae, 1883.

Pirhing, Enricus, *Jus Canonicum in V Libros Decretalium,* 4 vols., Dilingae, 1674-1678.

Reiffenstuel, Anacletus, *Jus Universum Canonicum,* 4 vols., Rome, 1831.

Roberti, Franciscus, *De Processibus,* 2 vols., Rome, 1926.

Santi, *Praelectiones Juris Canonici,* 2 vols., Ratisbon, 1886.

Scaccia, Sigmundus, *Tractatus De Judiciis,* 3 vols., Venice, 1663.

Schmalzgrueber, Franciscus, *Jus Ecclesiasticum Universum,* 12 vols., Romae, 1845.

Sebastianelli, G., *Praelectiones Juris Canonici,* 2 vols., Romae, 1906.

Serrigny, D., *Droit Public et Administratif Romain,* 2 vols., Paris, 1862.

Sherman, Charles Phineas, *Roman Law in the Modern World,* 2 ed., 3 vols., New Haven, 1922.

Smith, S. B., *Elements of Ecclesiastical Law,* 2 vols., New York, 1882.

——— *New Procedure in Criminal and Disciplinary Causes of Ecclesiastics in the United States,* New York, 1898.

——— *The Marriage Process in the United States,* New York, 1893.

Sole, Jacobus, *De Delictis et Poenis, Romae,* 1920.

Sperello, Alex., *Decisiones Fori Ecclesiastici,* 2 vols., Venice, 1666.

Strachan-Davidson, *Problems of Roman Criminal Law,* 2 vols., Oxford, 1912.

Van Espen, J., *Jus Universum Ecclesiasticum,* Lovanii, 5 vols., 1778.

Van Hove, A., *De Legibus Ecclesiasticis, Mechlin-Romae,* Dessain, 1930.

Vermeersch-Creusen, *Epitome Juris Canonici,* 4 ed., 3 vols., Romae, 1930.

Vromant, *De Matrimonio,* Louvain, 1931.

Wernz, Franciscus, *Jus Decretalium,* 2 ed., 6 vols., Romae, 1905.

Wernz-Vidal, *Jus Canonicum,* 6 vols., Romae, 1923-1928.

Woywod, Stanislaus, *A Practical Commentary on the Code of Canon Law,* 2 vols., New York, 1925.

Periodicals

American Ecclesiastical Review, The, Philadelphia, 1889—

Analecta Juris Pontificii, 28 vols., Paris, 1855-1888—

Apollinaris, Romae, 1928—

Archiv für katholisches Kirchenrecht (Afk KR.), Mainz, 1857—

Harvard Law Review, The, 48 vols., 1887-1935, Cambridge—

Homiletic and Pastoral Review, The, New York, 1900—

Il Diritto Ecclesiastico, Rome, 1890—

Il Monitore Ecclesiastico, Romae, 1879—

Jus Pontificium, Romae, 1921—

Nouvelle Revue Theologique (NRT), Paris, 1869—

Periodica de Re Morali, Canonica, Liturgica, Romae, 1905—

Revue des Sciences Ecclesiastiques, 70 vols., Lille, 1860-1897—

Theologisch-Praktische Quartalschrift (LQS), Linz, 1832—

ALPHABETICAL INDEX

BIOGRAPHICAL NOTE

John Carroll Glynn was born on May 6, 1907, in Bridgeport, Connecticut. He received his elementary education in the parochial school of St. Augustine and his high school training in Central High School of that city. He made his higher studies at St. Thomas Seminary, Hartford, and St. Mary's Seminary in Baltimore. He pursued his theological studies in the latter seminary, receiving his Bachelor of Arts in 1927 and his Baccalaureate of Sacred Theology in 1930. He was ordained to the priesthood on May 30, 1931, and two years later entered the School of Canon Law at the Catholic University of America in Washington, D. C., where he received the Baccalaureate in Canon Law in June, 1934, and the Licentiate the following June.

CANON LAW STUDIES

1. Freriks, Rev. Celestine A., C.PP.S., J.C.D., Religious Congregations in Their External Relations, 121 pp., 1916.
2. Galliher, Rev. Daniel M., O.P., J.C.D., Canonical Elections, 117 pp., 1917.
3. Borkowski, Rev. Aurelius L., O.F.M., J.C.D., De Confraternitatibus Ecclesiasticis, 136 pp., 1918.
4. Castillo, Rev. Cayo, J.C.D., Disertacion Historico-Canonica sobre la Potestad del Cabildo en Sede Vacante o Impedida del Vicario Capitular, 99 pp., 1919 (1918).
5. Kubelbeck, Rev. William J., S.T.B., J.C.D., The Sacred Penitentiaria and Its Relation to Faculties of Ordinaries and Priests, 129 pp., 1918.
6. Petrovits, Rev. Joseph, J.C., S.T.D., J.C.D., The New Church Law on Matrimony, X-461 pp., 1919.
7. Hickey, Rev. John J., S.T.B., J.C.D., Irregularities and Simple Impediments in the New Code of Canon Law, 100 pp., 1920.
8. Klekotka, Rev. Peter J., S.T.B., J.C.D., Diocesan Consultors, 179 pp., 1920.
9. Wanenmacher, Rev. Francis, J.C.D., The Evidence is Ecclesiastical Procedure Affecting the Marriage Bond, 1920 (Printed 1935).
10. Golden, Rev. Henry Francis, J.C.D., Parochial Benefices in the New Code, IV-119 pp., 1921 (Printed 1925).
11. Koudelka, Rev. Charles J., J.C.D., Pastors, Their Rights and Duties According to the New Code of Canon Law, 211 pp., 1921.
12. Melo, Rev. Antonius, O.F.M., J.C.D., De Exemptione Regularium, X-188 pp., 1921.
13. Schaaf, Rev. Valentine Theodore, O.F.M., S.T.B., J.C.D., The Cloister, X-180 pp., 1921.
14 Burke, Rev. Thomas Joseph, S.T.D., J.C.D., Competence in Ecclesiastical Tribunals, IV-117 pp., 1922.
15. Leech, Rev. George Leo, J.C.D., A Comparative Study of the Constitution "Apostolicae Sedis" and the "Codex Juris Canonici," 179 pp., 1922.
16. Motry, Rev. Hubert Louis, S.T.D., J.C.D., Diocesan Faculties According to the Code of Canon Law, II-167 pp., 1922.
17. Murphy, Rev. George Lawrence, J.C.D., Delinquencies and Penalties in the Administration and the Reception of the Sacraments, IV-121 pp., 1923.
18. O'Reilly, Rev. John Anthony, S.T.B., J.C.D., Ecclesiastical Sepulture in the New Code of Canon Law, II-129 pp., 1923.
19. Michalicka, Rev. Wenceslas Cyrill, O.S.B., J.C.D., Judicial Procedure in Dismissal of Clerical Exempt Religious, 107 pp., 1923.

20. Dargin, Rev. Edward Vincent, S.T.B., J.C.D., Reserved Cases According to the Code of Canon Law, IV-103 pp., 1924.
21. Godfrey, Rev. John A., S.T.B., J.C.D., The Right of Patronage According to the Code of Canon Law, 153 pp., 1924.
22. Hagedorn, Rev. Francis Edward, J.C.D., General Legislation on Indulgences, II-154 pp., 1924.
23. King, Rev. James Ignatius, J.C.D., The Administration of the Sacraments to Dying Non-Catholics, V-141 pp., 1924.
24. Winslow, Rev. Francis Joseph, O.F.M., J.C.D., Vicars and Prefects Apostolic, IV-149 pp., 1924.
25. Correa, Rev. Jose Servelion, S.T.L., J.C.D., La Potestad Legislativa de la Iglesia Catolica, IV-127 pp., 1925.
26. Dugan, Rev. Henry Francis, A.M., J.C.D., The Judiciary Department of the Diocesan Curia, 87 pp., 1925.
27. Keller, Rev. Charles Frederick, S.T.B., J.C.D., Mass Stipends, 167 pp., 1925.
28. Paschang, Rev. John Linus, J.C.D., The Sacramentals According to the Code of Canon Law, 129 pp., 1925.
29. Pointek, Rev. Cyrillus, O.F.M., S.T.B., J.C.D., De Indulto Exclaustrationis necnon Saecularizationis, XIII-289 pp., 1925.
30. Kearney, Rev. Richard Joseph, S.T.B., J.C.D., Sponsors at Baptism According to the Code of Canon Law, IV-127 pp., 1925.
31. Bartlett, Rev. Chester Joseph, A.M., LL.B., J.C.D., The Tenure of Parochial Property in the United States of America, V-108 pp., 1926.
32. Kilker, Rev. Adrian Jerome, J.C.D., Exteme Unction, V-425 pp., 1926.
33. McCormick, Rev. Robert Emmett, J.C.D., Confessors of Religious, VIII-266 pp., 1926.
34. Miller, Rev. Newton Thomas, J.C.D., Founded Masses According to the Code of Canon Law, VII-93 pp., 1926.
35. Roelker, Rev. Edward G., S.T.D., J.C.D., Principles of Privilege According to the Code of Canon Law, XI-166 pp., 1926.
36. Bakalarczyk, Rev. Richardus, M.I.C., J.U.D., De Novitiatu, VIII-208 pp., 1927.
37. Pizzuti, Rev. Lawrence, O.F.M., J.U.L., De Parochis Religiosis, 1927. (Not Printed.)
38. Bliley, Rev. Nicholas Martin, O.S.B., J.C.D., Altars According to the Code of Canon Law, XIX-132 pp., 1927.
39. Brown, Mr. Brendan Francis, A.B., LL.M., J.U.D., The Canonical Juristic Personality with Special Reference to its Status in the United States of America, VI-212 pp., 1927.
40. Cavanaugh, Rev. William Thomas, C.P., J.U.D., The Reservation of the Blessed Sacrament, VIII-101 pp., 1927.
41. Doheny, Rev. William J., C.S.C., A.B., J.U.D., Church Property: Modes of Acquisition, X-118 pp., 1927.

42. FELDHAUS, REV. ALOYSIUS H., C.PP.S., J.C.D., Oratories, IX-141 pp., 1927.
43. KELLY, REV. JAMES PATRICK, A.B., J.C.D., The Jurisdiction of the Simple Confessor, X-208 pp., 1927.
44. NEUBERGER, REV. NICHOLAS J., J.C.D., Canon 6 or the Relation of the Codex Juris Canonici to the Preceding Legislation, V-95 pp., 1927.
45. O'KEEFE, REV. GERALD MICHAEL, J.C.D., Matrimonial Dispensations, Powers of Bishops, Priests, and Confessors, VIII-232 pp., 1927.
46. QUIGLEY, REV. JOSEPH A. M., A.B., J.C.D., Condemned Societies, 139 pp., 1927.
47. ZAPLOTNIK, REV. JOHANNES LEO, J.C.D., De Vicariis Foraneis, X-142 pp., 1927.
48. DUSKIE, REV. JOHN ALOYSIUS, A.B., J.C.D., The Canonical Status of the Orientals in the United States, VIII-196 pp., 1928.
49. HYLAND, REV. FRANCIS EDWARD, J.C.D., Excommunication, Its Nature, Historical Development and Effects, VIII-181 pp., 1928.
50. REINMANN, REV. GERALD JOSEPH, O.M.C., J.C.D., The Third Order Secular of Saint Francis, 201 pp., 1928.
51. SCHENK, REV. FRANCIS J., J.C.D, The Matrimonial Impediments of Mixed Religion and Disparity of Cult, XVI-318 pp., 1929.
52. COADY, REV. JOHN JOSEPH, S.T.D., J.U.D., A.M., The Appointment of Pastors, VIII-150 pp., 1929.
53. KAY, REV. THOMAS HENRY, J.C.D., Competence in Matrimonial Procedure, VIII-164 pp., 1929.
54. TURNER, REV. SIDNEY JOSEPH, C.P., J.U.D., The Vow of Poverty, XLIX-217 pp., 1929.
55. KEARNEY, REV. RAYMOND A., A.B., S.T.D., J.C.D., The Principles of Delegation, VII-149 pp., 1929.
56. CONRAN, REV. EDWARD JAMES, A.B., J.C.D., The Interdict, V-163 pp., 1930.
57. O'NEIL, REV. WILLIAM H., J.C.D., Papal Rescripts of Favor, VII-218 pp., 1930.
58. BASTNAGEL, REV. CLEMENT VINCENT, J.U.D., The Appointment of Parochial Adjutants and Assistants, XV-257 pp., 1930.
59. FERRY, REV. WILLIAM A., A.B., J.C.D., Stole Fees, V-136 pp., 1930.
60. COSTELLO, REV. JOHN MICHAEL, A.B., J.C.D., Domicile and Quasi-Domicile, VII-201 pp., 1930.
61. KREMER, REV. MICHAEL NICHOLAS, A.B., S.T.B., J.C.D., Church Support in the United States, VI-136 pp., 1930.
62. ANGULO, REV. LUIS, C.M., J.C.D., Legislation de la Iglesia sobre la intencion en la application de la Santa Misa, VII-104 pp., 1931.
63. FREY, REV. WOLFGANG NORBERT, O.S.B., A.B., J.C.D., The Act of Religious Profession, VIII-174 pp., 1931.
64. ROBERTS, REV. JAMES BRENDAN, A.B., J.C.D., The Banns of Marriage, XIV-140 pp., 1931.
65. RYDER, REV. RAYMOND ALOYSIUS, A.B., J.C.D., Simony, IX-151 pp., 1931

66. Campagna, Rev. Angelo, Ph.D., J.U.D., Il Vicario Generale del Vescovo, VII-205 pp., 1931.
67. Cox, Rev. Joseph Godfrey, A.B., J.C.D., The Administration of Seminaries, VI-124 pp., 1931.
68. Gregory, Rev. Donald J., J.U.D., The Pauline Privilege, XV-165 pp., 1931.
69. Donohue, Rev. John F., J.C.D., The Impediment of Crime, VII-110 pp., 1931.
70. Dooley, Rev. Eugene A., O.M.I., J.C.D., Church Law on Sacred Relics, IX-143 pp., 1931.
71. Orth, Rev. Clement Raymond, O.M.C., J.C.D., The Approbation of Religious Institutes, 171 pp., 1931.
72. Pernicone, Rev. Joseph M., A.B., J.C.D., The Ecclesiastical Prohibition of Books, XII-267 pp., 1932.
73. Clinton, Rev. Connell, A.B., J.C.D., The Paschal Precept, IX-108 pp., 1932.
74. Donnelly, Rev. Francis B., A.M., S.T.L., J.C.D., The Diocesan Synod, VIII-125 pp., 1932.
75. Torrente, Rev. Camilo, C.M.F., J.C.D., Las Processiones Sagradas, V-145 pp., 1932.
76. Murphy, Rev. Edwin J., C.PP.S., J.C.D., Suspension Ex Informata Conscientia, XI-122 pp., 1932.
77. Mackenzie, Rev. Eric F., A.M., S.T.L., J.C.D., The Delict of Heresy in its Commission, Penalization, Absolution, VII-124 pp., 1932.
78. Lyons, Rev. Avitus E., S.T.B., J.C.D., The Collegiate Tribunal of First Instance, XI-147 pp., 1932.
79. Connolly, Rev. Thomas A., J.C.D., Appeals, XI-195 pp., 1932.
80. Sangmeister, Rev. Joseph V., A.B., J.C.D., Force and Fear as Precluding Matrimonial Consent, V-211 pp., 1932.
81. Jaeger, Rev. Leo A., A.B., J.C.D., The Administration of Vacant and Quasi-Vacant Episcopal Sees in the United States, IX-229 pp., 1932.
82. Rimlinger, Rev. Herbert T., J.C.D., Error Invalidating Matrimonial Consent, VII-79 pp., 1932.
83. Barrett, Rev. John D. M., S.S., J.C.D., A Comparative Study of the Third Plenary Council of Baltimore and the Code, IX-221 pp., 1932.
84. Carberry, Rev. John J., Ph.D., S.T.D., J.C.D., The Juridical Form of Marriage, X-177 pp., 1934.
85. Dolan, Rev. John L., A.B., J.C.D., The Defensor Vinculi, XII-157 pp., 1934.
86. Hannan, Rev. Jerome D., A.M., S.T.D., LL.B., J.C.D., The Canon Law of Wills, IX-517 pp., 1934.
87. Lemieux, Rev. Delisle A., A.M., J.C.D., The Sentence in Ecclesiastical Procedure, IX-131 pp., 1934.
88. O'Rourke, Rev. James J., A.B., J.C.D., Parish Registers, VII-109 pp., 1934.

89. TIMLIN, REV. BARTHOLOMEW, O.F.M., A.M., J.C.D., Conditional Matrimonial Consent, X-381 pp., 1934.
90. WAHL, REV. FRANCIS X., A.B., J.C.D., The Matrimonial Impediments of Consanguinity and Affinity, VI-125 pp., 1934.
91. WHITE, REV. ROBERT J., A.B., LL.B., S.T.B., J.C.D., Canonical Ante-Nuptial Promises and the Civil Law, VI-152 pp., 1934.
92. HERRERA, REV. ANTONIO PARRA, O.C.D., J.C.D., Legislacion Ecclesiastica sobra el Ayuno y la Abstinencia, XI-191 pp., 1935.
93. KENNEDY, REV. EDWIN J., J.C.D., The Special Matrimonial Process in Cases of Evident Nullity, X-165 pp., 1935.
94. MANNING, REV. JOHN J., A.B., J.C.D., Presumption of Law in Matrimonial Procedure, XI-111 pp., 1935.
95. MOEDER, REV. JOHN M., J.C.D., The Proper Bishop for Ordination and Dimissorial Letters, VII-135 pp., 1935.
96. O'MARA, REV. WILLIAM A., A.B., J.C.D., Canonical Causes for Matrimonial Dispensations, IX-155 pp., 1935.
97. REILLY, REV. PETER, J.C.D., Residence of Pastors, IX-81 pp., 1935.
98. SMITH, REV. MARINER T., O.P., S.T.Lr., J.C.D., The Penal Law for Religious, VII-169 pp., 1935.
99. WHALEN, REV. DONALD W., A.M., J.C.D., The Value of Testimonial Evidence in Matrimonial Procedure, XIII-297 pp., 1935.
100. CLEARY, REV. JOSEPH F., J.C.L., Canonical Limitations on the Alienation of Church Property, 1936.
101. GLYNN, REV. JOHN C., J.C.L., The Promoter of Justice, 1936.

www.ingramcontent.com/pod-product-compliance
Lightning Source LLC
LaVergne TN
LVHW050259080826
844660LV00012B/660

* 9 7 8 0 8 1 3 2 2 2 9 0 5 *